Race After the Internet

In this collection, Lisa Nakamura and Peter A. Chow-White bring together interdisciplinary, forward-looking essays that explore the complex role that digital media technologies play in shaping our ideas about race. *Race After the Internet* contains essays on the shifting terrain of racial identity and its connections to social media technologies like Facebook and MySpace, popular online games like World of Warcraft, YouTube and viral video, genetic ancestry testing, and DNA databases in health and law enforcement. Contributors aim to broaden the definition of the "digital divide" in order to convey a more nuanced understanding of access, usage, meaning, participation, and production of digital media technology in light of racial inequality.

Contributors: danah boyd, Peter A. Chow-White, Wendy Hui Kyong Chun, Sasha Costanza-Chock, Troy Duster, Anna Everett, Rayvon Fouché, Alexander Galloway, Oscar Gandy, Jr., Eszter Hargittai, Jeong Won Hwang, Curtis Marez, Tara McPherson, Alondra Nelson, Christian Sandvig, Ernest Wilson III.

Lisa Nakamura is Professor of Media and Cinema Studies and Director of the Asian American Studies Program at the University of Illinois, Urbana-Champaign. She is the author of *Digitizing Race: Visual Cultures of the Internet*, winner of the Association for Asian American Studies 2010 Book Award in Cultural Studies. She is also author of *Cybertypes: Race, Ethnicity, and Identity on the Internet* and co-editor, with Beth Kolko and Gilbert Rodman, of *Race in Cyberspace*, both published by Routledge.

Peter A. Chow-White is an Assistant Professor in the School of Communication at Simon Fraser University in Vancouver, Canada. His work has appeared in *Communication Theory*, the *International Journal of Communication, Media, Culture & Society, PLoS Medicine*, and *Science, Technology & Human Values*.

Race After the Internet

Edited by
Lisa Nakamura
and
Peter A. Chow-White

Routledge
Taylor & Francis Group

NEW YORK AND LONDON

First published 2012
by Routledge
711 Third Avenue, New York, NY 10017

Simultaneously published in the UK
by Routledge
2 Park Square, Milton Park, Abingdon, Oxon OX14 4RN

Routledge is an imprint of the Taylor & Francis Group, an informa business

© 2012 Taylor & Francis

Library of Congress Cataloging in Publication Data
Race after the Internet/edited by Lisa Nakamura and Peter Chow-White.
   p. cm.
   1. Race.   2. Race relations.   3. Internet—Social aspects.
   I. Nakamura, Lisa.   II. Chow-White, Peter.
   HT1523.R25123 2011
   302.23′1—dc23   2011013431

ISBN: 978-0-415-80235-2 (hbk)
ISBN: 978-0-415-80236-9 (pbk)
ISBN: 978-0-203-87506-3 (ebk)

Typeset in Minion Pro
by Florence Production Ltd, Stoodleigh, Devon

Printed and bound in the United States of America on acid-free paper
by Edwards Brothers, Inc.

SUSTAINABLE FORESTRY INITIATIVE
Certified Fiber Sourcing
www.sfiprogram.org

Contents

Introduction—Race and Digital Technology

Code, the Color Line, and the Information Society

LISA NAKAMURA

University of Illinois, Urbana-Champaign

PETER A. CHOW-WHITE

Simon Fraser University

Postracial America, Digital Natives, and the State of the Union

The current generation of young people is the first to have always had access to the Internet; these so-called digital natives are both hailed as omnipotently connected and decried as fatally distracted (see Palfrey and Gasser 2008). They are also the first to enter adulthood with a African American president in office. Yet digital natives are not an equally privileged bunch; like "natives" everywhere, they are subject to easy generalizations about their nature that collapses their differences. In contrast to former President Bill Clinton, who was colloquially known as the first black president, Obama was the first "wired" president. Unlike his opponent in the presidential election, John McCain, who fatally revealed that he didn't know how to use email, Obama was both our first black president and our first digital Commander in Chief, a harbinger of a new age in more ways than one. However, Obama's presidency coincides with some of the most racist immigration legislation seen in recent years, as well as a prison industrial complex that continues to thrive and target black males, and a financial and housing crisis that has disproportionately harmed black and Latino Americans. The paradox of race after the Age of the Internet, a period that some have defined as "postracial" as well as "postfeminist," lies in such seeming contradictions.

As the shift from analog to digital media formats and ways of knowing continues apace, continued social pressure is brought to bear on the idea of race as a key aspect of identity and an organizing principle for society. Yet no matter how "digital" we become, the continuing problem of social inequality along racial lines persists. As our social institutions and culture become increasingly digitally mediatized, regularly saturated with new platforms, devices, and applications that enable always-on computing and networking, digital media bursts the bounds of the Internet and the personal computer. The pervasiveness of the digital as a way of thinking and of knowing as well as a format for producing and consuming information forces intellectuals and scholars to produce new methodologies and ways of working to reflect current media realities. Equally important but often less discussed is this: the digital is altering our understandings of what race is as well as nurturing new types of inequality along racial lines.

Like many knowledge workers in the academy who came of age well before the Internet, the Human Genome Project (HGP), and digital cable, African American Studies scholar Henry Louis Gates has made the transition from old to new media, and his negotiation of this move encapsulates many of the contradictions of informatic understandings of race enabled by digital computing and the Internet. Formerly a producer of academic books such as *The Signifying Monkey* and the watershed anthology *Race, Writing, and Difference*, a staple text in critical race studies and literary theory in the 1980s and 1990s, he can now be found blogging on pbs.org, which hosts digital streams of his popular television programs. He started his television and new media career as the host and co-producer of the PBS documentary *Great Railroad Journeys* (2006), but his transition from writer to new media producer was signaled by his ongoing series about genealogical testing as a means for recovering the hidden life histories and backgrounds of well-known people of color. This series started out with a focus on African American genealogical testing. *African American Lives* (2006) and *African American Lives 2* (2008) traced "the lineage of more than a dozen notable African Americans . . . using genealogical and historic resources, as well as DNA testing."

In keeping with the rising popularity of reality television programming at this time, this series included celebrity guests as well and was narratively structured around several big "reveals," one of which involved Gates himself, who let the viewer in on the secret that he himself was not as "black" as he thought: In the first series, Gates learned of his high percentage of European ancestry due to his descent from the mulatto John Redman. In addition, he discussed findings about ancestry of his guests. This series featured similar "reveals" about other guests (Sara Lawrence-Lightfoot found out that she did not have any American Indian ancestry, and astronaut Mae Jemison found out that she was part Asian), complete with tears and other telegenic reaction shots after the news of each guest's genetic and racial truth was delivered.

The series proved so popular that it spawned both a spin-off series, ongoing at the time of this writing, entitled *Faces of America*, which examined the genealogy of twelve North Americans: Elizabeth Alexander, Mario Batali, Stephen Colbert, Louise Erdrich, Malcolm Gladwell, Eva Longoria, Yo-Yo Ma, Mike Nichols, Queen Noor, Dr Mehmet Oz, Meryl Streep, and Kristi Yamaguchi, as well as a trade book, available in both electronic and paper form, entitled *Finding Oprah's Roots: Finding Your Own* (2007). The similarity between the reality television format and *Faces of America* is right on the surface: the "reveal" of each star's genetic test results was read out to the celebrities by Gates himself, in much the same way as other reality television hosts have done. However, unlike *Dancing with the Stars*, a reality television program where Kristi

Yamaguchi distinguished herself earlier that year, *Faces of America* offered the truth of race as an informatic commodity and as a prize more for its viewers than for its subjects. The invitation to the viewer to synthesize the images of these stars that they saw on the screen with the "new" information provided by genetic testing produced race as a visual spectacle, one that could both be consumed pleasurably and cast into radical doubt by the test results.

Gates' explanation for his decision to start with African Americans as guests on this series of programs and as the first subjects for the genetic testing and historical research that formed the basis for his claims regarding the "truth" about racial identity was premised on the notion that slaves were uniquely deprived of information about their backgrounds and histories. African American slaves were rendered non-human or, as Orlando Patterson would put it, victims of social death, with the technique of historical erasure as part of the techne of racism. If racism is a technology, or rather, a systematic way of doing things that operates by mediating between users and techniques to create specific forms of oppression and discrimination, then enforced forgetting of the familial or historical past is surely a key part of its workings (see Hartman 1997).

Gates' engagement with race is digital in at least two ways: the subject matter of these programs is the use of bioinformatic technologies such as gene sequencing to tell individuals the "truth" about race, and the program itself is produced as a digital signal, as is much of the audiovisual content in circulation today, and is transcoded into various formats to fit different software platforms and viewing devices. Gates' videos can be viewed on YouTube.com as well as PBS.org, where they are discussed with great seriousness (as well as great flippancy, in keeping with the time-honored tradition of video comment boards) by users and viewers. The PBS website also hosts a "webinar" featuring Gates that it marketed specifically for educators, permitting Gates to enter into classrooms in a much different way than he had through his written work, a trajectory that many educators are being encouraged (or forced) into in an effort to reach "digital native" students.

Gates' new career as a digital media producer signals a new form of racial technology, posed as a curative to the older racist techne of enforced forgetting and information erasure or management—the genetic test or sequence, a digital technology with incredible resonance today as a truth-telling or re-membering device that can recover a lost past. Digital technology is here pressed into service as an identity construction aid; indeed, the immense popularity of home genetic tests for both paternity and dog breed determination (see www.canineheritage. com and www.wisdompanel.com) attests to their integration into everyday life. However, as the *African American Lives* series demonstrated, the racial truth revealed by these tests conflicted strongly and often painfully obviously with the subjects' experience of raced identity. This was true for its host as well. Gates mused aloud in *African American Lives* when receiving his results, "Does this mean that I'm not really black?" In the context of the program, this was a "teaching moment," and he employed it to discuss the complex nature of racial identity. However, he received a definitive answer to his question when he was arrested in Cambridge, Massachusetts, on July 16, 2009 for forcing his way into his own house when a jammed doorlock made it impossible for him to use his house key. The furor that resulted from this flagrant example of racial profiling (of a Harvard professor, as was noted prominently in the popular press) turned into a "national conversation" about race, as Barack Obama invited Gates to the White House to discuss the incident over beers with his arresting officer.

Clearly, race is more than genetics, and is composed of more than one kind of code, yet programs like *African American Lives* and *Faces of America* assert that the digital trumps all else. The biotechnical turn (like the visual turn) is born of a particular moment in history, one which privileges the technological and specifically the digital over other forms of knowledge, mediation, and interaction. Gates, a former MacArthur award-winner, the most prominent black critic in America, and the scholar most often credited with marrying African American Studies and critical theories such as postmodernism, has made this turn.

The replacement of the deconstructive turn with the digital one can be seen as well in the more recent work of media scholar and critical race scholar Paul Gilroy, who after a similarly long and illustrious career as a scholar of the African diaspora (his eloquent book *The Black Atlantic* was an invaluable resource for media scholars and critical race scholars, as it showed how black identity was a transnational cultural formation created and reflected by media products) made a similar move towards imagining race as less symbolic and more biological, but his turn was in a different direction. Instead of seeing race as a biological fact, in *Against Race* he cited the prevalence of digital technology as a reason that we could no longer talk about race as a sound descriptive category. Gates' and Gilroy's technobiological turns can be interpreted as critical exhaustion—let the scientists sort it out, since humanists and social scientists seem to have made little headway—as well as the adoption of a new strategy for racial politics. The technoscientific turns afford a new, seemingly more neutral or less contentious discourse about race to circulate in the public sphere. This move reflects the difficulty of having any sort of critical public conversation about race, with or without beers.

The conversation between Barack Obama, Henry Louis Gates, and the officer who arrested him did not produce either any great reconciliation or revelation. And though this was disappointing to many, it was not surprising, for as Bonilla-Silva (2001) writes, race has become literally impossible for many Americans to talk about; stammering, stuttering, or stymied muteness are common reactions to the topic. The techno-genetic turn offers a language for talking about race that feels safe for many, because it moves race comfortably out of the social and into another, seemingly less contentious realm. As Bonilla-Silva (2003) reminds us, the neoliberal ideology that defines our current political, economic, and socio-cultural moment moves race, like all other forms of personal identity, into the realm of the personal rather than the collective responsibility. Is it better to have a biotechnological conversation about race than none at all?

The media—television, radio, film, the Internet, digital games—are platforms for public conversations about race, for as Wendy Chun writes in her essay for this collection, "rather than the abatement of racism and raced images post WWII, we have witnessed their proliferation" (see also Chun 2006; Chun 2009). The visual turn and the technological turn are converging as images migrate and proliferate as well onto digital platforms. It is crucial that these images and modes of informatics be examined as it becomes increasingly inadequate and we become unwilling to have these conversations with each other, face to face. Mediatized conversations about race, whether on the Internet with human interlocutors or with the torrent of digitized media texts, have become an increasingly important channel for discourse about our differences. Race has itself become a digital medium, a distinctive set of informatic codes, networked mediated narratives, maps, images, and visualizations that index identity. Critical race scholarship, that is to say scholarship that investigates the shifting meanings of race and how it works in society, and proposes interventions in the name of social justice, must expand its scope to digital media and computer-based technologies. Gates and Gilroy's turns away from deconstruction and cultural analysis and towards genomic thinking really are affirmations that this is the case; they acknowledge that the digital turn has changed the game, and that race critique has to acknowledge this and respond to it meaningfully, or be left behind.

Similarly, projects like the MacArthur Digital Media and Learning Foundation, which supports critical scholarship on the impact of computing and networking on youth in education, titled its first conference in 2010 "Diversifying Participation" in order to establish that access to digital technologies is unevenly distributed, and that people of color and other groups are still denied equal opportunities in relation to digital media.

Measuring unequal access to digital media technologies across racial and ethnic lines is still a central part of the research contained within this book. In contrast to earlier scholarship on race and the Internet, it is not the only focus, and the work in here contains exciting new data about differential access to specific digital technologies, such as online journalism and SNSs (social network sites). When the Internet became widely adopted in the mid-1990s, research on the digital divide proceeded from both policy makers and scholars; monographs such as Van Dijk's *The Deepening Divide: Inequality and the Information Society* (2006), Lisa Servon's *Bridging the Digital Divide* (2002), Pew Research Center's Internet and American Life Project, and the U.S. Commerce Department's NTIA *Falling Through the Net* reports (1995, 1998, 1999) called attention to the problem of unequal access. While there is no doubt that access is important, a binary notion of access as either a yes or no proposition flies in the face of reason or usage, as Hargittai has shown with her empirical studies of web usage (see Hargittai 2008 and 2010). Reneta Mack's *The Digital Divide* (2001) shows how technology gaps for African Americans are connected to other "gaps" in economics and education. In any event, though the racial digital divide is narrowing, it has distinctly racialized contours, as youth flock to mobile digital platforms over fixed ones and begin to self-segregate into specific SNSs based on race, ethnicity, and other factors. As Watkins asserts in *The Young and the Digital: What the Migration to Social Network Sites, Games, and Anytime, Anywhere Media Means for Our Future* (2009) youth of color are rapidly adopting digital media technologies such as cellphones and games as part of their everyday lives, and in some cases use them more frequently than their white peers.

Critical race studies must take account of the digital, and digital media and technology studies must take account of race—though the essays in this book demonstrate that race is more than its technoscientific representation. Indeed, the essays in this book approach race and the digital from a variety of perspectives and disciplines: our authors come from departments of cinema and media studies, Asian American, Latino, and African American studies, communication, information studies, literary studies, and sociology. However, rather than taking the shift to digital and computer-mediated culture as new information which either invalidates the idea of race as a coherent category or encourages us to reduce it to a set of empirical data that reifies existing race categories, these essays explore the co-production of race and computing starting from the post-war U.S. period. This is a history that has deeper and older roots than had been previously thought.

The field of race and digital media studies was heralded by foundational collections about race and digital technologies such as Alondra Nelson and Thuy Linh Tu's excellent *Technicolor: Race, Technology, and Everyday Life* (2001), Nelson's special issue of *Social Text* entitled *Afrofuturism: A Special Issue of Social Text* (2002), and Kolko, Nakamura, and Rodman's *Race in Cyberspace* (2001). These collections focused on the pre-Web 2.0 period and the populariza-tion of the idea of the Internet as a "participatory medium," and much has changed since then. SNSs, YouTube, and Massively Multiplayer Online Role Playing Games had yet to become widely adopted, and Internet usage was not nearly as transnational as it is now. Since then the Internet has become even more widely adopted, digital convergence between media formats, devices, and genres has produced a truly transmedia environment (Jenkins 2006), and individual platforms other than email and websites have risen to prominence. Anna Everett's excellent *Learning, Race and Ethnicity: Youth and Digital Media*, part of the MacArthur/MIT Press Series on Digital Media and Learning (2008; available both for free online and in paper) updates earlier anthologies on race and the digital to include essays on racialized conflicts between transnational groups of users within MMOs (Doug Thomas), the formation of racialized communities on early race-based internet portals such as BlackPlanet (Dara Byrne) and the use of the Internet to encourage Native American digital literacy (Antonio Lopez). Rishab Aiyer Ghosh's innovative anthology *Code: Collaborative Ownership and the Digital Economy* (2005) takes a thoroughly transnational approach to digital media technologies and economies which is much needed in the field. Similarly, Pramod Nayer's (2010) *New Media and Cybercultures* anthology blends key essays on new media theory and racial difference in the U.S. context with a transnational approach that reflects the ongoing spread of the Internet and other digital technologies across the globe, while acknowledging the unevenness of its distribution. Collections like Ghosh's, Nayer's, and Landzelius' collection about indigenous and diasporic peoples, *Native on the Net*, internationalize Internet and race studies in much needed ways.

Monographs on race and the digital technologies such as Lisa Nakamura's *Cybertypes: Race, Ethnicity, and Identity on the Internet* (2002) and Anna Everett's *Digital Diaspora: A Race for Cyberspace* (2009) focused specifically on the Internet, and others blended media theory with software studies, such as Chun's brilliant *Control and Freedom: Power and Paranoia in the Age of Fiber Optics* (2006). Later monographs such as Jessie Daniel's *Cyber Racism: White Supremacy Online and the New Attack on Civil Rights* (2009) featured a more narrow focus on hate groups online, and others looked at specific racial groups' involvements and investments in digital mediaspace, such as Everett's book, which looked specifically at African American online cultures (see also Ignacio 2005). Nakamura's *Digitizing Race: Visual Cultures of the Internet* (2008a) did comparative work focusing on Asian Americans and combined it with a particular methodological approach—visual culture studies. Other authors included extensive analyses of race within books on digital media studies more broadly, such as Alex Galloway's chapter on simulation gaming and racial identity in his monograph *Gaming: Essays in Algorithmic Culture* (2006). These and other monographs traced the ways that new media industries, users, and platforms have co-created race from the Internet's early days and in the present, and we are happy to see that this area of study continues to grow apace.

Race After the Internet is part of a developing interdisciplinary critical conversation that started with a forceful critique of the utopian discourse that characterized early digital media studies. Ever since the now-iconic 1993 *New Yorker* cartoon that declared that "On the Internet Nobody Knows You're a Dog!" the Internet has been envisioned as a technology with a radical form of agency, endowed with the capacity to make kids smarter (or dumber), to make social life more playful and fluid (or more sexually corrupt and deceitful), and to create an ideal "information society" where everyone is radically equal. (See Nakamura

2008b for a more detailed review of scholarship on race and the Internet.) People of color were viewed in the 1990s as beneficiaries of the Internet's ability to permit anonymous communications, and much of the earlier scholarship focused on the issue of *race representation* on the Internet. The focus on the lack of images of blacks and other others in icons to be found on the Internet (see White 2006), as well as within video game avatars (see Everett 2009 and Leonard 2004) established that, indeed, users of color were hard put to find "good" representations of themselves, and thus had to choose between a default whiteness and a stereotyped form of blackness. Digital games are now a mainstream form of media (video games passed DVDs in global sales in 2010), and they show us the new racial order of avatar representation in interactive space in action: excellent essays by David Golumbia (2009), Tanner Higgin (2009), David Leonard (2006), Lisa Nakamura (2009), Jessica Langer (2008), and Alex Galloway (2006) describe how *World of Warcraft* and *Grand Theft Auto* are platforms for race as exotic spectacle (see also DeVane and Squire 2008 for an empirical study about how youth view race in *Grand Theft Auto*). While for some the world of Azeroth is a fantasy world of infinite possibility, a training ground for collaborative and managerial skill and teambuilding, or simply an immensely profitable and popular business, for others it is both a sweatshop and a minstrel show. The cybertyping of trolls and tauren as Caribbean exotics and Native Americans, complete with music, costumes, and accents, casts racial others as the bad guys on the wrong side of a racial war that is hard-coded into the game, but as Galloway's chapter in this essay shows, race is more than its representation, more than "screen deep," in Chun's words: it is part of the algorithmic logic of games and digital media themselves.

There are four main critical interventions that this collection adds to the existing and increasingly robust conversation on race and digital media technologies. The essays in Part I, "The History of Race and Information: Code, Policies, Identities" encourage a re-envisioning of race in digital technologies as a form of code, as well as a visual representation of a raced body. While earlier studies in race and digital media did the necessary work of identifying racist representations of samurai, gangsters, hookers, and other criminalized bodies as "colored," and calling for more even-handed and representative images of people of color on the dynamic screen, the study of stereotypes in digital media is intrinsically different from studies of representation in analog media. For code-based media is processual as well as visual; it does as well as appears. It executes race. Users don't just consume images of race when they play video games, interact with software, and program: instead, they perform them. While it still matters if your avatar can or cannot look like you, the ability to compose digital identities extends beyond what can be seen on the screen, and we must attend to how race operates as a set of parameters and affordances, ideological activities, and programmed codes. Indeed, as McPherson reminds us, media critics must force themselves to do more than read what's visible in new media's interfaces, for this work may distract us from the working of race within code itself.

McPherson's exciting essay "U.S. Operating Systems at Mid-Century: The Intertwining of Race and UNIX" mines the archive of software development history to expose how UNIX, an extremely important operating system, was based upon the paradigm of "encapsulation" that implemented increasingly modular systems. The high priority put upon separating different parts of the system from each other shows that

> this push toward modularity and the covert in digital computation also reflects other changes in the organization of social life in the 1960s. For instance, if the first half of the twentieth century laid bare its racial logics, from "Whites Only" signage to the brutalities of lynching, the second half increasingly hides its racial "kernel," burying it below a shell of neoliberal pluralism.

McPherson argues that scholars work against ongoing processes of encapsulation that separate disciplines from each other and racial populations from social and political alliance, reminding us that "computers are themselves encoders of culture," and that it is "at best naive to imagine that cultural and computational operating systems don't mutually infect one another."

Wendy Chun's "Race and/as Technology, or How to Do Things to Race" examines the "resurgence of the category of race within science and medicine" as an opportunity to read back into the archive of race science. As she writes, "segregation is an important U.S. racial technology, a clarifying spatial mapping that creates stark racial differences where none necessarily exist." Her formulation of race itself as a technology—a way of doing things—helps us to re-envision race as a form of encoding, rather than as a paint-by-numbers kit of stereotypes. Her incisive reading of hapa filmmaker Greg Pak's movie *Robot Stories* extends her work on techno-Orientalism; this film's all Asian American and African American cast have displaced whites in the film, forcing viewers to imagine a future where whiteness is no longer dominant, but is in fact absent. As she writes, the "invisibility and universality usually granted to whiteness has disappeared, not to be taken up seamlessly by Asian Americans and African Americans, but rather re-worked to displace both the technological and the human."

Archival work that traces the histories of digital technologies and race forces us to revise our ideas about innovation and creativity as somehow racially neutral and objectively defined. As Rayvon Fouché reminds us in his essay "From Black Inventors to One Laptop Per Child: Exporting a Racial Politics of Technology," technology has a pre-digital history that has long devalued the contributions and needs of African Americans, and these roots have borne fruit in digital uplift projects such as the One Laptop Per Child (OLPC) initiative. He posits that we map race and American culture into four periods: during the first of these,

1619–1865, slavery was a dominant technology in itself, and during the second period of formalized race-based segregation, from 1865 to 1954, many scientific and technological systems and infrastructures such as railroads became powerful forces for segregation. From 1954 to 2003 Fouché notes the unraveling of the biological connection to race and the UNESCO "Statement on Race" overlapping with the civil rights movement. Fouché marks the final period as heralding "new forms of segregation, a newly defined scientific foundation for the rebirth of race, and digital-age technological aid for the developing world" and concludes with a compelling critique of the OLPC project, asking us to question whether the "perceived universal nature of open source software [can] transcend region, language, space, and culture."

Curtis Marez's essay in this collection, "Cesar Chavez, the United Farm Workers, and the History of *Star Wars*," explores the industrial history of digital video-imaging technologies and its links to racialized labor practices in California's Valleys: the Central Valley, home of filmmaker George Lucas, and Silicon Valley. George Lucas, the producer of perhaps the most generative media franchise to hit both the big screen and digital screens around the world, grew up in Modesto, where Cesar Chavez was deploying DIY video in order to publicize and preserve the struggles of the United Farm Workers Union. Marez adeptly tells the story of how the *Star Wars* franchise and its lesser-known predecessors *THX-1138* and *American Graffiti* dramatize the struggles and eventual triumph of white masculinity, a narrative that was eagerly taken up by California conservatives during the Bush era. His essay reminds us that both digital and agricultural labor is overwhelmingly performed by racialized populations in California: chips are made by Asian women, Silicon Valley offices are cleaned by Latino and black workers, just as the UFW's workers harvested fruit in some of these same geographical spaces not long before.

Marez's brilliant critique of Lucas's oeuvre helps us see how the history of *Star Wars*, a frequently mined source text in participatory media produced by users and disseminated on YouTube and elsewhere (see Chad Vader) is not a neutral one: as he writes, "in contexts dominated by a *Star Wars* worldview it becomes harder to see and think about things like Justice for Janitors and, more broadly, digital culture's dependence on systems of racialized labor."

The digital divide is an attractive formulation because it promises an easy solution to a messy situation: it proposes that computer access in and of itself is a meaningful measure of informational power and privilege. Indeed, similar strains of idealism fueled by technological determinism are still to be found today, as Fouché notes in his excellent critique of the One Laptop Per Child program in this volume. We now know that computers themselves will not fix social and racial inequality, and indeed may produce new forms of inequality, as the essays in Part II, "Race, Identity, and Digital Sorting," by Alex Galloway, Oscar Gandy, Anna Everett, and Christian Sandvig show. The work in this section complicates and refines the question of access to digital technologies;

rather than viewing them as unambiguously good, the authors examine how computers enable new forms of social sorting. The essays in this section demand that we *rethink the rhetoric of the digital divide*.

Alex Galloway's essay in this section, "Does the Whatever Speak?" is structured around four key questions about race in the digital age. Galloway explains the intimate links between the "increased cultivation of racial typing" and the "recession of 'theory'," particularly identity politics and cultural studies. His provocative thesis is that the promiscuous production of digital racial imagery ought to be read as more than just the production of stereotypes, business as usual on the Internet, but rather as a form of *racial coding*, a logic of identity that has come to replace it more globally. In his brilliant reading of the role of race in the dress rehearsal for Obama's inauguration, he asserts that "racial coding has not gone away within recent years, it has only migrated into the realm of the dress rehearsal, the realm of pure simulation, and as simulation it remains absolutely necessary." If digital culture has taught us anything, it is that simulations are powerful. He addresses the issue of raced avatars within the most popular global Massively Multiplayer Role Playing Game *World of Warcraft* by asserting that "the most obvious thing to observe is precisely the way in which racial coding must always pass into fantasy before it can ever return to the real. The true is only created by way of an extended detour through falsity." This essay produces a theory of identity in the digital age that envisions the virtual as the "primary mechanism of oppression," yet ends on a hopeful note. Galloway encourages us to deploy theory's affordances to resist the marginalization of both critical theory and racial difference.

One of the most important new media technologies in the digital age that undergirds the Internet is the database. Most people rarely think about this technology that makes the storing, migration, collection, and analysis of data on the Internet possible. Oscar Gandy's chapter, "Matrix Multiplication and the Digital Divide," explores how data-mining practices that classify, sort, and evaluate populations reproduce racial inequality and generate new mechanisms of racial discrimination. Scholars working in surveillance studies explore the ways in which companies and state organizations use the information we put up on the Web to know a population of users. Oscar Gandy first referred to this practice as the *panoptic sort* in his foundational book on data mining and personal information published in 1993. Since then, data-mining technologies proliferated into all sorts of enterprises, especially marketing. When we purchase products, make wall posts on Facebook, update Twitter, or give personal information in exchange for services on the Web the data from those transactions enters into a matrix of information for social sorting. Once we lose control of that data, we lose control over the terms of our privacy and our identity online. In the early 2000s, concerns about privacy focused primarily on the security of credit card information and online shopping. A decade later, Facebook's privacy agreement is the main target in the struggle between users and corporations over the ownership of personal data. Users seek to gain control and ownership over their online identities and the information they put on the Web. Companies like Facebook package and sell the personal information from their users to other companies who then data mine the information to develop niche marketing strategies. While this may seem beneficial for individual consumers, scholars such as Joe Turow (2006) argue data-mining practices are creating new forms of consumer citizenship based on the economy of the marketplace rather than democratic principles. Marketers build group profiles to ascertain which population segments are preferred for companies and their products and which ones are less desirable. Gandy argues that this matrix of multiplication creates a cumulative disadvantage for African Americans.

Barack Obama's presidential campaign occurred at the same time that social media such as YouTube, SNSs, and social awareness tools such as Twitter ushered in a new media ecology. Obama supporters such as the "Obama Girl" disseminated viral video and leveraged other forms of social media, yet these same technologies have been deployed to spread hateful racist messages about the President, contributing both to his rise and the post-election dip in popularity, in Anna Everett's terms "voter's remorse." Anna Everett's essay "Have We Become Postracial Yet? Race and Media Technology in the Age of President Obama" examines user-generated content as well as traditional media coverage of Obama's presidency to examine how "Obama became the über-celebrity media text, one capable of testing the limits of new media's digital democracy credibility, while engendering a plethora of racial significations—novel and familiar." In this essay Everett explains how our first "digital" President, the first to use a laptop and a BlackBerry, both benefited from the "digital natives" who supported his campaign and suffered racist abuse from right-wing bloggers. Though many drew the conclusion that the United States had gone "beyond race" by electing Obama to the presidency, Everett's analysis of the social media scene in the years since demonstrates that black masculinity is still a deeply threatening (and threatened) identity in America.

Much of the early work on race and the Internet has tended to focus on more "majority" minority groups such as African Americans, Latinos, and Asian Americans, at the expense of considering other forms of difference in the U.S. and elsewhere. Sandvig's essay, "Connection at Ewiiaapaayp Mountain: Indigenous Internet Infrastructure," is based on ethnographic data gathered from an Internet collective based in California's San Diego County, a locale that has more distinct federally recognized Indian reservations than any other county in the United States. In his memorable formulation, comparing AT&T with the TDV (the Tribal Digital Village) helps us to compare dominant forms of Internet infrastructure provision with innovative new ones that operate under a different economic, cultural, and technological model. This essay tells the remarkable story of how 100 percent Internet penetration was achieved on an

Indian reservation that, in common with "Indian country" all over the U.S., had previously suffered from one of the most impoverished communication and general infrastructures to be found in the U.S. This work provides a useful challenge to the utopian notion of technological appropriation as always giving users from marginalized groups a variety of interesting new ways to be "other," and asserts that in the case of the TDV, "technological and cultural difference isn't celebrated—instead it is suppressed." Sovereignty, indigeneity, and locale are equally salient terms of identity to race in many parts of the world. Sandvig's work opens up new lines of inquiry into parts of the U.S. and elsewhere where racial identity has a different politics and composition: in the case of many native American groups, all individuals are mixed-race, and tribal enrollment signifies much more than race does.

The phrase "Let a thousand flowers bloom," much beloved of Internet enthusiasts who celebrate this platform's diversity, tolerance, and freedom to do what one wills, fails to take account of what sorts of flowers might be planted, where, and by whom. The essays in our third section, "Digital Segregations" explain how it is that Internet users are sorted and segregated into separate platforms or networks. The "digital divide" has been replaced by multiple divides or, as danah boyd puts it, bad and good neighborhoods, with users themselves envisioning the Internet as containing "ghettos" populated with lower-class, uneducated, potentially dangerous users of color and others as being safe, clean, and well supervised. boyd explains the history and trajectory of Facebook's rise to dominance over other social networks such as MySpace and Friendster by analyzing data gathered from youth who explained their decision process in choosing social networks in exactly these terms. This important and timely work debunks the myth that platforms succeed or fail based on their technological affordances, perceived convenience, or design, by documenting in users' own words why they moved from MySpace to Facebook. Her provocative title, "White Flight in Networked Publics: How Race and Class Shaped American Teen Adoption of MySpace and Facebook," updates earlier studies of race and the Internet by focusing on an influential and increasingly large and diverse population of Internet users—youth—as well as the immensely popular platforms for social networking that take up so much of our leisure and work time. The story of the Internet since the turn of the century is the story of the rise of social networks, and the mass movement of users from MySpace to Facebook reflects the increasingly segregated nature of Internet experience. boyd's research findings have proven controversial with readers of the *New York Times* online, for they threaten dearly held but incorrect assumptions about the inherent neutrality and democratic nature of social networks.

Eszter Hargittai investigates the differences among "digital natives" by surveying social network service use among a racially and ethnically diverse set of young adults. Her quantitative analysis in "Open Doors, Closed Spaces?

Differential Adoption of Social Network Sites by User Background" complements the findings of danah boyd's ethnographic study. Hargittai challenges the notion that as new web-based services emerge and become popular, most people shift their use accordingly and adoption is universal. By collecting two data sets across time and across a number of social networking service platforms, such as MySpace, Facebook, Xanga, and BlackPlanet, she is able to offer a unique and striking picture of racially segmented use over different time periods. This racial segmentation can have consequences for certain racial and ethnic groups if non-governmental, government, and business organizations wrongly assume that all populations use a site. The result could be systematic exclusion from access to different types of information.

Wilson and Costanza-Chock's chapter, "New Voices on the Net? The Digital Journalism Divide and the Costs of Network Exclusion," takes a different tack to the question of digital divides and the costs of digital inclusion and exclusion. Surveillance scholars focus on the effects for individuals and society in being caught in the panoptic Web. Wilson and Costanza-Chock examine the cumulative disadvantage of exclusion from the old and new media news networks. The authors survey the persistent problem of exclusion of people of color from the news media both as newsmakers and as owners of media companies. The recent economic crisis in the industry has put pressure on owners to reduce newsroom staff, sell to other organizations, or close their doors. Media companies are also turning to the Internet to create new online journalism platforms. The authors argue that participation in the news media is increasingly becoming a question of access to digital networks. They find that people of color are creating opportunities online for ownership and journalism, and emerging forms of community-based, non-professional journalism could potentially transform the media sector. However, the disparities in the mainstream of print and television persist online. Wilson and Costanza-Chock propose that this type of digital divide is best understood as a cost of network exclusion. As the networks of news media increasingly move online and continue to reproduce the racial inequality of representation in ownership and journalists, the costs for those outside the network grow exponentially.

Our last section, entitled "Biotechnology and Race as Information" picks up where this introduction started, that is, by taking account of the confluence of digital media's rise as a dominant cultural platform alongside rapid developments in racial genomics. The first parts of the book show some of the consequences and outcomes when race becomes information through the proliferation of digital media across institutional and user contexts. The domain of science is no exception as biology has gone digital. As Castells argues in his foundational trilogy on the rising information age, biology has become an informational science (Castells 2000). The questions we raised at the beginning of the introduction and explored by Chun in her essay about biology and race have become even more relevant today, especially since communication technologies, programming code, and digital data drive the new enterprise of genomics. The possibility of understanding race at the molecular level as mappable and quantifiable is premised on innovations and developments in computing and Internet technologies as race is recreated in digital media space.

Bowker and Star's foundational *Sorting Things Out* (2000) demonstrated that race is a process of social classification that relies upon an idea of scientific truth. Even when racial "science" turns out to be both spurious and overtly shaped by ideology, the idea that race classification rests upon some kind of an empirical base has been long enduring, and has worked strongly to form and re-form how race shapes people's lives. Troy Duster's foundational *Backdoor to Eugenics* (2003/1990) raised important questions about the combination of old scientific notions about race and emerging research into the new genetics in the 1980s and 1990s. Instead of the HGP finally confirming the spurious relationship between biology and race as Gilroy hoped in *Against Race,* it actually opened up a new line of inquiry into human differences. What began as a trickle of digital DNA into genome databases at the close of the twentieth century turned into a deluge in the first decade of the twenty-first. The scientific practice of classifying and comparing bodies using digital information in biomedical and pharmaceutical research is profoundly challenging earlier theories of social constructivism that viewed race as a purely imaginary construct. The technologies and scientific practices that sociologists Duster and Dorothy Nelkin (1989) investigated were in their infancy. Since the completion of the HGP, many have become reality and the rate of new racially based scientific and biomedical research and commercial products and services is accelerating. From the first race-based drug BiDil to Google's personal genomics company 23andMe, the consequences of this enormous shift in the concept of race are still emerging and have yet to be put into relation with digital technologies and the ways that they imbue everyday life with algorithmic logics.

Scientists have been constructing new forms of knowledge about biological differences between racialized groups, knowledges that define the intersection between digital media and digital biology. New DNA technologies are being developed in a techno-social context of digital media where information is the material for racial formation. In the cases of gaming and social media, for example, race operates as a social construct in fairly visible and concrete ways. The avatars users create and inhabit and the social networking sites they use are the result of socially enabled and constrained choices and performances. However, when scientists claim that there are differences in rates of disease between racialized groups, genetic notions of race tend to overshadow social causes. Even if scientists take great care in referring to study groups in non-racial terms, race tends to creep back into the discourse. This dynamic will become even more salient in the future, as the major hot button questions of intelligence, physical ability, and behavior come to the fore from the sidelines.

The chapters in this book by Nelson and Hwang, Chow-White, and Duster explain and critique some of the lines of inquiry that have been pursued by scholars working the "genome space" in the last ten years. These authors investigate how DNA technology is being used and shaped in a number of different enterprises such as direct to consumer genomic ancestry testing, biomedical and health research, and law enforcement.

In the 2000s a number of direct to consumer genomic biotechnology companies started up and offered genetic ancestry tests, such as Gate's biotech startup, African DNA. Consumers can send in a saliva swab and receive a genomic screen that tells them about the origins of their ancestral lineage. A number of companies inform customers of their racial makeup, from Asia, Europe, or Africa. In "Roots and Revelation: Genetic Ancestry Testing and the YouTube Generation," Alonda Nelson and Jeong Won Hwang explore how African American amateur genealogists combine genetic ancestry tests and the video-sharing social networking site to reveal information about their ancestry. They find that African Americans use companies such as African Ancestry to rediscover their "roots," a practice that became popular following the Alex Haley television mini series in the 1970s. While genealogy is primarily a hobby of older adults, the combination of cutting-edge technologies of genomic tests and confessional-style social networking is making it popular with youth. Nelson and Hwang explain how the reality TV format of the "reveal," where genealogists read out the results of their test and connect with their audience, is an important part of the revelation of finding out their genetic identity. Often, the genetic information confirms or disrupts their sense of their racial identity, just as it did with Henry Louis Gates' guests on his racio-genetic reality television programs.

In "Genomic Databases and an Emerging Digital Divide in Biotechnology," Peter Chow-White explains how scientists working on the Human Genome Project in the 1990s viewed genomic data as a public good rather than information that should be privately held by individual scientists or corporations. By making genome databases openly accessible through the Internet to anyone, they hoped that this would democratize science and prevent a global digital divide. While this is a laudable goal, Chow-White shows that the DNA data that scientists uploaded into public genome databases is primarily from European individuals. He argues this bias towards whiteness is a racial digital divide that has enormous consequences for understanding human health and making new medical discoveries.

While the DNA databases scientists use to study health are skewed towards whiteness, African Americans and Latinos are increasingly over-represented in forensic DNA databases used by federal and local law enforcement agencies. In "The Combustible Intersection: Genomics, Forensics, and Race," Troy Duster explains that DNA technology in crime scenes and the courts is largely seen as infallible, what he refers to as the "CSI effect." He explores the ideological and technical validity of DNA technologies and suggests new avenues of research for social science into the expanding surveillance net. Troy Duster's chapter addresses a decade of research by scholars into the proliferation of racialized DNA databases in the U.S. In the early 2000s, police collected DNA from convicted capital offence felons and sexual offenders. The collection mandate has crept over the last decade. Now, some state agencies collect DNA from people only arrested for much lesser infractions. In the context of over-policing of African American and Latino communities and high incarceration rates, the proliferation of DNA databanks puts African Americans and Latinos under increased surveillance.

Digital media are both long lived and ephemeral, fragmented, networked, and contingent. Digital media technology creates and hosts the social networks, virtual worlds, online communities, and media texts where it was once thought that we would all be the same, anonymous users with infinite powers. Instead, the essays in this collection show us that the Internet and other computer-based technologies are complex topographies of power and privilege, made up of walled communities, new (plat)forms of economic and technological exclusion, and both new and old styles of race as code, interaction, and image.

References

Bonilla-Silva, Eduardo. 2001. *White Supremacy and Racism in Post-Civil Rights Era*. Boulder, CO: Lynne Rienner.

——. 2003. *Racism Without Racists: Color-Blind Racism and the Persistence of Racial Inequality in the United States*. Boulder, Colorado: Rowman and Littlefield.

Bowker, Geoffrey C. and Susan Leigh Star. 2000. *Sorting Things Out: Classification and Its Consequences*. Cambridge, MA: MIT Press.

Castells, Manuel. 2000. *The Rise of the Network Society*, second edition. Oxford: Blackwell.

Chun, Wendy. 2006. *Control and Freedom: Power and Paranoia in the Age of Fiber Optics*. Cambridge, MA: MIT Press.

Daniel, Jessie. 2009. *Cyber Racism: White Supremacy Online and the New Attack on Civil Rights*. Lanham, MD: Rowman and Littlefield.

DeVane, Ben, and Kurt D. Squire. 2008. "The Meaning of Race and Violence in *Grand Theft Auto San Andreas*." *Games and Culture* 3.3–4: 264–285.

Duster, Troy. 2003/1990. *Backdoor to Eugenics*, second edition. New York: Routledge.

Everett, Anna, ed. 2008. *Learning, Race and Ethnicity: Youth and Digital Media, Digital Media and Learning*. Cambridge, MA: MacArthur Foundation and MIT Press.

——. 2009. *Digital Diaspora: A Race for Cyberspace*. Albany, NY: SUNY Press.

Galloway, Alex. 2006. *Gaming: Essays in Algorithmic Culture*. Minneapolis: University of Minnesota Press.

Gandy, Oscar H. 1993. *The Panoptic Sort: A Political Economy of Personal Information*. Boulder, CO: Westview Press.

Gates, Henry Louis. 1986. *"Race," Writing, and Difference*. Chicago: University of Chicago Press.

Gates Jr, Henry Louis. 1988. *The Signifying Monkey: A Theory of Afro-American Literary Criticism*. New York: Oxford University Press.

——. 2007. *Finding Oprah's Roots: Finding Your Own*. New York: Crown.

Ghosh, Rishab Aiyer, ed. 2005. *Code: Collaborative Ownership and the Digital Economy*. Cambridge, MA: MIT Press.

Gilroy, Paul. 2000. *Against Race: Imagining Political Culture Beyond the Color Line*. Cambridge, MA: Belknap Press of Harvard University Press.

Golumbia, David. 2009. "Games Without Play." *New Literary History* 40.1: 179–204.

Hargittai, Eszter. 2008. "The Digital Reproduction of Inequality," in D. Grusky, ed., *Social Stratification*. Boulder, CO: Westview Press.

——. 2010. "Digital Na(t)ives? Variation in Internet Skills and Uses among Members of the 'Net Generation'." *Sociological Inquiry* 80.1: 92–113.

Hartman, Saidiya. 1997. *Scenes of Subjection: Terror, Slavery, and Self-Making in Nineteenth-Century America*. Oxford: Oxford University Press.

Higgin, Tanner. 2009. "Blackless Fantasy: The Disappearance of Race in Massively Multiplayer Online Role-playing Games." *Games and Culture* 4.1: 3–26.

Ignacio, Emily Noelle. 2005. *Building Diaspora: Filipino Community Formation on the Internet*. Piscataway, NJ: Rutgers University Press.

Jenkins, Henry. 2006. *Convergence Culture: Where Old and New Media Collide*. New York: NYU Press.

Kolko, B.E., L. Nakamura, and G.B. Rodman, eds. 2000. *Race in Cyberspace*. New York: Routledge.

Landzelius, Kyra, ed. 2006. *Native on the Net: Indigenous and Diasporic Peoples in the Virtual Age*. New York: Routledge.

Langer, Jessica. 2008. "The Familiar and the Foreign: Playing (Post)Colonialism in *World of Warcraft*," in H. Corneliussen and J.W. Rettberg, eds, *Digital Culture, Play, and Identity: A World of Warcraft Reader*. Cambridge, MA: MIT Press.

Leonard, David J. 2004. "High Tech Blackface: Race, Sports Video Games and Becoming the Other." *Intelligent Agent* 4: 1–5.

——. 2006. "Virtual Gangstas, Coming to a Suburban House Near You: Demonization, Commodification, and Policing Blackness," in N. Garrelts, ed., *The Meaning and Culture of Grand Theft Auto: Critical Essays*. Jefferson, NC: McFarland.

Mack, Raneta Lawson. 2001. *The Digital Divide: Standing at the Intersection of Race & Technology*. Durham, NC: Carolina Academic Press.

Nakamura, Lisa. 2002. *Cybertypes: Race, Ethnicity, and Identity on the Internet*. New York: Routledge.

——. 2008a. *Digitizing Race: Visual Cultures of the Internet*. Minneapolis: University of Minnesota Press.

——. 2008b. "Cyberrace." *PLMA* 123.5: 1673–1682.

——. 2009. "Don't Hate the Player, Hate the Game: The Racialization of Labor in *World of Warcraft*." *Critical Studies in Media Communication* 26.2: 128–144.

Nayar, Pramod K., ed. 2010. *The New Media and Cybercultures Anthology*. Malden, MA: Wiley-Blackwell.

Nelkin, Dorothy, and Laurence Tancredi. 1989. *Dangerous Diagnostics: The Social Power of Biological Information*. New York: Basic Books.

Nelson, Alondra, Thuh Linh N. Tu, and Alicia Headlam Hines. 2001. *Technicolor: Race, Technology, and Everyday Life*. New York: New York University Press.

NTIA U.S. Department of Commerce. 1995. *Falling through the Net I: A Survey of the "Have Nots" in Rural and Urban America*. Available at: www.ntia.doc.gov/ntiahome/fallingthru.html

——. 1998. *Falling through the Net II: New Data on the Digital Divide*. Available at: www.ntia.doc.gov/ntiahome/net2

——. 1999. *Falling through the Net III: Defining the Digital Divide*. Available at: www.ntia.doc.gov/ntiahome/fttn99/

Palfrey, John, and Urs Gasser. 2008. *Born Digital: Understanding the First Generation of Digital Natives*. New York: Basic Books.

Servon, Lisa. 2002. *Bridging the Digital Divide: Technology, Community, and Public Policy*. New York: Blackwell.

Turow, Joseph. 2006. *Niche Envy: Marketing Discrimination in the Digital Age*. Cambridge, MA: MIT Press.

Van Dijk, Jan. 2006. *The Deepening Divide: Inequality and the Information Society*. Thousand Oaks, CA: Sage.

Watkins, Craig. 2009. *The Young and the Digital: What the Migration to Social Network Sites, Games, and Anytime, Anywhere Media Means for Our Future*. Boston, MA: Beacon Press.

White, Michelle. 2006. *The Body and the Screen: Theories of Internet Spectatorship*. Cambridge, MA: MIT Press.

I
The History of Race and Information
Code, Policies, Identities

1

U.S. Operating Systems at Mid-Century

The Intertwining of Race and UNIX

TARA MCPHERSON

University of Southern California

I begin with two fragments cut from history, around about the 1960s. This essay will pursue the lines of connection between these two moments and argue that insisting on their entanglement is integral to any meaningful understanding of either of the terms this volume's title brings together: the internet and race. Additionally, I am interested in what we might learn from these historical examples about the very terrains of knowledge production in the post-World War II United States. The legacies of mid-century shifts in both our cultural understandings of race and in digital computation are still very much with us today, powerful operating systems that deeply influence how we know self, other and society.

Fragment One

In the early 1960s, computer scientists at MIT were working on Project MAC, an early set of experiments in Compatible Timesharing Systems for computing. In the summer of 1963, MIT hosted a group of leading computer scientists at the university to brainstorm about the future of computing. By 1965, MULTICS (Multiplexed Information and Computing Service), a mainframe timesharing operating system, was in use, with joint development by MIT, GE, and Bell Labs, a subsidiary of ATT. The project was funded by ARPA of the Defense Department for two million a year for eight years. MULTICS introduced early ideas about modularity in hardware structure and software architecture.

In 1969, Bell Labs stopped working on MULTICS, and, that summer, one of their engineers, Ken Thompson, developed the beginning of UNIX. While there are clearly influences of MULTICS on UNIX, the later system also moves away from the earlier one, pushing for increased modularity and for a simpler design able to run on cheaper computers.

In simplest terms, UNIX is an early operating system for digital computers, one that has spawned many offshoots and clones. These include MAC OS X as well as LINUX, indicating the reach of UNIX over the past forty years. The system also influenced non-UNIX operating systems like Windows NT and remains in use by many corporate IT divisions. UNIX was originally written in assembly language, but after Thompson's colleague, Dennis Ritchie, developed the C programming language in 1972, Thompson rewrote UNIX in that language. Basic text-formatting and editing features were added (i.e. early word processors). In 1974, Ritchie and Thompson published their work in the *Journal of the Association for Computing Machinery*, and UNIX began to pick up a good deal of steam.[1]

UNIX can also be thought of as more than an operating system, as it also includes a number of utilities such as command line editors, APIs (which, it is worth noting, existed long before our Google maps made them sexy), code libraries, etc. Furthermore, UNIX is widely understood to embody particular philosophies and cultures of computation, "operating systems" of a larger order that we will return to.

Fragment Two

Of course, for scholars of culture, of gender and of race, dates like 1965 and 1968 have other resonances. For many of us, 1965 might not recall MULTICS but instead the assassination of Malcolm X, the founding of the United Farm Workers, the burning of Watts, or the passage of the Voting Rights Act. The mid-1960s also saw the origins of the American Indian Movement (AIM) and the launch of the National Organization for Women (NOW). The late 1960s mark the 1968 citywide walkouts of Latino youth in Los Angeles, the assassinations of Martin Luther King, Jr. and Robert F. Kennedy, the Chicago Democratic convention with its police brutality, the Stonewall Riots, and the founding of the Black Panthers and the Young Lords. Beyond the geographies of the United States, we might also remember the Prague Spring of 1968, Tommie Smith and John Carlos at the Mexico Summer Olympics, the Tlatelolco Massacre, the execution of Che Guevara, the Chinese Cultural Revolution, the Six-Day War, or May '68 in Paris, itself a kind of origin story for some genealogies of film and media studies. On the African continent, thirty-two countries gained independence from colonial rulers. In the U.S., broad cultural shifts emerged across the decade, as identity politics took root and counter-cultural forces challenged traditional values. Resistance to the Vietnam War mounted as the decade wore on. Abroad, movements against colonialism and oppression were notably strong.

The history just glossed as 'Fragment One' is well known to code junkies and computer geeks. Numerous websites archive oral histories, programming manuals, and technical specifications for MULTICS, UNIX, and various mainframe and other hardware systems. Key players in the history, including Ken Thompson, Donald Ritchie and Doug McIlroy, have a kind of geek-chic celebrity status, and differing versions of the histories of software and hardware development are hotly debated, including nitty-gritty details of what really counts as "a UNIX." In media studies, emerging work in "code studies" often resurrects and takes up these histories.

Within American, cultural and ethnic studies, the temporal touchstones of struggles over racial justice, anti-war activism, and legal history are also widely recognized and analyzed. Not surprisingly, these two fragments typically stand apart in parallel tracks, attracting the interest and attention of very different audiences located in the deeply siloed departments that categorize our universities.

But Why?

In short, I suggest that these two moments cut from time are deeply interdependent. In fact, they co-constitute one another, comprising not independent slices of history but, instead, related and useful lenses into the shifting epistemological registers driving U.S. and global culture in the 1960s and after. Both exist as operating systems of a sort, and we might understand them to be mutually reinforcing.

This history of intertwining and mutual dependence is hard to tell. As we delve into the intricacies of UNIX and the data structures it embraces, race in America recedes far from our line of vision and inquiry. Likewise, detailed examinations into the shifting registers of race and racial visibility post-1950 do not easily lend themselves to observations about the emergence of object-oriented programming, personal computing, and encapsulation. Very few audiences who care about one lens have much patience or tolerance for the other.

Early forays in new media theory in the late 1990s did not much help this problem. Theorists of new media often retreated into forms of analysis that Marsha Kinder has critiqued as "cyberstructuralist," intent on parsing media specificity and on theorizing the forms of new media, while disavowing twenty-plus years of critical race theory, feminism and other modes of overtly politicized inquiry. Many who had worked hard to instill race as a central mode of analysis in film, literary, and media studies throughout the late twentieth century were disheartened and outraged (if not that surprised) to find new media theory so easily retreating into a comfortable formalism familiar from the early days of film theory.

Early analyses of race and the digital often took two forms, a critique of representations *in* new media, i.e. on the surface of our screens, or debates about access to media, i.e., the digital divide. Such work rarely pushed toward the analyses of form, phenomenology or computation that were so compelling and lively in the work of Lev Manovich, Mark Hansen, or Jay Bolter and Richard Grusin. Important works emerged from both "camps," but the camps rarely intersected. A few conferences attempted to force a collision between these areas, but the going was tough. For instance, at the two Race and Digital Space events colleagues and I organized in 2000 and 2002, the vast majority of participants and speakers were engaged in work in the two modes mentioned above. The cyberstructuralists were not in attendance.

But what if this very incompatibility is itself part and parcel of the organization of knowledge production that operating systems like UNIX helped to disseminate around the world? Might we ask if there is not something *particular to the very forms* of electronic culture that seems to encourage just such a movement, a movement that partitions race off from the specificity of media forms? Put differently, might we argue that the very structures of digital computation develop at least in part to cordon off race and to contain it? Further, might we come to understand that our own critical methodologies are the heirs to this epistemological shift?

From early writings by Sherry Turkle and George Landow to more recent work by Alex Galloway, new media scholars have noted the parallels between the ways of knowing modeled in computer culture and the greatest hits of structuralism and post-structuralism. Critical race theorists and postcolonial scholars like Chela Sandoval and Gayatri Spivak have illustrated the structuring (if unacknowledged) role that race plays in the work of poststructuralists like Roland Barthes and Michel Foucault. We might bring these two arguments together, triangulating race, electronic culture, and post-structuralism, and, further, argue that race, particularly in the United States, is central to this undertaking, fundamentally shaping how we see and know as well as the technologies that underwrite or cement both vision and knowledge. Certain modes of racial visibility and knowing coincide or dovetail with specific ways of organizing data: if digital computing underwrites today's information economy and is the central technology of post-World War II America, these technologized ways of seeing/knowing took shape in a world also struggling with shifting knowledges about and representations of race. If, as Michael Omi and Howard Winant argue, racial formations serve as fundamental organizing principles of social relations in the United States, on both the macro and micro levels (1986/1989: 55), how might we understand the infusion of racial organizing principles into the technological organization of knowledge after World War II?

Omi and Winant and other scholars have tracked the emergence of a "race-blind" rhetoric at mid-century, a discourse that moves from overt to more covert modes of racism and racial representation (for example, from the era of Jim Crow to liberal colorblindness). Drawing from those 3-D postcards that bring two or more images together even while suppressing their connections, I have earlier termed the racial paradigms of the post-war era "lenticular logics." The ridged coating on 3-D postcards is actually a lenticular lens, a structural device that makes simultaneously viewing the various images contained on one card nearly impossible. The viewer can rotate the card to see any single image, but the lens itself makes seeing the images *together* very difficult, even as it conjoins them at a structural level (i.e. within the same card). In the post-Civil Rights

U.S., the lenticular is a way of organizing the world. It structures representations but also epistemologies. It also serves to secure our understandings of race in very narrow registers, fixating on sameness or difference while forestalling connection and interrelation. As I have argued elsewhere, we might think of the lenticular as a covert mode of the pretense of "separate but equal," remixed for mid-century America (McPherson 2003: 250).

A lenticular logic is a covert racial logic, a logic for the post-Civil Rights era. We might contrast the lenticular postcard to that wildly popular artifact of the industrial era, the stereoscope card. The stereoscope melds two different images into an imagined whole, privileging the whole; the lenticular image partitions and divides, privileging fragmentation. A lenticular logic is a logic of the fragment or the chunk, a way of seeing the world as discrete modules or nodes, a mode that suppresses relation and context. As such, the lenticular also manages and controls complexity.

And what in the world does this have to do with those engineers laboring away at Bell Labs, the heroes of the first fragment of history this essay began with? What's race got to do with that? The popularity of lenticular lenses, particularly in the form of postcards, coincides historically not just with the rise of an articulated movement for civil rights but also with the growth of electronic culture and the birth of digital computing (with both—digital computing and the Civil Rights movement—born in quite real ways of World War II). We might understand UNIX as the way in which the emerging logics of the lenticular and of the covert racism of colorblindness get ported into our computational systems, both in terms of the specific functions of UNIX as an operating system and in the broader philosophy it embraces.

Situating UNIX

In moving toward UNIX from MULTICS, programmers conceptualized UNIX as a kind of tool kit of "synergistic parts" that allowed "flexibility in depth" (Raymond 2004: 9). Programmers could "choose among multiple shells. . . . [and] programs normally provide[d] many behavior options" (2004: 6). One of the design philosophies driving UNIX is the notion that a program should do one thing and do it well (not unlike our deep disciplinary drive in many parts of the university), and this privileging of the discrete, the local, and the specific emerges again and again in discussions of UNIX's origins and design philosophies.

Books for programmers that explain the UNIX philosophy turn around a common set of rules. While slight variations on this rule set exist across programming books and online sites, Eric Raymond sets out the first nine rules as follows:

1. Rule of Modularity: Write simple parts connected by clean interfaces.
2. Rule of Clarity: Clarity is better than cleverness.

3. Rule of Composition: Design programs to be connected to other programs.
4. Rule of Separation: Separate policy from mechanism; separate interfaces from engines.
5. Rule of Simplicity: Design for simplicity; add complexity only where you must.
6. Rule of Parsimony: Write a big program only when it is clear by demonstration that nothing else will do.
7. Rule of Transparency: Design for visibility to make inspection and debugging easier.
8. Rule of Robustness: Robustness is the child of transparency and simplicity.
9. Rule of Representation: Fold knowledge into data so program logic can be stupid and robust. (2004: 13)

Other rules include the Rules of Least Surprise, Silence, Repair, Economy, Generation, Optimization, Diversity, and Extensibility.

These rules implicitly translate into computational terms the chunked logics of the lenticular. For instance, Brian Kernighan wrote in a 1976 handbook on software programming that "controlling complexity is the essence of computer programming" (quoted in Raymond 2004: 14). Complexity in UNIX is controlled in part by the "rule of modularity," which insists that code be constructed of discrete and interchangeable parts that can be plugged together via clean interfaces. In *Design Rules, Vol. 1: The Power of Modularity*, Carliss Baldwin and Kim Clark argue that computers from 1940 to 1960 had "complex, interdependent designs," and they label this era the "premodular" phase of computing (2000: 149). While individuals within the industry, including John von Neumann, were beginning to imagine benefits to modularity in computing, Baldwin and Clark note that von Neumann's ground-breaking designs for computers in that period "fell short of true modularity" because "in no sense was the detailed design of one component going to be hidden from the others: all pieces of the system would be produced 'in full view' of the others" (2000: 157). Thus, one might say that these early visions of digital computers were neither modular nor lenticular. Baldwin and Clark track the increasing modularity of hardware design from the early 1950s forward and also observe that UNIX was the first operating system to embrace modularity and adhere "to the principles of information hiding" in its design (2000: 324).

There are clearly practical advantages of such structures for coding, but they also underscore a world view in which a troublesome part might be discarded without disrupting the whole. Tools are meant to be "encapsulated" to avoid "a tendency to involve programs with each other's internals" (Raymond 2004: 15). Modules "don't promiscuously share global data," and problems can stay "local" (2004: 84–85). In writing about the Rule of Composition, Eric Raymond advises programmers to "make [programs] independent." He writes, "It should be easy to replace one end with a completely different implementation without disturbing the other" (2004: 15). Detachment is valued because it allows a cleaving from "the particular . . . conditions under which a design problem was posed. Abstract. Simplify. Generalize" (2004: 95). While "generalization" in UNIX has specific meanings, we might also see at work here the basic contours of a lenticular approach to the world, an approach which separates object from context, cause from effect.

In a 1976 article, "Software Tools," Bell Lab programmers Kernighan and Plauger urged programmers "to view specific jobs as special cases of general, frequently performed operations, so they can make and use general-purpose tools to solve them. We also hope to show how to design programs to look like tools and to interconnect conveniently" (1976b: 1). While the language here is one of generality (as in "general purpose" tools), in fact, the tool library that is being envisioned is a series of very discrete and specific tools or programs that can operate independently of one another. They continue, "Ideally, a program should not know where its input comes from nor where its output goes. The UNIX time-sharing system provides a particularly elegant way to handle input and output redirection" (1976b: 2). Programs

> can profitably be described as filters, even though they do quite complicated transformations on their input. One should be able to say
> program-1 ... | sort | program-2 ...
> and have the output of program-1 sorted before being passed to program-2. This has the major advantage that neither program-1 nor program-2 need know how to sort, but can concentrate on its main task. (1976b: 4)

In effect, the tools chunk computational programs into isolated bits, where the programs' operations are meant to be "invisible to the user" and to the other programs in a sequence (1976b: 5): "the point is that this operation is invisible to the user (or should be). . . . Instead he sees simply a program with one input and one output. Unsorted data go in one end; somewhat later, sorted data come out the other. It must be *convenient* to use a tool, not just possible" (1976b: 5). Kernighan and Plauger saw the "filter concept" as a useful way to get programmers to think in discrete bits and to simplify, reducing the potential complexity of programs. They note that "when a job is viewed as a series of filters, the implementation simplifies, for it is broken down into a sequence of relatively independent pieces, each small and easily tested. This is a form of high-level modularization" (1976b: 5). In their own way, these filters function as a kind of lenticular frame or lens, allowing only certain portions of complex datasets to be visible at a particular time (to both the user and the machine).

The technical feature which allowed UNIX to achieve much of its modularity was the development by Ken Thompson (based on a suggestion by Doug McIlroy) of the pipe, i.e., a vertical bar that replaced the "greater than" sign in the operating system's code. As described by Doug Ritchie and Ken Thompson in a paper for the Association of Computing Machinery in 1974 (reprinted by Bell Labs in 1978),

> A *read* using a pipe file descriptor waits until another process writes using the file descriptor for the same pipe. At this point, data are passed between the images of the two processes. Neither process need know that a pipe, rather than an ordinary file, is involved.

In this way, the ability to construct a pipeline from a series of small programs evolved, while the "hiding of internals" was also supported. The contents of a module were not central to the functioning of the pipeline; rather, the input or output (a text stream) was key. Brian Kernighan noted "that while input/output direction predates pipes, the development of pipes led to the concept of tools— software programs that would be in a 'tool box,' available when you need them" and interchangeable.[2] Pipes reduced complexity and were also linear. In *Software Tools*, Kernighan and Plauger extend their discussion of pipes, noting that "a pipe provides a hidden buffering between the output of one program and the input of another program so information may pass between them without ever entering the file system" (1976a: 2). They also signal the importance of pipes for issues of data security:

> And consider the sequence
> decrypt key <file | prog | encrypt key > newfile
> Here a decryption program decodes an encrypted file, passing the decoded characters to a program having no special security features. The output of the program is re-encrypted at the other end. If a true pipe mechanism is used, no clear-text version of the data will ever appear in a file. To simulate this sequence with temporary files risks breaching security. (1976a: 3)

While the affordances of filters, pipes, and hidden data are often talked about as a matter of simple standardization and efficiency (as when Kernighan and Plauger argue that "Our emphasis here has been on getting jobs done with an efficient use of people" (1976a: 6)), they also clearly work in the service of new regimes of security, not an insignificant detail in the context of the Cold War era. Programming manuals and UNIX guides again and again stress clarity and simplicity ("don't write fancy code"; "say what you mean as clearly and directly as you can"), but the structures of operating systems like UNIX function by hiding internal operations, skewing "clarity" in very particular directions. These manuals privilege a programmer's equivalent of "common sense" in the Gramscian sense. For Antonio Gramsci, common sense is a historically situated process, the way in which a particular group responds to "certain problems posed by reality which are quite specific" at a particular time (1971: 324). I am here arguing that, as programmers constitute themselves as a particular class of workers in the 1970s, they are necessarily lodged in their moment, deploying common sense and notions about simplicity to justify their innovations in code. Importantly, their moment is over-determined by the ways in which the U.S. is widely coming to process race and other forms of difference in more covert registers, as noted above.[3]

Another rule of UNIX is the "Rule of Diversity," which insists on a mistrust of the "one true way." Thus UNIX, in the word of one account, "embraces multiple languages, open extensible systems and customization hooks everywhere," reading much like a description of the tenets of neoliberal multiculturalism if not poststructuralist thought itself (Raymond 2004: 24). As you read the ample literature on UNIX, certain words emerge again and again: modularity, compactness, simplicity, orthogonality. UNIX is meant to allow multitasking, portability, time-sharing, and compartmentalizing. It is not much of a stretch to layer these traits over the core tenets of post-Fordism, a process which begins to remake industrial-era notions of standardization in the 1960s: time–space compression, transformability, customization, a public/private blur, etc. UNIX's intense modularity and information-hiding capacity were reinforced by its design: that is, in the ways in which it segregated the kernel from the shell. The kernel loads into the computer's memory at startup and is "the heart" of UNIX (managing "hardware memory, job execution and time sharing"), although it remains hidden from the user (Baldwin and Clark 2000: 332). The shells (or programs that interpret commands) are intermediaries between the user and the computer's inner workings. They hide the details of the operating system from the user behind "the shell," extending modularity from a rule for programming in UNIX to the very design of UNIX itself.[4]

Modularity in the Social Field

This push toward modularity and the covert in digital computation also reflects other changes in the organization of social life in the United States by the 1960s. For instance, if the first half of the twentieth century laid bare its racial logics, from "Whites Only" signage to the brutalities of lynching, the second half increasingly hides its racial "kernel," burying it below a shell of neoliberal pluralism. These covert or lenticular racial logics take hold at the tail end of the Civil Rights movement at least partially to cut off and contain the more radical logics implicit in the urban uprisings that shook Detroit, Watts, Chicago, and Newark. In fact, the urban center of Detroit was more segregated by the 1980s than in previous decades, reflecting a different inflection of the programmer's vision of the "easy removal" or containment of a troubling part. Whole areas of the city might be rendered orthogonal and disposable (also think post-Katrina New Orleans), and the urban Black poor were increasingly isolated in "deteriorating city centers" (Sugrue 1998: 198). Historian Thomas Sugrue traces the increasing unemployment rates for Black men in Detroit, rates which rose dramatically from the 1950s to the 1980s, and maps a "deproletarianization" that "shaped a pattern of poverty in the postwar city that was surprisingly new" (1998: 262). Across several registers, the emerging neoliberal state begins to adopt "the rule of modularity." For instance, we might draw an example from across the Atlantic. In her careful analysis of the effects of May 1968 and its afterlives, Kristin Ross argues that the French government contained the radical force of the uprisings by quickly moving to separate the students' rebellion from the concerns of labor, deploying a strategy of separation and containment in which both sides (students and labor) would ultimately lose (2004: 69).

Modularity in software design was meant to decrease "global complexity" and cleanly separate one "neighbor" from another (Raymond 2004: 85). These strategies also played out in ongoing reorganizations of the political field throughout the 1960s and 1970s in both the Right and the Left. The widespread divestiture in the infrastructure of inner cities might be seen as one more insidious effect of the logic of modularity in the post-war era. But we might also understand the emergence of identity politics in the 1960s as a kind of social and political embrace of modularity and encapsulation, a mode of partitioning that turned away from the broader forms of alliance-based and globally-inflected political practice that characterized both labor politics and anti-racist organizing in the 1930s and 1940s.[5] While identity politics produced concrete gains in the world, particularly in terms of civil rights, we are also now coming to understand the degree to which these movements curtailed and short-circuited more radical forms of political praxis, reducing struggle to fairly discrete parameters.

Let me be clear. By drawing analogies between shifting racial and political formations and the emerging structures of digital computing in the late 1960s, I am not arguing that the programmers creating UNIX at Bell Labs and in Berkeley were *consciously* encoding new modes of racism and racial under-standing into digital systems. (Indeed, many of these programmers were themselves left-leaning hippies, and the overlaps between the counterculture and early computing culture run deep, as Fred Turner has illustrated.) I also recognize that their innovations made possible the word processor I am using to write this article, a powerful tool that shapes cognition and scholarship in precise ways. Nor am I arguing for some exact correspondence between the ways in which encapsulation or modularity work in computation and how they function in the emerging regimes of neoliberalism, governmentality and post-Fordism. Rather, I am highlighting the ways in which the organization of information and capital in the 1960s powerfully responds—across many registers—to the struggles for racial justice and democracy that so categorized the U.S. at the time. Many of these shifts were enacted in the name of liberalism, aimed at distancing the overt racism of the past even as they contained and cordoned off progressive radicalism. The emergence of covert racism and its rhetoric of colorblindness are not so much intentional as systemic. Computation is a primary delivery method of these new systems, and it seems at best naïve to imagine that cultural and computational operating systems don't mutually infect one another.

Thus we see modularity take hold not only in computation but also in the increasingly niched and regimented production of knowledge in the university after the Second World War. For instance, Christopher Newfield comments on the rise of New Criticism in literature departments in the Cold War era, noting its relentless formalism, a "logical corollary" to "depoliticization" (2004: 145) that "replaced agency with technique" (2004: 155). He attributes this particular tendency in literary criticism at least in part to the triumph of a managerial impulse, a turn that we might also align (even if Newfield doesn't) with the workings of modular code (itself studied as an exemplary approach to "dynamic modeling systems" for business management in the work of Baldwin and Clark cited above).[6] He observes as well that this managerial obsession within literary criticism exhibits a surprising continuity across the 1960s and beyond. Gerald Graff has also examined the "patterned isolation" that emerges in the university after World War II, at the moment when New Criticism's methods take hold in a manner that de-privileges context and focuses on "explication for explication's sake." Graff then analyzes the routinization of literary criticism in the period, a mechanistic exercise with input and output streams of its own (1989: 227). He recognizes that university departments (his example is English) begin to operate by a field-based and modular strategy of "coverage," in which subfields proliferate and exist in their own separate chunks of knowledge, rarely contaminated by one another's "internals" (1989: 250). (He also comments that this modular strategy includes the token hiring of scholars of color who are then cordoned off within the department.) Graff locates the beginning of this patterned isolation in the run-up to the period that also brought us digital computing; he writes that it continues to play out today in disciplinary structures that have become increasingly narrow and specialized. Patterned isolation begins with the bureaucratic standardization of the university from 1890 to 1930 (1989: 61–62), but this "cut out and separate" mentality reaches a new crescendo after World War II as the organizational structure of the university pushes from simply bureaucratic and Taylorist to managerial, a shift noted as well by Christopher Newfield. Many now lament the over-specialization of the university; in effect, this tendency is a result of the additive logic of the lenticular or of the pipeline, where "content areas" or "fields" are tacked together without any sense of intersection, context, or relation.

It is interesting to note that much of the early work performed in UNIX environments was focused on document processing and communication tools and that UNIX is a computational system that very much privileges text (it centers on the text-based command line instead of on the Graphical User Interface, and its inputs and outputs are simple text lines). Many of the methodologies of the humanities from the Cold War through the 1980s also privilege text while devaluing context and operate in their own chunked systems, suggesting telling parallels between the operating systems and privileged objects of the humanities and of the computers being developed on several university campuses in the same period.

Another example of the increasing modularity of the American university might be drawn from the terrain of area studies. Scholars including Martin W. Lewis and Kären Wigen have recently mapped the proliferation of area studies from the onset of the Cold War era to the present. They show how a coupling of government, foundations and scholars began to parse the world in finer and finer detail, producing geographical areas of study that could work in the service of the "modernization and development" agenda that was coming to replace the older models of colonial domination, substituting the covert stylings of the post-industrial for the overtly oppressive methods of earlier regimes. By 1958, government funding established university-based "area-studies centers" that grew to "some 124 National Resource Centers [by the 1990s] . . . each devoted to the interdisciplinary study of a particular world region" (Lewis and Wigen 1999: 164). John Rowe has convincingly argued that area studies thrived by operating through a kind of isolationism or modularity, with each area intently focused within its own borders.

Lev Manovich has, of course, noted the modularity of the digital era and also backtracked to early twentieth-century examples of modularity from the factory line to the creative productions of avant garde artists. In a posting to the Nettime list-serve in 2005, he frames modularity as a uniquely twentieth-century phenomenon, from Henry Ford's assembly lines to the 1932 furniture designs of Belgian designer Louis Herman De Kornick. In his account, the twentieth century is characterized by an accelerating process of industrial modularization, but I think it is useful to examine the digital computer's privileged role in the process, particularly given that competing modes of computation were still quite viable until the 1960s, modes that might have pushed more toward the continuous flows of analog computing rather than the discrete tics of the digital computer. Is the modularity of the 1920s really the same as the modularity modeled in UNIX? Do these differences matter, and what might we miss if we assume a smooth and teleological triumph of modularity? How has computation pushed modularity in new directions, directions in dialogue with other cultural shifts and ruptures? Why does modularity emerge in our systems with such a vengeance across the 1960s?

I have here suggested that our technological formations are deeply bound up with our racial formations, and that each undergo profound changes at mid-century. I am not so much arguing that one mode is causally related to the other, but, rather, that they both represent a move toward modular knowledges, knowledges increasingly prevalent in the second half of the twentieth century. These knowledges support and enable the shift from the overt standardized bureaucracies of the 1920s and 1930s to the more dynamically modular and covert managerial systems that are increasingly prevalent as the century wears on. These latter modes of knowledge production and organization are powerful racial and technological operating systems that coincide with (and reinforce) (post-)structuralist approaches to the world within the academy. Both the computer and the lenticular lens mediate images and objects, changing their relationship but frequently suppressing that process of relation, much like the divided departments of the contemporary university. The fragmentary know-ledges encouraged by many forms and experiences of the digital neatly parallel the lenticular logics which underwrite the covert racism endemic to our times, operating in potential feedback loops, supporting each other. If scholars of race have highlighted how certain tendencies within poststructuralist theory simultan-eously respond to and marginalize race, this maneuver is at least partially possible because of a parallel and increasing dispersion of electronic forms across culture, forms which simultaneously enact and shape these new modes of thinking.

While the examples here have focused on UNIX, it is important to recognize that the core principles of modularity that it helped bring into practice continue to impact a wide range of digital computation, especially the C programming language, itself developed for UNIX by Ritchie, based on Thompson's earlier B language. While UNIX and C devotees will bemoan the non-orthogonality and leakiness of Windows or rant about the complexity of C++, the basic argument offered above—that UNIX helped inaugurate modular and lenticular systems broadly across computation and culture—holds true for the black boxes of contemporary coding and numerous other instances of our digital praxis.

Today, we might see contemporary turns in computing—neural nets, clouds, semantics, etc.—as parallel to recent turns in humanities scholarship to privilege networks over nodes (particularly in new media studies and in digital culture theory) and to focus on globalization and its flows (in American studies and other disciplines). While this may simply mean we have learned our mid-century lessons and are smarter now, we might also continue to examine with rigor and detail the degree to which dominant forms of computation—what David Golumbia has aptly called "the cultural logic of computation" in his recent update of Frankfurt School pessimism for the twenty-first century—continue to respond to shifting racial and cultural formations. Might these emerging modes of computation be read as symptoms and drivers of our "post-racial" moment, refracting in some way national anxieties (or hopes?) about a decreas-ingly "white" America? We should also remain alert to how contemporary techno-racial formations infect privileged ways of knowing in the academy. While both the tales of C.P. Snow circa 1959 and the Sokal science wars of the 1990s sustain the myth that science and the humanities operate in distinct realms of knowing, powerful operating systems have surged beneath the surface of what and how we know in the academy for well over half a decade. It would be foolish of us to believe that these operating systems—in this paper best categorized by UNIX and its many close siblings—do not at least partially over-determine the very critiques we imagine that we are performing today.

Moving Beyond Our Boxes

So, if we are always already complicit with the machine, what are we to do?

First, we must better understand the machines and networks that continue to powerfully shape our lives in ways that we are ill-equipped to deal with as media and humanities scholars. This necessarily involves more than simply studying our screens and the images that dance across them, moving beyond studies of screen representations and the rhetorics of visuality. We might read representations seeking symptoms of information capital's fault lines and successes, but we cannot read the logics of these systems and networks solely at the level of our screens. Capital is now fully organized under the sign of modularity. It operates via the algorithm and the database, via simulation and processing. Our screens are cover stories, disguising deeply divided forms of both machine and human labor. We focus exclusively on them increasingly to our peril.

Scholars in the emerging field of "code studies" are taking up the challenge of understanding how computational systems (especially but not only software) developed and operate. However, we must demand that this nascent field not replay the formalist and structuralist tendencies of new media theory circa 1998. Code studies must also take up the questions of culture and meaning that animate so many scholars of race in fields like the "new" American studies. Likewise, scholars of race must analyze, use and produce digital forms and not smugly assume that to engage the digital directly is in some way to be complicit with the forces of capitalism. The lack of intellectual generosity across our fields and departments only reinforces the "divide and conquer" mentality that the most dangerous aspects of modularity underwrite. We must develop common languages that link the study of code and culture. We must historicize and politicize code studies. And, because digital media were born as much of the Civil Rights era as of the Cold War era (and of course these eras are one and the same), our investigations must incorporate race from the outset, understanding and theorizing its function as a "ghost in the digital machine." This does not mean that we should "add" race to our analysis in a modular way, neatly tacking it on, but that we must understand and theorize the deep imbrications of race and digital technology even when our objects of analysis (say, UNIX or search engines) seem not to "be about" race at all. This will not be easy. In the writing of this essay, the logic of modularity continually threatened to take hold, leading me into detailed explorations of pipe structures in UNIX or departmental structures in the university, taking me far from the contours of race at mid-century. It is hard work to hold race and computation together *in a systemic manner*, but it is work that we must continue to undertake.

We also need to take seriously the possibility that questions of representation and of narrative and textual analysis may, in effect, be a distraction from the powers that be—the triumph of the very particular patterns of informationalization evident in code. If the study of representation may in fact be part and parcel of the very logic of modularity that such code inaugurates, a kind of distraction, it is equally plausible to argue that our very intense focus on visuality in the past twenty years of scholarship is just a different manifestation of the same distraction. There is tendency in film and media studies to treat the computer and its screens as (in Jonathan Beller's terms) a "legacy" technology to cinema. In its drive to stage continuities, such an argument tends to minimize or completely miss the fundamental material differences between cinematic visuality and the production of the visual by digital technologies.

To push my polemic to its furthest dimensions, I would argue that to study image, narrative and visuality will never be enough if we do not engage as well the non-visual dimensions of code and their organization of the world. And yet, to trouble my own polemic, we might also understand the workings of code to have already internalized the visual to the extent that, in the heart of the labs from which UNIX emerged, the cultural processing of the visual via the register of race was already at work in the machine.

In extending our critical methodologies, we must have at least a passing familiarity with code languages, operating systems, algorithmic thinking, and systems design. We need database literacies, algorithmic literacies, computational literacies, interface literacies. We need new hybrid practices: artist-theorists; programming humanists; activist scholars; theoretical archivists; critical race coders. We have to shake ourselves out of our small field-based boxes, taking seriously the possibility that our own knowledge practices are "normalized," "modular," and "black boxed" in much the same way as the code we might study in our work. That is, our very scholarly practices tend to undervalue broad contexts, meaningful relation and promiscuous border crossing. While many of us "identify" as interdisciplinary, very few of us extend that border crossing very far (theorists tune out the technical, the technologists are impatient of the abstract, scholars of race mock the computational, seeing it as corrupt). I'm suggesting that the intense narrowing of our academic specialties over the past fifty years can actually be seen as an effect of or as complicit with the logics of modularity and the relational database. Just as the relational database works by normalizing data—that is by stripping it of meaningful context and the idiosyncratic, creating a system of interchangeable equivalencies—our own scholarly practices tend to exist in relatively hermetically sealed boxes or nodes. Critical theory and post-structuralism have been powerful operating systems that have served us well; they were as hard to learn as the complex structures of C++, and we have dutifully learned them. They are also software systems in desperate need of updating and patching. They are lovely, and they are not enough. They cannot be all we do.

In universities that simply shut down "old school" departments—at my university, German and Geography; in the UK, Middlesex's philosophy program; in Arizona, perhaps all of ethnic studies—scholars must engage the vernacular digital forms that make us nervous, *authoring* in them in order to better understand them and to recreate in technological spaces the possibility of doing the work that moves us. We need new practices and new modes of collaboration; we need to be literate in emerging scientific and technological methodologies, and we'll gain that literacy at least partially through an intellectual generosity or curiosity toward those whose practices are not our own.

We must remember that computers are themselves encoders of culture. If, in the 1960s and 1970s, UNIX hardwired an emerging system of covert racism into our mainframes and our minds, then computation responds to culture as much as it controls it. Code and race are deeply intertwined, even as the structures of code work to disavow these very connections. Politically committed academics with humanities skill sets must engage technology and its production, not simply as an object of our scorn, critique, or fascination, but as a productive and generative space that is always emergent and never fully determined.

Notes

1   UNIX developed with some rapidity, at least in part because the parent company of Bell Labs, AT&T, was unable to enter the computer business due to a 1958 consent decree. Eric Raymond notes that "Bell Labs was required to license its nontelephone technology to anyone who asked" (2004: 33). Thus a kind of "counterculture" chic developed around UNIX. Eric Raymond provides a narrative version of this history, including the eventual "UNIX wars" in his *The Art of UNIX Programming* (2004). His account, while thorough, tends to romanticize the collaborative culture around UNIX. For a more objective analysis of the imbrications of the counterculture and early computing cultures, see Fred Turner's *From Counterculture to Cyberculture* (2006). See also Tom Streeter (2003) for a consideration of liberal individualism and computing cultures.

2   This quote from Kernighan is from "The Creation of the UNIX Operating System" on the Bell Labs website. See www.bell-labs.com/history/unix/philosophy.html

3   For Gramsci, "common sense" is a multi-layered phenomenon that can serve both dominant groups and oppressed ones. For oppressed groups, "common sense" may allow a method of speaking back to power and of re-jiggering what counts as sensible. Kara Keeling profitably explores this possibility in her work on the Black femme. Computer programmers in the 1970s are interestingly situated. They are on the one hand a subculture (often overlapping with the counterculture), but they are also part of an increasingly managerial class that will help society transition to regimes of neoliberalism and governmentality. Their dreams of "libraries" of code may be democratic in impulse, but they also increasingly support post-industrial forms of labor.

4   Other aspects of UNIX also encode "chunking," including the concept of the file. For a discussion of files in UNIX, see *You Are Not a Gadget* by Jaron Lanier (2010). This account of UNIX, among other things, also argues that code and culture exist in complex feedback loops.

5   See, for instance, Patricia Sullivan's *Days of Hope* (1996) for an account of the coalition politics of the South in the 1930s and 1940s that briefly brought together anti-racist activists, labor organizers, and members of the Communist Party. Such a broad alliance became increasingly difficult to sustain after the Red Scare. I would argue that a broad cultural turn to modularity and encapsulation was both a response to these earlier political alliances and a way to short-circuit their viability in the 1960s. My *Reconstructing Dixie* (2003) examines the ways in which a lenticular logic infects both identity politics and the politics of difference, making productive alliance and relationality hard to achieve in either paradigm.

6   To be fair, Newfield also explores a more radical impulse in literary study in the period, evident in the likes of (surprisingly) both Harold Bloom and Raymond Williams. This impulse valued literature precisely in its ability to offer an "unmanaged exploration of experience" (2004: 152).

Bibliography

Baldwin, Carliss and Kim Clark. 2000. *Design Rules, Vol. 1: The Power of Modularity*, Cambridge, MA: MIT Press.

Beller, Jonathan. 2009. "Re: Periodizing Cinematic Production." Post to IDC Listserve. September 2. Archived at https://lists.thing.net/pipermail/idc/2009-September/003851.html.

Bolter, Jay and Richard Grusin. 2000. *Remediations: Understanding New Media*. Cambridge, MA: MIT Press.
"The Creation of the UNIX Operating System" on the Bell Labs website. Available at: www.bell-labs.com/history/unix/philosophy.html.
Galloway, Alex. 2006. *Protocol: How Control Exists after Decentralization*. Cambridge, MA: MIT Press.
Golumbia, David. 2009. *The Cultural Logic of Computation*. Cambridge, MA: Harvard University Press.
Graff, Gerald. 1989. *Professing Literature: An Institutional History*. Chicago, IL: University of Chicago Press.
Gramsci, Antonio. 1971. *Selections from the Prison Notebooks*. Translated and edited by Q. Hoare and G. Nowell Smith. London: Lawrence and Wishart.
Hansen, Mark B.N. 2000. *Embodying Technesis: Technology Beyond Writing*. Ann Arbor: University of Michigan Press.
Keeling, Kara. 2007. *The Witch's Flight: The Cinematic, the Black Femme, and the Image of Common Sense*. Durham, NC: Duke University Press.
Kernighan, Brian and Rob Pike. 1984. *The Unix Programming Environment*. Englewood Cliffs, NJ: Prentice Hall.
Kernighan, Brian and P.J. Plauger. 1976a. *Software Tools*. Reading, MA: Addison-Wesley.
——. 1976b. "Software Tools." *ACM SIGSOFT Software Engineering Notes* 1.1 (May): 15–20.
Kernighan, Brian and D.M. Ritchie. 1978. *The C Programming Language*. Englewood Cliffs, NJ: Prentice Hall. Second edition 1988.
Kinder, Marsha. 2002. "Narrative Equivocations Between Movies and Games," in Dan Harries, ed., *The New Media Book*, London: BFI.
Landow, George. 1991. *Hypertext: The Convergence of Contemporary Critical Theory and Technology*. Baltimore, MD: Johns Hopkins University Press.
Lanier, Jaron. 2010. *You Are Not A Gadget: A Manifesto*. New York: Knopf.
Lewis, Martin W. and Kären Wigen. 1999. "A Maritime Response to the Crisis in Area Studies." *The Geographical Review* 89.2 (April): 162.
McPherson, Tara. 2003. *Reconstructing Dixie: Race, Place and Nostalgia in the Imagined South*. Durham, NC: Duke University Press.
Manovich, Lev. 2002. *The Language of New Media*. Cambridge, MA: MIT Press.
——. 2005. "We Have Never Been Modular." Post to Nettime Listserve, November 28. Archived at www.nettime.org/Lists-Archives/nettime-l-0511/msg00106.html.
Newfield, Christopher. 2004. *Ivy and Industry: Business and the Making of the American University, 1880–1980*. Durham, NC: Duke University Press.
Omi, Michael and Howard Winant. 1986/1989. *Racial Formation in the United States: From the 1960s to the 1980s*. New York: Routledge.
Raymond, Eric. 2004. *The Art of UNIX Programming*. Reading, MA: Addison-Wesley. 2004.
Ritchie, Dennis. 1984. "The Evolution of the Unix Time-sharing System," *AT&T Bell Laboratories Technical Journal* 63.6 (2): 1577–1593. Available at: http://cm.bell-labs.com/cm/cs/who/dmr/hist.html
Ritchie, D.M. and K. Thompson. 1978. "The UNIX Time-Sharing System." *The Bell System Technical Journal* 57.6 (2, July–August).
Ross, Kristin. 2004. *May '68 and Its Afterlives*. Chicago: University of Chicago Press.
Rowe, John Carlos. Forthcoming. "Areas of Concern: Area Studies and the New American Studies," in Winfried Fluck, Donald Pease, and John Carlos Rowe, eds, *Transatlantic American Studies*. Boston: University Presses of New England.
Salus, Peter H. 1994. *A Quarter-Century of Unix*. Reading, MA: Addison-Wesley.
Sandoval, Chela. 2000. *Methodology of the Oppressed*. Minneapolis: University of Minnesota Press.
Spivak, Gayatri. 1987. *In Other Worlds: Essays in Cultural Politics*. New York: Routledge.
Streeter, Thomas. 2003. "The Romantic Self and the Politics of Internet Commercialization." *Cultural Studies* 17.5: 648–668.
Sugrue, Thomas J. 1998. *The Origins of the Urban Crisis: Race and Inequality in Post-War Detroit*. Princeton: Princeton University Press.
Sullivan, Patricia. 1996. *Days of Hope: Race and Democracy in the New Deal Era*. Chapel Hill, NC: UNC Press.
Turkle, Sherry. 1997. *Life on the Screen: Identity in the Age of the Internet*. New York: Simon and Schuster.
Turner, Fred. 2006. *From Counterculture to Cyberculture: Stewart Brand, the Whole Earth Network, and the Rise of Digital Utopianism*. Chicago: University of Chicago Press.

2
Race and/as Technology or How to Do Things to Race

WENDY HUI KYONG CHUN

Brown University

This essay poses the questions: to what degree are race and technology intertwined? To what extent can race be considered a technology and mode of mediatization, that is, not only a mechanism, but also a practical or industrial art? Could "race" be not simply an object of representation and portrayal, of knowledge or truth, but also a technique that one uses, even as one is used by it—a carefully crafted, historically inflected system of tools, of mediation, or of "enframing" that builds history and identity?

"Race *and/as* technology" is a strange, and hopefully estranging, formulation, but its peculiarity does not stem from its conjoining of race and technology. There already exists an important body of scholarship that simply addresses "race *and* technology" within science and technology, film and media and visual culture, and African American and ethnic studies, ranging, just to give some examples, from analyses documenting the resurgence of race as a valid scientific category to those tracing the historically intersecting truth claims of phrenology and photography, from investigations uncovering the centrality of data processing to the execution of the Holocaust to those analyzing the importance of raced images to mass-mediated consumer culture.[1] These works have mapped the ways in which race and technology impact each other's logic and development, especially in relation to enterprises that seek to establish the "truth" of race as a scientific fact or cultural phenomenon.

Yet the consideration of "race *as* technology," in contrast, brings other questions forward. Crucially, "race as technology" shifts the focus from the *what* of race to the *how* of race, from *knowing* race to *doing* race by emphasizing the similarities between race and technology. Indeed, "Race as technology" is a simile that posits a comparative equality or substitutability—but not identity— between the two terms. "Race as technology," however, is not simply an example of a simile; it also *exemplifies* similes by encapsulating the larger logic of comparison that makes both race and similes possible. "Race as technology" reveals how race functions as the "as," how it facilitates comparisons between entities classed as similar or dissimilar. This comparison of race and technology also displaces claims of race as either purely biological or purely cultural because technological mediation, which has been used to define humankind as such ("man" as a "tool-using" animal), is always already a mix of science, art, and culture. Humans and technology, as Bernard Stiegler has argued, evolve together.[2] Race has never been simply "biological" or "cultural"; it has rather been crucial to negotiating and establishing historically variable definitions of "biology" and "culture." Thus, by framing questions of race *and* technology, as well as by reframing race *as* technology, this essay wagers that not only can we theoretically and historically better understand the forces of race and technology and their relation to racism, we can also better respond to contemporary changes in the relationships between human and machine, human and animal, media and environment, mediation and embodiment, nature and culture, visibility and invisibility, privacy and publicity.

Race, within the biological and medical sciences, has returned as a new form of "natural history," that is, as a means to track "the great human diaspora" through mainly invisible (non-expressed) genetic differences or as a way to weigh risk factors for certain diseases.[3] As Jenny Reardon has noted, these biological "confirmations" have disturbed the post-WWII, cross-disciplinary "consensus" on the physical non-existence of race, catching off-guard many humanities scholars, whose critiques rested in part on "scientific evidence."[4] In response, some, such as philosopher of science Lisa Gannett, have analyzed the ways in which race never left population science; similarly, some historians of science and medicine, such as Evelyn Hammonds, have highlighted the biases underpinning the use of current and historical race.[5] Others, such as Henry Louis Gates, Jr, have embraced DNA tracing in order to write a more comprehensive African American history, and still others, such as Paul Gilroy, have argued that these new biological categorizations, because they view the body from a nanological perspective from which race may exist but is not "visible," defy the epidermal logic that has traditionally defined race and thus offer us an opportunity to shelve race altogether.[6] That is, if race—like media—has involved linking what is visible to what is invisible, then Gilroy's argument is that race, as an invisible entity, can no longer buttress this logic of revelation. This debate over the ontology of race is important, and this article supplements it by analyzing race's utility regardless of its alleged essence, and by investigating how race itself has been key to the modern concept of essence that is apparent in discourses of science and art. Most importantly, understanding race and/as technology enables us to frame the discussion around ethics rather than ontology, on modes of recognition and relation, rather than being. In what follows, I offer a historical and theoretical context for this reframing for these interventions by outlining the ways in which race has been framed as both biology and culture, and how this dichotomy also relies on and is disturbed by race as technology. I further outline the stakes of this reconfiguration of race by considering the ways in which/how race can be considered a "saving" grace. Inspired by the groundbreaking work by Beth Coleman on race as technology,

I conclude by considering Greg Pak's feature film *Robot Stories* as an engagement of race as technology—specifically, Asians as robot-like—that displaces the techno-Orientalism it embraces.[7]

Making the Visible Innate

At a certain level, the notion of race as technology seems obvious, for race historically has been a tool of subjugation. From Carl Linnaeus' eighteenth-century taxonomy of human races in *Systema Naturae* to Charles Davenport's early twentieth-century "documentation" of the disastrous effects of miscegenation, from the horrors of the Holocaust to continuing debates over the innateness of intelligence, "scientific" categorizations of race have been employed to establish hierarchical differences between people, rendering some into mere objects to be exploited, enslaved, measured, demeaned, and sometimes destroyed.[8] In the United States, racist theories maintained the contradiction at the heart of the nation's founding, that of all men being created equal and black slaves counting as three-fifths human (thus allowing them to be accounted *for*, but not themselves count). Even after emancipation, racist legislation and bureaucratic practices such as segregation, with its validation of discrimination within social and private spaces as "natural antipathies," maintained inequalities in a facially equal democratic system. Race in these circumstances was wielded—and is still wielded—as an invaluable mapping tool, a means by which origins and boundaries are simultaneously traced and constructed, and through which the visible traces of the body are tied to allegedly innate invisible characteristics.

Race as a mapping tool stems from its emergence as a scientific category in the eighteenth century, although it has consistently designated relations based on perceived commonalities. According to Bruce Dain, race first denoted a group of people connected by common descent (e.g. a noble house, family, kindred); then, in the fifteenth and sixteenth centuries, the Era of Exploration, it roughly corresponded to "geographical groups of people marked by supposedly common physical characteristics" (e.g. the English race); lastly, in the eighteenth century, it designated all of humankind (in distinction to animals), as well as sub-species of *homo sapiens* (such as *homo sapiens asiaticus*; according to Linnaeus, a male of this subset is "yellowish, melancholy, endowed with black hair and brown eyes . . . severe, conceited, and stingy. He puts on loose clothing. He is governed by opinion").[9] As science moved from eighteenth-century natural history, which based its species classifications on visible structures, to nineteenth-century science, which pursued the invisible processes of life itself, race became an even more important means by which the visible and the invisible were linked.[10]

The modern value of race stemmed from its ability to link somatic differences to innate physical and mental characteristics. According to Samira Kawash:

In this shift to a modern, biologized understanding of race, skin color becomes visible as a basis for determining the order of identities and differences and subsequently penetrates the body to become the truth of the self . . . race is on the skin, but skin is the sign of something deeper, something hidden in the invisible interior of the organism (as organic or ontological). To see racial difference is therefore to see the bodily sign of race but also to see more than this seeing, to see the interior difference it stands for.[11]

This "seeing" of internal difference makes accidental characteristics essential, prescriptors rather than descriptors. In terms of U.S. slavery, dark skin became the mark of the natural condition of slavery through which all kinds of external factors—and the violence perpetrated on African slaves—became naturalized and "innate." As Saidiya Hartmann has argued, "the wanton use of and the violence directed toward the black body come to be identified as *its* pleasures and dangers"—that is, the expectations of slave property are ontologized as the innate capabilities and inner feelings of the enslaved, and moreover, the ascription of excess and enjoyment to the African effaces the violence perpetrated against the enslaved.[12] For many anti-racists, then, the key to loosening the power of racism was (and still is) to denaturalize race, to loosen the connection between the bodily sign of race and what it signified.

Within the United States, there has been a long history of this attempt at denaturing, from the work of radical abolitionists in the nineteenth to that of cultural anthropologists in the twentieth century. Frederick Douglass, in his commencement address at Western Reserve College in 1854, famously contended that similarities between the bodies of Irish workers and black slaves undermined theories of racial traits as inherent or natural.[13] To Douglass, the congruence between the "deformed" physical features of the American slave and the common Irish man revealed the importance of education and class to bodily form, and the accomplishments of many Irish thinkers (and implicitly himself) testified to the potential of emancipated and educated slaves. For Douglass, racist arguments about the inherent inferiority of Africans were also a case of media bias, since they would always feature images of the "best" Caucasians next to those of the most oppressed African slaves. Franz Boas also deployed arguments against "natural" reasons for visible racial traits in the 1930s. Boas's work, which was key to transforming race from a biological to an anthropological category, argued against the innateness of both racial traits and racism.[14] Challenging those who advocated racism as a form of natural selection, Boas contended that antagonism between closed social groups may be innate, but what constituted a social group was not.

After WWII and the public renunciation by many scientists of overtly racist science within various UNESCO statements, race as a cultural, rather than bio-logical, fact seemed universally accepted, and the "two cultures" of the sciences and the humanities coalesced together around this common understanding.

Indeed many humanists in the late twentieth century rested their own critique of race as ideological on scientific definitions of race. Henry Louis Gates Jr, for instance, argued:

> Race has become a trope of ultimate, irreducible difference between cultures, linguistics groups, or adherents of specific belief systems, which—more often than not—also have fundamentally opposed economic interests. Race is the ultimate trope of difference because it is so very arbitrary in its difference. The biological criteria used to determine "difference" in sex simply do not hold when applied to "race." Yet we carelessly use language in such a way as to *will* this sense of *natural* difference into our formulations.[15]

By calling race a careless use of language, Gates implies that the problem of racism (which stems from race) could be fixed by a more careful use of language. Racism, in other words, stems from faulty media representations, and thus the best way to combat racism is to offer more realistic portrayals of "raced others" and to produce media critiques that expose the fallacies of racial thinking.

As mentioned previously, the resurgence of the category of race within science and medicine has troubled this position, which rests, as Reardon notes, on a separation between what are evaluated as "ideological" and "true" scientific statements—a separation that work across media and cultural studies has repeatedly emphasized is impossible.[16] Even more damning, despite the good intentions behind the reformulation of race as culture, the conceptualization of race as culture has been no less effective at creating social divisions than the notion of race as biology. Racist arguments have adeptly substituted culture for nature, creating what Etienne Balibar has called "neo-racism."[17] For instance, as Anne Anlin Cheng has pointed out, the psychological evidence used in *Brown v. Board of Education*, the "doll test"—which was pivotal to the juridical overturning of segregation in schools—is now used to justify segregation as granting "black children the opportunity to develop a stronger, 'healthier,' more independent black identity."[18] Rather than the abatement of racism and raced images post-WWII, we have witnessed their proliferation. As Toni Morrison notes:

> Race has become metaphorical—a way of referring to and disguising forces, events, classes, and expressions of social decay and economic division far more threatening to the body politic than biological "race" ever was. Expensively kept, economically unsound, a spurious and useless political asset in election campaigns, racism is as healthy today as it was during the Enlightenment. It seems that it has a utility far beyond economy, beyond the sequestering of classes from one another, and has assumed a metaphorical life so completely embedded in daily discourse that it is perhaps more necessary and more on display than ever before.[19]

Although Morrison here argues that race has become metaphorical, it is important to note the ways in which race, cultural or biological, acts as a trope. Even when understood as biological, race was not simply indexical, but rather still served as a sign, as a form of mediation, as a vehicle for revelation.

On the Limits of Culture

Race, conceived either as biology or as culture, organizes social relationships and turns the body into a signifier. Michael Omi and Howard Winant have influentially argued that race is "a fundamental *organizing principle* of social relationships,"[20] and they have used the term "*racial formation* to refer to the process by which social, economic and political forces determine the content and importance of racial categories, and by which they are in turn shaped by racial meanings."[21] Race, like media, is also a heuristic, a way to understand, to reveal, the world around us. To return to Samira Kawash's argument regarding skin color:

> the modern conception of racial identity maintains an uneasy relation to the visual; the visible marks of the racialized body are only signs of a deeper, interior difference, and yet those visible marks are the only differences that can be observed. The body is the sign of a difference that exceeds the body. The modern concept of race is therefore predicated on an epistemology of visibility, but the visible becomes an insufficient guarantee of knowledge. As a result, the possibility of a gap opens up between what the body says and what the body means.[22]

By linking outside to inside in an effort to make the body transparent, the body becomes a signifier: by creating a gap between what one sees and what one knows, racial markers are placed in an ever-shifting chain of signification.

Crucially, this gap between what the body says and what the body is taken to mean underlies the force of racism. As Ann Laura Stoler has argued, racism's force lies in the productive tension between the somatic and the essential. Reflecting on how racial discourse slips between discussions of somatic and visual difference and notions of inner, essential qualities, Stoler argues:

> the ambiguity of those sets of relationships between the somatic and the inner self, the phenotype and the genotype, pigment shade and psychological sensibility are not slips in, or obstacles to, racial thinking but rather conditions for its proliferation and possibility . . . The force of racisms is not found in the alleged fixity of visual knowledge, nor in essentialism itself, but on the *malleability* of the criteria of psychological dispositions and moral sensibilities that the visual could neither definitively secure nor explain.[23]

Racial discourse has always been polyvalently mobile and capable of thriving in the face of uncertainty. Race as biology and race as culture are similarly mobile and flexible technologies. Focusing on race as a technology, as mediation, thus allows us to see the continuing function of race, regardless of its "essence." It also highlights the fact that race has never been simply biological or cultural, but rather a means by which both are established and negotiated.

Creating Differences: Eugenics and Segregation

Like technology, race has never been merely cultural or biological, social or scientific. Indeed, the strict conceptual separation of culture from biology—nurture from nature, development from transmission—is a fairly recent phenomenon, stemming from the acceptance of Mendelian genetics. Focusing on U.S. eugenics and segregation in the twentieth century as technologies of difference, this section outlines how accepting race as biology also makes race technological.

Race did not simply move from a biological to a cultural concept. The early "mixed" nature of notions of race is evident in Linnaeus' foundational description of the male variant of *homo asiaticus* cited earlier: "yellowish, melancholy, endowed with black hair and brown eyes . . . severe, conceited, and stingy. He puts on loose clothing. He is governed by opinion." This description treats interchangeably visible physical traits ("yellowish"), psychological characteristics ("melancholy"), and cultural traditions ("loose clothing"). Similarly, Thomas Jefferson, writing in the eighteenth century, argued against incorporating African slaves into the nation using a mix of both historical and natural reasons.[24] Even in the nineteenth century, race was seen as encompassing both cultural and biological transmission: as George W. Stocking, Jr, has argued, the terms "race" and "nation" were not different by nature but by degree, since both intersected with questions of "blood."[25] Both environmentalists and extreme hereditarians, that is,

> started from the same inclusive idea of race as an integrated physical, linguistic, and cultural totality. Furthermore, because science—to paraphrase a number of contemporary social scientists—no longer separated the phenomena of the body from those of the mind, both hereditarians and environmentalists tended to assume that racial mental differences were related to racial physical differences.[26]

The clear separation of biology from culture and, transmission from development stemmed from Mendelian genetics' strict separation of germ from somatic cells.[27] This emphasis on the chromosomes as unchanging from generation to generation both made possible and relied on a belief in unchanging "eternal" features, many of which were racialized.[28]

The premise of eugenics—which seemingly defined race as biological—was the breedability of the human species. Charles Davenport, the father of U.S. eugenics, argued:

Eugenics is the science of the improvement of the human race by better breeding or, as the late Sir Francis Galton expressed it: "The science which deals with all influences that improve the inborn qualities of a race." The eugenical standpoint is that of the agriculturalist who, while recognizing the value of culture, believes that permanent advance is to be made only by securing the best "blood." Man is an organism—an animal; and the laws of improvement of corn and of race horses hold true for him also. Unless people accept this simple truth and let it influence marriage selection human progress will cease.[29]

This notion of traits in the blood, which can be manipulated through proper breeding, places eugenics within what Michel Foucault has called an "analytics of sexuality."[30] The term "breeding" exemplifies human races as technologically manipulable, while also muddying the boundary between culture and biology, human and animal. Agriculture, Davenport's favorite metaphor—"the human babies born each year," he writes, "constitute the world's most valuable crop"— nicely encapsulates the intertwining of the natural and the cultivated that is necessary to human civilization.[31] Eugenics is necessary because biology is not enough.[32] Davenport's work also exemplifies the difficulty of separating the natural from the cultivated: in the end, he argues that every characteristic, such as vagrancy, evident in more than one generation, is transmitted through blood. Although Davenport's work is now considered to be ideologically corrupt, race and breeding are still intertwined in more modern understandings of race. According to modern population genetics, a human race is a "breeding population" marked by certain gene frequencies.[33]

However, as the history of segregation and anti-miscegenation legislation in the U.S. makes clear, breeding populations, if they exist, are never simply natural, but rather result from a complex negotiation between culture, society and biology. Importantly, segregation was a response to failures of biological theories of the innate physical degeneracy of mulattos and Africans. It is also a response to the "confusion" brought about by emancipation. As Hartmann argues:

the conception of race engendered by slavery and abolished by the Thirteenth Amendment made "black" virtually synonymous with "slave" and "white" with "free" ... Now that race no longer defined status, classificatory schemes were required to maintain these lines of division. The effort to maintain the color line, or, properly speaking, black subordination, involved securing the division between the races and controlling the freed population. Central to this effort was the codification of race, which focused primarily on defining and containing blackness.[34]

This codification—especially its "one drop" formulation—widened the gap between what the body says and what it means, since it became increasingly difficult to read the signifier, let alone the signification.

Segregation is an important U.S. racial technology, a clarifying spatial mapping that creates stark racial differences where none necessarily exist. As Grace Elizabeth Hale has argued, "whites created the culture of segregation in large part to counter black success, to make a myth of absolute racial difference, to stop the rising." Segregation made "race dependent on space, and the color bar became less a line than the ground on which southern people were allowed to drink and buy and stand."[35] Segregation, importantly, did not only map space, but was a reaction to the transgression of space brought about by modern technologies, such as trains. It fought mobility with immobility. Hale, analyzing the importance of segregation on trains, argues:

> For southern whites, however, more was at stake than comfortable plushy cushions and clean-carpeted aisles. Whiteness itself was being defined in late nineteenth-century first-class train cars. When middle-class blacks entered the semi-public space of railroads, they placed their better attire and manners in direct juxtaposition with whites' own class signifiers. Because many whites found it difficult to imagine African Americans as anything other than poor and uneducated, finely dressed blacks riding in first-class cars attracted their particular ire . . . Greater mobility made the poorest whites more visible to the rising white middle class as well . . . Class and race, then, became more visibly unhinged as railroads disrupted local isolation. Confusion reigned.[36]

Racist technologies thus sought to make clear distinctions in society, where none necessarily existed. Segregation and eugenics are therefore examples of what Foucault has called modern racism, a racism fostered to allow states, which are supposedly dedicated to the social welfare of their populations, to exercise sovereign power—that is, to punish and destroy. He writes,

> Racism is bound up with the workings of a State that is obliged to use race, the elimination of races and the purification of the race, to exercise its sovereign power. The juxtaposition of—or the way biopower functions through—the old sovereign power of life and death implies the workings, the introduction and activation, of racism.[37]

Importantly, though, for Foucault, modern racism did not simply apply to those who were subjugated. Extrapolating from Nazism, he argues that race wars became "a way of regenerating one's own race. As more and more of our number die, the race to which we belong will become all the purer."[38] Also, in terms of an analytics of sexuality, eugenics applies to everyone: Davenport's eugenics textbook, for instance, is directed to those middle-class readers who want to know "how to fall in love intelligently." Eugenics also redefined all humans as the carriers of eternal characteristics, making the base unit not the human but the trait. Racism renders everyone into a standing reserve of genes to be stored and transmitted.

Mimicking Standing Reserves

According to Heidegger in his 1955 "The Question Concerning Technology," the essence of technology is not technological. Indeed, by examining tools, we miss what is essential about technology, which is its mode of revealing or "enframing." This mode of revealing, he argues, "puts to nature the unreasonable demand that it supply energy that can be extracted and stored as such"; once transformed into energy, it is also transmitted and circulated.[39] Technology also changes the nature of essence as such, making what is essential that which endures rather than its generic type, shrinking causality from the rich fourfold system discussed by Aristotle to one mode: "a reporting—a reporting challenged forth—of standing-reserves that must be guaranteed either simultaneously or in sequence."[40] Most damningly, enframing endangers man by rendering man himself into a standing reserve:

> As soon as what is unconcealed no longer concerns man even as object, but does so, rather, exclusively as standing-reserve, and man in the midst of objectlessness is nothing but the order of the standing reserve, then, he comes to the brink of a precipitous fall; that is, he comes to the point where he himself will have to be taken as standing-reserve. Meanwhile man, precisely as the one so threatened, exalts himself to the posture of lord of the earth. In this way the impression comes to prevail that everything man encounters exists only insofar as it is his construct. This illusion gives rise to one final delusion: It seems as though man everywhere and always encounters only himself . . . *In truth, however, precisely nowhere does man today any longer encounter himself.*[41]

This endangerment, though, not only reduces man to a standing and circulating source of energy: it also makes impossible his recognition of another kind of revealing, since it "conceals that revealing which, in the sense of *poiesis*, lets what presences come forth into appearance."[42] Poiesis, art, enables a revelation that does not reduce nature into a standing reserve, but rather lets it stand against man as an object.

The resonances between Heidegger's post-World War II reflections on the dangers of technology and analyses of race and racism are profound (and perhaps not surprising, given Heidegger's involvement with National Socialism). In a 1949 lecture on technology, Heidegger argued,

> agriculture is now a motorized food industry, the same thing in its essence as the production of corpses in the gas chambers and the extermination camps, the same thing as blockades and the reduction of countries to famine, the same thing as the manufacture of hydrogen bombs.[43]

The National Socialist program reduced all humans to standing reserves: some to be "destroyed," others to be optimized and made more productive. Intentionally or unintentionally, race too, understood as a set of visible or invisible genetic characteristics, is a mode of revealing that renders everyone into a set of traits that are stored and transmitted; and also race is then seen as what allows man to endure through time as a set of unchanging characteristics. Further, Heidegger's discussion of the experience of the human as not even an object resonates with the historical experience of people of color. Hortense Spillers, writing on the situation of slaves in the Middle Passage, argues, "under these conditions, one is neither female, nor male, as both subjects are taken into 'account' as quantities."[44] During this period, the captives are "culturally unmade." The pain of non-recognition, which makes one neither object nor subject, has also been eloquently enunciated by Frantz Fanon:

> I came into the world imbued with the will to find a meaning in things, my spirit filled with the desire to attain to the source of the world, and then I found that I was an object in the midst of other objects.
>
> Sealed into that crushing objecthood, I turned beseechingly to others. Their attention was a liberation, running over my body suddenly abraded into nonbeing, endowing me once more with an agility that I had thought lost, and by taking me out of the world, restoring me to it. But just as I reached the other side, I stumbled, and the movements, the attitudes, the glances of the other fixed me there, in the sense in which a chemical solution is fixed by a dye. I was indignant; I demanded an explanation. Nothing happened. I burst apart.[45]

In addition, race understood as a set of visible or invisible genetic characteristics, is a mode of revealing that renders everyone into a set of traits that are stored and transmitted; race is then seen as what allows man to endure through time as a set of unchanging characteristics.

Yet crucially, for Heidegger, understanding the essence of technology also makes salvation possible: although enframing conceals poiesis, it also makes poiesis a saving power. "Because the essence of technology is nothing technological," he writes, "essential reflection upon technology and decisive confrontation with it must happen in a realm that is, on the one hand, akin to the essence of technology and, on the other, fundamentally different from it. Such a realm is art."[46] According to Heidegger, poiesis "brings forth truth into the splendor of radiant appearing."[47] Similarly, Fanon writes:

> The crippled veteran of the Pacific war says to my brother, "Resign yourself to your color the way I got used to my stump; we're both victims."
>
> Nevertheless with all my strength I refuse to accept that amputation. I feel in myself a soul as immense as the world, truly a soul as deep as the deepest of rivers, my chest has the power to expand without limit.[48]

Thus the question becomes: to what extent can ruminating on race as technology make possible race as poiesis, or at least as a form of agency? Can race become a different mode of creation or revealing? Race has historically enabled subversive action. Homi Bhabha, for instance, has influentially argued that colonial mimicry—the mimicking of the colonizers by the colonized, demanded by the colonizers—"is at once resemblance and menace."[49] Understood as something that is repeatedly performed, race, like gender, opens up the space of parody and agency. Intriguingly, Fanon describes his strength in terms that trouble the boundary between nature and human: his soul as "deep as the deepest rivers." This simile suggests an embracing of factors not usually considered human. That is, if race as technology does make it possible to expand without limit, could this power stem not from asserting the difference between humans and technology, technology and poiesis, but rather through an acceptance of their similarities—through race as prosthesis?

Donna Haraway has influentially argued that we must embrace the breakdown in boundaries between human and animal, natural and artificial, mediation and embodiment. According to Haraway, "late twentieth-century machines have made thoroughly ambiguous the difference between natural and artificial, mind and body, self-developing and externally designed, and many other distinctions that used to apply to organisms and machines."[50] Rather than condemning this situation, as does Heidegger, she argues for the cyborg as a utopian figure precisely because it reworks nature and culture so that

> the one can no longer be the resource for appropriation or incorporation by the other. The relationships for forming wholes from parts, including those of polarity and hierarchical domination, are at issue in the cyborg world . . . The cyborg would not recognize the Garden of Eden; it is not made of mud and cannot dream of returning to dust.[51]

As she notes, however, "the main trouble with cyborgs . . . is that they are the illegitimate offspring of militarism and patriarchal capitalism, not to mention state socialism."[52] Thus, in dealing with cyborgs, one must always see things doubly and "see from both perspectives at once because each reveals both dominations and possibilities unimaginable from the other vantage point."[53] To see race as technology, thus, is always to see double: to see possibilities (reworkings) and domination (eugenics) together.

In an effort to do so, I conclude by rethinking arguments I've made in the past regarding high-tech Orientalism—the high-tech abjection of the Asian/Asian America other—through Greg Pak's 2003 feature film *Robot Stories*, which explores the extent to which high-tech Orientalism might be the ground from which some other future can be created; the ground from which dreams can be made to fly, flower, in freaky, queer unexpected ways.[54]

Loving Robots

High-tech Orientalism would seem to be the limit case for race as technology, for it literally figures the raced other as technology. Stemming from 1980s' anxiety over rising Japanese dominance, its most dominant strain figures the Asian other as a robotic menace, so that s/he literally becomes the technology s/he produces.

In my first book, *Control and Freedom: Power and Paranoia in the Age of Fiber Optics*, I examined the importance of high-tech Orientalism to cyberpunk fiction and film, and to the emergence of the Internet as cyberspace. High-tech Orientalism is the obverse of the "scenes of empowerment" that flooded the airwaves in the mid- to late-1990s—conflations of racial and technological empowerment that argued that technology would eradicate racial difference. Foundational cyberpunk pre-visions, from William Gibson's 1984 *Neuromancer* to Neal Stephenson's 1993 *Snow Crash*, I contended, use "Asian," "African" and "half-breed" characters to create seductively dystopian near futures. Gibson's fiction in particular perpetuates and relies on this high-tech Orientalism, a "navigate-by-difference" tactic in which disembodied heroes/console data cowboys emerge through disembodied representations of "local" people of color, irrevocably fixed in the past, and cyberspace is made desirable and exotic through relentless comparisons between it and Ninsei.[55] Importantly, Gibson's vision of cyberspace has little to nothing in common with the Internet—other than a common 1990s fan base. Inspired by the early 1980s Vancouver arcade scene, Gibson sat at his typewriter and outlined a 3D chessboard/consensual visual hallucination called the Matrix or "cyberspace," in which corporations exist as bright neon shapes, and console cowboys steal and manipulate data. In *Neuromancer*, cyberspace is a "graphic representation of data abstracted from the banks of every computer in the human system."[56]

Even though Gibson's cyberspace does not coincide with the Internet, its seductive vision of a consensually hallucinated network in which U.S. cowboys thrive in an unfriendly, Asian-dominated corporate world made it an origin myth in the 1990s. Cyberpunk literature, which originated the *desire for* cyberspace as a frontier rather than cyberspace itself, seductively blinds users to their circulating representations through dreams of disembodiment (freedom from one's body), sustained by representations of others as disembodied information. Cyberpunk offers unnerving, disorienting yet ultimately readable "savage" otherness in order to create the mythic user. Rather than brush aside fear of strange locations, strangers, and their dark secrets by insisting that we are all the same, these narratives, like the detective fiction on which they are often based, romanticize and make readable, trackable and solvable the lawlessness and cultural differences that supposedly breed in crowds and cities. Racial and ethnic differences, emptied of any link to discrimination or exclusion, make these spaces "navigable" yet foreign, readable yet cryptic. Difference as a simple database category grounds cyberspace as a "navigable space"; through racial difference we steer, and sometimes conquer.

High-tech Orientalism offers the pleasure of exploring, the pleasure of being somewhat overwhelmed, but ultimately "jacked-in." Crucially, this pleasure

usually compensates for *lack* of mastery—*Neuromancer* was written at a time
when the U.S. seemed to be losing its status as the number one financial power.
The future in *Neuromancer* seemingly belongs to Japanese and other non-U.S.-
corporations—the status of the U.S. as a nation-state is unclear—although U.S.
console cowboys still ride high in cyberspace. High-tech Orientalism is not
colonialism, but rather a paranoid reaction to global economic and data flows.
High-tech Orientalism promises intimate knowledge, sexual concourse with the
"other," which it reduces to data, to a standing resource. This will-to-knowledge
structures the plot of many cyberpunk novels, as well as the reader's relation
to the text; the reader is always "learning," always trying understand these
narratives that confuse the reader. The reader eventually emerges as a hero/ine
for having figured out the landscape, for having navigated these fast-paced texts,
since the many unrelated plots (almost) come together at the end and
revelations abound. This readerly satisfaction generates desire for these vaguely
dystopian futures. Thus, if online communications threaten to submerge users
in representation—if they threaten to turn users into media spectacles—high-
tech Orientalism allows people to turn a blind eye to their own vulnerability
and to enjoy themselves while doing so, to enjoy one's emasculation. Silicon
Valley readers are not simply "bad readers" for viewing these texts as utopian,
for they do not necessarily desire the future as described by these texts; rather,
they long for the ultimately steerable and sexy cyberspace, which always seems
within reach, even as it slips from the future to past. They also yearn for
cyberspace as the space of "biz."

To put it slightly differently and to draw from the work of Karen Shimakawa
on abjection and Asian American performance, high-tech Orientalism is a
process of abjection—a frontier—through which the console cowboy, the
properly human subject, is created. Shimakawa, drawing from the work of Julia
Kristeva, argues that abjection is

> both a state and a process—the conditions/position of that which is
> deemed loathsome and the process by which that appraisal is made . . .
> It is . . . the process by which the subject/"I" is produced: by establishing
> perceptual and conceptual borders around the self and "jettison[ing]" that
> which is deemed objectionable.[57]

The human is constantly created through the jettisoning of the Asian/Asian
American other as robotic, as machine-like and not quite human, as not quite
lived. And also, I would add, the African American other as primitive, as too
human.

The question this essay asks in rethinking of race as technology is: can the
abject, the Orientalized, the robot-like data-like Asian/Asian American other
be a place from which something like insubordination or creativity can arise?
To put it slightly differently, can the formulation of Asian as technology, Asians
as the future, be turned from something terrifying to something like what

Judith Butler calls a future horizon—"a . . . horizon . . . in which the violence of exclusion is perpetually in the process of becoming overcome"?[58] Can the abject, as Shimakawa argues, be a place for a critical mimesis—can we critically assume the role of the abject in order to call into question the larger system of representation and its closure? That is, can Asian/Asian American as robots, as data, be a critical mimesis of mimesis itself—a way for all to embrace their inner robot?

To explore this possibility, I turn to the work of HAPA filmmaker Greg Pak. His feature film *Robot Stories* explores the parallel between robots and Asians that lies at the core of high-tech Orientalism. Although at times relentlessly sentimental—the promotional materials that claim "everything is changing . . . except for the human heart"—*Robot Stories* asserts Asian American as human by emphasizing their alleged similarities and their opposition to robots *and* at the same time deconstructs the opposition between human and robots. That is, his stories play with the stereotypes of Asian Americans as relentless, robotic workers, as looking all the same (can't tell them apart), as dragon ladies, in order to create a livable future—literally a future in which Asian Americans and African Americans live as the non-abject.

Robot Stories consists of four shorts, which create an intriguing progression. Since this progression is central to my argument, I will spend some time outlining the plot of the film. The first story is "Robot Child," in which an Asian American couple—Roy and Marcia Ito—take care of a robot baby for a month in hopes of being given a real baby to adopt. Taking care of this robot, it is hoped, will make these stereotypically work-driven people human, especially the non-maternal Marcia Ito, who is scarred by memories of her own mother. Symbolically, at the adoption agency, for instance, Roy Ito turns to Marcia and says that this adoption of a robot baby will make them real people, a real family— just as the camera focuses on the image of a white blond baby. Although Roy seems the most committed to having a child and to non-traditional gender roles (the child and he bond quickly, and the child and Marcia reject each other's awkward gestures; Marcia drops the baby a couple of times), Roy soon leaves for Japan, in proper husbandly fashion, to pursue a project that will secure the child's future. Turning to her own father to find a software solution to baby care (the robot becomes hooked to their iMac, which simulates feeding, caring, etc.), Marcia returns to the office. On her return home, however, she is confronted by a robot/child gone mad. Deciding in the end not to return the robot and thus disappoint Roy by jeopardizing their chance of ever adopting, Marcia goes after the "little fucker," to find it, like herself so many years ago, crying in a closet (see Figures 2.1 and 2.2). Breaking down in tears herself as she identifies with the robot, the "mother" and robot finally bond. In this story, white figures are still very much in positions of control: the white nurse who oversees the adoption controls the gaze and she, in the end, will decide whether or not they are "good parents."

FIGURE 2.1 Marcia in closet

Still from *Robot Stories*

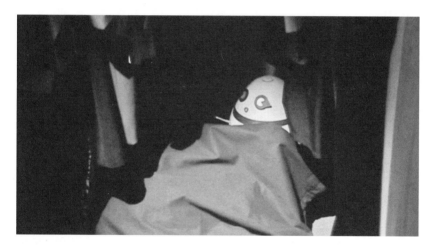

FIGURE 2.2 "Baby" robot in closet

Still from *Robot Stories*

In the next story, "Robot Fixer," a mother, stricken with grief, guilt and anger over her comatose son, is driven to obsessively complete and repair her son's toy robot collection. Fixing these robots—showing them the care she felt her son Wilson was never able to give—becomes a way for the mother to deal with her son's accident and his failure to live up to her dreams. Through these robots, however, she comes to respect the interests and ways of her son, who seems to have been a bit of a robot himself: one co-worker describes him as a "G9," an office robot; as a child he played endlessly with these robots and perhaps dreamed of them. The mother becomes fixated on one robot in particular, whose wingless condition stems from her own carelessness during vacuuming. Stealing a rare female figure for her wings, she accidentally handicaps it as well. As the son's body parts are distributed to needy Asian Americans, the mother returns home, carrying a prized one-winged robot which she no longer feels the need to fix. Insisting on the importance of parts, as both a human and robot condition, "Robot Fixer," like "Robot Child," pursues Asian Americans as robots, as ideal workers, to break down the opposition between robot and human; Asian American and white.

The next story, "Robot Love," moves from an Asian American son like a G9 to a pair of G9s like Asian Americans, and also breaks down the barrier between Asian American and white. The G9 robot coders, who look Asian, are perfect workers (much better than their real Asian American equivalents who, like their white counterparts, play video games in their spare time). They work continuously, following the commands of their bosses and their "inner" female voice that reminds them "you have work," and they accept sexual harassment (both male and female robots are objects of scopic desire and physical molestation). The attempts of the male G9, Archie, at interactions are rebuked by all, except the nerdy white sysop Bob, who sympathizes and identifies with Archie—Bob allows Archie to address him as "Bob" (after Bob is teased by his co-workers), and he also allows Archie to leave the building to pursue the female G9 (after Bob's co-worker calls the pair of them "fucking freaks"). The audience too is made to identify with Archie: not only are many shots taken from Archie's point of view, but the audience's view goes dark when Archie has been turned off. This story brings out nicely the relationship between sexual exploitation and reduction to information brought about by high-tech Orientalism.

Interestingly the actors who play the mother in "Robot Fixer" and the husband in "Robot Child" re-used in this story, playing with the notion that "we" can't tell Asian Americans apart, but also emphasizing that *Robot Stories* demands the suspension of disbelief. The entry of Asian American-like robots at this point of the film both buttresses the status of and places some Asian Americans as non-abject (defined as human in opposition to the G9s and to Bob), but also attacks the notion of, and critically mimics, the robotic as abject (as frontier). This move from abject happens at the conclusion of this story, and is most clear in the scene in which robots finally get together and "make love" (see Figure 2.3). In this scene, love—which is implied earlier as making one human—is reworked into "robot love." In robot love, slurs ("freaky," "they could've put a bigger rack on her") move from being that which separates humans and robots, to that which with care—robot-like humanism—can be reworked into loving statements. They inhabit the slur and the insult, turning them into the basis for love. Following Judith Butler's call to become the bad copy, robot love, in other words, seems to claim robots as a fake or bad copy in order to rework claims of human love as originary and unique. The queerness of robot love is also physically queer: explicit in its physical manifestation, which

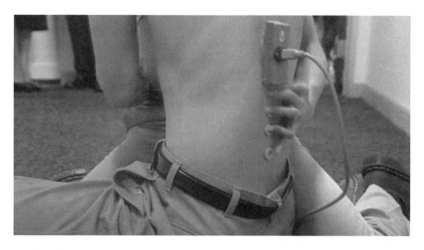

FIGURE 2.3 Robot sex

Still from *Robot Stories*

comprises the mutual stimulation of female plugs. It displaces heterosexual normativity within an ostensibly heterosexual coupling—it also troubles the boundary between private and public. With robot love, Archie and his female counterpart are finally also granted the privacy denied to them during their love-making scene. As everyone watches the coupling, "Bob" requests that they give Archie and the female robots some privacy and everyone leaves, even though he stays to watch for a little while. Intriguingly, though, the robots don't seem to care (privacy is something granted, not demanded); privacy is also something violated by Bob's look, but respected by the camera's—rather than it showing what Bob sees, Bob himself becomes the spectacle.

The sentimentality of the series becomes most clear in the last story, which is set farthest in the future (in 2027), at a time in which antibiotics no longer work but humans have reached immortality by being "scanned" into data banks. From there they can supposedly see everything, do everything, know everything. The story centers around an Asian American sculptor, dying of pneumonia, who is fighting against being scanned, and his African American wife, who has already been scanned. Rather than representing the "natural other," his African American wife represents a certain embrace of technology: the traditional roles have been reversed. What is truly remarkable about this story, however, is that there are *no white people portrayed in this future*. Even more remarkably, *no one seems to have noticed*. All the critics reviewing *Robot Stories* emphasize its universal "human heart" angle and its differences from blockbuster sci-fi films, rather than its status as an "ethnic film," or its relationship to other Asian American films—certainly not as a film in which white people have disappeared. This is because Asian Americans and African Americans have come to represent humanity as seamlessly as the scanned people have come to take the place of the robotic. What is abject here is not death, which is embraced, but informatic immortality—even as the notion of humans as robot-like has been embraced.

Clearly, this raises some questions: for instance, to what extent is sentimentalizing humanism key to this reworking of high-tech Orientalism? To what extent is this displacing of abjection dependent on a reification of humanity as original? Regardless, what is remarkable here is that the invisibility and universality usually granted to whiteness has disappeared, not to be taken up seamlessly by Asian Americans and African Americans, but rather to be reworked to displace both what is considered to be technological and what is considered to be human. The opening credits of *Robot Stories*, which begins with the now stereotypical stream of 1s and 0s, encapsulates Pak's methodology nicely. Rather than these 1s and 0s combining to produce the name of the actors etc. (as in *Ghost in the Shell* and *The Matrix*), the credits interrupt this diagonal stream (this stream mimics the path of the flying robots in "Robot Fixer"). As the sequence proceeds, little robots are revealed to be the source of the 1s and 0s. Shortly after they are revealed, one malfunctions, turnings a different color, and produces a 2 (Figure 2.4). Soon, all the robots follow, turn various colors and produce all sorts of colorful base-10 numbers. Thus, robots turn out in the end to be colorful and to operate in the same manner—and in the same numerical base—as humans. The soundtrack features a Country and Western song telling Mama to let herself go free. The 1s and 0s, rather than being readable, are made to soar, to color the robots that are ourselves.

Race as technology thus problematizes the usual modes of visualization and revelation, while at the same time making possible new modes of agency and causality. Race as technology is both the imposition of a grid of control and a lived social reality in which kinship with technology can be embraced. Importantly, it displaces ontological questions of race—debates over what race

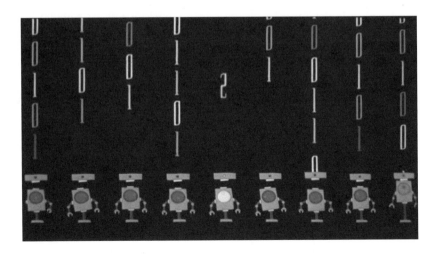

really is and is not, focused on separating ideology from truth—with ethical questions: what relations does race set up? As Jennifer González has argued, race is fundamentally a question of relation, of an encounter, a recognition, that enables certain actions and bars others.[59] The formulation of race as technology also opens up the possibility that, although the idea and the experience of race have been used for racist ends, the best way to fight racism might not be to deny the existence of race, but to make race do different things. Importantly, though, this is not simply a private decision, because race has been so key to the definition of private and public as such. In order to reformulate race, we need also to reframe nature and culture, privacy and publicity, self and collective, media and society.

Notes

1 For examples, see Jennifer Reardon, *Race to the Finish: Identity and Governance in an Age of Genomics* (Princeton: Princeton University Press, 2005); Coco Fusco and Brian Wallis, eds. *Only Skin Deep: Changing Visions of the American Self* (New York: Harry N. Adams, 2003); Aly Gotz and Karl Heinz Roth, *The Nazi Census: Identification and Control in the Third Reich* (Philadelphia: Temple University Press, 2003).

2 See Bernard Stiegler, *Technics and Time, 1: The Fault of Epimetheus*, trans. Richard Beardsworth and George Collins (Stanford: Stanford University Press, 1998).

3 See Luca Cavalli-Sforza and Francesco Cavalli-Sforza. *The Great Human Diasporas* (Reading, MA: Addison-Wesley, 1995); Alan Templeton, "Human Races: A Genetic and Evolutionary Perspective," *American Anthropologist* 100.3 (1999): 632–650.

4 See Reardon, *Race to the Finish.*

5 See Lisa Gannett, "Making Populations: Bounding Genes in Space and Time," *Philosophy of Science* 70 (December 2003): 989–1001; and Evelyn Hammonds "Straw Men and their Followers: The Return of Biological Race," SSRC, June 7, 2006, available at: http://raceandgenomics.ssrc.org/Hammonds

6 See Henry Louis Gates, Jr, *African American Lives*, PBS series; and Paul Gilroy, *Against Race: Imagining Political Culture Beyond the Color Line* (Cambridge, MA: Harvard University Press, 2000).

7 Beth Coleman "Race as Technology," *Camera Obscura* 70, 24:1 (2009): 177–207.

8 See Charles Davenport and Morris Steggerda, *Race Crossing in Jamaica* (Washington: Carnegie Institution of Washington, 1929); Edward Black, *IBM and the Holocaust* (New York: Crown Publishing, 2001); Richard J. Hermstein and Charles Murray, *The Bell Curve: Intelligence and Class Structure in American Life* (New York: Free Press, 1994).

9 Bruce Dain. *A Hideous Monster of the Mind: American Race Theory in the Early Republic* (Cambridge, MA: Harvard University Press, 2002), 7.

10 See Michel Foucault, *The Order of Things: An Archaeology of the Human Sciences* (New York: Pantheon, 1971); and François Jacob, *The Logic of Life: A History of Heredity*, trans. Betty E. Spillman (New York: Pantheon, 1973).

11 Samira Kawash, *Dislocating the Color Line* (Stanford: Stanford University Press, 1997), 130.

12 Saidiya Hartmann, *Scenes of Subjection: Terror, Slavery, and Self-Making in Nineteenth-Century America* (Oxford: Oxford University Press, 1997), 26.

13 Relaying his experience of speaking on temperance before "the common people of Ireland," Douglass stated:

> Never did human faces tell a sadder tale. More than five thousand were assembled; and I say, with no wish to wound the feelings of any Irishman, that these people lacked only a black skin and woolly hair, to complete their likeness to the plantation negro. The open, uneducated mouth—the long, gaunt arm—the badly formed foot and ankle—the shuffling gait—the retreating forehead and vacant expression—and, their petty quarrels and fights—all reminded me of the plantation, and my own cruelly abused people. Yet, *that* is the land of GRATTAN, of CURRAN, of O'CONNELL, and of SHERIDAN . . . The Irishman educated, is a model gentleman; the Irishman ignorant

and degraded, compares in form and feature, with the negro! (The Claims of the Negro: An Address, Before the Literary Societies of Western Reserve College, at Commencement, July 12, 1854 (Rochester, NY: Lee, Mann, 1854), 30.)

14 Responding to arguments that racism was key to the evolution of the species, Boas contended:

> I challenge him [Sir Arthur Keith] to prove that race antipathy is "implanted by nature" and not the effect of social causes which are active in every closed social group, no matter whether it is racially heterogeneous or homogeneous. The complete lack of sexual antipathy, the weakening of race consciousness in communities in which children grow up as an almost homogeneous group; the occurrence of equally strong antipathies between denominational groups, or between social strata—as witnessed by the Roman patricians and plebeians, the Spartan Lacedaemonians and Helots, the Egyptian castes and some of the Indian castes—all these show that antipathies are social phenomena. If you will, you may call them "implanted by nature," but only in so far as man is a being living in closed social groups, leaving it entirely indetermined [sic] what these social groups may be. ("Race and Progress," *Science* 74 (1931): 8)

Importantly, this argument highlighted race's functioning: race was a tool for creating social groupings to enclose "man" into social groupings, which could then coincide with a natural antipathy to other closed social groupings.

15 Henry Louis Gates, Jr, "Writing 'Race' and the Difference It Makes," *"Race," Writing, and Difference,* ed. Henry Louis Gates, Jr (Chicago: University of Chicago, 1986), 5.

16 Reardon, *Race to the Finish,* 18–19.

17 Etienne Balibar, "Is There a Neo-Racism?" *Race, Nation, Class: Ambiguous Identities* (London: Verso, 1991), 17–28.

18 Anne Anlin Cheng. *The Melancholy of Race: Psychoanalysis, Assimilation, and Hidden Grief* (Oxford: Oxford University Press, 2001), 5. The same group of white parents argued, "major differences exist in the learning ability patterns of white and Negro children." As Cheng notes, "this line of argument advanced by white segregationists aimed to transform psychical damage as the result of social injury into a notion of inherent disability" (ibid.).

19 Toni Morrison, *Playing in the Dark* (New York: Vintage, 1993), 63.

20 Michael Omi and Howard Winant, *Racial Formation in the United States: From the 1960s to the 1980s* (New York: Routledge, 1986/89), 66.

21 Ibid., 61–62.

22 Samira Kawash, *Dislocating the Color Line,* 130.

23 Ann Laura Stoler, "Racial Histories and their Regimes of Truth," *Political Power and Social Theory* 11 (1987): 187, 200.

24 Thomas Jefferson, arguing against the incorporation of freed black slaves into the nation-state, argued,

> deep rooted prejudices entertained by the whites; the thousand recollections, by the blacks, of the injuries they have sustained; new provocations; the real distinctions which nature has made; and many other circumstances, will divide us into parties, and produce convulsions which will probably never end but in the extermination of one race or the other. (Dain, *A Hideous Monster of the Mind,* 31)

25 He writes:

> In 1896, the processes and the problems of heredity were little understood, and "blood" was for many a solvent in which all problems were dissolved and all processes commingled. "Blood"—and by extension "race"—included numerous elements that we would today call cultural; there was not a clear line between cultural and physical elements or between social and biological heredity. The characteristic qualities of civilizations were carried from one generation to another both in and with the blood of their citizens. (George W Stocking, Jr, "The Turn-of-the-Century Concept of Race," *Modernism/Modernity* 1.1 (1994): 6)

26 Ibid., 15.

27 To be clear, this is not to say that understandings of race prior to the widespread acceptance of Mendelian genetics did not assert racial differences as biological: the polygenesist argument is a perfect example of this. Yet importantly, the polygeneticist argument did not strictly separate

biologically transmitted racial traits from cultural ones—that is, racial characteristics were considered mutable.

28 Charles Davenport's studies of the transmission of traits, for instance, revealed how eye color, skin color, feeblemindedness, and so on, moved unchanged from generation to generation. These unit characteristics allegedly formed a stable link between individuals across time. These unit characteristics, however, also reveal that, although eugenics is now popularly conceived as pitting race against race, it also made unstable the concept of race. Davenport, for instance, consistently wrote about the need to better the race, but also argued:

> two very light "colored" parents will have (probably) only light children, some of whom "pass for whites" away from home. So far as skin color goes they are as truly white as their greatgrandparent and it is quite conceivable that they might have mental and moral qualities as good and typically Caucasian as he had. Just as perfect white skin can be extracted and a typical Caucasian arise out of the mixture. However, this result will occur only in the third, or later, hybrid generation and the event will not be very common. (Charles Davenport, *Heredity in Relation to Eugenics*. New York: Arno, 1972, 37–38)

In this passage, the race of a typical Caucasian is viewed as something that is "recoverable" from a mixture of other races—a notion that is diametrically opposed to the "one drop rule" used in many Southern states and that is also against the percentage logic that drove Nazi anti-semitism (although later, arguing against hybrid vigor in offspring between black and white Jamaicans, Davenport would write about the disharmonies in mulattos, thus implying that racial types comprised a certain balance of racial features (Davenport and Steggerda, *Race Crossing in Jamaica*, 471)). This passage also reveals the connection between visible differences—white skin—and mental characteristics. Yet, importantly, what this passage suggests is that the move to separate biology from culture did not designate the biological as unchangeable, but rather as technological—as something that could be bred and improved upon.

29 Charles Davenport, *Heredity in Relation to Eugenics*, 1.

30 Michel Foucault, *The History of Sexuality*, Vol. 1, trans. Alan Sheridan (New York: Vintage, 1978), 148. Foucault argues that, within a sovereign society, blood relation was paramount because:

> differentiation into orders and castes, and the value of descent lines were predominant . . . It [blood] owed its high value at the same time to its instrumental role (the ability to shed blood), to the way it functioned in the order of signs (to have a certain blood, to be of the same blood, to be prepared to risk one's blood) . . . blood was *a reality with a symbolic function*. We, on the other hand, are in a society of "sex," or rather a society "with a sexuality": the mechanisms of power are addressed to the body, to life, to what causes it to proliferate, to what reinforces the species, its stamina, its ability to dominate, or its capacity for being used. (Ibid., 147)

Given Davenport's argument, it would seem, however, that the society of sex does not forego blood, but rather resignifies it.

31 Charles Davenport, *Heredity in Relation to Eugenics*, 2.

32 Breeding is an "unnatural" product of human ingenuity, needed because natural and sexual selection are not sufficiently rational: "the general program of the eugenist is clear—it is to improve the race by inducing young people to make a more reasonable selection of marriage mates; to fall in love intelligently" (ibid., 4). This falling in love intelligently implies that any "natural" phenomenon can be cultured, cultivated, in order to produce something better—that biology, in other words, can never be completely separated from culture.

33 See Lisa Gannett, "Making Populations."

34 Saidiya Hartmann, *Scenes of Subjection*, 187.

35 Grace Elizabeth Hale. *Making Whiteness: The Culture of Segregation in the South, 1890–1940* (New York: Vintage, 1999), 21.

36 Ibid., 128–129. This technology of segregation was also accompanied, Hales contends, by modern technological spectacles such as the lynch festival, which represented the consequences of crossing racial lines through a perverse "crossing" of the black lynched body.

37 Michel Foucault, *Society Must Be Defended: Lectures at the College de France, 1975–1976* (New York: Macmillan, 2003), 258.

38 Ibid., 257.

39 Martin Heidegger, "The Question Concerning Technology," in *The Question Concerning Technology and Other Essays*, trans. William Lovitt (New York: Harper & Row, 1977), 14.

40 Ibid., 31 and 23.

41 Ibid., 27.

42 Ibid., 27.

43 As cited in Philippe Lacoue-Labarthe, *Heidegger, Art and Politics: The Fiction of the Political* (Oxford: Blackwell, 1990), 34.

44 Hortense Spillers, "Mama's Baby, Papa's Maybe: An American Grammar Book," *Diacritics* 17.2 (Summer 1987): 72.

45 Frantz Fanon, *Black Skin White Masks*, trans. Charles Lam Markmann (New York: Grove, 1967), 109.

46 Martin Heidegger, "The Question Concerning Technology," 35.

47 Ibid., 34.

48 Frantz Fanon, *Black Skin White Masks*, 140.

49 Homi Bhabha, "Of Mimicry and Man," *The Location of Culture* (New York: Routledge, 1994), 86.

50 Donna Haraway, "A Cyborg Manifesto: Science, Technology, and Socialist-Feminism in the Late Twentieth Century," in *Simians, Cyborgs and Women: The Reinvention of Nature* (New York: Routledge, 1991), 152.

51 Ibid., 151.

52 Ibid.

53 Ibid., 154.

54 *Robot Stories*, DVD, directed by Greg Pak (2003; NY, NY: Kino Video, 2005).

55 Wendy Hui Kyong Chun, *Control and Freedom: Power and Paranoia in the Age of Fiber Optics* (Cambridge, MA: MIT, 2006), William Gibson, *Neuromancer* (New York: Ace Books, 1984), Neal Stephenson, *Snow Crash* (New York: Bantam Books, 1992).

56 William Gibson, *Neuromancer*, 51.

57 Karen Shimakawa, *National Abjection: The Asian American Body Onstage* (Durham: Duke University Press, 2002), 3.

58 Judith Butler, *Bodies that Matter: On the Discursive Limits of "Sex,"* (New York: Routledge, 1993), 53.

59 Jennifer González, "The Face and the Public: Race, Secrecy, and Digital Art Practice," *Camera Obscura* 70, 24:1 (2009).

3

From Black Inventors to One Laptop Per Child

Exporting a Racial Politics of Technology

RAYVON FOUCHÉ

University of Illinois, Urbana-Champaign

> It is a well-know fact that the horse hay rake was first invented by a *lazy negro* [sic] who had a big hay field to rake and didn't want to do it by hand.[1]

The epigraph is one representative snapshot of the historical relationship that African Americans have had with technology and the institutions that support these technologies. The lawyer who spoke this statement in a patent rights battle involving an African American inventor at the turn of the twentieth century probably did not recognize the irony in his utterance. He clearly intended it to come off as a slight against African American work ethics; instead it reads completely the opposite. Outside of the "lazy negro" phrase, the comment can be interpreted as a smart and innovative labor-saving solution to a problem of fieldwork. Thus, the hay rake inventor—if there is actually one person who "invented" the hay rake—may have been lazy, but I would think of this person as being industrious, innovative, and simply smart. The idea of not wanting to clean up something by hand has brought the world a plethora of mechanical, automated, and robotic vacuuming devices. What is most important about this quote has less to do with the rake and more to do with the perceived technological limitations of African American people. Beyond the basic insult, the lawyer is contending that African Americans are technologically incompetent. Understanding that this quote comes from the late nineteenth century, it is just an extension of the tradition of African American inability that deemed these people incapable of caring for themselves.[2] This quote not only reflects the historic connections between race and technology in the United States, but can reference similar relationships throughout the globe. Laziness has been a pejorative term deployed by Western colonizers in Africa, Asia, and India long before the group of people transported to North America became known as Negroes.[3] Of course, deeming someone as lazy is an effective technique to substantiate unequal treatment and subjugation. The racial politics of difference and inferiority that allow one group to enslave or subjugate another manifest themselves within historical and contemporary discussions of technology creation and use. These historical assumptions about the meager mental capacities of the world's brown people were easily and effectively reproduced in technological realms. The creative ability to invent, innovate, and merely use technology—thought of as a god-given ability well into the twentieth century— has regularly been denied to so-called intellectually inferior peoples of color who could only survive through the benevolent assistance of others not like themselves. Well before the twentieth century white Westerners brought (and still do) Christianity to the unsaved brown people of the world.[4] By the late twentieth century this missionary zeal had been reborn in a desire to save the same people through science and technology rather than religion.[5] Brown people, once attended to by bibles and missionaries, now receive the proselytizing efforts of computer scientists wielding integrated circuits in the digital age.

This chapter will examine one strand of race and technology. It will be argued that technology and race within an American context have moved through four eras. In the first era humans, as in the case of slaves, were the technologies of production and dominant cultural communities controlled the meanings of race in the United States. During the following era—from the development of early electrical devices to early computing—racial segregation stabilized within the United States. The next era began with the first digital computing devices and strengthened with the proliferation of personal digital technologies and correlated with the supposed end of racial discrimination. Similarly as these digital devices get smaller, our perceptions of race and racism become harder to see. The fourth—which I argue we have just recently entered—produces digital devices that nostalgically reference the analog realm—such as the (re)production of the multiple sounds of an SLR camera by a digital camera and a nostalgia of in-need ethnic others to be saved. Currently, American society is struggling to move away from the biological underpinnings of race to ethnicity, culture, and community. However, similar to the ways in which technologies hark back to the analog period and reconjure it in digital guise, the move to ethnicity and culture licenses the analog period's discriminatory practices. Moreover, as ethnicity and culture are commodities traded within a global economy, ethnicity and culture—as in the case of a fast food franchise like Taco Bell—becomes less associated with peoples and bodies, but a disembodied consumable. It is in this final moment that the politics of race and technology in the United States have produced efforts to extend technological "aid" to the developing world.

The One Laptop Per Child (OLPC) program will be examined as an example of this new technological missionary work. OLPC presents a case that unfortunately reflects the comment by the attorney in the epigraph, and illustrates how we have come full circle in the digital age and seemingly altruistic work continues to be laced with racial overtones. In the desire to make history

relevant and meaningful to our current state of affairs globally, I will outline a framework of technology and race that locates OLPC within the most recent period of race and technology evolutions.

As the United States has grown to become a global power on multiple fronts, the dynamics of race have clearly changed. People of African heritage at different times in American history have been black, negro, colored and African American.[6] Indigenous American populations have been red, Indian, Native American, or defined by a tribal affiliation.[7] Even once disdained European others, like those of Jewish and Irish heritage, have now been lumped into the broad category of "white."[8] For most reading this volume, many of these changes are quite obvious and well documented historically. But scholars are just in the process of sorting through the changing dynamics of race in this new "multicultural" century.[9]

In many ways the election of Barack Obama as the forty-fourth president of the United States heralded this new multicultural moment. In the most optimistic reading of this moment, President Obama's election signaled a seismic shift in American racial consciousness. Images of the multi-hued crowd triumphantly celebrating on a cold Washington, DC, February day cemented this vision that the collective "we" had crossed the transom into a new era. But was this shift real or illusory? Arguably it was a bit of both. The election of President Obama conceivably correlated with a sense of, dare I say, "change." Similarly, the question that arises is a change of or to what? I would contend that the changes occurring are less about the emergence of a post-racial America than about the belief that although the United States is far from a racially inclusive oasis it is much closer to the century-old melting pot that it has been called for the past century. This essay will not debate whether or not the United States is closer to a mythological melting pot, but is interested in how this post-Obama election rhetoric connects to the relationships between technology and the racially marginalized in the current historical moment. Some have argued that the election of Barack Obama confirms that social programs like affirmative action have successfully run their course.[10] Closely related to these discussions is that technology, once seen as a gateway through which the American underclass could pass to lift themselves from their impoverished condition, is for the most part in place. Technology had overcome the old and often overused term of digital divides, to provide access to those in need. With the significant decrease in the price of computing equipment and the ubiquity of computers and training in public and private space (from universities and libraries), the question of access has become less of a question. With the proliferation of these technologies, the lack of proficiency in the use of these tools and the effective integration of these objects into one's existence is no longer being viewed as a byproduct of institutionalized racism, but as a product of an individual's lack of motivation or laziness. Thus in this opened digital age, with much in place to turn someone's American nightmare into an American dream, it is now the responsibility of the individual to harness the power and courage to—in Booker T. Washington language—pull oneself up by his or her bootstraps because "buckets" of technology had been cast down across the United States. The casting down of technological buckets has been very strong in the United States and if the "problem" of technological access has been solved State-side, a new place to be fixed is the developing world. This is one of the multiple contexts in which the OLPC program emerged. The American-based OLPC has aims to enable the material and ideological power of computing to leave American shores and transform the developing world. Beginning with the lives of African Americans, this essay will follow one trajectory of race and technology to discern how the rhetoric of technology as racial salvation is reproduced by American technological visionaries.

The Power of the Black Inventor Myth

As I am an African American historian of technology—who has written about black inventors, this transition is made plain to me every year before Black History Month. I have traditionally met the run-up to Black History Month with some trepidation. In a period designed to focus on the greatest of African American achievements, black inventors have become one of the most popular circulated historical connections between blackness and technology. What does this actually mean in practice? Black History Month is rightfully about honoring and celebrating black achievement, but often has no place for critical commentary on black life. As a result, I am generally invited to retell a version of the heroic black inventor myth, which, unbeknownst to many, I loathe. I struggle with the simplified representation of humanity that this perspective demands.

In the past few years, requests have shifted from the black inventor "greats" of the late nineteenth and early twentieth centuries to anyone who has anything to do with "computers." For me, this marks a partially positive evolution in the contemporary representations of African American people and technology. At one level, it shows that turn-of-the-twentieth-century patented objects no longer resonate with school-age children as much as they excite their teachers. At another, it indicates a recognition of the power of computing upon African American life. Yet unfortunately, most still would like today's black computer geniuses swathed in the same uplift rhetoric and mythology that wraps early twentieth-century African American inventors. The aim is, of course, to inspire young people to emulate African American technological successes, but it is also about a need to confirm the belief that the access problem in the United States has been solved with African Americans. To understand this need and desire for this story, the black inventor myth is quite instructive.

This myth has evolved and changed over time, but is sustained by four main themes: (1) a patent equals financial success; (2) black inventors were race champions and invented to uplift the race; (3) a patent by a black inventor is one of a kind; (4) all black inventors have similar racial experiences.[11] The black inventor myth began innocently enough with Henry E. Baker. Baker, born in 1859 in Columbus, Mississippi, initially set his sights on becoming a military officer. In 1875, Baker was the third and final black man to pass the entrance exam and enter the United States Naval Academy before the First World War.[12] After leaving the Naval Academy in 1877 through the racism of his fellow cadets, he began working at the United States Patent Office as a copyist. In 1879, he enrolled at Howard University to study law, graduated at the top of his class in 1881, and eventually became one of the first, if not the first, black patent examiners. Baker, under the auspices of then Commissioner of Patents Hon. Charles H. Duell, compiled the first official list of black inventors in 1900. The United States Commission to the Paris Exposition of 1900 requested that Commissioner Duell provide a list of patents issued to "colored" inventors. The commission used the list in preparing the "Negro Exhibit." Baker indicated that the list was overdue. The Patent Office evidently received regular inquiries about black inventors, but the general response was that the Patent Office did not keep records documenting racial heritage. Yet, there had been informal lists of black patentees compiled by the Patent Office. Lists had been created for Negro exhibits at the World's Industrial and Cotton Centennial Exposition at New Orleans in 1884, the World's Fair at Chicago in 1893, and the Cotton States and International Exposition at Atlanta in 1895. On January 26, 1900, the Patent Office sent requests to two-thirds of the nearly twelve thousand registered patent attorneys for information about any black inventor with whom they had worked. The Patent Office demanded a prompt reply, which certainly had to do with the fact that the Paris Exposition was set to begin on April 15. The Patent Office charged Baker with the responsibility for managing the correspondence with the attorney and compiling the list. Baker indicated that several thousand patent attorneys replied to the request. After verifying the information presented Baker created the first "definitive" black inventor list.[13] The Patent Office duplicated the same procedure in 1913 at the request of the Pennsylvania Commission for the Emancipation Exposition in Philadelphia.

I have disappointed many by not retelling the underlying myth this list supports. I am invested in moving our collective understanding of African Americans and technology past black inventors and the simple representations of names, patent numbers, and objects. These pieces of information dominate the historical understandings about black inventors' lived experiences. The historical reduction of their lives into these elements is the major problem in the already problematic consumption and appropriation of black inventors. This historical reduction conceals the difficulties they endured while gaining the patent protection that would, in the best situations, enable them to profit from their work. This historical reduction also denies black inventors their humanity—their frailties and strengths—and produces disembodied icons celebrated merely for their patented material production. But more importantly, reinscribing a narrow understanding of black inventors into our collective knowledge of African American people curtails more important discussions about the historical and contemporary meanings of technology within American society and culture at large. It also over-emphasizes technology as unequivocally good and a non-socially or culturally constructed object. Finally, imbedded in these lists and the myth is the idea that technology can liberate underserved and impoverished communities.

General lists of black inventors, which have taken on lives of their own, have been added to and transformed from word of mouth to paper to email, and circulated for more than a hundred years. The glee with which they are exchanged raises interesting questions about how, in a digital age, the historically rooted narratives of the relationships between African Americans and technology can inform studies of race and technology at the current moment globally. This myth is not as powerful as it once was because black technological ability is easily confirmed. Since it is so easily verified, African American difficulties within this digital age are no longer viewed as an effect of a historically racist society but a byproduct of not pulling hard enough on one's bootstraps. What this means for American underclasses is that technologies do not have politics in the way that Langdon Winner wrote about Robert Moses and the construction of bridges with racist affordances.[14] The new politics are the libertarian politics of freedom and empowerment championed by technological futurists and popular magazines like *Wired*.[15] By the turn of the twenty-first century, the idea that limited access was a hindrance to success—in the multiple ways success is constructed—had been washed away in the United States. For all intents and purposes the access problem had been solved by the technological altruism of the past few decades. The OLPC programs fit nicely into the moment of technological triumph in the United States and OLPC's visionaries see the developing world as the next frontier to subdue and conquer.

How do we get from Henry E. Baker and black inventors to OLPC and portable laptops with endearing green and white enclosures? The simple answer is: in many ways, but this essay aims to follow one strand of this story through the lives of African Americans and contribute to the body of scholarship invested in critically broadening the dialogues on race and technology. In specific, this paper considers the relationships between race and technology and discusses how technological changes influence our perceptions of racial and cultural relations. It contends that technological change references and reflects the fluid meanings of race and the nature of race relations in the United States. However, the ever-shifting racial terrain of the United States in the twenty-first century and the transnational flow of technology and culture demand that scholars consider technological change and race relations more globally. Arguably, analysis of the workings of race and technology has to move beyond examining one group of people, in one geographically bound location, at one specific moment in time. But in thinking about how to do this, it is important to steer clear of promoting a Kuhnian paradigm shift where the prior state of existence is surpassed and forgotten.[16] By charting the changing nature of race in relation to technology from the United States to impoverished parts of the world, this essay supports a middle ground, a synergy of the past, present, and future that embraces the value of history, while championing contemporary critical engagements.

Periodization has been a successful way of conceptualizing and historicizing technological change. Lewis Mumford in *Technics and Civilization* named eotechnic (wood and water), paleotechnic (coal and iron), and neotechnic (electricity and alloys) as defining moments in the global evolution of technology.[17] The writing of Thomas Kuhn has propelled the language of paradigm shift. More recently, Science and Technology Studies scholars have championed the social construction of technology as a means to understand how relevant social groups negotiate which technologies become old and which are deemed new.[18] One of the most interesting ways of conceptualizing modern technological change, as David Harvey has so eloquently illustrated, can be characterized by the pre-Fordist, Fordist, and post-Fordist historical eras.[19] What is fascinating about Harvey's periodization is that these points in time map nicely onto black and white race relations in the United States. During the pre-Fordist era the dominant racialized regime circulated around the effects and outcomes of the American slavery system. The Fordist era began shortly after the "separate but equal" decision of *Plessy v. Ferguson* institutionalizing racial segregation. Finally, the current post-Fordist era that took hold by the oil crisis of 1973 maps onto the illusionary triumphs of civil rights movements. However, as interesting and effective as this approach has been for studying African American civil rights' era experience with technology, this genealogy does not work very well for our current global racial moment, where race and racial identity are being supplanted by the less volatile terms of ethnicity, culture, and community.

Periodizing Racing and Technology

A new mapping of race and American culture opens avenues of analysis to more effectively incorporate the current historical moment. I will use African American life to conceptualize eras of race and technological change in the United States. These eras are not meant to be fixed or static, but to provide a historically informed structure from which to examine the evolution of the politics of race as American technological visions migrate from the underprivileged in the contiguous United States to the developing world.

The first era begins roughly in 1619, the year the first African slaves were brought to the "new world," and concludes in 1865, the year that the United States Congress ratified the Emancipation Proclamation. This period is characterized by the ways that institutionalized racial discrimination based on the biological concept of race became a dominant way of explaining difference in the West. During this period, the dominant institution that influenced, directed, and controlled the lives of the enslaved Africans was slavery. In understanding the ways African American lives have been affected by science and technology, American slavery is a critical starting point because networks of science and technology like guns and the slave ships helped create the diverse groups of people now known as African Americans.

However, in thinking about this racial/technological moment it is necessary not only to examine the basic scientific and technological devices developed to control black bodies, like shackles and whips, but also explore slavery as a technology itself. To think broadly about the connections between race, science, and technology it is important to move from the simple discussions of how and why specific scientific and technological design decisions were made to subjugate African Americans, to how slavery was a scientific and technological system in which African Americans played the role of a replenishable resource. The system of slavery would not have worked without a dehumanized enslaved labor force providing the "power." Sadly, enslaved African Americans were the cogs in a system that fundamentally contributed to their subjugation and solidified the perceptions of intellectual inferiority. By interpreting slavery through the lens of science and technology, other relevant questions arise. For instance, could slavery have stunted early American innovation? On the other hand, did the rising prices for slaves, the growing complexities of controlling slaves, and Abolitionist efforts to end slavery create a great demand for technologies that eliminated the need for slave labor? During this period of American history, where the political structure had socially and culturally invested in the technological system of slavery, the end of slavery could have been an important step forward in American technological development but the overarching belief in wholesale black inferiority was nearly impossible to dismantle.

The second era, defined by the formalization of a race-based system of segregation, is bound by 1865 and 1954—the year the Supreme Court of the United States declared in the *Brown v. Board of Education* decision that separate educational facilities were inherently unequal and that they violated the guarantee in the Fourteenth Amendment to the United States Constitution that all citizens would be equally protected under the law. Much work on African Americans, science, and technology has focused on this era and the ways that African American inventors negotiated the racial terrain of the late nineteenth and early twentieth centuries. This research has investigated not only the lives of black inventors, but also the ways their inventions affected black people in the United States. For example, many African Americans patented inventions, like those that improved railway transportation, which at best only partially benefited African Americans, and at worst, contributed to the maintenance of racial segregation.[20]

During this period, many scientific and technological systems like those associated with transportation became powerful forces of segregation. For instance, trains and buses with segregated or "Jim Crow" cars and seating became battlegrounds for black/white identity and citizenship. Moments like the removal of the well-to-do black woman Ida Wells-Barnett from the all-white "ladies" car in 1884, the trial of black professional Homer Plessy in 1892 when he tested the constitutionality of the Louisiana Separate Car Act of 1890, the imprisonment of the nine black "Scottsboro Boys" on trumped-up charges of raping two white women on a moving train in 1931, and the arrest of Montgomery, Alabama, seamstress Rosa Parks for not giving up her seat to a white man in 1955 are instances where black American identity was negotiated with and through scientific and technological artifacts of transportation during this era.[21] Thus, efforts to maintain racially defined technological space within the United States came under attack by African Americans who reclaimed science and technology for their own social and cultural agendas.

During the third era, loosely bound by 1954 and the completion of the sequencing of the human genome in 2003, we see reluctant integration and a desire to end the biological connection to race. By the middle of the twentieth century, the biological connection to race began to unravel. Organizations like the United Nations challenged the scientific basis of race. To reconstitute the ways race had been constructed, the United Nations Educational, Scientific, and Cultural Organization (UNESCO) convened a panel of social and natural scientists, and charged them with producing a definitive statement on racial difference. The panel produced two statements: *Statement on Race* (1950) and *Statement on the Nature of Race and Race Difference* (1951). These documents declared that race had no scientific basis and called for an end to racial thinking in scientific and political thought. Within the next two decades UNESCO would release two more papers: *Proposal on the Biological Aspects of Race* (1964) and *Statement on Race and Racial Prejudice* (1967). Although deeply important, these statements did not immediately influence social policy or ingrained public attitudes about race.

It is interesting that during a period when there was a desire to end the biological connection to race, African Americans increasingly embraced their identity as a racially defined group.[22] Moreover, new information sciences and technologies of representation became important outlets for African Americans to publicly display their struggles to the larger, primarily white, American society. For instance, the technologically mediated televisual representation of African American people during the protests of the Civil Rights Movement changed the way white America saw and viewed African Americans. Black people went from docile, invisible, and silent laborers to vocal and outspoken protesters.[23] These images were a stark contrast to Hattie McDaniel in *Gone With The Wind* or Alvin Childress, Spencer Williams, and Tim Moore in *Amos 'n' Andy*, which were the preferred images of African American people.[24] However, these new and quickly reproduced images of blackness assisted in condensing multiple protests into one dominant televisual event: the "March on Washington." Similarly Martin Luther King, Jr, has been condensed to sound bites from his "I Have a Dream" speech of 1963. Unfortunately, it also condemns King's life to end in 1963 and overlooks his other ideas, particularly his writing about science and technology in his last published book in 1968, *Where Do We Go From Here?*[25]

Also during this and other periods, African American people used technologies to redefine the public representation of blackness. The Black Panther Party effectively seized the scientific and technological power of the gun. Guns were instruments that historically had been used to control black bodies, but the Black Panther Party members inverted this power. They used one of the most potent and visible symbols of power and appropriated that power to create a sense of fear—the same fear that many African Americans had felt for generations—among many white Americans. The Black Panther Party appropriated the material and symbolic power of the gun and redeployed it against those who had used it so powerfully to control African Americans. As a result the Black Panther Party claimed a level of technological power African Americans infrequently accessed.[26]

The final period—the period that the OLPC program fits within—begins in 2003 and is structured by the new forms of segregation, a newly defined scientific foundation for the rebirth of race, and digital-age technological aid for the developing world. In the 1990s, research performed by the National Telecommunications and Information Administration began to show the United States resegregating along a race/technology digital divide.[27] This body of work has told us a great deal about those on both sides of the divide; however, these studies do not adequately discern the various needs, uses, and information-seeking strategies of racially and ethnically marginalized communities. Recent studies have begun to reexamine the connections between race and technology to move past the traditional framing of the issues as an "access and use" problem.[28] But the issues of access, use, and capability still circulate around these debates and inform individual and institutionalized policy decisions. Yet to more completely understand the relationships between racially marginalized peoples like African Americans, science, and technology, a comparative historical foundation needs to be built upon a firmer footing of earlier analog and digital information and communication technologies like newspapers, radio, telephony, and television to more effectively assess current and future barriers to technological access, use, development, and deployment.

Race has also begun to reemerge in a new way with the completion of the DNA sequence of the human genome by the Human Genome Project (HGP) in 2003. Some of the most promising and troubling outcomes of the HGP in the context of race have to do with genetic therapy. Genetic researchers contend that the human genome consists of chromosome units or haplotype blocks. Haplotype maps (HapMaps) can possibly provide a simple way for genetic researchers to quickly and efficiently search for genetic variations related to common diseases and drug responses. The danger of this research is to re-ensconce the biological concept of race within scientific practice and knowledge production. It is already common practice for physicians to make clinical decisions based on a patient's perceived race. The positive potential of HapMaps could be overshadowed by the manipulation of genetic data to support racialized stereotypes, renew claims of genetic differentiation between races, and add biological authority to ethnic stereotypes. These pitfalls arise when genetic data become the techno-scientific basis upon which racially specific drugs or treatments are designed. In 2003, the United States Food and Drug Administration proposed guidelines that would require all new drugs be evaluated for the effects on different racial groups. In the modern world, the genetic origins of race reappear much more quickly than they are eliminated. What this has also meant is that the confluence of race, identity, and technology has produced a corporate organization that attempts to trace African American heritage back to Africa.[29] The desire to create an origin story is very strong for African American people, many of whom do not feel as if they know where they come from, and has led to the current moment where the politics of race and technology have moved beyond national borders to transnational exchanges.

This periodization aims to create a way to address the connections between race, science, and technology in America, while thinking carefully about the methods, tools, and techniques used to examine these relationships. For African Americans, knowledge about technological life must also be examined anew because it is inextricably intertwined with relations of power that are regularly applied to regulate black existences. Most of what we know about the relations between black people, science and technology primarily comes from dominant subject positions, which tells us more about the ways African Americans are and have been controlled and oppressed than how black people interact, have interacted, and will interact with science and technology from their locations within American society. What this has meant in practical terms is that African Americans, like other groups marginalized in the United States, have not been written into studies of technology because they do not easily fit into the traditional historical narratives.

To uncover, explore, and understand technological experiences among African American people, it is essential to lessen the emphasis on examining larger institutional structures. Often one cannot cull much intellectual purchase by examining traditional institutions of scientific and technological production and development, because they are traditionally invested in the racialized structure of American society. It is critical to examine how African American people, overtly and tacitly, reacted, interacted, resisted, and fought the systems of oppression enforced through the application and use of science and technology, as well as how African Americans contributed to their own oppression and subjugation and that of others. By gaining a more complete understanding of the varied experiences of African Americans with science and technology, it is possible to understand how African Americans, as culturally and historically constituted subjects, become scientific and technological agents for their own benefit and demise. By focusing on the disenfranchised margins and uncovering the multiple layers of communities and their interactions with science and technology, this research intends to make productive interventions into our collective understanding of the connections between race, science, and technology. These connections between African Americans, race, and technology relate to similar experiences by racially marginalized peoples around the world. As the world has become "smaller" through the reach of technology, the racial politics that constitute a critical component of technological use and implementation travel with the artifacts.[30] As the perceptions of racial divides reconfigure, due to the growing multiracialness in America, the place to express American desires to save the underprivileged through technology (or any other means) has in certain instances migrated from the United States to Africa in the case of the OLPC program. Of course, aid, technology or otherwise, is not new. The early appropriate technology movement is one of many seemingly well-thinking enterprises endeavoring to enable the world's underprivileged to pull themselves up by their bootstraps that unfortunately did not take the needs of the communities to heart.

The OLPC program fits within the last of the four periods and is an interesting location to explore the historical and contemporary circulation of technology and race in a global context. The OLPC program displays how certain technologies embody historically constituted American racial politics and transport these politics to the developing world. Reflecting Edward Said's writings about the ways Orientalism retains racialized histories of othering, presumed American technological aid and assistance retains racialized assumptions about developing-world competence and capacity.[31] Said importantly indicated that the processes of othering are necessary configurations for subjugation. Similarly OLPC demands belief in an altruistic illusion of American technology, African technological incapability, and its value neutrality to embark on a program to create a computer to change the lives of children in the developing world. So how do we get to the One Laptop Per Child program?

OLPC, Race and the Transnational Flow of Western Technological Aid

In January 2005, at the World Economic Conference in Davos, Switzerland, Nicholas Negroponte announced the radical idea of a solar-power/crank-powered low-cost laptop for the developing world. The press dubbed this the $100 laptop.[32] From his initial announcement many questioned if the project could be realized. Nearly three years later, in December 2007, the first set of XO laptops were distributed to consumers in the United States under the give-one, get-one program (G1G1). Thus, Negroponte fulfilled the promise of delivering a laptop. The OLPC program had lofty goals from the beginning. This non-profit organization contended,

> OLPC is not, at heart, a technology program, nor is the XO a product in any conventional sense of the word. OLPC is a non-profit organization providing a means to an end—an end that sees children in even the most remote regions of the globe being given the opportunity to tap into their own potential, to be exposed to a whole world of ideas, and to contribute to a more productive and saner world community.[33]

The rhetoric links OLPC to a troubled history of Western "advanced" technology and its deliverers as saviors. Similar to the efforts aimed at ameliorating access problems within impoverished communities in the United States, the social, cultural, and political forces that have created these "remote regions of the globe" are at best pushed aside. At worst, they are ignored because the bringers of the artifact believe that technology and computing will build a direct path to a Western-styled promised land. These programs driven by the "if only they had . . ." mantra, sadly, though not purposefully, construct the receivers of these technological tools as empty vessels into which Western technological knowledge must be poured.

The OLPC program has many origins, but one within which I would like to situate it is the work of Seymour Papert. His early work on the relationships between children, computing, and learning as well as his connection to Negroponte and the OLPC project make him an important historical node of genesis. Beginning in the late 1960s, Papert worked with Daniel Bobrow and Wally Feurzeig to develop Logo, a computer programming language specifically for children. Over the last several decades Papert has been a strong advocate for educational technologies that empower children to investigate, experiment, and learn. He sees the archaic and outcome-driven assessment of school systems as one of the biggest hindrances to innovative education. Papert argues that education is still "largely committed to the educational philosophy of the late nineteenth and early twentieth centuries."[34] The primary problem is that methods of learning concentrate, focus, and promote a single way of knowing and knowledge production. Papert champions partial, interconnected, intuitive, personal, and nonformalized ways of learning and knowing. His approach, "constructionism," is deeply indebted to Jean Piaget and Piaget's work on constructivist learning theories. Constructionism, for Papert,

> is built on the assumption that children will do best by finding ("fishing") for themselves the specific knowledge they need. Organized or informal education can help most by making sure that children receive moral, psychological, material, and intellectual support for their efforts.[35]

Papert aims to invert traditional educational processes by having children spend more time learning than having teachers instruct. His approach relies heavily on educational technologies to restructure educational power dynamics. He wants to design and build new machines to reform the tradition of children being instructed by a teacher or doing non-interactive math problems. Papert's abstractly theorized "Knowledge Machines" aimed to usher children into new forms and modes of intellectual exploration. The OLPC project fit perfectly with Papert's claim that technologies, in specific the computer, enable children of all ages to create "personal media" that contributed to and supported multiple forms of learning. Clearly this is what Negroponte had in mind when he hatched the OLPC idea in 2004.

The use of computing to increase literacy and shrink digital divides has been on philanthropic agendas for some time. This language can be traced to the National Telecommunication and Information Administration (NTIA) early reports on technology usage by America's "have-nots." The first *Falling Through the Net* report in 1995 moved the discussion from debates about universal telephone service and telephone penetration to the need for increased access, accumulation, and assimilation of information; or, as the report stated, "[w]hile a standard telephone line can be an individual's pathway to the riches of the Information Age, a personal computer and modem are rapidly becoming the keys to the vault."[36] The follow-up reports in 1998 and 1999 solidified the language and policy and began using the all too familiar term the *digital divide*. These discussions directly and indirectly implied that potentially large groups of people were incapable of keeping up with the digital revolution. The solution to this problem was to send more computers. In the burgeoning digitally driven information age, more terminals and connections to the "net" (or computer clubs or community technology centers) could solve the problem. But, of course, this was not simply a technical problem. It was a technical problem inflected by social, cultural, and economic realities. The real problem was that no one spoke to the members of these communities to devise a substantive and sustainable digital agenda. Ron Eglash has written a wonderful critique of this approach by describing it as a one-way bridge, where technology goes in but usually very few substantive conversations address community needs.[37] I remember reading these reports and being distressed at the way the discussions were playing out. It appeared as if it was impossible to stop the seemingly self-regenerating representation of African Americans as technological infants who had nothing to say about technology and needed guidance to figure out how to use it. Shortly after the NTIA released its 1999 report, two articles, one by Anthony Walton in the *Atlantic Monthly* and the other by Henry Louis Gates in *The New York Times* catalyzed my thinking on the issues circulating around African Americans and technology.

Gates's article, "One Internet, Two Nations," latched onto the *Falling Through the Net* reports, contending that

[t]he Internet is the 21st century's talking drum, the very kind of grassroots communication tool that has been such a powerful source of

education and culture for our people since slavery. But this talking drum we have not yet learned to play. Unless we master the new information technology to build and deepen the forms of social connection that a tragic history has eroded, African-Americans will face a form of cybersegregation in the next century as devastating to our aspirations as Jim Crow segregation was to those of our ancestors.[38]

So for Gates, as for many others, it was about access, enrollment, and literacy. But his essay on the Internet as a twenty-first-century talking drum completely misses the point about the drum and African technological innovation. Africans conceived, designed, and built those talking drums. Someone from outside their community did not determine that these devices would be the only way to communicate in the future and deliver them to the people without community input.

Similarly the Walton article, "Technology Versus African-Americans," argued that "[t]he history of African-Americans since the discovery of the New World is the story of their encounter with technology, an encounter that has proved perhaps irremediably devastating to their hopes, dreams, and possibilities."[39] This pessimistic view of African American experiences with technology leaves no space to consider technological agency, creativity or control. Technology as subjugation is only part of the story, but it is unfortunately this ideological position that has digitally divvied up the world. Alondra Nelson in writing about the divide contended,

> the rhetoric of the digital divide does more than assume that, in the best of all worlds, technology can and should eliminate racial distinctions. It also assumes that "race is a liability in the twenty-first century" and that blackness is "always oppositional to technologically-driven chronicles of progress."[40]

This reality is troubling because digital rhetoric has become a dominant note in public discourse. Nicholas Negroponte, who in 1995 (the same year the NTIA released the first *Falling Through the Net* report) published *Being Digital*, presented a case for why everything can, should, and will be digitized. One of the most extreme versions can be seen in *The Singularity Is Near: When Humans Transcend Biology*, Ray Kurzweil's guide for surviving to the middle of the century, when digital technology will enable immortality. Of course, the binary opposite of digital is analog. Futurists like Negroponte and Kurzweil, and organizations like the Foresight Nanotech Institute, see people's reliance and connection to the analog past as an anchor preventing them from embracing the unbridled potential of the digital age. Some would even argue that we have "crossed over," as *Wired* magazine illustrated in 2003.[41] As problematic as the analog digital binary is, I find the language useful because of its popular significance and resonance with multiple discussions of generational shifts.[42] By the turn of the twenty-first century it was no surprise that many of these digital theorists began to embrace the "digital divide" language spawned by the *Falling Through the Net* report and export it to the developing world. It is within this desire to digitally improve the lives of the "deserving" have-nots of the developing world that we get the OLPC program.

In 2004 Negroponte approached Intel about the possibility of producing a low-cost/low-power chip to be used in a laptop distributable to the developing world. Negroponte contends that Intel was only mildly interested and then only if the device for this chip would not be called a laptop. After waiting months for a response, Negroponte moved onto Intel competitor AMD who agreed to join the project almost immediately. When he announced the XO laptop in January 2005, it had an AMD chip (Intel contend that Negroponte did not give them a full opportunity to participate). By early 2005, he had also secured commitments from Google and Red Hat. Each, along with AMD, pledged to contribute two and a half million dollars to Negroponte's philanthropic enterprise. This corporate trio, along with a growing list of contributors and collaborators, created a potent network of volunteers whose intellectual and financial resources would be invaluable for the realization of this project.[43]

Now that Negroponte had corporate and institutional buy-in, he proceeded to sell the device, not as a grassroots project but as a state investment plan. He worked his way around the globe convincing leaders in countries like Argentina, Brazil, Nigeria, Thailand, and Pakistan that he would be able to deliver a $100 laptop for each country's children to use. He sold the technology as a way for each country to quickly enter the digital age by creating a technologically savvy population. Twenty-first-century citizens would bring twenty-first-century riches to each country. Initially, he appeared to have been extremely successful. Early on, he had commitments in batches of 100,000 from a host of countries. Negroponte had planned to supply the third world with 150 million laptops by the end of 2008, but soon his plan began to unravel.

The technology was highly innovative, something which some have argued was part of the program's downfall. In addition to AMD's low-power chipset, the OLPC team under the direction of Mary Lou Jepson was able to design a long-lasting battery, a reliable mesh network, and a screen viewable in direct sunlight. It was the lowest-power laptop made to date. As much as the hardware amazed, the software underwhelmed. Sugar, the Linux-based open source operating system, was far from dazzling in comparison to the smile-inducing white and green enclosure. For those unfamiliar with Linux, it was far from intuitive. Furthermore, developing countries were less than enthusiastic about their children learning Linux as opposed to a more mainstream set of tools. The Nigerians were more interested in their students learning to work in Windows. In many ways, this is where the technological visionaries and computer scientists missed the mark. The project had now been so deeply ensconced in the idea that Papert's Knowledge Machine would win the day, and create the third world as a new generation of mobile-ly connected thinkers, that they could not see the fundamental social and cultural issues that were of primary concern. The dream of creating a non-geographically-bound digital technological citizen from a clean slate of third-world children excited OLPC developers, but did not impress developing-world leaders in their attempt to build a population capable of quickly entering the global technological mainstream. It is around these issues that the firm foundation that Negroponte had built did not quite turn to sand, but now had a much softer consistency.

As they developed early prototypes and marched them through testing, OLPC had amassed an image cache of wide-eyed, happily computing, brown children from around the globe reveling in the magical worlds their meshed networks allowed them to explore. As compelling as these images were, the orders promised never fully materialized. In 2005, OLPC required countries to buy a minimum of 1 million laptops. By the beginning of 2007, the number had shrunk to 250,000 and by summer further reduced to 100,000. To generate interest and move some units, OLPC announced the give-one, get-one program in chosen North American countries. The program allowed American consumers to purchase these cute laptops as long as they purchased one for an undetermined, developing-world child. As someone who purchased an XO-1 through the G1G1 program, I soon realized the $100 laptop quickly became the $423.95 laptop. Numbers have never been fully verified, but various journalists believe that around 370,000 have been distributed.[44]

Over the past years, the OLPC has struggled. Mary Lou Jepson left to form Pixel Qi to commercialize the screen technology. Intel produced a competing Windows-based laptop named the Classmate and carried on a rather public battle with OLPC. Libya and Nigeria backed out of their commitments for OLPC machines and opted for the Classmate and Windows. But the biggest tensions were of the ideological variety. At the April 1, 2008 meeting, the board of directors agreed to make all of their machines dual boot Sugar and a Windows-based operating system. As result OLPC President Walter Bender and software security leader Ivan Krstić, two of the key players in OLPC development, resigned. The decision to partner with Microsoft set off a firestorm of critiques from within the OLPC community. For some, OLPC was selling its soul to the devil. Many of those who deeply believe in constructionism, including Papert, left OLPC when they saw the program focus migrate from learning to laptop penetration.[45]

On my campus in January 2008, I organized a panel on the OLPC program to discuss many of the issues circulating around its give-one, get-one program. The program had wide appeal on and off campus. The audience ranged from members of community organizations like the NAACP, interested in the potential to equip inner-city children with affordable computers, to computer scientists delighted with the open source potential of a smaller more portable device, to educational technologists excited about the desire to globally disseminate educational computing, and intrigued undergraduates. However,

I found the most fascinating folks in the crowd were the techno/gadget enthusiasts who brought their newly delivered XO-1s to the event to "connect" at multiple levels. It was not only about participating in a discussion about the newly acquired gadget, but also connecting with people who could also appreciate their techno-consumptive desires.

The main paper, by Langdon Winner, and the subsequent comments by Bill Hammack and Robert Markley, brought a series of tensions to the fore. Many of those in the audience expected the panel to confirm their unbridled enthusiasm for all things technological. However, the panelists' commentaries presented a more critically and concerned tone that questioned the desire to once again save the "rest" of the world by distributing a new salvation technology. The panelists queried: what does it mean to make a universal technology useable by all children around the globe? To what degree did the children in the locations contribute to the design of the technology that would supposedly bring them into the twenty-first century? Such questions placed OLPC within an existing set of debates about appropriated technology and participatory design.[46] At the end of the panel some in the audience announced that within the week the newly formed Champaign-Urbana XO-1 user group would have its first meeting. However, it was not apparent whether this organization would survive past its first meeting. Would the technological fetish of portable green laptops or the technological altruism of participating in a movement aimed at leading the developing world into the digital age drive the organizations? Unable to find a common ground, many user groups around the country have come and gone in the past years, while others have disbanded because members moved onto the next "must have" gadget or became disillusioned with the D movement.

Currently, OLPC satisfies no one. Peru, OLPC's biggest national supporter, is struggling to integrate the laptop into the cultural environment. In 2009, OLPC's annual budget shrank from 12 million to 5 million U.S. dollars. OLPC no longer develops the Sugar operating system; it will now rely on the open source community to move it forward. Many American techno fans have either given up on OLPC since the announced collaboration with Microsoft or have just moved onto the next exciting technological gadget. The precarious position that OLPC currently holds reminds us of the true limitations of a technological fix to a social and cultural problem.[47] However, all is not lost. Currently, most of the approximately 380,000 primary school students in Uruguay have received an OLPC laptop. The devices have brought home computing to many impoverished households and reduced the level of truancy. But there have been problems. From the laptops without Spanish software to older teachers uncomfortable with this technology incursion, the idea of hinging a generation's future on this specific technology is precarious.[48] As of late 2009, Rwanda announced that it wants every child between the ages of nine and twelve (1.3 million) to have an OLPC laptop. Since the price of the devices has nearly doubled, to U.S. $181, their estimated start-up cost is U.S. $313 million. Yet, concern that the "present version of the OLPC machine is too expensive, too clunky, and too slow" will continued to dog the program.[49]

The reception and interpretation of new technologies or technological networks often fall between the two poles of saving or destroying society or, as Mélanie Roustan has called them, the messianic and apocalyptic imaginaries. Early on the OLPC team's messianic vision contended that laptops, specifically the ones their team designed and developed, would provide a solution to the widening gap between the global haves and have-nots. These devices would enable developing-world children to overcome the history of global inequality in one simple technological leap. Critics of the program argued that the developing world does not need another savior technology. These computers would continue the tradition of technologies of domination and alienation introduced into the developing world by the "West." Yet, these perspectives give too much agency to the technology itself and "position technology as a cause of social changes, thus somewhat neglecting to consider how technology itself is the product and outcome of social organization."[50] Clearly, race is one of the social organizations that is overlooked. The OLPC program's technological determinism is embedded within a racial determinism that is continually being reshaped.

Both sides of this continuum appeared on the OLPC wiki discussion. For instance, one writer produced a critical commentary on the politics of the program. The author of the post wrote:

> Whilst I applaud the innovative nature of the project and particularly the conceptual model surrounding "Sugar", it worries me that it is being foisted upon the so-called third-world communities; it all smacks too much of the flavour of some kind of social pedagogical "experiment". There is, I suppose, a great deal of sense in the argument that such communities have not been exposed to and pre-conditioned by existing interfaces and their established standards, and will thus be more amenable to alternatives. However, I can't help feeling that strategies for optimum learning are by their very nature culturally dependent, as indeed are any notions of what might be considered valuable knowledge. I can't help thinking that it is unlikely that these "third-world" communities have had much genuine say in the OLPC project's design and planning . . . Once again, "wisdom" seems to be in the hands of the rich, generous, patriarchal white nations of the "West". Perhaps the "experiment" would have been better carried out in the US?[51]

In response, an OLPC insider brushed aside the criticisms of those prodding OLPC to see the racial politics in the program by arguing,

> OLPC pedagogy is based upon Constructionism, the gist of which is that you learn through doing, so if you want more learning, you want more

doing. While this approach is not epistemologically agnostic, it is for the most part culturally agnostic: it is—by design—amenable to adaptation to local cultural values in regard to what "doing" is appropriate . . . The role of Sugar is simply to provide some affordances that enable children to explore, express, and communicate. Sugar is a community project that has contributors from a diverse base; feedback from teachers and students in roughly one-dozen trials in the developing world has greatly influenced the design. Further, it is—by design—free and open.[52]

This response is troubling. The idea of a technology being culturally agnostic runs against volumes of work within Science and Technology Studies. But it also fits into the perspective that deploying OLPC in the United States was too culturally and racially tricky, so the plan was to take this experiment to a location where race and culture were seemingly meaningless, which could not be further from the truth.

The One Laptop Per Child (OLPC) program, as a way to think through one relationship between emerging technology and global society, raises a set of interesting and unanswered questions about information technology, computer design, global markets, international relations, democracy, technological innovation, and mobility. In specific, can you build a technology for "the" developing world? Does the perceived universal nature of open source software transcend region, language, space, and culture? How do corporate desires manage cultural needs within technologically mediated spaces? Has the XO laptop become an unsatisfying and unnecessary gadget for American technological consumers? Why is technological colonialism, as opposed to participatory design, a dominant model of aid in the developing world? How does American dreaming racially infused technological imperialism become mobile with the OLPC program?

We live in a contemporary historical moment where all things digital, and now all things digital and mobile, have been loaded with the power of connecting, empowering, and ultimately saving the world. The OLPC XO-1 laptop represents one form of this technological desire. This mobile computing device, in the most optimistic terms, would enable the next generation of third-world children to experience, enjoy, and appropriate the mobile technological world that had passed their parents by. However, OLPC is an exemplar of the tension between global capitalism and philanthropy in the developing world, and technological hopes, dreams and desires. It also illustrates that the developing world no longer has to blindly accept American technological efforts. The OLPC program misjudged the illusory transcendent power of artifacts and assumed that American technological "philanthropy" would be uncritically embraced. As with the early misperceptions of technological ability in the United States, people of color have much to contribute to discussions about how and why technology will alter their lives. Not surprisingly, as the world becomes smaller through technology, more groups of people have become empowered through technology in the digital age. Thus this digital moment may eventually be seen as a watershed moment in developing world technological agency.

Notes

1   Woods' Testimony in Surrebuttal, Interference cases #18,207 and #18,210, 253, NARA-S, Record Group 241, taken from "A Colored Man's Invention," *New York Recorder*, February 13, 1892.
2   This was one of the many arguments against abolishing slavery. Many of those who supported chattel slavery in the United States voiced strong concerns that, once freed, the former slaves would have no idea of how to take care of themselves without the structure of the plantation system and the firm benevolence of their owners. See Frederick Douglass, "What Shall be Done with the Slaves if Emancipated?" *Douglass' Monthly*, January 2, 1862.
3   Albert Memmi, *The Colonizer and the Colonized* (Boston: Beacon Press, 1965).
4   Jehu Hanciles, *Euthanasia of a Mission: African Church Autonomy in a Colonial Context* (West Port, CT: Praeger, 2002); Martin Ballard, *White Men's God: The Extraordinary Story of Missionaries in Africa* (West Port, CT: Greenwood Press, 2008).
5   Kelvin W. Willoughby, *Technology Choice: A Critique of the Appropriate Technology Movement* (London: IT Publications, 1990).
6   Randall Kennedy, *Nigger: The Strange Career of a Troublesome Word* (New York: Vintage, 2003).
7   Jack D. Forbes, *Africans and Native Americans: The Language of Race and the Evolution of Red–Black Peoples* (Urbana, University of Illinois Press: 1993).
8   David R. Roediger, *Working Toward Whiteness: How America's Immigrants Became White: The Strange Journey from Ellis Island to the Suburbs* (New York: Basic Books, 2006).
9   Beth E. Kolko, Lisa Nakamura, and Gilbert B. Rodman, eds, *Race in Cyberspace* (New York: Routledge, 2000); Alondra Nelson, Linh N. Thuya, and Alicia Headlam Hines, eds, *Technicolor: Race, Technology and Everyday Life* (New York: New York University Press, 2001).
10 Joseph Williams and Matt Negrin, "Affirmative Action Foes Point to Obama: Say Candidate is Proof Effort No Longer Needed," *Boston Globe*, March 18, 2008. Available at: www.boston.com/news/nation/articles/2008/03/18/affirmative_action_foes_point_to_obama/ (accessed December 30, 2009).
11 Rayvon Fouché, *Black Inventors in the Age of Segregation* (Baltimore, MD: Johns Hopkins University Press, 2003), 1–8.
12 Bernard C. Nalty, *Strength for the Fight: A History of Black Americans in the Military* (New York: Simon and Schuster, 1989), 82.
13 Henry E. Baker, "The Negro as an Inventor," in D.W. Culp, ed., *Twentieth Century Negro Literature* (Naperville, IL: J.L. Nichols, 1902), 401–402.
14 Langdon Winner, *The Whale and the Reactor: A Search for Limits in an Age of High Technology* (Chicago: University of Chicago Press, 1986), 19–39.
15 Fred Turner, *From Counterculture to Cyberculture: Stewart Brand, the Whole Earth Network, and the Rise of Digital Utopianism* (Chicago: University of Chicago Press, 2006).
16 Thomas Kuhn, *The Structure of Scientific Revolutions* (Chicago: University of Chicago Press, 1996), 136–143.
17 Lewis Mumford, *Technics and Civilization* (New York: Harvest Books, 1963), 109.
18 Wiebe E. Bijker and Trevor Pinch, "The Social Construction of Facts and Artefacts: or How the Sociology of Science and the Sociology of Technology Might Benefit from Each Other," *Social Studies of Science* 14 (August 1984): 399–441.
19 David Harvey, *The Condition of Postmodernity: An Enquiry into the Origins of Cultural Change* (Oxford: Blackwell, 1990), 121–200.
20 Fouché, *Black Inventors in the Age of Segregation*, 26–81.
21 Patricia Ann Schechter, *Ida B. Wells-Barnett and American Reform, 1880–1930* (Chapel Hill, NC: University of North Carolina Press, 2000), 43; Mark M. Smith, *How Race Is Made: Slavery, Segregation, and the Senses* (Chapel Hill, NC: University of North Carolina Press, 2006), 66–95; Dan T. Carter, *Scottsboro: A Tragedy of the American South* (Baton Rouge, LA: Louisiana State University Press, 1979); Jo Ann Gibson Robinson, *Montgomery Bus Boycott and the Women Who Started It: The Memoir of Jo Ann Gibson Robinson* (Knoxville, TN: University of Tennessee Press, 1987), 19–52.

22 Ron Eyerman, *Cultural Trauma: Slavery and the Formation of African American Identity* (Cambridge: Cambridge University Press, 2002).

23 Sasha Torres, *Black, White, and in Color: Television and Black Civil Rights* (Princeton: Princeton University Press, 2003), 13–35.

24 Melvin Patrick Ely, *Adventures of Amos 'n' Andy: A Social History of an American Phenomenon* (New York: The Free Press, 1991).

25 Martin Luther King, Jr, *Where Do We Go from Here: Chaos or Community?* (New York: Harper & Row, 1967).

26 Timothy B. Tyson, *Radio Free Dixie: Robert F. Williams and the Roots of Black Power* (Chapel Hill, NC: University of North Carolina Press, 1999), 4–25.

27 National Telecommunications and Information Administration, *Falling Through the Net: A Survey of the "Have Nots" in Rural and Urban America* (Washington, DC: U.S. Commerce Department, 1995); National Telecommunications and Information Administration, *Falling Through the Net II: New Data on the Digital Divide* (Washington, DC: U.S. Commerce Department, 1998); National Telecommunications and Information Administration, *Falling Through the Net: Defining the Digital Divide* (Washington, DC: U.S. Commerce Department, 1999); National Telecommunications and Information Administration, *Falling Through the Net: Toward Digital Inclusion* (Washington, DC: U.S. Commerce Department, 2000).

28 Adam J. Banks, *Race, Rhetoric, and Technology: Searching for Higher Ground* (New York: Lawrence Erlbaum Associates, 2005), 68–85

29 Deborah Bolnick, Duana Fullwiley, Troy Duster, Richard Cooper, Joan H. Fujimura, Jonathan Kahn, Jay S. Kaufman, Jonathan Marks, Ann Morning, Alondra Nelson, *et al.*, "The Business and Science of Genetic Ancestry Testing," *Science* 318.5849 (2007): 399–400.

30 Langdon Winner, "Upon Opening the Black Box and Finding It Empty: Social Constructivism and the Philosophy of Technology," *Science, Technology, & Human Values* 18.3 (Summer 1993): 370–371.

31 Edward W. Said, *Orientalism* (New York: Vintage Books, 1979), 284–328.

32 Jo Twist, "UN Debut for $100 Laptop for Poor," *BBC News*, November 17, 2005. Available at: *http://news.bbc.co.uk/2/hi/technology/4445060.stm* (accessed August 15, 2009).

33 OLPC promotional material, December 2007.

34 Seymour Papert, *The Children's Machine: Rethinking School in the Age of the Computer* (New York: Basic Books, 1993), 139.

35 Ibid., 139.

36 *Falling Through the Net: A Survey of the "Have Nots" in Rural and Urban America*, July 1995. Available at: www.ntia.doc.gov/ntiahome/fallingthru.html (accessed August 15, 2009).

37 Ron Eglash, "A Two-Way Bridge Across the Digital Divide," *The Chronicle of Review*, June 21, 2002.

38 Henry Louis Gates, Jr, "One Internet, Two Nations," *The New York Times*, October 31, 1999, final edition.

39 Anthony Walton, "Technology Versus African-Americans," *The Atlantic Monthly* 283.1 (1999): 16.

40 Alondra Nelson, "Introduction: Future Texts," *Social Text*, 20 (Summer 1971): 1.

41 "The Great Crossover: Digital Technology Finally Surpasses Analog," *Wired* (November, 2002), 58–59.

42 Don Tapscott, *Grown Up Digital: How the Net Generation is Changing Your World* (New York: McGraw-Hill, 2008), 9–72.

43 John Markoff, "For $150, Third-World Laptop Stirs Big Debate," *The New York Times*, November 30, 2006. Available at: www.nytimes.com/2006/11/30/technology/30laptop.html (accessed August 11, 2009).

44 Brian Appleyard, "Why Microsoft and Intel Tried to Kill the XO $100 Laptop," *The Times* (London), August 10, 2008. Available at: http://technology.timesonline.co.uk/tol/news/tech_and_web/article4472654.ece (accessed August 9, 2009).

45 Ivan Krstić "Sic Transit Gloria Laptopi." Available at: http://radian.org/notebook/sic-transit-gloria-laptopi (accessed September 25, 2008).

46 Ron Eglash, Jennifer L. Croissant, Giovanna Di Chiro, and Rayvon Fouché, eds, *Appropriation Technology: Vernacular Science and Social Power* (Minneapolis: University of Minnesota Press, 2004).

47 Lisa Rosner, ed., *The Technological Fix: How People Use Technology to Create and Solve Problems* (New York: Routledge, 2004).

48 "Laptops for All," *The Economist* 393.8651 (October 1, 2009): 46.
49 "Rwanda's Laptop Revolution: Upgrading the Children," *The Economist* 393.8660 (December 3, 2009): 60.
50 Phillip Vannini, *Material Culture and Technology in Everyday Life* (New York: Peter Lang, 2009), 90.
51 Mcewanw, 19:26, 13 September 2007 (EDT), http://wiki.laptop.org/go/OLPC_myths (accessed September 10, 2009).
52 Walter, 04:11, 15 September 2007 (EDT), http://wiki.laptop.org/go/OLPC_myths (accessed September 10, 2009).

4
Cesar Chavez, the United Farm Workers, and the History of Star Wars

CURTIS MAREZ

University of California, San Diego

Many of the companies in California's Silicon Valley that invented and manufacture the hardware and software of digital cultures have taken an active interest in archiving and presenting their corporate histories. Silicon Valley's Intel Corporation, for example, is the world's largest maker of semiconductor chips, the inventor of the microprocessors in most personal computers, and a pioneer in the fabrication of historical memory. It operates the Intel Museum and Intel Corporate Archives, which includes both online components and a material incarnation, at company headquarters. The Museum's mission is to collect, preserve, and exhibit "Intel corporate history for the purpose of increasing employee, customer and public awareness of Intel innovations, technologies and branding in an interactive and educational manner." It has been increasingly geared toward parents and children or teachers and students, thousands of whom visit the Museum every year where, among other things, they get to simulate the experience of working at Intel. A multimedia presentation in the "Intel Culture Theater" promises to let visitors "see what it's like to work at the world's largest computer chip manufacturer, and learn more about Intel's risk-taking and results-oriented—yet fun—business environment." The "fun" part is represented by the figure of the bunny-suited worker. The white suits, which cover workers from head to toe and include a visored helmet with a battery-operated air filter unit, are worn in the company's large white clean rooms or microchip fabrication facilities. In the gift store one can buy plush dolls representing clean room workers and t-shirts decorated with dancing workers. An interactive exhibit devoted to the company's "Brand Program" prominently features its successful trademark image of an excited bunny-suited worker jumping in the air with up stretched arms and splayed fingers. One particularly popular exhibit is of a simulated employee locker room where adults are invited to help children "try on a bunny suit and imagine you are going to work in an Intel fab." The Museum's website depicts a little girl of color being helped into a bunny suit. A subsequent photo shows a bunny-suited child, body and face obscured by the costume, leaping in the air in imitation of the Intel trademark. While it is hardly surprising that a corporation would attempt to persuade people to identify with its products, Intel encourages museum visitors to interact with both Intel hardware and a virtual version of the work process. Or more precisely, the Museum invites people to take pleasure in performing an Intel "brand" based on images of happy workers.[1]

In contrast with conventional Marxist accounts of fetishism, where commodities obscure the labor of the workers who produce them, Intel has incorporated its workers into its various advertising materials, making an idealized image of its labor relations part of the pitch for its products in ways that exclude the material costs and consequences of working in clean rooms. The image of the little girl of color in the bunny suit is part of a corporate memory-making machine that disappears the work-related illnesses and injuries of low-wage Asian and Latin American migrant workers in Silicon Valley, not only in the clean rooms but also among the poorly paid janitors and service workers who support the regional high-tech economy. The Museum's positive spin on Valley labor relations forms part of a broad cultural offensive against organized labor. The company's Museum and Internet Archive are self-consciously aimed at (re)producing an historical memory of Intel innovation in labor relations and visitors are repeatedly informed about how the company was founded in opposition to hierarchical, east coast firms and hence developed in a more open and egalitarian manner that supported both teamwork and a meritocratic system of individual achievement. Even though the benefits of this unique business culture have not extended to low-wage workers of color, their images and simulated experiences are nonetheless incorporated into the Museum in ways that make labor a kind of playful risk-taking or heroic play and that implicitly suggest that labor unions are obsolete relics of the past.

Even though—or perhaps *because*—low-wage clean-room workers are relatively marginalized within the material process of production, they have been symbolically central to the way Intel reconstructs its history and, by extension, to the historical origins of the digital "revolution."[2] Intel founder Robert Noyce, himself an amateur photographer, worked closely with several commercial photographers who produced images for ads, annual reports, and celebrations of company anniversaries, many of which prominently featured bunny-suited employees.[3] For example, a glossy 1984 magazine marking Intel's fifteenth anniversary entitled "Revolution in Progress . . . A History of Intel to Date" included the portrait of a bunny-suited worker on its cover and a section about the history of the bunny suit inside. The magazine also included a 1977 photo of a "start-up team" of fab workers in white bunny suits and Storm Trooper masks surrounding their "leader," a computer engineer wearing a Darth Vader mask.

Why would the company want to dress up its history in *Star Wars* costumes? From one perspective this choice suggests that, like Lucas Films or Industrial

Light and Magic, Intel is a dominant corporate empire. Indeed, the photo illustrates a story about the history of the company's international expansion titled "The Sun Never Sets on Intel." But here the blunt celebration of corporate imperialism is softened by association with a nostalgic image reminiscent of boyish fun. At the same time the image tells us something about the corporation's historical view of company labor relations. In a section titled "Inside Intel: The Evolution of a Culture," Intel's "corporate values" of openness, individual meritocracy, and teamwork are enumerated in ways that seemingly dissolve differences between management and labor. Similarly, in the caption to the *Star Wars* photo, workers become members of a "start-up team" and the manager becomes "team leader." The magazine thus displaces an actual history of labor struggles in Silicon Valley with an image representing the mythic struggles in *Star Wars*.

As this example suggests, *Star Wars* has become an important reference point for corporations and workers in the Silicon Valley. As Michael Kanellos, a journalist who covers the IT industries there, argues, the film "stands as perhaps one of the greatest influences, if not the greatest force, on the development of the high-technology industry. Released in 1977, the original *Star Wars* inspired thousands with the belief that a better life lay beyond the junior high school cafeteria. The trickle-down effect can be seen all over Silicon Valley."[4] This fascination with the space opera among Silicon Valley companies and IT enthusiasts more generally is extensively represented in the pages of *Wired* magazine while, at the same time, *Star Wars* has inspired a host of digital filmmakers, most notably George Lucas himself, as well as scholars such as Henry Jenkins, who celebrate its generative possibilities for subsequent new media creations.

In what follows I argue that the popularity of *Star Wars* in Silicon Valley as well as the success of the film itself responds to and shapes race and class formations in California that originate in the history of its agribusiness economy and which continue to shape contemporary digital cultures. I situate *Star Wars* in relationship to the history of struggles between agribusiness and farm workers in California. The epic battles between the United Farm Workers (UFW) and agribusiness corporations have been a prominent feature of the regional mediascape and Lucas's early history overlaps or converges with the movement, its distorted remains visible in his films. I focus on elements of Lucas's biography, then, not only because it has been an important part of the way meaning has been made out of the *Star Wars* phenomenon, but also as part of an effort to analyze the kinds of race and class subjectivities *Star Wars* presupposes and encourages. The film appeals to a broad audience in part because it provides resources for multiple, often contradictory interpretations and uses, but a study of its historical context suggest its tendency to encourage in particular a form of free market white individualism with origins in the agribusiness-dominated political economy of California's Central Valley. *Star*

Wars provides a revealing fantasy rendering of a dominant subject formation in the recent history of California and national politics: a kind of pastoral, free-market, white individualism partly defined in dialectical relation to Mexican migrant labor. Drawing both on insights generated by appropriations of *Star Wars* by digital artist and filmmaker Alex Rivera and on historical research into the UFW in California media and politics, I suggest that the film helps make visible the ideological and affective appeals of a kind of agrarian white populism identified with capitalism and against labor, the very formation that has helped bring right-wing politicians to power in California and the world, from Ronald Reagan to Arnold Schwarzenegger. And traces of the historically sedimented race and class formations that crystallized in *Star Wars* can be found, I conclude, not only in Silicon Valley labor politics but also in the recent history of digital filmmaking and digital cultural criticism based on it.

Not So Long Ago, in a Valley Nearby . . .

In 2009, George Lucas joined his friend Stephen Spielberg to help dedicate a new building for the School of Cinematic Arts at the University of Southern California. Lucas is its most famous alumnus and the School plays an important part in the familiar story about the Central Valley farm boy who became a famous director. He contributed 75 million dollars to the construction of the building, which is based on his design and includes a large "Spanish-style" courtyard, a tribute to old Hollywood's enthusiasm for Spanish revival architecture.[5] In the courtyard there is a life-size statue of School founder Douglas Fairbanks, who often played exotic "Latin" characters, including Zorro, a romantic hero of nineteenth-century "Spanish" California.[6] In keeping with this star image, the Fairbanks statue features the actor looking as though he is ready for one of his Latin roles, sporting a pencil-thin moustache and holding a scrolled document (a script?) in one hand and a sword (as opposed to a light saber?) in the other.

Historians and cultural critics have often interpreted the California vogue for all things "Spanish," particularly in Hollywood, as part of a contradictory social formation that appropriated elements of a Spanish fantasy past while remaining indifferent or even hostile to the contemporary Mexican working class, as if the fantasy helped white Angelenos deny that part of their contemporary reality.[7] But rather than reading Lucas's design in relationship to the history of Hollywood, I want to instead foreground another kind of historical juxtaposition involving the UFW. The new Lucas building is not far from a small marker commemorating Cesar Chavez's three visits to USC in 1982, 1986, and 1989 to promote the grape boycott. Los Angeles was the second largest market for table grapes in the world and as a result, in the 1970s and 1980s, Chavez and the UFW were highly visible in and around Hollywood, where they cultivated the support of entertainment industry liberals and others. Chavez's final visit to USC occurred when he was recovering from his longest fast ever and was part of a renewed push to publicize the dangers of pesticides and, through the boycott, force agribusiness to negotiate with the union.

The Chavez memorial at USC, along with the establishment of a Chicano/ Latino major, was partly a response to demands by Latino students in the wake of the Rodney King uprisings near campus, at a time when the public image of the university with respect to race relations was undergoing scrutiny. The memorial was announced in 1994 and by the time it was completed in 1998, USC was involved in a dispute with a largely Latino labor union that self-consciously invoked the memory of Chavez. Maria Elena Durazo, the president of the Hotel Employees and Restaurant Employees (HERE) Local 11, led the union in a conflict with USC that started when the university refused to guarantee that the jobs of HERE's 350 workers would not be subcontracted out. After a year of negotiations without an agreement, Durazo expanded the struggle by building an alliance with a newly formed student group, the Student Coalition Against Labor Exploitation (SCALE). The faculty advisor to SCALE was Professor Laura Pulido, a USC geographer and historian of the UFW's battles against pesticides. In the spring of 1998, workers protested at the USC graduation and students staged an alternative graduation in solidarity with HERE. That fall there was a large march of students, workers, and clergy in support of the union, while 135 national religious leaders signed a statement critical of USC for "valuing the bottom line over and above human dignity." When still no progress was made, Durazo, who as a child had worked in the fields of Oregon and California with her migrant farm-worker parents, borrowed Cesar Chavez's tactic of the rolling hunger strike. On May 10, 1999, with the help of veteran UFW organizers, she and 40 others began a fast that, according to Randy Shaw, was "likely the most highly publicized such event since Chavez's 1988 effort." On the eleventh day, she passed the fast on to California state assemblyperson Gilbert Cedillo, who passed it on to L.A. County Federation of Labor head Miguel Contreras, and so on. The rolling fast ultimately involved over 200 participants and lasted for 150 days. According to Shaw, students "would pass the fast to each other in a ceremony at the statue of Tommy Trojan, the symbol of USC." When UFW cofounder Dolores Huerta attended the dedication of the Chavez memorial on campus she blasted the university for its hypocrisy.[8] USC finally agreed to safeguard the union members from subcontracting in October 1999, leading Shaw to conclude that "like Chavez's effort, Durazo's spiritual fast had changed the momentum of the struggle, and proved decisive in changing her adversary's position."[9]

In light of this backstory, the Cinema building, with its "Spanish" courtyard and statue of a white actor in Latin drag, almost seems to mock the Chavez memorial. But what if we read this strange juxtaposition differently, as the sign of a secret connection? What if we imagined that the Chavez memorial was part of the unconscious or the suppressed of the new Lucas building? What if the Lucas world was linked to the history of Chavez and the UFW, the absent presence distantly animating the drama of *Star Wars*?

What at first seems an unlikely comparison becomes plausible when we consider in greater detail where their histories overlap. *Star Wars* emerges from a regional history in which agribusiness has been a dominant political-economic and cultural force in California since the early decades of the twentieth century, roughly paralleling the history of the development of the film industry in Southern California. During the 1930s there were hundreds of agricultural strikes in the state among male and female farm workers and cannery workers, strikes often led by Mexicans and which partly inspired John Steinbeck's famous novel, *The Grapes of Wrath*.[10] But the strikes also provoked a brutal response that Carey McWilliams called "fascism in the fields," a combination of public and private police violence and aggressive efforts to use the media to control public opinion.[11] Movie theaters represented the region's most popular commercial entertainment and one of the few public spheres that included farm workers, in however subordinated a fashion, and agribusiness exercised significant influence over what was screened.[12] Central to corporate agriculture's efforts to control the media was the California Associated Farmers, a statewide interest group that denounced *The Grapes of Wrath* as communist propaganda. In Kern County, its members even helped to ban the novel in public libraries. The CAF further attempted to stop the making of the film version of *The Grapes of Wrath* and, when this effort failed, the group organized a boycott against the studio that made the film and tried to prevent it from screening in the Valley.[13] Meanwhile, the CAF's "carefully organized propaganda department" cranked out regular bulletins for members and the general public and distributed publications and a steady flow of statements and releases for the press.[14]

In such a context, farm worker unions struggled to organize workers and produce their own media—press, photography, and film—in order to combat the agribusiness media monopoly.[15] Farm workers have been among the lowest paid and most vulnerable workers in the United States, regularly subjected to extreme forms of violence at the hands of police and agribusiness vigilantes. Unlike other workers, they did not have the legal right to organize unions and bargain collectively with employers until the 1970s, as a result of the UFW's activities. Hence in the post-World War II context, media technology became increasingly important to farm worker struggles, not only to combat agribusiness propaganda but also to intervene in a civil society dominated by state institutions aligned with agribusiness and actively hostile to farm worker interests. This is the world that Lucas and other California baby boomers of his generation were born into, where often violent conflicts between agribusiness and labor loomed large in the local mediascape.

1944

In his earliest recorded act of civil disobedience, a teenaged Cesar Chavez is arrested at a movie theater in the Central Valley town of Delano after refusing to move from the "Whites Only" section to the section reserved for blacks, Filipinos and Mexicans.[16]

George Lucas is born in Modesto, another Central Valley town, also with segregated movie theaters, to George Sr, who owns a local stationery store and walnut ranch, and Dorothy Bomberger, the daughter of a prominent local family.[17]

1948

Chavez joins an automobile caravan of support for a strike against the mammoth DiGiorgio Fruit Company by the National Farm Labor Union, led by Ernesto Galarza. The union collaborates with Hollywood unions to make a documentary about the strike, *Poverty in the Valley of Plenty*, but is ultimately bankrupted when the Company successfully sues for libel and the film is banned.[18]

1952–1962

Chavez becomes a community organizer in San Jose, near what is becoming Silicon Valley. At the end of this period, he returns to Delano and, along with Dolores Huerta and others, founds the National Farm Workers Association, the immediate precursor to the UFW.

During the same years, Lucas reads comic books and ultimately tinkers with cameras and cars on his family's walnut farm.

1963

A teenaged Lucas begins to frequent bohemian San Francisco, including counter-cultural film screenings at City Lights Bookstore and San Francisco State.[19] The following year, after two years at Modesto Junior College, he transfers to USC, where he studies film.

1965

The Delano grape strike begins, with farm workers demanding they be paid the Federal minimum wage. It lasts five years and results in agreements with major growers.

1966

Farm workers walk 300 miles north from Delano, through Modesto, to the state capital in Sacramento as part of a pilgrimage that ends on Easter Sunday. Seemingly overnight Chavez becomes a huge media celebrity and the first documentary about the UFW, *Huelga*, is produced and broadcast on public TV.

In the same year Lucas returns to USC as a graduate film student, where he begins making short experimental films.

1967

Striking farm workers and supporters begin a national boycott of California table grapes. The pro-UFW documentary *Decision at Delano* is released and plays on college campuses and in public schools.

Lucas completes several student films including *The Emperor*, which is about an L.A. radio disc jockey who, at one point, delivers an ad for the United Fruit Company which leads to a surreal scene, set in a cornfield, where two Latino characters, "Rodriguez" and "Dominguez," prepare to execute a third man. Rodriguez is dressed as Che Guevara, while Dominguez is dressed like Pancho Villa.[20]

1968

In the face of suggestions from some strikers that the union consider adopting violent tactics, Chavez rededicates the movement to nonviolence by fasting for 25 days. When he finally breaks his fast he is joined by Robert Kennedy, who hands Chavez a piece of bread, resulting in some of the most iconic visual images of the 1960s.

1969

Francis Ford Coppola founds the production company American Zoetrope in San Francisco. Imagined as an alternative to the Hollywood studios, this "film making 'commune'" is where Lucas will do post-production work on his first feature film, *THX 1138*.[21]

1970

Chavez is jailed for fourteen days in Salinas, California for refusing to obey a court order to end a boycott, an incident that is widely reported in the media. He is visited in his cell by Coretta Scott King and Ethel Kennedy. While leaving, Kennedy is surrounded and physically threatened by opponents of the boycott, including a group from the local John Birch Society—all captured for broadcast on the national evening TV news. At the same time, the growers and their allies, the Teamsters, employ thugs to menace and beat picketers and their supporters.[22] Released after winning an appeal, Chavez tells NBC that the prison was a "disgrace" that reminded him of farm labor camps.[23]

1971

Lucas releases *THX 1138*, a futuristic drama about a white man called THX (Robert Duvall) who rebels against a totalitarian society and ultimately escapes from one of its prisons. Lucas says it is about situations where people are "in cages with open doors" and that its theme is "the importance of self and being able to step out of whatever you're in and move forward rather than being stuck in your little rut."[24]

In June, the UFW establishes a film department and begins plans to build its own film and video production facilities. It also helps produce the film *Nosotros Venceremos* (*We Shall Overcome*) about the Delano grape strike, the march to Sacramento, Chavez's first fast and the union's first victorious contracts.

1972

Chavez once again fasts for 25 days, this time in Phoenix, in opposition to an Arizona law that effectively prevents farm workers from organizing, striking, and boycotting. During the fast he utters the now famous phrase "*si se puede*" (yes we can), which Huerta takes up as a rallying slogan in the concurrent protests.[25]

1973

The UFW releases two films, *Si Se Puede* and *Fighting for Our Lives*. The sound for *FFOL* is mixed at American Zoetrope and the film includes dramatic

footage of police beating farm workers in scenes that echo images from *THX 1138*. The UFW also launches a highly publicized boycott of the Gallo Wine Corporation of Modesto.

Lucas releases *American Graffiti*, a nostalgic film about white teens cruising the streets of Modesto in 1962, the year Chavez and Huerta established their first union in the Central Valley. Lucas says that the film celebrates "all that hokey stuff about being a good neighbor, and the American spirit" and that the heroes of both *THX 1138* and *AG* show that "(a)nybody who wants to do anything can do it. It's an old hokey American point of view, but I've sort of discovered that it's true."

1975

In order to pressure Gallo to come to the bargaining table, a few thousand UFW members march from San Francisco to Modesto. By the time they arrive, they have been joined by over 15,000 people. The march is widely covered in the media, including the national TV news, and helps to build support for passage of the California Agricultural Labor Relations Act (CALRA), which establishes the right of farm workers to collective bargaining.[26]

Lucas founds Industrial Light and Magic and writes the first draft of the *Star Wars* trilogy.

This partial parallel history indicates that Chavez and the UFW were vital actors in regional and national media in ways that would be hard to ignore, particularly for an aspiring filmmaker from a California agricultural community. Moreover, my timeline suggests that both Lucas and Chavez were directly involved in alternative 1960s film cultures that, while distinct in many ways, partly converged in others. The audience members for the kinds of experimental films Lucas watched in San Francisco, a center of UFW support, would also have been likely to attend UFW screenings and events. And yet, there are also many differences between the Lucas universe and the UFW, starting with the distinction between the collective address of "*Si Se Puede*" (Yes It Can be Done), and the individualist cliché, "(a)nybody who wants to do anything can do it." Which is to say that the Lucas trajectory combines the countercultural affiliations and rebellious impulses of the San Francisco scene, on the one hand, with the kinds of middle-class white conservatism characteristic of nearby agricultural towns such as Modesto, on the other.

This combination of counter-culture rebellion and conservative individualism is well represented by *THX 1138*.[27] In its mode of production the film constitutes a sort of rebellion against the Hollywood studio system, which is how Lucas described it both then and subsequently.[28] The title character also rebels against an oppressive system, figured here by a futuristic totalitarian State. *THX 1138* is a reactionary dystopia that melds a Cold War demonology of Soviet society with a kind of anti-big government white male individualism defined in opposition to women, homosexuals, blacks, and, implicitly, Mexican farm workers. One sign of oppression in the film is the erasure of gender differences —men and women have identical uniforms and shaved heads and answer to unisex codes in place of gendered names. The State forcibly separates THX and his partner, LUH (Maggie McOmie), and seemingly murders her. At the same time, THX must resist the sexual advances of a male superior, SEN (Donald Pleasence), who attempts to arrange it so that the two men will be forced to live together in State-controlled housing. This is in fact why SEN is ultimately imprisoned, where he continues to pursue THX. There the men are joined by a black male figure named SRT (Don Pedro Colley), who turns out to be a hologram. SRT recalls an earlier scene where, as a sign of his debasement within a mass society, THX masturbates while watching the hologram of a naked black woman dancing to the sound of drums. The bizarre implication is that the State uses illusory racial representations to control the white hero in ways that alienate him from himself and from "real" human relationships, defined as heterosexual relations with his white wife. Ultimately THX escapes the tyranny of mass society and becomes a free man only after losing his wife and literally racing away from the film's gay and black characters. The gay character is the first to fall by the wayside when he is arrested by the robot police. SRT is next: together he and THX steal police cars but the black hologram quickly crashes whereas the white male hero outdistances both him and the police. In the concluding scenes, THX eludes the police and climbs up a long ladder, out of what is revealed to have been a society constructed underground, and into the light and fresh air of the "real" world on the surface. The final shots suggest the quasi-religious resurrection of the white male hero: the silhouette of a lone individual is defined against the background of the setting sun while the solemn choral music of Bach's *St Matthew Passion* plays on the soundtrack. In these ways the film uses counter-cultural tropes of resistance to State power to deify a lone white man in rebellion against a government that violates his personal freedom by treating everyone—white men, women, gays, people of color— the same.

In the present context the most uncanny figures in the film are the so-called "shell dwellers" who live on the edge of the underground world. The film's sound editor and co-writer Walter Murch explains that the human characters have moved underground in response to "some kind of radiological or ecological disaster," and they are surrounded by a "society of dwarf people who live at the outer edges of society in the shell, which means up near the surface of the earth and presumably they're closer to what ever troubles have beset the surface of the earth and they're looked upon as a nuisance by the rest of society." As THX makes his final escape he must evade a group of shell dwellers that attack him and momentarily impede his progress. Their role in the narrative, combined with their depiction as grotesque and animalistic, suggests that the shell dwellers are fictionalized versions of farm workers. Their marginal social status and proximity to ecological disaster recalls farm worker vulnerability to pesticide poisoning and the UFW's highly visible campaigns against their use in California agriculture. The fact that the characters are played by little people with dark hair and beards recalls historical representations of Mexican farm workers as small in stature and hence constitutionally well suited for so-called "stoop labor." Similarly, the shell dwellers are dehumanized within the film's narrative (human characters react with visceral disgust to their perceived smell) and sound design (their voices are supplied by recordings of bears and apes) in ways that recall depictions of farm workers as dirty and animalistic. Ultimately, the freedom and individuality of the film's white male hero depends upon the distance he puts between himself and the shell dweller as farm worker.

Lucas compared the character of THX to Curt from *American Graffiti*, claiming they both represent the "American point of view" where "anybody who wants to do anything can do it," which he refers to elsewhere as the "Horatio Alger myth" of pulling yourself up by the bootstraps.[29] In interviews then and later, Lucas narrates his own life in similar terms. He has often, for example, figured himself as a rebel and an outsider, striving for freedom of expression.[30] "Freedom" is a keyword for Lucas, particularly individual freedom, but "equality" is not, perhaps because he associates it with a kind of State-imposed uniformity as in *THX 1138*.[31] Lucas's early career thus embodies an ideological shift analyzed by David Harvey in his *Brief History of Neoliberalism*. Harvey argues that the social movements of the 1960s represented an unstable combination of struggles *against* structural inequalities and *for* individual freedom, and that over the course of the 1970s such tenuous coalitions were broken as countercultural individualism morphed into neoliberalism:

> For almost everyone involved in the movement of '68, the intrusive state was the enemy and it had to be reformed. And on that, the neoliberals could easily agree. But capitalist corporations, business, and the market system were also seen as primary enemies requiring redress if not revolutionary transformation: hence the threat to capitalist class power. By capturing ideals of individual freedom and turning them against the interventionist and regulatory practices of the state, capitalist class interests could hope to protect and even restore their position.[32]

Lucas, I would argue, is a central figure in this history and his career makes visible the conflicted historical emergence of neoliberalism in relationship to the political economy of California's Central Valley, where individual white market freedoms are defined in relationship to Mexican farm workers.

Lucas constructed his own history in ways that obscure material inequalities so that all that remains are white individuals proving themselves in a free market. He expresses such sentiments in the formula that people are in "cages with open doors," prisons of their own making that can be transcended through individual initiative. This kind of facile idealism forcibly disappears otherwise highly visible counter-evidence of material inequalities (low wages, no rights or legal protections, state and vigilante violence) and the necessity of a collective response. And yet traces of such inequalities remain in the form of Latino characters in Lucas's early films that indirectly reference the UFW and its struggles with agribusiness. In two instances, Latino characters symbolically mediate the countercultural rebelliousness of '68 and the emergent neoliberal individualism of the 1970s. On the one hand, his student film *The Emperor* suggests an identification between film school rebels and Latino revolutionaries fighting against an agribusiness corporation. On the other hand, the film also others the Latin characters, who speak in exaggerated Spanish accents, wear theatrical costumes, and ultimately execute another character. From this perspective *The Emperor* seems like a demeaning parody of the Latino and Latin American movements of the period, including the UFW and Chavez. Similarly, in *American Graffiti* Curt at first partly identifies with, but then ultimately distances himself from, Latino gangsters. During his last night in Modesto before leaving for college, Curt is kidnapped by three "hoods" from a car club called the Pharos—made up of Joe Young (Bo Hopkins) and two Latinos, Carlos (Manuel Padilla) and Ants (Beau Gentry)—when he mistakenly sits on the car of an absent fourth Pharo, Gil Gonzales.[33] The group gives Curt a choice: either destroy a police car or Ants will drag him behind *his* car. After he successfully demolishes the cop car the gang offers to make him a member, but since he is bound for college in the morning Curt declines, leaving behind those, like the Latino gangsters, who cannot escape the "cage" of small town life.

While images of Latino revolutionaries and gangsters may seem far removed from Chavez and the UFW, conservative and agribusiness media in fact represented them in just such terms. During the 1960s and 1970s, agribusiness and its allies produced a constant stream of press releases, pamphlets, and books suggesting that Chavez was an authoritarian dictator, the leader of a gang of thugs, a revolutionary, a communist, and a crook.[34] Perhaps most famously, Governor Ronald Reagan, a staunch supporter of agribusiness, announced in a 1968 press conference that the boycott was "illegal," "immoral," and "attempted blackmail." Using the rhetoric of Cold War anti-communism, he further called it "the first domino" threatening to spread labor unrest throughout California agriculture. In order to demonstrate his opposition to the boycott, he publicly ate grapes for the news cameras.[35] Like other conservatives, Reagan represented the UFW as a kind of subversive criminal conspiracy in ways that are echoed by Lucas's Latino revolutionaries and hoods.

In these ways, Lucas's Latino characters partly represent fictional versions of Chavez and the UFW that serve to mediate a decisive shift from counterculture to neoliberalism, Central Valley style. With this last phrase I mean to suggest a regional social formation, with national influence, that combines myths of white male individualism, agrarian values, and market freedoms in opposition to Mexican farm workers. While by the 1940s, corporate agriculture had largely destroyed the material preconditions for agrarian populism in the West, images of the yeoman farmer have continued to play an influential role within right-wing political discourses in California and other parts of the United States. Most recently, with his fishing trips, cowboy boots, and bouts of brush clearing on his Texas ranch, George W. Bush seemed to mimic the similar performances of Ronald Reagan in his attempts to appeal to white male voters in the South and the West within a tradition of agrarian populism. And while agrarian populism has historically been associated with men, the Bush administration's former Agricultural Secretary Ann Veneman described herself as "'a poor little peach farmer's daughter" from California's Central Valley. Born and raised in Modesto and reportedly Lucas's second cousin, Veneman began her career working as a lawyer for the local firm representing Gallo in its battle with the UFW and, according to journalist Laura Flanders, she has "spent her entire adult life taking big business's side in a battle that pits the largest corporations in the world against the smallest farmer."[36] As Bush's agrarian political style and Veneman's reference to her father suggest, even though agribusiness threatens small farmers, images of the white male farmer as the bedrock of democracy have helped cement a conflicted alliance between white populism and corporate capitalism.

One of the most influential proponents of such an alliance is Victor Hanson, a one-time Bush administration advisor emeritus, Fresno State classicist specializing in agrarian communities, Hoover Institute Fellow, and a former employer of Mexican farm workers. Indeed, Hanson's personal history as a farmer is often cited as lending credibility to the anti-immigrant views articulated in his popular books, *National Review* columns, and blog. He is "a classicist, but also a farmer, who was born, lives, and works on a family farm in California's Central Valley" and in his writings Hanson attempts to "make sense" of the world from an "agrarian vantage point" that has been "handed down from some five previous generations."[37] In his book *Fields Without Dreams: Defending the Agrarian Ideal,* he argues that the small family farm is the "foundry of the country—its values, its militia, its very resilience." The life of a farmer, who is generally male in this account, is "a struggle with a purpose, where self and family have clear roles prescribed by the wisdom of the ages," while farms "forge family ties, the notion that blood above all is to be honored and protected, feuds, divorces, and alienation to be avoided." Farmers are "natural bedrock conservative(s)" who distrust "fashion and trend—whether it be multiculturalism or leveraged buyouts."[38]

While he is sometimes critical of the way agribusiness corporations have undermined family farms, Hanson attempts to bridge the gap between agrarian populism and corporate power by demonizing Mexican farm workers. In *Mexifornia: A State of Becoming* (2003), his paranoid dystopian account of the near-future immigrant takeover of California, he forecloses a broader, critical discussion of corporate capitalism by instead blaming migrants for a host of social problems, including violent crime, theft, STDs, drunk driving, monopolizing emergency medical resources, littering, abandoning dogs and cats on his farm, and even stealing a copy of one of his book manuscripts from his rural mailbox. Echoing a familiar narrative of countercultural disenchantment, Hanson notes that when he was an adolescent he secretly put pro-UFW bumper stickers on his uncle's farm truck and later he and his brother attended a UFW rally. But as he got older and wiser, he started to question the heroic image of Chavez presented in the public schools, claiming to discover that the UFW leader was an ambitious opportunist, a sort of "Mexican George Meany, in charge of a vast empire of stoop laborers," who, in combination with liberal politicians, helped "loot" union dues.[39] Here the figure of the Mexican farm worker anchors a neoconservative psychobiography, a Central Valley variation on neoliberalism that attacks state tyranny but embraces the tyranny of the market.

Hanson represents an influential kind of Valley Republicanism, where Mexicans are hyper-visible as phobic objects that organize nativist political projects and subjectivities. By contrast, Lucas has been more closely aligned with liberal Democrats, while Latinos are marginal to his films. Even so, the comparison with Hanson is revealing since Hanson renders in explicit and extreme terms the relationship between white farm boy and Mexican farm worker that is also represented, although in much more implicit and indirect ways, in *Star Wars*, to which I now turn.

The Migrant Farm Worker in Star Wars

There are no farm workers in *Star Wars* but their power as an animating absence is still important. The UFW challenged a hegemonic white agrarianism in the Valley by foregrounding images of farm workers rather than romantic images of a white yeomanry. UFW media implicitly negated the figure of the white farmer that helped shore up corporate agribusiness and I would argue that Luke represents the negation of the negation and *Star Wars* the return of the white farm boy. At the same time, traces of Chavez and the UFW are disseminated across the landscape of the Manichean world the film imagines.

Alex Rivera's film *Sleep Dealer* (2008) illuminates the potential significance of farm workers in *Star Wars*. *Sleep Dealer* develops a scenario Rivera first presented in *Why Cybraceros?* (1997), a short film in which a fictional corporation promises to use new computer technology to solve the "immigration problem" by enabling Mexicans to operate, *from Mexico*, farm worker robots in the United States. A satiric response to the "Internet utopianism" of the late 1990s, it incorporated footage from the UFW film *Fighting for Our Lives* showing police and Teamsters attacking strikers. Building on his earlier work, Rivera's first feature film, *Sleep Dealer*, focuses on the character of Memo (Luis Fernando Peña), a young peasant farmer living in the interior of a near-future Mexico where water has been privatized and a large pipeline has been built to

transport it to the United States. When a group of rebels emerges to fight water privatization, the United States launches a war on terror in Mexico, including attacks on suspected rebel strongholds by automated drones like those currently used in Pakistan. Near the beginning of the film, a military drone, remote-controlled from the U.S. by a Mexican American soldier named Rudy (Jacob Vargas), destroys Memo's home and kills his father. This tragedy turns Memo into a migrant who travels from his rural home to the border city of Tijuana. There he meets Luz, a sort of futuristic media maker who downloads other people's memories and sells them on the equivalent of the Internet; she introduces Memo to a brave new world of work, helping him implant electronic nodes all over his body so that he can perform remote labor. Soon he has a job working for a company called Cybraceros, where he is hooked up to cables and a sort of virtual reality mask, enabling him to operate, from Tijuana, construction bots in the United States. Meanwhile, Luz has been selling Memo's memories on the Internet, where they come to the attention of Rudy the drone pilot, who, consumed with guilt, migrates to Mexico to find Memo and make amends. Together, the three characters break into Cybraceros' facilities and commandeer the technology in order to fly a drone to Memo's village and destroy a massive, heavily guarded dam.

As Rivera has explained, *Sleep Dealers* is partly a reworking of *Star Wars*, with the destruction of the dam standing in for the destruction of the Death Star. Moreover, Memo's character arc, in which an imperial army destroys his family's farm and initiates his migration toward the center of the empire, recalls Luke's odyssey.[40] Rivera's reappropriation of *Star Wars* thus in turn suggests that the Skywalker story appropriates the structure of a migrant worker narrative for the story of the white farm boy, but rather than being based in the fields of Mexico, the imaginary world of *Star Wars* begins in the farm lands of California. According to *Wired* writer Steve Silberman, though filmed in Tunisia, the scenes of Luke's home planet of Tatooine, where he initially lives on a small family farm with his aunt and uncle, were modeled on "the dusty Central Valley flatlands."[41] However, in the film's fantastic, revisionary reversal, the figure of the white farm boy occupies a position that more closely resembles that of a migrant farm worker. Landless and dispossessed, vulnerable to extreme forms of militarized police power, and forced by material conditions to leave home in order to survive, Luke's story sounds like that of many farm workers. And yet in *Star Wars*, the noble white farm boy appropriates for agrarian populism the pathos of exploitation and marginalization that was previously attached to the farm worker movement. Or more precisely, Luke's fate at the start of the film is made more tragic, and his ultimate rise more heroic, in part because he is a white farm boy who has fallen to the level of a migrant farm worker. This reading is supported by the analysis of *THX 1138*, which suggests a similar kind of racialized reversal, whereby the film's white male hero experiences extreme forms of police violence that recall iconic period images of black and brown civil rights protesters being beaten by the police. And substituting an oppressed white farm boy for oppressed people of color recalls the contemporaneous emergence of discourses of reverse discrimination that rearticulated civil rights rhetoric in order to argue that state efforts to redress prior histories of inequality violated the rights of white men.[42] The early films of Lucas thus help make visible an influential historical shift from the social movements for radical transformation of the 1960s to an emergent neoconservative reaction of tactical reversals.

Displacing migrant farm workers by mimicking them, the white farm boy proceeds to fight a brutal empire represented by a ruthless "black" villain. A number of critics have argued that the Darth Vader character is shaped by ideas about racialized blackness and I would argue that the figure references Latinos as well.[43] Just as Chavez was symbolically and practically linked to civil rights and anti-colonial leaders (Gandhi, MLK, Coretta Scott King, Huerta, Bobby Seale of the Black Panthers), I would speculate that Vader condenses a variety of racialized or third world movements for social transformation, including the UFW, that are often represented by the shorthand of "1968." And the *Star Wars* villain is contradictory in ways that recall Chavez's conflicted public image. On the one hand, with his disfigured body and audibly labored breathing, Vader seems to require the life support help of his elaborate costume. On the other hand, he speaks in a powerful, commanding voice and exercises a charismatic, quasi-religious power over a vast army of minions. Similarly, many of the iconic media images of Chavez from the 1960s represent him weakened by one of his fasts and being supported by other people, and yet at the same time agribusiness interests and their allies used hyperbolic rhetoric and imagery in order to demonize the UFW. Whereas McWilliams had argued that agribusiness was responsible for fascism in the fields, conservatives constructed a counter-narrative in which Chavez's public commitment to nonviolence and self-sacrifice was a sham that masked a charismatic dictator's will to power. And in ways even more extreme and explicit than Reagan's language about falling dominos, right-wing books with titles such as *Little Cesar: The Farm Worker Movement* (1971) and *Little Cesar and his Phony Strike* (1974) compared Chavez to an imperial dictator and a mafioso.[44] Hanson recently echoed such period pieces when he claimed that the union leader's public image was at odds with his ambition to control "a vast empire of stoop laborers." All of which is to suggest that Darth Vader can be read as a demonological rendering of Chavez as dictatorial union boss.

And yet, recalling Milton's Satan, Darth Vader has perhaps proven to be the most interesting character to viewers and consumers of *Star Wars*, and I would wager that the villain has sold more merchandise, inspired more imitations, and generally generated more global cultural attention than any of the heroes. Michael Rogin's claims about the forms of political demonology that have dominated California and ultimately the United States are helpful for understanding the Vader effect. Taking Reagan as exemplary, Rogin analyzes a conservative political formation that has historically demonized people of color, radicals, and labor unions in its devotion to "counter subversion." He identifies a counter-subversive tradition in U.S. politics and films that project forms of violence and aggression onto social groups that challenge the status quo and then promotes the use of their own vilified tactics against them. From this perspective, the threat posed by subversive others licenses government officials to mimic the demons they have created.[45] Which seems like a revealing gloss on *Star Wars*, where the figure of the white farm boy, threatened with displacement by the UFW and other forces of transformation, serves to energize investments in Darth Vader. How else can we understand the narrative of Lucas's transformation from rebellious farm boy to the head of a vast corporate empire? As he explained on a 2004 DVD release of *Star Wars*,

> I'm not happy that corporations have taken over the film industry, but now I find myself being the head of a corporation, so there's a certain irony there. I have become the very thing that I was trying to avoid. That is Darth Vader—he becomes the very thing he was trying to protect himself against.[46]

Meanwhile, Back at Skywalker Ranch, or the UFW in Contemporary Digital Culture

According to USC film scholar David James, Lucas recreated his film school experience in grandiose ways, first with major donations to USC and then

> in the idealized version of film school at the Skywalker Ranch, with its own offices, editing, and post production facilities. Here the conditions of USC in the 1960s were replicated on a corporate scale, and here he

made his own hypertrophied experimental films. So *Star Wars* reads as the projection of a childhood fantasy and also an allegory of his own career: Luke and Lucas get to play with the toys of industrial light and magic, destroy the bad guys from Hollywood, and return the movies to the mentality of pubescence.[47]

As James persuasively argues, Lucas's ideal is a corporate one, with origins in his own history and self-narration. Based on my own research, I would say that the corporate ideal represented by Skywalker Ranch is imaginatively based in agribusiness. The Ranch, which cost over 100 million dollars and sits on over 4,000 acres of land in rural Marin County, is anchored by a massive Victorian farmhouse with an expansive front porch. In 1986 Lucas told a visitor he thought the ranch should "have a good story," so before building it he constructed an imaginary history in which "the estate would have started as a monastery, but was later converted into a mansion and vineyard for wine-making. As the vineyard's family grew, new homes and cottages were built."[48] The website for Skywalker Sound at the Ranch prominently features images of the vineyards (minus workers), including a QuickTime film that presents a panoramic view of them from the porch.[49] Skywalker Ranch is thus not just a corporate fantasy of the family farm on steroids, but also represents Lucas's media empire as an idealized version of Gallo Wines, the Modesto company that fought the UFW for so long.

Which is to suggest that the history of pre-digital race and labor formations continues to influence contemporary digital culture, starting with Lucas' own digital filmmaking. Like Silicon Valley companies, Lucas has been deeply invested in his own corporate history, and to that end has released digitally revised versions of almost all of his major, pre-digital films—much to the chagrin of many fans and critics.[50] In 2004, for example, he released into theaters and on DVD *THX 1138: The George Lucas Director's Cut*, which makes a number of digital additions, many of which serve to intensify the kinds of racial representations analyzed earlier. The white hero now masturbates to a digitally enhanced hologram of the naked black dancing woman, for example, while the shell dwellers that attack him have been replaced by menacing CGI apes.[51] This last change has contradictory implications since, on the one hand, it obscures the connections between Lucas and the UFW suggested by the shell dwellers in the original version of *THX 1138*, while on the other hand the very substitution of digital monkeys seems to recall the more recent past of anti-immigrant discourse in California and the United States more generally. The 1980s and 1990s saw the rearticulation of older race and class ideologies in the form of white anti-immigrant nativism directed at workers from Latin America and often framed in the language of animality (especially parasites and vermin), filth, waste, and other expressions of racialized disgust. At the same time, and partly in response to such populist nativism, state and federal immigration enforcement became increasingly militarized, incorporating high-tech military weaponry and surveillance equipment (including flying drones). And so the 2004 director's cut of *THX 1138* roughly coincided both with Hanson's nativist best-seller, *Mexifornia*, and the establishment of U.S. Immigration and Customs Enforcement (ICE), which has unleashed what Rachel Buff calls a new "deportation terror" against migrant workers.[52]

While historically CGI has been used in SF films to create a variety of effects, it has often been deployed in figural ways, to represent exotic or fantastic characters and creatures. This practice has lent itself to the creation of racialized digital characters, most infamously the figure of Jar Jar Binks, which was widely criticized for being a CGI version of a blackface minstrel.[53] Jar Jar Binks recalls the black holograms, suggesting that Lucas has used CGI not only to produce a kind of enhanced realism but also as a means of derealizing race and class conflict, which is to shift focus away from whether this or that use of CGI is realistic or persuasive and to instead ask what it means to render race and class differences as special effects.[54] In the case of *THX 1138*, the original had already represented farm workers in fantastic SF terms and when new digital tools became available they were used in ways that made the shell dwellers even more "unreal," like the holograms. Here, however, the substitution of digital apes for human actors displaces workers literally and symbolically. Or, more precisely, in the director's cut figures representing farm workers are digitally incorporated into the film in ways that drain them of humanity and disconnect them from political economic contexts. Analyzing Lucas in relationship to Chavez and the UFW thus suggests the extent to which he has increasingly used digital technology to create compelling fictional worlds that draw upon the "real world" but ultimately replace it. Recalling the ways that Intel incorporated fictionalized versions of low-wage workers of color into its corporate brand, we might say that the corporate development and deployment of CGI sublates social and material histories of race and class, simultaneously preserving and canceling them out, in ways that ultimately deny their reality. Meanwhile, cultural criticism celebrating the centrality of *Star Wars* to a new participatory digital culture risks reproducing the ideologies encoded in its source material.[55]

Which returns us to where we began—the popularity of *Star Wars* in the corporate world of Silicon Valley. Before the rise of the high-tech industry there, the region was largely known as an agricultural area with a significant population of migrant farm workers and low-wage cannery workers, and so, like Lucas's corporate empire, Silicon Valley originated out of an agribusiness culture and economy. And according to Manuel Castells, Silicon Valley companies developed a new work model, limited to their more privileged employees, that drew upon elements of the 1960s counter cultures but melded them to capitalist entrepreneurship in ways that recall Lucas' own historical morphing.[56]

Starting in the Cold War period, high-tech companies in Silicon Valley, including Intel, have been aggressively devoted to combating organized labor, becoming what David Bacon has called "laboratories for developing personnel-management techniques for maintaining a union-free environment." Along with older tactics of incorporating sham company unions in order to displace independent union organizing, new union-busting techniques have been created, including the so-called "team method" of organizing workers on plant floors, represented by the "team" of workers in *Star Wars* masks. As a result of such efforts, IT industries in the Valley remain largely un-unionized. The force of corporate anti-unionism is suggested by the fact that many clean-room workers are low-paid and made vulnerable to premature death because of toxic chemicals in ways that most people would do everything they could to avoid if they had other options.[57]

The situation has been different, however, in the case of the largely Latino janitors who clean Silicon Valley buildings and offices. For decades tech companies there have contracted outside firms to provide cleaning services, and so janitors aren't part of the company "team." On the one hand, this arrangement favors corporations because it relieves them of responsibility for providing benefits to the janitors and because competition among janitorial subcontractors keeps costs (and hence wages) low. On the other hand, the janitors' exclusion from a corporate work culture organized around labor control has perhaps contributed to the historic success of the "Justice for Janitors" movement. "Justice for Janitors" is an ongoing campaign to organize janitors in various locations, including Silicon Valley, where it began in 1988 as an organizing drive by the Service Employees International Union (SEIU) and led by several former UFW organizers. In an important early victory, the union promoted boycotts of Apple products and organized janitors in highly visible protests at Apple headquarters, MacWorld Expo, and annual shareholder meetings during the early 1990s. Anticipating the similar strike among mostly Latino service workers at USC near the end of the decade, in 1991 the union initiated a hunger strike on Apple corporate grounds in Cupertino. Both Huerta and Chavez made visits to Silicon Valley to support the strikers, which ultimately helped force Apple and their janitorial company to renegotiate a new more favorable contract with the janitors, leading to a number of other Valley companies following suit. (A few years later, as if to symbolically ward off future labor problems, Apple incorporated an iconic image of Chavez into its "Think Different" advertising campaign.)

Throughout the 1990s, during the dot.com boom, striking janitors could be seen wearing red t-shirts to protest their invisibility to employers and the broader public. As Mike Garcia, an SEIU organizer, explained at the time, many janitors "were working two to three jobs and trying to raise a family. Meanwhile, they're cleaning the edifices of the filthy rich, the overnight billionaires and millionaires. How could they explain that their janitors are living two to three families in a garage?" Under these conditions, and in ways that directly drew upon the UFW struggles with agricultural corporations, janitors in Silicon

Valley, some of the poorest and most vulnerable workers in the United States, have often beaten big corporations at their own game of media manipulation and public relations. Unfortunately, in contexts dominated by a *Star Wars* worldview it becomes harder to see and think about things like "Justice for Janitors" and, more broadly, digital culture's dependence on systems of racialized labor.

Notes

1 Intel Museum and Corporate Archives, www.intel.com/museum (accessed September 6, 2009).
2 See the website for the Intel Museum and Corporate Archives. Similarly, a keyword search for "Intel" at the "Silicon Valley History" site yields numerous such photos: www.siliconvalleyhistory.org (accessed September 6, 2009).
3 Interview with Steve Allen, Lawrence Bender, and Richard Steinheimer, "Silicon Genesis: An Oral History of Semiconductor Technology," Special Collections, Stanford University. Available at: http://silicongenesis.stanford.edu/complete_listing.html#semi (accessed February 5, 2010).
4 Michael Kanellos, "Silicon Valley's Misplaced *Star Wars* Lust," *CNET News*, May 10, 1999. Available at: http://news.cnet.com/Silicon-Valleys-misplaced-Star-Wars-lust/2010-1071_3-281231.html (accessed February 5, 2010).
5 Michael Cieply, "A Film School's New Look is Historic," *New York Times*, February 8, 2009. Available at: www.nytimes.com/2009/02/09/movies/09film.html (accessed August 7, 2009).
6 On the racial politics of Fairbanks' star image, as well as the actor's racism, see Lary May, *Screening Out the Past: The Birth of Mass Culture and the Motion Picture Industry* (Chicago: University of Chicago Press, 1980), 216, 96–146.
7 Carey McWilliams, *Southern California: An Island on the Land* (Salt Lake City: Peregrine Smith, 1995; first edition 1946); John R. Chávez, "The Spanish Southwest," *The Lost Land: The Chicano Image of the Southwest* (Albuquerque: University of New Mexico Press, 1984), 85–106; William Deverell, *Whitewashed Adobe: The Rise of Los Angeles and the Remaking of Its Mexican Past* (Berkeley: University of California Press, 2005).
8 Laura Pulido, email correspondence.
9 Randy Shaw, *Beyond the Fields: Cesar Chavez, the UFW, and the Fight for Justice in the 21st Century* (Berkeley: University of California Press, 2008), 94–5.
10 John Steinbeck, *The Harvest Gypsies: On the Road to the Grapes of Wrath* (Berkeley: Heyday Books, 1988; first edition 1936); Carey McWilliams, *Factories in the Fields: The Story of Migratory Farm Labor in California* (Berkeley: University of California Press, 2000; first edition 1939), 211–229; Vicki Ruiz, *Cannery Women, Cannery Lives: Mexican Women, Unionization, and the California Food Processing Industry, 1930–1950* (Albuquerque: University of New Mexico Press, 1987); Devra Weber, *Dark Sweat, White Gold: California Cotton, Farm Workers and the New Deal, 1919–1939* (Berkeley: University of California Press, 1996).
11 McWilliams, *Factories in the Fields*, 230–263.
12 Walter Goldschmidt, *As You Sow* (Glencoe, IL: The Free Press, 1946), 117–119.
13 Richard Steven Street, "Poverty in the Valley of Plenty: The National Farm Labor Union, DiGiorgio Farms, and Suppression of Documentary Photography in California, 1946–1966," *Labor History* 48.1 (February 2007): 30–31.
14 McWilliams, *Factories in the Fields*, 234–237; Ernesto Galarza, *Farm Workers and Agri-business in California, 1947–1960* (Notre Dame, IN: University of Notre Dame Press, 1977), 47–55; and Goldschmidt, *As You Sow*, 181–183.
15 Street, "Poverty in the Valley of Plenty" and *Photographing Farm Workers in California* (Stanford: Stanford University Press, 2004).
16 Richard Griswold del Castillo and Richard A. Garcia, *César Chávez: A Triumph of the Spirit* (Norman, OK: University of Oklahoma Press, 1997), 13. Except where otherwise stated, the information in this section about Chavez and the UFW comes from this source.
17 John Baxter, *Mythmaker: The Life and Work of George Lucas* (New York: Spike Books, 1999), 21–29; Dale Pollack, *Skywalking: The Life and Films of George Lucas* (New York: Da Capo Press, 1999), 11–40. Unless otherwise noted all biographical information about Lucas comes from these two biographies.

18 Ernesto Galarza, *Spiders in the House and Workers in the Field* (Notre Dame, IN: University of Notre Dame Press, 1970); Street, "Poverty in the Valley of Plenty."

19 Steve Silberman, "Life After Darth," *Wired* magazine 13.05 (May 2005). Available at: www.wired.com/wired/archive/13.05/lucas.html (accessed February 6, 2010).

20 George Lucas, *The Emperor*, Cinema Library, University of Southern California.

21 *American Cinematographer*, October 1971; reprinted in Sally Kline, ed., *George Lucas: Interviews* (Jackson, MI: University Press of Mississippi, 1999), 9.

22 *NBC Evening News*, December 7, 1970, Vanderbilt Television News Archive. Available at: http://tvnews.vanderbilt.edu/?SID=20090918509796142 (accessed September 18, 2009); Mike Davis, "Beating the UFW," in Mike Davis and Justin Akers Chacón, eds, *No One is Illegal: Fighting Racism and State Violence on the U.S.–Mexican Border* (Chicago: Haymarket Books, 2006), 79.

23 *CBS Evening News*, December 4, 1970; *NBC Evening News*, December 4, 1970; *NBC Evening News*, December 24, 1970, Vanderbilt Television News Archive.

24 Quoted by Judy Stone, "George Lucas," *San Francisco Chronicle*, May 23, 1971; reproduced in Kline, *George Lucas: Interviews*, 5.

25 See www.chavezfoundation.org/uploads/Si_Se_Puede_History.pdf.

26 CBS Evening News, February 28, 1975, Vanderbilt Television News Archive.

27 My reading of *THX 1138* is indebted to Janani Subramanian, who analyzes racial representation in the film in the context of theories of the avant-garde. See her "The Fantastic Avant-Garde: Riddles of Representation in Fantastic Media" (PhD dissertation, USC 2009). See also her essay "Alienating Identification: Black Identity in *The Brother from Another Planet* and *I Am Legend*," *Science Fiction Film and Television* 3.1: 37–56.

28 David James, *The Most Typical Avant-Garde: History and Geography of Minor Cinemas in Los Angeles* (Berkeley: University of California Press, 2005), 208–212.

29 See Lucas quoted by Faber in Kline, *George Lucas: Interviews*, 38, and by Michael Pye and Linda Miels, "George Lucas," *The Movie Brats* (New York: Holt Rinehart and Winston, 1979), reprinted in Kline, *George Lucas: Interviews*, 68.

30 Stone, "George Lucas," in Kline, *George Lucas: Interviews*, 5, 6–7.

31 See Farber, in Kline, *George Lucas: Interviews*, 38.

32 David Harvey, *A Brief History of Neoliberalism* (Oxford: Oxford University Press, 2005), 42.

33 As a teen in Modesto Lucas was on the margins of a car club called the Faros (Spanish for lights, as in headlights), and the name was changed to "Pharos" for the film; Dale Pollock, *Skywalking: The Life and Times of George Lucas* (New York: Da Capo Press, 1999), 27–28. My father, Paul Marez, who grew up in the same area at the same time, recalls that the members of the club were largely Portuguese, but Lucas seems to have Mexicanized them.

34 "Opposition Propaganda" (file 15, box 31) and "Anti-Union Propaganda" (file 40, box 34), UFW Administration Papers, Walter Reuther Library, Wayne State University, Detroit.

35 "The Little Strike that Grew to La Causa," *Time* magazine, July 4, 1969. Available at: www.time.com/time/magazine/article/0,9171,840167-2,00.html (accessed August 15, 2009); *Bitter Harvest: Chavez Fights On* (1976), BBC Video, UFW VHS Collection, Box 1, Reuther Library.

36 Laura Flanders, "FLAVR SAVR—Ann Veneman," *Bushwomen: Tales of a Cynical Species* (New York: Verso Press, 2004), 113–146. The quotations in the preceding sentence are on 113.

37 Victor Hanson, *An Autumn of War: What America Learned from September 11 and the War on Terrorism* (New York: Anchor Books, 2002), xvi. See also Hanson, *Field without Dreams: Defending the Agrarian Ideal* (New York: Free Press, 1997); and *Mexifornia: A State of Becoming* (New York: Encounter Books, 2004).

38 Hanson, *Field without Dreams*, xxi, 17, xx.

39 Hanson, *Mexifornia*, 97–98.

40 Interview with Alex Rivera, *SF 360*. Available at: www.sf360.org/features/qa-alex-rivera-sleep-dealer (accessed June 19, 2008); director's commentary, *Sleep Dealer* DVD (Maya Entertainment, 2009).

41 Silberman, "Life After Darth."

42 Michael Omi and Howard Winant, *Racial Formations in the United States: From the 1960s to the 1990s* (New York: Routledge, 1994), 116.

43 Clyde R. Taylor, *The Mask of Art: Breaking the Aesthetic Contract—Film and Literature* (Bloomington: Indiana University Press, 1998), 148–150; Martin Kevorkian, *Color Monitors: The Black Face of Technology in America* (Ithaca: Cornell University Press, 2006), 123–126.

44 George Mariscal, *Brown Eyed Children of the Sun: Lessons of the Chicano Movement* (Albuquerque: University of New Mexico Press, 2005), 156–159.

45 Michael Rogin, *Ronald Reagan, the Movie*, xiii, 10, 39–40.

46 Quoted in Silberman, "Life After Darth."

47 James, *The Most Typical Avant-Garde*, 213.

48 George Perry, "A Day at Lucas Films." Available at: www.insideskywalkerranch.com/skywalker-ranch-tour.htm (accessed September 17, 2009).

49 Skywalker Sound, http://skysound.com/qtvr/qtvr_tour_front_porch.html (accessed September 17, 2009).

50 The one exception here is *American Graffiti*, which has been released on DVD with a digitally remastered soundtrack but apparently no other changes or additions.

51 YouTube user "Videosteni" has produced a useful comparison of the two versions of the film. See www.youtube.com/watch?v=kIfTT8EGj3A (accessed February 5, 2010).

52 Rachael Ida Buff, "The Deportation Terror," *American Quarterly* 60.3 (September 2008): 523–552.

53 See, for example, Patricia J. Williams, "Racial Ventriloquism," *The Nation*, July 5, 1999. Available at: www.thenation.com/doc/19990705/Williams (accessed February 5, 2010).

54 See Michele Pierson's *Special Effects: Still in Search of Wonder* (New York: Columbia University Press, 2002), for a critique of understandings of CGI solely in realist terms.

55 See Henry Jenkins, "Quentin Tarantino's *Star Wars*? Grassroots Creativity Meets the Media Industry," in *Convergence Culture: Where Old and New Media Collide* (New York: NYU Press, 2006), which makes claims for a new participatory digital culture that reduces democracy to market freedoms and affirms forms of corporate capitalism.

56 Manuel Castells, *The Internet Galaxy: Reflections on the Internet, Business, and Society* (New York: Oxford University Press, 2001), 36–63.

57 David Bacon, "The New Face of Union Busting," available at: http://dbacon.igc.org/Unions/02ubust0.htm (accessed February 5, 2010); Lisa Sun-Hee Park and David Nabuib Pellow, *The Silicon Valley of Dreams: Environmental Injustice, Immigrant Workers, and the High-Tech Global Economy* (New York: New York University Press, 2002); Curtis Marez, "The Homies in Silicon Valley: Figuring Styles of Life and Work in the Information Age," *Aztlan: A Journal of Chicano Studies* 31.2 (Fall 2006): 134–148.

II
Race, Identity, and Digital Sorting

5
Does the Whatever Speak?

ALEXANDER R. GALLOWAY

New York University

"Do we really need another analysis of how a cultural representation does symbolic violence to a marginal group?" This is how one colleague recently put it, suggesting that the cultural studies and identity politics movements of the 1980s and 1990s had at last exhausted their utility.

But how could an ostensibly liberal, broad-minded person say such a thing? How did we get here? How did the world slip away from the 1960s mould, in which the liberation of desire (and thus affective identities of various kinds) was considered a politically progressive project to undertake? At the turn of the new millennium we have a different destiny, for today under the new postfordist economies desire and identity are part of the core economic base and thus woven into the value chain more than ever before.[1] What cruelty of fate. If marginal groups are now "normalized" within the mode of production, what would it mean to offer criticism of the present situation? Is there any outside anymore? Any subaltern?

These are some of the questions I aim to address here. The inquiry centers around a specific tableau, the so-called "Chinese gold farmer." The Chinese gold farmer is a gamer who plays video games day and night in order to earn virtual gold and sell it for real money. In particular I am interested in the ideological work that such a tableau performs within contemporary culture.

To get there I offer four questions. The first is an inquiry into the contemporary status of race, in parallel with a few observations about the state of cultural theory. The second and third questions deal directly with representations of race in video games and elsewhere. And the final question offers something of a suggestion, a possible reassessment of the situation itself, not so much a "way out" of the problems presented here, but an alternate beginning that shows, if I am successful, how some of the problems might not actually be problems in the first place, provided we are willing to leave them be.

First Question: Ubinam Gentium Sumus? Or, Where In the World Are We?

So how did we get here? Allow me to step back and sketch two larger points of socio-historical context that inform the present debate. The first concerns the question of how race is represented today in culture, while the second concerns the so-called failure of theory and the turn, in recent years, away from identity politics and cultural criticism.

For the first point of context, recall the inauguration of the American President Barack Obama—not the ceremony itself, but the rehearsal that took place just prior to the event in January 2009. I was struck in seeing photographs of the rehearsal. Three figures appear on the platform, the same three who would be present during the swearing-in. Barack Obama's stand-in is a black man, Michelle Obama's a black woman, and Justice John Roberts' a white man.

Who are these people? Who orchestrated this event, and why go to such lengths to enforce such racial specificity body by body? This black man for that black man, this black woman for that black woman, this white man for that white man?

Have we not achieved, in Obama's inauguration rehearsal, the most perfect form of racial typing? At the point in which race no longer matters, it matters more than anything else. In the most prosaic dress rehearsal of who steps when and where, of moving television cameras around, of determining the temporal

Figure 5.1 Stand-ins for President-elect Barack Obama, his wife Michelle Obama and Chief Justice John Roberts rehearse the swearing-in ceremony for the inauguration on the West Front of the U.S. Capitol, Monday, January 19, 2008, in Washington, DC. (AP/World Wide Photos, used with permission.)

sequences of events—at this very moment of absolute banality, the logic of race nevertheless holds sway.

Consider the logic of superstition. Of course, you claim, *I'm* not superstitious. I know that it doesn't *really* matter if I step on a crack, or walk under a ladder, or place a hat on a bed. Occult ritual—doing one thing to ward off another—has *nothing* to do with how the world really works. We all know this. But all the more reason to adhere militantly to the rules of correct behavior. The fact that the decision is not obligatory makes it all the more necessary to choose correctly. Of course it is absolutely meaningless, so why risk it—why *would* you walk under a ladder rather than not, when the two paths are equivalent and one may just as easily avoid it?

This is the logic of race today. "Of course race doesn't matter, which is why it must be globally cemented at all cost." Within global neoliberalism we have reached a state in which race matters absolutely, but only because it does not matter at all anymore. The very lack of necessity drills forward like an irresistible force. Racial coding has not gone away in recent years, it has only migrated into the realm of dress rehearsal, the realm of pure simulation, and as simulation it remains absolutely necessary. The Obama body doubles, as pure simulation, *must be black.*

Perhaps this indicates the next phase in racial typing. After Jim Crow, after civil rights, race today has been liberated, but only so it may persist in a purely digital form. Perhaps now this is the phase of pure racial coding, no longer the dirty racism of actual struggle. Perhaps now after what Marxists call the "formal" subsumption of racial logic we have the "real" subsumption. With Obama racism is finally liberated so that it may exist in a purely ideological form. In essence, the most perfect racism is that which lives inside a mediated simulation.

The reason for this is that the virtual can *only* exist within the absolute; the virtual *needs* the absolute. The trouble is that conventional wisdom often suggests the reverse, that the virtual is the thing that stands "above" or apart from the real, that all anxieties about the real ultimately find their escape in the virtual, and so on. But here conventional wisdom is totally wrong. For the exact opposite is true. The virtual can only be possible, not in relation to the real, but in relation to the absolute.

To formalize this slightly, one can say that (1) the absolute is responsible for the "perfection" (i.e. "completion" or "accomplishment") of racial simulation, and that (2) the virtual is responsible for the projection-forward of race within digital simulation or, in other words, for race having entered into the enterprise of value creation (i.e. the virtual as pure energy, as part of the productive forces). I will say more about how race enters the sphere of value creation in a moment.

First, let me put on the table a second bit of socio-historical context. The second point concerns the so-called failure of theory and the turn, in recent years, away from identity politics and cultural theory.

Consider again the quotation given at the outset. "Do we really need another analysis of how a cultural representation does symbolic violence to a marginal group?" Instead of passing this off as the insensitivity of a white liberal academic turning a blind eye to matters of racial and cultural injustice, it is important to point out a far more fundamental trend that is at work here. For in certain philosophical circles there exists today a newfound desire to divorce politics from ontology. There exists a desire to neuter the force of critique by removing dialectical reason from the structure of being. As this particular individual put it, the terms of the new philosophy will be: "a rejection of textual analysis or linguistic structures, a positive ontology and desire to attain the Absolute, and an attempt to shed all anthropocentrism." But what does this mean? The first term, a rejection of textual analysis, refers to literary criticism and the perception that textual approaches gained too much ground in recent years, so much so that they must be curtailed in favor of realist or non-interpretive approaches. The second term, a positive ontology, refers (as best I can surmise) to the "affirmative" ontology of someone like Deleuze, who removes the dialectical negative entirely from his theory of being. While the third term, the shedding of all anthropocentrism, refers to a demotion of the human, such that humankind is on an equal footing with all other objects in the world, no more privileged and no less privileged than other kinds of entities.

Should we be surprised that the identity politics and cultural theory movements have experienced such a crisis of faith? Even the most hard-line defenders of leftist theory admit the same thing, that no one really believes in postmodernism any more. Even Fredric Jameson, in his *A Singular Modernity*, put forward a new take on the postmodern as something of an echo of the modern, something to be folded back, something to be reversed and reincorporated into a singular periodization. It was easy to sneer at those who slowed the march of civil rights, or cluck at a politically incorrect remark. But perhaps a total reversal has taken place without anyone knowing. Perhaps the bottom has fallen out. Perhaps we are all Alan Sokal now.

So is it any surprise that, just at the moment when identity and affect become incorporated into the digital markets of postfordism, the utility of identity and affect as critical categories comes into question? Shall we not discard our discussions of affective "faciality" in favor of a new defacement? Is the sixties-era liberation of affect really a new kind of obscenity, a new pornography in which all must be exposed for speculation and investment?

Michael Hardt and Antonio Negri fired one of the first volleys in this new skirmish over the utility of certain critical tactics, specifically the elevation of multiple affects and subjectivities by those working within leftist cultural theory:

> We suspect that postmodernist and postcolonialist theories may end up in a dead end because they fail to recognize adequately the contemporary object of critique, that is, they mistake today's real enemy. What if the modern form of power these critics (and we ourselves) have taken such

pains to describe and contest no longer holds sway in our society? What if these theorists are so intent on combating the remnants of a past form of domination that they fail to recognize the new form that is looming over them in the present? What if the dominating powers that are the intended object of critique have mutated in such a way as to depotentialize any such postmodernist challenge? In short, what if a new paradigm of power, a postmodern sovereignty, has come to replace the modern paradigm and *rule through differential hierarchies of the hybrid and fragmentary subjectivities* that these theorists celebrate? In this case, modern forms of sovereignty would no longer be at issue, and the postmodernist and postcolonialist strategies that appear to be liberatory would not challenge but in fact coincide with and even unwittingly reinforce the new strategies of rule! . . . This new enemy not only is resistant to the old weapons but actually thrives on them, and thus joins its would-be antagonists in applying them to the fullest. Long live difference! Down with essentialist binaries![2]

As might be expected, Hardt and Negri were met by a considerable amount of resistance for taking this position, particularly from those scandalized by the notion that postmodernist theories about cultural identity might not be as effective as once thought, and may even add fuel to systems of power and domination. But they were not speaking alone; other voices soon added themselves to the chorus. Both Alain Badiou and Slavoj Žižek, for example, have made it clear that they oppose so-called postmodern theory and the fragmentary subjectivities and liberated affects that supposedly go along with it. With his book *In Defense of Lost Causes* Žižek advocates a return to universal truth, leftist theory's erstwhile enemy, and thus an end to postmodernism's skepticism toward "grand narratives," a skepticism which he rightly associates with the corrosive properties of capitalism.[3] Badiou goes even further, staking much of his work on a theory of the subject bound not by "fragmentary subjectivities" but grounded in the universality of truth. This newfound interest in a singular, universal truth is also shared by Susan Buck-Morss in her recent *Hegel, Haiti, and Universal History*:

Can we rest satisfied with the call for acknowledging "multiple modernities," with a politics of "diversality," or "multiversality," when in fact the inhumanities of these multiplicities are often strikingly the same? Critical theoretical practice today is caught within the prisonhouse of its own academic debates . . . We exist behind cultural borders, the defense of which is a boon to politicians. The fight to free the facts from the collective histories in which they are embedded is one with exposing and expanding the porosity of a global social field, where individual experience is not so much hybrid as human . . . It is not that truth is multiple or that the truth is a whole ensemble of collective identities with partial perspectives. Truth is singular, but it is a continuous process of inquiry because it builds on a present that is moving ground. History keeps running away from us, going places we, mere humans, cannot predict. The politics of scholarship that I am suggesting is neutrality, but not of the nonpartisan, "truth lies in the middle" sort; rather, it is a *radical* neutrality that insists on the porosity of the space between enemy sides, a space contested and precarious, to be sure, but free enough for the idea of humanity to remain in view.[4]

Truth is thus singular, Buck-Morss suggests, and it is achieved through a "radical neutrality" of the human, a point I will return to at the end.

But perhaps the most forceful push away from subject-oriented, relativistic, and correlationist thinking has come from Quentin Meillassoux, in his *After Finitude*. Through a highly technical intervention, Meillassoux rejects the hegemony of finitude and urges us to awake from our slumber and reconcile ourselves with the absolute.[5]

I cite this series of authors merely to outline a trend, to accentuate the contrast between a dawning set of concerns and those of the immediate past. Consider for example Gayatri Chakravorty Spivak's much cited essay "Can the Subaltern Speak?"[6] an article that helped set the stakes for a whole field of critical race theory, particularly in the area of postcolonialism. Spivak's "subaltern" refers not simply to the historically disenfranchised. Subaltern is not simply the subordinate position within any given structural relationship, such as that of Woman, Proletarian, or Gay. There is another level of remove. The subaltern is that quasi-subject structured as Other through a relationship of difference vis-à-vis imperial power. The subaltern is precisely the one who does not have a seat at the table. The one who cannot petition the powers-that-be. The one who is not—or is not yet—a wage slave for capital.

If Spivak's "Can the Subaltern Speak?" is taken to be emblematic of the critical 1980s and 1990s period of cultural politics, today the very terms of the question have changed dramatically. The question today is not so much *can* the subaltern speak, for the new global networks of technicity have solved this problem with ruthless precision, but *where* and *how* the subaltern speaks, or indeed *is forced* to speak. It is not so much a question of *can* but *does*. (And to be clear: "speech" means something entirely different under this new regime.) Not so much a politics of exclusion, as a politics of subsumption. The crucial political question is now therefore not that of the liberation of affect, as it was for our forebears in the civil rights movement, the gay liberation movement, or the women's movement, in which the elevation of new subject positions, from out of the shadows of oppression, was paramount. The crucial question now is— somehow—the reverse. Not exactly the repression of affect, but perhaps something close. Perhaps something like a politics of subtraction or a politics of disappearance. Perhaps the true digital politics of race, then, would require us to *leave it be*. Before defining it explicitly, we can say provisionally that something else is necessary, a *something* of the political. In short, Obama's body double doesn't have to be black. It can be whatever it is.

So where in the world are we?[7] To summarize the two points of socio-historical context: (1) there comes an increased cultivation of racial typing and a triumph of the decades-long quest to liberate affect, concurrent with (2) the recession of "theory," particularly identity politics and cultural studies. At first glance these two phenomena might appear unconnected. They might appear as merely contradictory effects, pushing each other apart, tied together only by historical coincidence. It is thus necessary to pose the question explicitly: Are these two forces connected? And the answer is most certainly yes.

Second Question: Why Do Games Have Races and Classes?

To pull back the curtain a bit, I turn now to cultural production and the digital infrastructure, particularly video games and the kinds of worlds they create. Game designers talk about things called races and classes. They design them and construct complex software algorithms to model them effectively. Why?

In a game, a race designates a set of representational proclivities—across both diegetic and nondiegetic representation—that are closely followed in matters of narrative, character modeling and animation, gamic elements such as weapons and resources, *mises en scène*, algorithmic personalities, styles of gameplay, AI behaviors, and so on. These types of software artifacts are then "metaphorically patched"[8] into games as coherent, contained "races."

Gamic races are often essentialist in nature, paralleling certain offline retrograde notions of naturally or physiologically determined and unchangeable human races. In a game like *World of Warcraft* race is conditioned largely by the demands of aesthetic representation of certain "ethnic" intangibles like voice, visage, and so on (the world is still waiting for an explanation of why the game's troll race speaks with a Jamaican accent), and only secondarily intersects with informatic modeling of behavior in so-called racial traits. Yet in a game like *StarCraft* race is much more algorithmically foundational.[9] In *StarCraft* one speaks of a race's "way of doing things." Or their unique combat strategies. (To be sure, we are admittedly speaking about "race" in an entirely gamic context, a context which is altogether different from but in some senses determined by offline race.) *StarCraft* is more sinister in this sense, in that it provides a much more direct mapping of race onto machinic variables, whereas *World of Warcraft* offloads almost all of this functionality to the sister concept, class, retaining race largely for the window dressing of diegetic representation.

After these software clusters are metaphorically patched into the game as distinct races, the game designers seek balance in game play by fine tuning different variables within each software cluster, reducing a value in one faction and augmenting it in an oppositional faction. The races are brought into balance. For example, if one *StarCraft* race is inordinately powerful certain racial variables may be quantitatively increased or decreased. The goal is to create a better sense of equilibrium in play. Since each software cluster is apt to be quite complex, the techniques of racial balancing generally operate in a rather roundabout way, eschewing any neat and tidy trade-off between this or that trait mirrored across two or more races. Instead, balance is achieved through the delicate art of exchanging qualitatively different values: for example, shaving *time* off one racial ability and transmutating it into a *damage* boost in another race's ability. If the simulated system involves three races, as in *StarCraft*, or an even larger number of classes as in *World of Warcraft*, the art of balance can be exceedingly difficult, ultimately measurable in certain global statistics such as win–loss percentages for each race or that intangible statistic known elusively as fun.

Certainly much more could be said here about races and classes in games, and the distinction between them, but I will offer just one more observation, that these games subscribe to a specific notion of race and class (and one not dissimilar to the offline): *race is static and universal, while class is variable and learned.* So in *World of Warcraft* racial traits do exist and have a bearing on game play, but they are unmodifiable (alas, the troll-Jamaican alliance is incorruptible), while class traits are configurable in a number of significant ways including the talent tree and the boosting of class abilities via consumables or wearables. What this means is that race is "unplayable" in any conventional sense, for all the tangible details of gamic race (voice, visage, character animation, racial abilities, etc.) are quarantined into certain hardcoded machinic behaviors, what I have elsewhere called the "diegetic machine act."[10] One cannot "play" race in *World of Warcraft*. One must accept it as such. Certainly the enterprising gamer can "play with" race via the chat channel, fan comics, and so on. But to *play* with race and to play *with* race are two entirely different things.

The worrisome conclusion is that this view on race is typically what we would call, in the offline context, racism, in that the game assigns from without certain identifiable traits to distinct classes of entities and then builds complex machineries for explaining and maintaining the natural imperviousness of it all. That the game pleads innocence by placing the narrative in a fantasy world of fantasy races (trolls, gnomes, elves) does not absolve it from foregrounding a systemic, "cybertype"[11] logic of naturalized group definition and division, as in a dream when the most important or traumatic details are paraded before the mind's eye in such flagrant obviousness that one is blind to them in their very immediacy. The "innocence" of the sublimation is in fact apropos because it illustrates the neoliberal, digirati notion that race must be liberated via an uncoupling from material detail, but also that the logic of race can never be more alive, can never be more *purely* actualized, than in a computer simulation. Apparently one must leave this world in order to actualize more fully its mechanisms of management and discipline. Let me stress, the most interesting thing to observe here is *not* that *World of Warcraft* is racist. That would be absurd. The interesting thing to observe is precisely the way in which racial

coding must always pass into fantasy before it can ever return to the real. The true is only created by way of an extended detour through falsity.

(An interesting rejoinder to address at this point is the notion that the race problem in gaming is merely a nominal one, that "race" is simply an unfortunate word choice for what is ultimately a pragmatic design requirement: games often require clusters of algorithmic representational proclivities to designate distinct players and player types. If the game designers had used a different word ["archetype," "species," "family"] would we be having this conversation? The answer lies certainly in the deployment of what Lisa Nakamura calls "menu-driven identities"—with or without reference to race—but also in the disheartening discovery that ethnic and racial coding seem always to be synonymous with mediation itself.[12] The one implies the other. With an allusion to the *Star Wars* movies, this is what one might call the "Jar Jar Binks" problem of fantasy representation: the more one seems to extricate oneself from the mire of terrestrial stereotyping, the more free and flexible the bigotry machine becomes, able to repopulate one's racialized imagination with "aliens," but aliens that conveniently still stick to the gangly comic relief of the blackface minstrel complete with exaggerated facial features and a Jamaican accent [Jar Jar Binks borrows the voice, but not the body, of black actor Ahmed Best]. Similar scenarios occur in any number of other digital animations, as in the 2001 animated feature *Shrek* where Eddie Murphy quite literally plays the ass. Apparently computers are much better at this than we ever could have imagined. In this sense, I would suggest that the contemporary format of animation, both cinematic and gamic, is one of the most important sites today where racial coding is worked out in mass culture. Until this issue is addressed, the "race" problematic in gaming will be alive and well, no matter what name it goes by.[13])

Third Question: Who Is the Chinese Gold Farmer?

But what of the market system in general, where does it appear? Most all games are markets of some form or another. Markets are places where the standardized exchange of qualitatively different entities takes place in a naturalized, unfettered fashion. One might make the claim that real-time strategy (RTS) games—races and all—are essentially simulations of markets. To be sure this is entirely different from the claim, issuing from certain economists, that games like *Everquest* or *World of Warcraft* are markets due to the circulation of virtual gold within them.[14] Rather, this is the claim that RTS games (a genre shared not by *World of Warcraft* but by its predecessor *Warcraft III* as well as *StarCraft*) are markets because the algorithms of game play themselves are structured around an economy of resources and productive capabilities. Resources circulate, objects and agents are produced, destroyed and replenished, all without the exchange of "gold" or the existence of virtual "marketplaces" in any proper sense. The market analogy is significant because

it highlights the problem of how to "control" that which is uncontrollable, or how to shift from top-down control to organic, bottom-up control.

A common way of addressing the question of markets in games is through the so-called problem of the Chinese gold farmer. Somewhere off in another land, beyond the sea—the story goes—there are legions of Chinese gamers, working in near sweat-shop conditions, playing games to earn real cash for virtual objects. I do not wish to dispute this on purely empirical grounds. Of course such rooms exist, here, there and elsewhere. But of much greater importance, it seems, is the ideological work being performed by the tableau itself: "the problem of the Chinese gold farmer." A certain amount of ideological demystification is in order, if not to shrug off the xenophobia latent in such a formulation, then to invert the terms entirely.

What if something else is really happening? What if the "problem of the Chinese gold farmer" is really a decoy for what is actually going on? In order to tackle the problem directly, I offer the first of two affirmations: *(1) We are the gold farmers.* (And by "we" I mean the gamers and users of the developed and undeveloped worlds alike, the unified mass of whites and nonwhites alike.)

What does this mean, that *we are the gold farmers*? It means that in the age of postfordist capitalism it is impossible to differentiate cleanly between play and work. It is impossible to differentiate cleanly between nonproductive leisure activity existing within the sphere of play and productive activity existing within the sphere of the workplace. This should be understood in both a general and a specific sense. In general, postfordist workspaces are those that have ballooned outward into daily life to such a high degree that labor is performed via phone in the car, on email walking down the street, or at home after putting the children to bed; and also crosscutting this outward expansion is an internal collapse of the workspace itself, as the "bored at work" classes invent new ways to slack off on the job, surfing the web, and otherwise circumventing the necessities of workplace always-on performance. But also in a more specific sense, postfordism is a mode of production that makes life itself the site of valorization: that is to say, it turns seemingly normal human behavior into monetizable labor. The new consumer titans Google or Amazon are the masters in this domain. No longer is one simply a blogger, one is performing the necessary labor of knitting networks together. No longer is one simply a consumer, browsing through links on an e-commerce site, one is offloading one's tastes and proclivities into a data-mining database with each click and scroll. No longer are we simply keeping up our email correspondence with friends, but rather we are all the middle-management clerks for the creation and maintenance of codified social relationships. Each and every day, anyone plugged into a network is performing hour after hour of unpaid micro labor. And in this sense are we not gold farmers too? Why are our dreary hours spent in front of the screen any different? We troll and scroll, tagging and clicking, uploading and contributing, posting and commenting. They spider

us and mine us, extracting value from pure information. Our drudgery is rewarded from time to time, of course, with bribes of free this and free that, a free email account or a free ring tone. I do not dispute the existence of a business plan. I dispute the ideological mystification that says: we are the free while the Chinese children are in chains, our computers are a life-line and their computers are a curse. This kind of obscenity must be thrown out. We are all gold farmers. And all the more paradoxical, for we do it willingly and for no money at all.

Now a second affirmation: *(2) It's not the gold, it's the Chinese.* In order to understand further the kind of ideological force behind the so-called problem of the Chinese gold farmer, one must acknowledge that it is not the gold that is being farmed, it is the "Chinese" that is being farmed. The purely economic claim from the first affirmation must now be supplemented. As I have hinted thus far, there is a new kind of speech online, the speech of the body, the codified value it produces when it is captured, massified, and scanned by systems of monetization. The purely economic claim, then, that we all perform scads of unpaid micro labor, merely through the act of living inside the digital cradle, must be supplemented via an examination of the very quality of that act. So the hunter becomes the hunted, migrating from a situation in which we farm, to a situation in which we are being farmed. For, under postfordism, the act of life is always already an act of affective identity. A body is always "cybertyped"— that is to say, it is always tagged with a certain set of affective identity markers. It is not just simply that a body must always be speaking, a body must always be speaking-*as*. Whenever a body speaks, it always already speaks as a body codified with an affective identity (gendered, ethnically typed, and so on), determined as such by various infrastructures both of and for identity formation.

Before continuing, let me be absolutely clear on this point: I advocate not for the elimination of difference, racial or otherwise; what I am critical of is, on the one hand, when difference becomes fodder for injustice, and on the other hand, when difference is mobilized as fuel for value creation in the marketplace. The goal, then, would be to uncouple difference from both injustice and valorization, something which seems more and more possible through the figure of the "whatever," which I will take up in the final question.

With the postfordist colonization of affect and the concomitant valorization of affective difference, a body has no choice but to speak. A body speaks whether it wants to or not. This is the genius of the "page rank" algorithm used by search engines: use graph theory to valorize pure heterogeneity, show how quality is an emergent property of quantity, as Barbara Cassin has written in her book on Google.[15] We think of data mining in terms of location and extraction of nuggets of information from a sea of background noise. But this metaphor is entirely wrong. Data mining is essentially a plastic art, for it responds to the sculpture of the medium itself, to the background noise itself.

It valorizes the pure shape of relationships. Not "can" but "does" the body speak? Yes, it has no choice.

Making a phone call from the slums of Cairo or Mumbai or Paris, the subaltern "speaks" into a database—just as much as I do when I pick up the phone. The difference for difference is no longer actual, it is technical. The subaltern speaks, and somewhere an algorithm listens.

Final Question: Does the Whatever Speak?

At the very moment of the digital, at the very moment of the prohibition of the negative, from out of the trenches of forced speech, of enforced behavior, of networks reinforced with apparatuses of capture and protocols for ebb and flow, here rises a new politics of disappearance. It is no longer the Hegel of history, where everything is "post-" this and "post-" that, but the Hegel of the negative, where everything is "un-" or "non-." What was once a logic of supersession is now a logic of cancellation. We seek not the posthuman, but the nonhuman. We are not post identity, but rather subtractive of it. The operative political question today, in the shadow of digital markets, is not that of confrontation on equal footing, not "what are they going to do to us?" or even "what are we going to do to them?" but rather the exodus question: first posed as "what are we going to do *without* them?" and later posed in a more sophisticated sense as "what are we going to do without *ourselves*?" Cease trying to buttress presence with new predicates, it is time now to abandon it, to leave it be. It is time now for leaving-being.

The virtual (or the new, the *next*) is not the site of emancipation. Rather, it is the primary mechanism of oppression. And so even in the face of those who seek alternatives to this world of debasement and exploitation, one must stress that it is not the job of politics to invent a new world. On the contrary, it is the job of politics to make all these new worlds irrelevant. No politics can ever be derived from a theory of the new. The reason is simple: we have never known any form of modernity except that form of modernity subservient to the new. We have never known any form of modernity except that of market accumulation, increased profit margins, development of the productive forces, rises in productivity, new jingles, the latest fads, and on and on. These are the currency of the realm. We must subtract from this world, not add to it. Our challenge is not one of political or moral imagination, for this problem was solved ages ago—kill the despots, surpass capitalism, inclusion of the excluded, equality for all of humanity, end exploitation. And here I diverge from the progressive theorization of utopia by Fredric Jameson and others. We don't need new ideas. Our challenge is simply to realize what we already know to be true.

That silly slogan of the left, "another world is possible," should be scrapped. Another world is not possible. The political is that thing that cannot happen. It cannot be produced and it cannot take place. But why? Because "production"

and "taking place" are the domain of anti-political forces. The political does not arise from the domain of production, nor does it exist in any place or situation. Another vocabulary is required. So like the Deleuzians one might speak of political becoming in terms of the virtual, or like the Badiousians one might speak of the political in terms of the event.

The "me" today is the *whatever*. Recall Buck-Morss's concept of a "singular" truth reached via "radical neutrality." This was our first hint as to the meaning of this elusive concept. But what exactly is the whatever? It is now time to answer the question more fully.

The concept of the whatever comes from the writing of a number of different authors, all working roughly in the terrain of continental philosophy and political theory. While the concept has roots in the scholastics and can be found in thinkers as divergent as Pierce, Levinas, and Lyotard, the whatever gained traction in the current discourse largely because of Deleuze and then later via more sustained considerations by Agamben. Deleuze uses the concept of the "whatever" and the "any-space-whatever" in his *Cinema* books, and deploys related terminology in other texts, such as the "something" (*aliquid*) and the "neutral" in *Logic of Sense*, and "haecceity" (the Latinate term borrowed from Duns Scotus, meaning "thisness") in *A Thousand Plateaus*. In *The Coming Community* Agamben explains his use of the term in greater detail: "The Whatever in question here relates to singularity not in its indifference with respect to a common property (to a concept, for example: being red, being French, being Muslim), but only in its being *such as it is*."[16] And later:

> Whatever is the figure of pure singularity. Whatever singularity has no identity, it is not determinate with respect to a concept, but neither is it simply indeterminate; rather it is determined only through its relation to an *idea*, that is, to the totality of its possibilities.[17]

The whatever follows a logic of belonging (*x* such that it belongs to *y*), not a logic of predication (*x* is identified as *y*, or more simply, *x* is *y*).

The trick of the whatever is thus to abstain from the assignation of traits, to abstain from the system of biopolitical predication, to abstain from the bagging and tagging of bodies. This does not mean that all bodies are now blank. Quite the opposite. All bodies are full. But their fullness is a generic fullness, a fullness of whatsoever they are.[18]

It might be helpful to oppose the whatever to two kinds of subjects with which it is often confused. The first is the postfordist economic subject. It would be a mistake to think that the whatever is merely the fully unique, customized, qualitatively special postfordist consumer—what Tiqqun calls the "Bloom," the subject for whom everything is tailored and targeted.[19] For each affective predilection of the postfordist economic subject there is a corresponding marketplace that will satisfy it. And here we might list, with sour cynicism, the Pyrrhic victories of identity politics: each woman a woman consumer, each black a black consumer, each gay a gay consumer, each chicano a chicano consumer. For in our delivery from oppression, were we not also delivered to a new site of consumption? This was precisely the point I tried to make above about the Chinese gold farmer: every economic transaction today is also an affective transaction (which is to say a transaction that will likely deal with aspects such as, but not limited to, racial identity).

Second is the liberal political subject. It would also be a mistake to think that the whatever is akin to something like the "original position" and "veil of ignorance" described by John Rawls in his theory of justice, but evident as well in other forms across a number of different liberal social theories. The veil-of-ignorance subject must hold in suspension its gender, its ethnicity, its religious affiliation, its class position, etc. In the digital context it is often summed up by the slogan "on the Internet nobody knows your identity." (This position was famously parodied by one magazine as "on the Internet nobody knows you're a dog.") The Rawlsian liberal fantasy is thus that of the transcendental subject par excellence, the subject who is able to step out of his skin, suspending social relations in order to observe them from a position of supposed neutrality. (The dilemma with Rawls is that some models of social relations are *not* suspended, specifically those borrowed from liberal political economy and game theory: respect for individual liberty, the maximization of advantage, rational choice, and so on. So again we have the demon of simulation, which only ever appears neutral when it is *least* neutral.) Given this characterization of the liberal political subject it would be a mistake to think that it has much at all in common with the whatever.

Remember that, after the old enemy of transcendental essentialism, racial justice has a new enemy, transient anti-essentialism. Recall the conceit of white privilege: to cast off the fetters of race and retreat to the original position behind a veil of ignorance (as in Rawls). Such a theory reveals not only the ignorance of the veil, but also the ignorance of the position, for it is only certain select bodies, certain select subjects, who are free to cast off their earthly fetters and go blank, like a white sheet of paper. What of those bodies of color for whom this is not an option? Or what about those who simply have no desire to abandon themselves, to abandon their culture, to abandon their history— for whom would this be justice? What even of those bona fide whatever bodies who nevertheless are constructed and viewed as such from the perspective of the dominant? Did they bring it upon themselves? Do they wish it to be so? We know already that such subaltern positions exist entirely within normative discursive structures.

The rebuttal from the whatever is: yes, the old system of transcendental essentialism is still our enemy, we do not want to return to a politics of essential purity in which only certain subjects are dominant and all others are consigned to alterity; but at the same time, the new system of transient anti-essentialism is our enemy too, for we also reject the new customized micropolitics of identity management, in which each human soul is captured and reproduced as an autonomous individual bearing affects and identities. The whatever rejects the symbolic violence of Facebook just as much as it rejects the real violence of Jim Crow. The whatever rejects the farming of "Chinese" just as much as the farming of gold.

In short what we have today is universality without collectivity. The whatever is an attempt to work through this dilemma, not by eliminating universality, but by showing how collectivity is the natural outcome of the generic, how the common is only achieved by those who have nothing in common.

So I underline that the whatever should be read *not* as simply a new spin on the same old white liberal hobbyhorse: for all the world's people to appear in our image, for us all to join in a chorus of "we are the world." No, as George Yúdice wrote, we are *not* the world. The world does not appear in our image. By contrast, the whatever is an attempt to avoid the trap of affect—that is to say, the trap of the "image" of the identity-bound individual. It is an attempt to avoid the trap of racialized universalism. The sooner we realize these things, the sooner we can return to what we are, *whatever* that may be.[20]

Again let me be absolutely clear: the whatever does not eliminate difference. The whatever is a synonym neither for the universal, nor for the transcendental, the white, the blank, the empty, or the whole. The whatever begins when the system of predication ends.

To be sure, the whatever is not a panacea. It is not a heroic subject position. The whatever is not a gateway to a utopia. This is not a new kind of Maoism, a call to go forth and disentangle oneself from ideology and privilege, to live among the peasant classes, those who have no qualities except their own authentic history. The whatever is merely a practical suggestion, an ethos. Demilitarize being. Stand down. Cease participating in the system of subjective predication. Stop trying to liberate your desire. Forget 1968. Don't "let it be," *leave* it be.

So we ask again finally, was the subaltern able to speak? No, not exactly. What of today's digital class? It has no choice but to speak, continuously and involuntarily.

And the whatever? The whatever fields no questions and leaves very little to say. Let's try to keep it that way.

Notes

1 Nancy Fraser charts this historical shift with great facility and insight in her article "Feminism, Capitalism and the Cunning of History," *New Left Review* 56 (March–April 2009): 97–117.
2 Michael Hardt and Antonio Negri, *Empire* (Cambridge: Harvard University Press, 2000), 137–138, emphasis added.
3 Slavoj Žižek, *In Defense of Lost Causes* (New York: Verso, 2008).
4 Susan Buck-Morss, *Hegel, Haiti, and Universal History* (Pittsburgh: University of Pittsburgh Press, 2009), 138–139, 149, 150.
5 Quentin Meillassoux, *After Finitude: An Essay on the Necessity of Contingency*, trans. Ray Brassier (London: Continuum, 2008), 128.

6 Gayatri Chakravorty Spivak, "Can the Subaltern Speak?" in Cary Nelson and Lawrence Grossberg, eds, *Marxism and the Interpretation of Culture* (Urbana, IL: University of Illinois Press, 1988), 271–313.

7 With the essay well underway I may now reference the source of this quotation, Cicero's famous lament from the *Catiline Orations* where with much pomp and flourish he decries the abominations besetting the city: *O di immortales, ubinam gentium sumus? Quam rem publicam habemus? In qua urbe vivimus?* ("Oh immortal gods, where in the world are we? What kind of commonwealth do we have? In what sort of city do we live?") Or perhaps for our purposes today a slightly more literal translation of *gentium* is appropriate: "Where are we among all the races?" Are we barbarians? Do you think this is *China*?

8 "Metaphorically patched artifacts [are] technological narrative elements that are brought to fit into the diegesis by the deployment of a metaphor." See Eddo Stern, "A Touch of Medieval: Narrative, Magic and Computer Technology in Massively Multiplayer Computer Role-Playing Games," available at www.c-level.cc/~eddo/Stern_TOME.html; reprinted in Frans Mayra, ed., *Computer Games and Digital Cultures Conference Proceedings* (Tampere, Finland: Tampere University Press, 2002).

9 The *StarCraft* universe contains two playable races in addition to the Zerg: Terran, a human colonizing force with Marines, tanks, and the like; and Protoss, a cybernetic race steeped in arcane psionics.

10 A diegetic machine act is an action performed by the game within the world of the story. For more on this concept see the chapter "Gamic Action, Four Moments" in my *Gaming: Essays on Algorithmic Culture* (Minneapolis: University of Minnesota Press, 2006).

11 See Lisa Nakamura, *Cybertypes: Race, Ethnicity, Identity on the Internet* (New York: Routledge, 2002).

12 Ibid., 101–135.

13 I thank David Parisi for raising the problem of nominalism in this context.

14 See in particular Edward Castronova, *Synthetic Worlds: The Business and Culture of Online Games* (Chicago: University of Chicago Press, 2005). A precursor to *World of Warcraft*, *Everquest* is a massively multiplayer online role-playing game released in 1999 by Sony Online Entertainment.

15 See Barbara Cassin, *Google-moi: La deuxième mission de l'Amérique* (Paris: Albin Michel, 2007), 100, 102.

16 Giorgio Agamben, *The Coming Community*, trans. Michael Hardt (Minneapolis: University of Minnesota Press, 1993), 1. Agamben is relying here on the Latin word *quodlibet*; the Italian cognate is *qualunque*, the French *quelconque*. Agamben suggests that the root *libet* indicates that the whatever being has a relationship to desire, yet it carries a slightly softer connotation than that, as *libet* signifies not so much full-fledged desire (a word so loaded with meaning these days) as the fact of being pleased by something or finding something agreeable. Thus one should not see the whatever as a code word for desire in the strongest sense, particularly not in the way that desire was picked up by poststructuralism. *Quodlibet* is literally: "what you please"; or more loosely, "whatever you want."

17 Agamben, *The Coming Community*, 67.

18 Agamben says that the whatever is neither particular nor general, neither individual nor "generic." Yet it is important to point out that Badiou uses the term "generic" too, and when he does he means something very similar to the whatever. So a superficial false-friend incompatibility should not deter us from making a connection between the two terms. See Alain Badiou, *Being and Event*, trans. Oliver Feltham (New York: Continuum, 2005), and also Nina Power's essay "What is Generic Humanity? Badiou and Feuerbach," *Subject Matters* 2.1 (2005): 35–46, in which she follows an interesting path back to Marx and Feuerbach's *Gattungswesen*, man's "generic nature," or as it is more commonly rendered in English, his "species-being."

19 See in particular Tiqqun, *Theorie du Bloom* (Paris: La Fabrique, 2004). The Tiqqun group also deploy the concept of the whatever in their writing.

20 Here I diverge—if perhaps not substantively then in a few points of emphasis—from the critique of Agamben and Mark Hansen in the excellent paper by Jennifer González titled "Surface: Slippery Ethics and the Face" given at the "Visual and Cultural Studies: The Next 20 Years" conference at the University of Rochester on October 2, 2009, and published in alternate form as "The Face and the Public: Race, Secrecy, and Digital Art Practice," *Camera Obscura* 70.24(1) (2009): 37–65. In my reading of Agamben, the whatever is not a universally same

subject, as González's critique of Agamben and Hansen would imply. The whatever is the subject of unassigned difference, not sameness. The whatever is never the same, it never transcends what it is, it always disidentifies itself into the generic. Again, this is a far cry from both the blank, universal sameness of the transcendental ego on the one hand (the Cartesian, Kantian, Rawlsian variant), and the infinitely customizable granular individuality of the postfordist "dividual" on the other (the cybernetic, behaviorist, game-theoretical, protocological variant).

6
Matrix Multiplication and the Digital Divide

OSCAR H. GANDY, JR

University of Pennsylvania

Introduction

In *The Matrix*, Neo struggles to maintain his grasp on the distinctions between what is real, and what is a well-constructed illusion. Surveillance theorists have also struggled to define the differences between our representations and our true identities. While there has been much debate, there has also been some convergence of opinion with regard to critical distinctions between online and offline behavior and experience. However, there continues to be considerable disagreement about the extent to which representation within the matrix shapes the nature of our existence within "the real world."

In the movie, Neo comes to understand that death within the matrix can mean death in the material world. Some of us also believe that injury within the shadow world of credit scores and customer relationship management will certainly be experienced as harm in the world of consumer capitalism. This chapter is an attempt to illustrate some of the ways in which computer analyses of transaction-generated information (TGI) that often involve sophisticated techniques based on matrix multiplication and linear algebra help to determine the quality of life that many of us get to enjoy. Although the emphasis is on the ways in which these matrices affect peoples of color, no one really escapes their reach.

Matrix multiplication is just one of the statistical resources used in the identification, classification and evaluation of individuals on the basis of the populations or groups to which they have been assigned through analysis. Of course, the relevant matrix here is the one generated after a series of operations uncover and then define a complex set of relationships between variables that appear to be stable across a large number of individuals. Indeed, the goal driving the analysis is the development of an optimal number of "groups" or categories that are characterized by a high degree of similarity within each group, and to the greatest extent possible, the least similarity, or overlap between those groups.

More sophisticated techniques seek to go beyond differentiation to the identification of likely customers with maximum lifetime value to the firm

(Novak *et al.* 1992). Other users "invert" these matrices in order to identify groups and individuals that represent the most substantial risks. Although government agencies are active users of these technologies, their activities represent a declining fraction of a rapidly expanding market.

The assignment of individuals to groups is known by a variety of names, but whatever the name, the primary function is to improve the reliability, efficiency, and effectiveness of the discriminatory choices that are made on the basis of what are often invidious distinctions among people. As Charles Raab suggests (2009: 237), it is important for us to examine the ways "in which identity is established and inscribed in information systems that relate to decisions and judgments that are made concerning citizens or customers."

It is also important to understand this process within the theoretical space being shaped within the sphere of contemporary surveillance studies (Gandy 2010; Lyon 2006). Surveillance is a twin-edged sword. It facilitates the individualization of each person it encounters as it moves forward through a complex web of interactions. On its backswing, it compares the data gathered from these individuals against others within this, or some other database. This comparative assessment is part of a process of norm generation. Individuals are characterized in relation to as many norms as are deemed relevant to the theoretical and statistical generation of groups within a particular analytical model. What we are just beginning to understand is that "surveillance produces both discipline (that is conformity to the norm), and the disciplines (related fields of knowledge and expertise) . . . It renders us visible—it identifies us— in relation to the norms it produces" (Phillips 2009: 308). This process of identification, classification and evaluation helps to generate and reinforce patterns of inequality (Bailey 2008), and this chapter is committed to expanding on the work that has already been done in this regard.

It begins with a brief introduction to the means by which the identification, classification, and assessment of individuals is being accomplished—increasingly by autonomous expert and decision support systems (Gandy 2010). After characterizing the primary use of this discriminatory technology in terms of its use as an aid to consumer segmentation, a brief discussion invites consideration of the distinction between the kinds of authentic segmentation that might facilitate organization for social or political ends, and the corrupt segmentation that is optimized for economic exploitation. Social Networking Sites (SNS), especially those targeted at minority populations, are seen to exhibit especially troublesome signs of corruption.

A consideration of the role of trust, as the aspect of a relationship between an agent and its clients that moderates our concerns about the misuse of our transaction-generated information (TGI), leads to some critically important questions that need to be raised about our reliance on Google, and other dominant providers of search. After an examination of some of the roles that corrupt segmentation plays with regard to the cumulative disadvantage that

African Americans and other poor peoples of color tend to bear (Gandy 2009), the chapter concludes with some reflection on the sociotechnical alternatives we may wish to pursue.

The Technology of Identification and Classification

As Charles Raab (2009: 233) notes, in a world such as ours, one that is "perceived to be unsafe," many believe that it is important to "establish the 'truth' of someone's identity." This means, of course, that in general "persons cannot be trusted to give an unquestioned account of who they are." This emerging environment of distrust means that transaction systems, especially those dependent upon third-party payments, are especially concerned about having access to the most reliable means of identification. Because the interest in identification goes well beyond the determination of "who you are," to a determination of "what you are," the amount of information required to achieve confidence continues to expand. Ironically, much of that information is generated by the same transaction management systems that are demanding reliable identification in the first place.

A family of techniques generally referred to as data mining transforms this transaction-generated information (TGI) into meaningful intelligence (Gandy 2003a; Millar 2009). Data mining's special value is its ability to derive knowledge from the patterns and relationships in data that would be invisible without the aid of software designed to become more accurate through use. The demand for improvements in this technology expanded quite dramatically in the wake of the terrorist attack on September 11, 2001 (Gandy 2003a). The subsequent application of these techniques to other management concerns within business and government bureaucracies has contributed to a literal explosion in the development and spread of the technology (Millar 2009). Our emphasis here will be on the uses of the technology as an aid to market segmentation and targeting.

As Adam Arvidsson (2006: 60–61) notes, a fairly recent transformation in the nature of market research involved the decoupling of distinct consumer cultures from particular class positions. Beyond claiming a rupture in traditional Marxist or materialist notions regarding the origins of class-consciousness, this emerging view "meant that consumers were no longer depicted as structured according to some over-riding principle." This observation may have important implications for the role that racial identification plays in the construction of market segments. For most people, their personal identity includes their racial or ethnic group. However, the salience of racial identity tends to be higher for African Americans and other people of color than it is for whites (Cornell and Hartmann 2007), and this fact determines the role that racial identification plays in the marketing matrix.

To the extent that market research has shifted its attention from individuals whose needs and preferences could be assumed on the basis of their social "situation," to the "gathering of a large variety of variables linked not so much to particular individuals as to particular meanings or practices—purchasing patterns, values, media consumption, and so on" (Arvidsson 2006: 64), new means of identification have had to be developed (Mobasher 2007).

Data mining facilitates the identification of individuals as members of "groups" on the basis of the similarity of their "profiles." These profiles can be quite complex given the fact that various targets of interest can be differentiated along multiple dimensions. The challenge for analysts is to identify a set of features, or "signatures" of membership within a particular segment or group. Simple demographic classification no longer fills the need for accuracy and precision. Additional requirements emerge when the identification, classification and evaluation of individuals is focused on the rapidly changing media environment.

Measuring the audience and assessing its value

Fernando Bermejo (2007) provides considerable detail regarding what he describes as the active and passive forms of audience or user identification and measurement that have been developed specifically for the internet. Passive methods refer primarily to the information that is derived from the interactions between computers. He emphasizes data generated by an analysis of web server log files, advertisement server log files, and the log files that are generated by electronic "tags" that can be read by web browsers (Bermejo 2007: 119–139). Server log files can capture a substantial amount of information about these computer-to-computer interactions. Some of this TGI might be characterized as personally identifiable information (PII) even though it may not include the user's name or email address.

Bermejo (2007) identifies a number of attributes of this TGI that limit its utility as an accurate assessment of the size and character of the "audience" for internet content. His concerns about the inability of most server log files to identify a unique individual indexically (Phillips 2004), or in ways that allow some interested party to "reach out and touch" someone in particular, seem likely to be overcome in the near future.

Surveillance scholars and privacy activists are especially concerned about the probability that popular web resources, including online social networks, are facilitating the association of personal information with TGI. Earlier assumptions regarding the extent to which identification was limited to the user's computer/browser have been challenged by a series of studies by Krishnamurthy and Wills (2009). They conclude that the use of tracking cookies by third-party aggregators, like DoubleClick, is the primary means by which the leakage of PII takes place.

Arvind Narayanan and Vitaly Shmatikov (2009) describe the remarkable success with which members of popular social networking sites (SNS), in this case Flickr and Twitter, could be reliably identified despite the claims that the

Twitter graphs had been "anonymized." Their high success rate (88 percent) was accomplished in part through the use of widely available auxiliary information. The authors were especially critical of the extent to which information about SNS group members is shared with third parties, a group that includes advertisers as well as the growing number of application providers. Even greater concern was expressed about the emergence of a number of information "aggregators" that capture and combine accessible information about SNS group members.

As many critical observers have noted "Since many sites are commercial enterprises that have a business model based on harvesting personal information for marketing purposes, many users' half cogitated belief that what happens on these sites stays on these sites is, to put it mildly, naïve" (Mooradian 2009: 6). Of particular interest and concern is the extent to which the information being leaked to these aggregators includes identification of the SSN members' "friends and associates."

Obviously, the identification, classification and evaluative assessment of individuals are not accomplished solely through approaches based on data mining. The supply of alternative technologies to the market for applied statistical analysis appears to be expanding at an incredible rate. One source for insights about the kinds of technological advances that are likely to appear on the horizon are the patents that are being applied for in the area of personalized search, automated text analysis, and ad selection and pricing.

Because market researchers have determined that some "6 percent of the online population accounts for 50 percent of all clicks" and, even more troublesome, these "heavy clickers" are not the most desirable responders because they tend to be among the poorer households (Fulgoni and Mörn 2009: 134), there is a powerful incentive for web marketing to become more precise and selective. A recent patent application promised to deliver a system and method where web publishers and advertisers can continually "optimize ad cost and placement to yield the best possible result for all parties involved, and to provide for the seamless delivery of advertisements inline with a publisher's main web page content" (Powell *et al.* 2009).

Emphasizing the special character "Cost-per Click-Through" (CPC) versus "Cost-per-Mile" or cost-per-impression forms of pricing common to the print advertising, this system promised to enhance the ability of advertisers to benefit from value-driven bidding as a way of determining the prices they would pay per click. This bidding is clearly governed by the degree to which they are able to "target their ads to a specific audience" and to accomplish this through a process that allows them to "seamlessly serve the advertisement with the content."

What is important to keep in mind is that, with this kind of technology, advertisers would be able to routinely adjust their bids, and ultimately their financial support for web publishers that provide them with access to just the "right" audience. As the inventors put it, if statistics show that user traffic coming from one web site is twice as likely to make a purchase as compared to visitors coming from other web sites, the advertiser can raise their cost per click on the more profitable site and lower their bid on the others ... [thereby] maximizing the profitability of their advertising campaign. (Powell *et al.* 2009)

We should expect that this and similar inventions will find a ready market among marketers seeking to maximize the impact of their online budgets by minimizing their exposure to less desirable consumers, however they might define themselves.

Authentic vs. Corrupt Segmentation

It has to be recognized that not all efforts at segmentation and targeting are associated with commercial exploitation, marketplace discrimination and cumulative disadvantage (Gandy 2009). There is an important role for social and political organization on the basis of common experiences, needs and interests, and this kind of mobilization generally involves segmentation. Michael Dawson (1994) has examined this rationale in considerable detail with regard to the sense of "linked fate" that exists among African Americans. Anita Allen (2003) has examined it more broadly with regard to the role that "accountability" plays in shaping an individual's relationship to her identity group. But there is no escaping the fact that our relationships with our various identity groups are being transformed and challenged as a function of the enlarged role that market actors and government agencies have come to play (Gandy 2007).

C. Edwin Baker (2002) explores the distinctions between republican democracy and liberal pluralism with regard to the role that diversity and segmentation are thought to play within different idealized forms of a democratic public sphere. He introduces the notion of "corrupted diversity," where the distinctions that are drawn are arguably inauthentic because they do not reflect the genuine interests or identities of individuals within a given segment.

It should be clear that racial classification is not the same as racial identification. The fact that racial identity varies, and its strength explains the kinds of social, economic and political choices that we make, is reflected in the role that it plays in a revealed preference for racially targeted internet sites. Osei Appiah (2004) observed that blacks with "weak ethnic identities" did not differ in the amount of time they spent browsing black- or white-targeted sites, or in their evaluations of the sites or the stories they contained. His findings suggest that racial identification would be more useful than racial classification as a basis for segmenting consumers.

Arguably, authentic segmentation based on racial identification would involve a high degree of reflective awareness of the existence, history, and nature of an individual's identity or reference group. Many of the groups to which individuals are assigned by relationship management software and other resources used by marketers would undoubtedly not be recognizable to their members. In some cases, as with the labeling of geodemographic market clusters, discovery of the names or labels that have been assigned to the "communities" with which individuals have been associated has stimulated a widespread expression of outrage (Gandy 2007, 2010).

In Baker's words, corruption "occurs when segmentation reflects the steering mechanisms of bureaucratic power or money rather than the group's needs and values" (Baker 2002: 180). Thus, under conditions of corruption, decisions about what kinds of communications vehicles and content will be supplied to audience segments defined by race, class, or gender, will be determined primarily with regard to profit potential, rather than on the basis of the scale and intensity of identifiable needs. So, as Baker suggests "Market-determined segmentation predictably disfavors, for example, media focusing on political ideology, non-market valued ethnic and cultural divisions, economically poorer groups, or any life-style needs and interests not easily exploited for marketing purposes" (Baker 2002: 184). Even the exploitation of communities defined by sexual orientation reflects the same kinds of corrupting influence (Campbell 2005).

On the other hand, authentic segmentation within the public sphere has been associated with enhanced levels of political participation. For example, Joel Waldfogel (2007) has provided evidence to suggest that people are more likely to vote if they have their "own" targeted media. The same patterns are observed with regard to the availability of local, rather than nationally oriented media.

Whether the election of an African American as the President of the United States in 2008 marked the nation's transition into a post-racial society is a question that has yet to be answered. It is clear, however, that there is an opening for public questioning of the necessity or appropriateness of segmentation by race. The recent introduction of a black-targeted web browser, Blackbird, generated an active debate within the blogosphere about whether the development of such a targeted resource was actually a racist act (Benton 2008; Forte 2008). There was also some pointed criticism of this enterprise as an exercise in target marketing, rather than actually being a resource for "building online communities and bringing Black people together" (The Angry Black Woman 2008).

Social Networks and their Vulnerable Members

Some researchers have explored the extent to which social networking sites (SNS) actually serve what Baker (2002), Dawson (1994), and Waldfogel (2007) might see as legitimate community interests. Dara Byrne (2007) has provided an analysis of discourse on BlackPlanet, in part because it is one of the oldest and largest SNS providing specialized content to a population group thought to be underserved by mainstream portals and search engines. Byrne sought to compare this black-targeted SNS to offline social clubs and organizations that

"have promoted networking as a means to strengthen black identity, providing forums for civic engagement and for facilitating social action" (Byrne 2007: 6). In framing her analysis, Byrne notes (2007: 7) that BlackPlanet is black-targeted but not a black-owned enterprise. It is one of a number of sites dedicated to youthful sub-cultural markets defined by race, ethnicity, and sexual orientation that are owned by Community Connect, Inc.

Because she was concerned about the extent to which this SNS helped to cultivate a politically active black identity, Byrne focused her analysis on the discussions within a subset of the popular forums on BlackPlanet and noted the extent to which they addressed ten issues of common concern to African Americans. Not surprisingly, given the youthful focus of the site as a whole, most of the threads she examined were focused on "relationships," while "current events" accounted for less than 5 percent of the threads. "Heritage and Identity" did account for 9 percent of the threads and around 12 percent of the responses (Byrne 2007: 13–14). Overall, Byrne's analysis of the discussions within these threads led her to characterize the level of civic engagement on the site as "limited." In fact, there was a generalized tendency for the participants in many of these forums to be dismissive of calls for specific forms of social or political action. And, as might be expected, those threads that were actually focused on strategic political actions like boycotts had the lowest levels of participation (Byrne 2007: 20).

As Christian Fuchs observes (2009: 84), "social networking has an ideological character: its networking advances capitalist individualization, accumulation and legitimization. An alternative would be platforms that allow group profiles, joint profile creation, group blogging, and that are explicitly oriented towards collective political and social goals."

It is not that political groups, or political activity, are in some way banned, or officially discouraged within cyberspace. The availability of such groups does reflect, to some extent, the interaction of supply and demand. Back in 2001, when the commercial character of cyberspace was just beginning to emerge, the most popular kinds of sites were those designed to meet the needs of trade associations and professional groups, or people who shared interests in a hobby, or in popular culture pursuits. Even then, political groups were being visited by less than 25 percent of the population (Chadwick 2006: 97).

The kinds of groups that Fuchs prefers already exist, but they fail to capture the kinds of participants that marketers feel a need to reach at a price that covers the costs of their attraction. The development, and sustainable operation of such networks remains desirable and imaginable, even if not a particularly likely development in the current sociopolitical environment.

Agents: Trusted and Otherwise

Again, let's be clear here: most of us would be pleased to have a "trusted agent" that knows us well, and responds with minimal error to our requests for

information. We would want to be confident, however, that this agent is never conflicted: not torn between meeting our needs as it understands them, and meeting the needs of some other client (or controller).

Infomediaries

John Campbell and Matt Carlson (2002) described the role of "internet ad servers and infomediaries" like DoubleClick in shaping the development of online commerce with their ability to identify, characterize, and assess the profit potential of consumers in cyberspace. It is their description of the business model for infomediaries exemplified by Lumeria that influences our thinking about the role of the trusted agent.

Where internet ad servers capture TGI for the purposes of classification, and often do so without the knowledge or consent of data subjects, infomediaries build extensive profiles on the basis of information supplied voluntarily by their clients. The assumption in this relationship is that personal information is a commodity that can be packaged and sold, and that data subjects will receive something of value in exchange. At least, that was the idea as initially promoted by Hagel and Singer (1999).

In their view, each consumer would have her own "agent," an information intermediary who would negotiate the sale, or rental of consumer attention to marketers seeking to offer products and services. The same agents might be compensated for providing their clients with the best deals when they are actually in the market for something specific.

Most of us are probably familiar with the kind of infomediary that assists online shoppers with price comparisons, and with the mechanics of completing a transaction. The assumption is that the "agent" has no financial interest in the outcome of the transaction beyond the satisfaction of the desire of the consumer to find the best quality at the best price under the most favorable conditions of exchange (Palvia and D'Aubeterre 2007). This assumption is a necessary, if occasionally unwarranted, expression of trust that the agent or infomediary does not make use of asymmetries in information to the disadvantage of the consumer.

The importance of trust between the agent and the consumer is recognized by Hagel and Singer (1999), but they are remarkably silent about the ways in which that trust might be abused beyond the failure to provide security for their client's PII. The extent to which infomediaries might participate in the delivery of their client's information in support of adverse price discrimination is barely considered. Other ways in which a conflicted agent might limit a client's access to opportunity were apparently not matters of substantial concern.

It seems likely that infomediaries associated with the portals or SNS that are used primarily or exclusively by members of minority groups who are more likely to be younger, less wealthy, and less sophisticated about the nature of the markets they are entering, are more likely to take advantage of their "clients."

Indeed, in an analysis of responses of more than 16,000 customers who had used an online infomediary as an aid to their recent purchase of an automobile, this is precisely what the data revealed. "Portals appear to contribute the least to consumer welfare as their users pay a higher price despite a lower product fit." This finding held even after controlling for consumer psychographics and demographics (Viswanathan *et al.* 2005: 21). This is the kind of mistreatment of the most vulnerable that contributes what is referred to as cumulative disadvantage (Gandy 2009).

Consider the relationship between the readers of consumer-oriented magazines and the publishers. In an ideal world, the magazine publishers would be acting as the agents of the consumers, providing them with the best information about price and quality. In reality, specialist magazines are also, and in some cases primarily, in the business of helping advertisers to gain access to the awareness or attention of their readers. There is no reason to expect much difference in the relationship between print and electronic media in this regard as long as the publishers depend upon income from advertising. Indeed, the fact that online publishers rely almost entirely on revenue from advertisers would lead us to expect that the interests of advertisers dominate the interests of readers in the decisions made by these publishers.

Although research designed to verify this tendency is difficult to find, it is beginning to emerge. A recent study of financial media that included both magazines and newspapers provides rather impressive evidence to support the assumptions of media critics, at least with regard to the magazines (Reuter and Zitzewitz 2006). Apparently consumers tend to follow the recommendations of the magazines they read with regard to making investments in particular mutual funds, despite the fact that these recommendations bear no relationship to the actual future performance of those funds. In addition, these magazines tended to bias the granting of favorable recommendations toward the funds that had recently purchased advertising space in their publications. These are agents that clearly should not be trusted—at least not by their readers.

Personalized search

Personalization is what you expect from a "trusted agent." There is no expectation that this agent, seeking to maximize income, including income from third parties, will act in ways that reduce your net benefit. That is, they will not discriminate in ways that do you harm. The generation and distribution of harm has been the primary concern of this chapter. It has been focused on identifying the ways in which knowing "who and what you are, and what you are interested in" may be used to "do you harm." The production and distribution of harms matter, even if each individual "harm" is no more than a fractional disadvantage such as longer waiting time, higher prices, or marginally lower quality in the resources acquired as the result of a personalized search experience.

As John Battelle (2005: 273) makes quite clear, "Google and most other consumer-facing search engines are obsessively focused on understanding user intent" despite however poorly a user query might actually convey that information. This idealized "perfect search" is most likely to emerge as the result of increasingly comprehensive "histories" of our behavior in cyberspace. That is, "by tracking not only what searches you do, but also what sites you visit, the engines of the future will be able to build a real-time profile of your interests from your past Web use."

In one sense, because of ways in which future searches will be improved on the basis of insights derived from all of your web-enabled activities, what you would actually be searching is the equivalent of "your own personal Web." Of course, improvements in the searches of any individual will depend on analyses of the searches and transactions of millions of others as well (Battelle 2005: 261–262). This "collaborative" approach depends upon the ability of the search provider to identify sets of similar users, or similar sets of information needs (Micarelli *et al.* 2007).

And, while we might recognize the value of an interactive system in which users explicitly evaluate the results of each search, it seems more likely that we would prefer search engines that would learn about our preferences with a minimal amount of effort, including reflective assessments on our part. Such an agent would provide more efficient searches, and might even anticipate our needs by making recommendations regarding media content that we are likely to find useful at some future point, given what our behavior in the past might suggest. This is certainly the kind of service that predictive data mining techniques seem likely to make economically viable for a firm like Google (Millar 2009: 112). The fact that Google depends almost entirely on revenue from advertising, however, makes it less likely that the company could actually serve as a trusted agent (Tene 2008; Zimmer 2008).

In the absence of a relationship with an uncompromised trusted agent, concerns about the ways in which the providers of personalized search manage a user's TGI begin to take on considerable weight (Andrejevic 2007a, 2007b). It is one thing to respond to questions from your physician, or other service provider because you believe that information will enable an enhanced level of service. It is quite something else to provide information as a condition of using a resource, without any assurance, or reasonable expectation, that its use will be limited to enhancing your well-being.

Still, it has become something of a commonplace, despite the surprise expressed by observers like Andrejevic (2007b: 306), who observes: "it seems to pass without any serious challenge that the content we provide to companies like Google becomes their property." It seems like it ought to be a matter of concern that the capture of this information allows marketers to either target, or bypass

specific individuals based on details about their online browsing habits, combined with the content of their e-mail messages, the shape of their time–space path throughout the course of the day, and any other details of their personal and professional lives that can be gleaned from an increasing array of overlapping digital enclosures. (Andrejevic 2007b: 313)

As we suggested, part of the problem online is that there is usually no formal agent relationship. There is no meaningful contract; there is certainly no agreement to pay. This is the kind of problem that emerges when the consumer's agent is paid by a third party—the advertiser. We hardly need to be reminded of the adage that whoever pays the piper is most likely to call the tune. Control over the collection and use of TGI increasingly defaults to the third party providers of marketing services, and the consumer of information or communications services has little if anything to say about it (Kane and Delange 2008–2009).

We do need to be reminded, however, that within commercial systems, those who pay the piper are more likely to be governed by concerns about the needs and interests of their owners and investors than they are about the needs and interests of their customers or clients. The fact that this relationship shifts further toward the owner/investors, and away from the client/consumers as a function of the size of the contribution that the client/consumer makes to the bottom line, places those disadvantaged by race and class near the bottom of the distribution of concern.

We certainly need to be reminded that those who find themselves at the bottom of the distribution of value with regard to information are likely to be even more firmly entrenched at the bottom of other distributions of resources that determine our quality of life. This is at the heart of our concerns about cumulative disadvantage.

Discrimination and Cumulative Disadvantage

Based on the observations made by Byrne (2007), and other assessments of the behavior of marketers (Gandy 2004), a general lack of interest and support for the audiences produced by politically engaged content will help to ensure that the supply of such content will be suboptimal, especially for the audiences with the greatest need for the benefits it would likely supply.

Despite the fact that young African Americans are among the more politically active members of their age cohort (Dawson 2001; Gandy 2007; Gray 2005), it is somewhat troublesome to observe that the most commercially attractive SNS seem to be the least likely to provide a welcoming environment for the development and expression of this group's political interests. They are welcome only in their roles as consumers (Luke 2002).

The impact of this commercial orientation is amplified by the oft-noted fact that when online, "African Americans, Hispanics, and Asian Americans generally participate more often in activities coded as 'fun'" (Nakamura 2004:

76). We are reminded that "the percentage of African Americans in the population who read about politics online is consistently lower than the percentage of whites" from 2000–2006 (Mossberger 2009: 176).

It is hard to explain the differential use of web resources as being determined primarily by limitations on access to either the technology or the skills needed to take advantage of the opportunities that the network represents, although it is clear that education, and the capabilities and motivations established and enhanced by educational development play a significant role in shaping the use of informational resources. It is not clear what role education plays in the development of more active political participation or engagement.

Part of the explanation may be found in the notion of cumulative disadvantage, or in its inversion, the Matthew Principle, "those that have, get more," and "those that don't do without." Waldfogel (2007) even finds in this pattern a challenge to mainstream economic assumptions about the performance of markets. His detailed analyses demonstrate that people are more likely to be able to find and afford the things that they like and need as a function of how many other people happen to like the same thing. This "tyranny of the majority" ensures that minority tastes and preferences tend not to be served in the marketplace that we experience in life, in comparison with the markets we are presented with in mainstream economic theory. As Mossberger notes (2009: 176) with young people as an important exception, "online politics largely replicates existing patterns of participation," and more critically, "prior disparities may be exacerbated online."

The systems developed for the identification, classification, and evaluative assessment of users of networked information systems are used for one fundamental purpose—the enhancement of discriminatory choices regarding whose interests are to be met and whose needs are to be set aside. These decisions are arguably rational, at least for those with the power to decide. At the same time, these decisions are based on morally suspect justifications regarding the efficiency, effectiveness, and social value of the outcomes being maximized or limited. This is the claim that I make with regard to the bulk of the decisions being made with the aid of advanced analytics (Gandy 2009).

Of particular concern is the use of informed segmentation to identify targets for predation, or the marketing of harmful products. Although there have been attempts to "blame the victims" for their role in the Great Recession that began in the housing market, the fact is that target marketing of predatory loans to minority communities was at the heart of a rapidly spreading cancer that placed the global economy at risk. The evidence seems quite compelling with regard to the targeting of low quality, high-risk products to segments of the population with lower levels of income, information, and power (Culliton 2005; Petty *et al.* 2003). The fact that these segments happen to also be composed primarily of racial and ethnic minority group members underscores the fact that disadvantage cumulates over time and space.

What Is There to be Done?

I have argued that formal restrictions should be established that would limit the use of matrix multiplication and other tools of applied statistics in support of marketplace discrimination (Gandy 2009, 2010). Many will disagree. For many, blaming the victim is the most common response to data and evidence of gross disparities in both opportunity and results in the markets for opportunity. This dismissive tendency offers little hope that critical scholars and activists will easily succeed in reframing debates about privacy and surveillance in terms of the impact of matrix manipulation on socioeconomic disparities between groups defined by race and class (Bailey 2008; Hoofnagle 2009). Corporate influence over whatever legislative initiatives we may see on the horizon also seems likely to grow in the wake of massive investments in the management of public opinion and its representation to members of Congress (Gandy 2003b).

Alas, the courtroom does not appear to be a promising path through which users of discriminatory technologies will be forced to internalize the costs or compensate the victims for the collateral damages that befall them. Class action suits hold little promise in the current era of tort reform (Rubin and Shepherd 2008). And, although there may be a nascent social movement developing within the community of surveillance scholars, we appear to be a long way from any "takeoff to growth" in this particular sphere of engagement with the law (Haggerty 2006).

Part of the problem, of course, is that the growth of social networking and other information sharing features of Web 2.0 help to reduce the importance that web users place on their privacy, and their expectations of control over personal information (Kane and Delange 2008–2009). Social networking resources reinforce the value of visibility as an index of popularity and self-worth. Youngsters are especially vulnerable to the promise of instant fame, and they seem to be largely unaware and unconcerned about the attendant long-term costs of this exposure. Indeed, in the language of those who "tweet" on Twitter, popularity means being "followed" by larger and larger groups of strangers. While sizeable majorities of youth and adult web users are actually opposed to advertisers "following" them around the internet without their permission, many remain open to the possibility that the benefits exceed the costs of this kind of visibility (Turow *et al.* 2009).

A large survey of Canadian undergraduates revealed that these students were largely unconcerned about who has access to their SNS profiles, although they did seem to share Helen Nissenbaum's view (2004) that what goes on within a social network should remain within it. Although they are aware of some of the consequences that may flow from actual and potential employers gaining access to this information, the unconcerned far outnumber the more wary or cautious users (Levin *et al.* 2008).

In addition to the vulnerabilities associated with the multiplication of detailed profiles that will be accessible through SNS, the move toward "cloud computing," or the storage of personal files on the remote computers of network service providers will only serve to weaken the control that individuals can expect to have over the information that they generate or are associated with (Kane and Delange 2008–2009). The move toward web-based television promises an even more substantial expansion of network user visibility and subsequent vulnerability to being trapped within the matrix.

Beyond this, I would add that information generated and then accumulated about individuals and the communities and the groups to which they belong will be multiplied quite dramatically as the network of networks expands in still other directions. A virtual flood of TGI will emerge as we make our ways through the built environment and its networked sensors. This flood will both enable and require continuous adjustments of the matrix that will emerge from the operation of automated AmI or ambient intelligence systems (Gandy 2010; Rouvroy 2008).

There is some slight possibility, however, that enlightened self-interest will lead marketers to understand that the public does indeed value its privacy, and that value is reflected in the price that consumers are willing to pay for commodities acquired through online vendors who can assure them that their personal information will not be shared with third parties (D'Souza and Phelps 2009).

In the meanwhile, we will have to rely on the efforts of the more technologically savvy and socially concerned scholar/activists who are willing to add to the defensive resources for individuals previously identified by Gary Marx (2003). Daniel Howe and Helen Nissenbaum (2009), for example, have developed an extension for the Firefox browser that is designed to make it more difficult for search engines and other aggregators to develop accurate user profiles. The TrackMeNot (TMN) extension sends out simulated "decoy" search requests, accompanied by additional simulated search behaviors that essentially turn the user's actual search queries into the proverbial "needles in a haystack."

The developers of TMN are quite aware of the possibility that marketers and the search engines they rely upon for sorting the seekers of goods and services are likely to invest in countermeasures, including the hammers and fences we experience as law (Gandy and Farrall 2009). Yet they declare their interventions to be political acts of the sort that constitutions are meant to protect: "TMN provides for some users a means of expression, akin to a political placard or a petition" (Howe and Nissenbaum 2009: 431).

Although I am far from being a First Amendment absolutist, I do hope that not only are they correct in their assessment, but they attract an army of open-source imitators who will help them to improve this defensive technology.

References

Allen, A. 2003. *Why Privacy Isn't Everything: Feminist Reflections on Personal Accountability.* Lanham, MD: Rowman and Littlefield.

Andrejevic, M. 2007a. *iSPY: Surveillance and Power in the Interactive Era.* Lawrence, KS: University Press of Kansas.

——. 2007b. "Surveillance in the Digital Enclosure." *The Communication Review* 10.4: 295–317.

Appiah, O. 2004. "Effects of Ethnic Identification on Web Browsers' Attitudes toward and Navigational Patterns on Race-targeted Sites." *Communication Research* 31.3: 312–337.

Arvidsson, A. 2004. "On the 'Prehistory of the Panoptic Sort': Mobility in Market Research." *Surveillance & Society* 1.4: 456–474.

——. 2006. *Brands: Meaning and Value in Media Culture.* New York: Routledge.

Bailey, J. 2008. "Towards an Equality-enhancing Conception of Privacy." *The Dalhousie Law Journal* 31: 267–309.

Baker, C.E. 2002. *Media, Markets and Democracy.* Cambridge: Cambridge University Press.

Battelle, J. 2005. *The Search: How Google and its Rivals Rewrote the Rules of Business and Transformed Our Culture.* New York: Penguin.

Benton, A. 2008. "Race and the Web: Going after Niche Markets or Practicing Digital Segmentation?" *Target Marketing News.* Available at: www.targetmarketnews.com/storyid12150801.htm

Bermejo, F. 2007. *The Internet Audience: Constitution and Measurement.* New York: Peter Lang.

Byrne, D. 2007. "Public Discourse, Community Concerns, and Civic Engagement: Exploring Black Social Networking Traditions on BlackPlanet.com." *Journal of Computer-Mediated Communication* 13.1: article 16. Available at: http://jcmc.indiana.edu/vol13/issue1/byrne.html.

Campbell, J. 2005. "Outing PlanetOut: Surveillance, Gay Marketing and Internet Affinity Portals." *New Media & Society* 7.5: 663–683.

Campbell, J. and M. Carlson. 2002. "Panopticon.com: Online Surveillance and the Commodification of Privacy." *Journal of Broadcasting and Electronic Media* 46.4: 586–606.

Chadwick, A. 2006. *Internet Politics: States, Citizens, and New Communication Technologies.* New York: Oxford University Press.

Cornell, S. and D. Hartmann. 2007. *Ethnicity and Race: Making Identities in a Changing World.* Thousand Oaks, CA: Pine Forge Press.

Culliton, K. 2005. "The Impact of Alcohol and Tobacco Advertising on the Latino Community as a Civil Rights Issue." *Berkeley La Raza Law Journal* 16 (Fall): 71–117.

Dawson, M. 1994. *Behind the Mule: Race and Class in African-American Politics.* Princeton, NJ: Princeton University Press.

——. 2001. *Black Visions: The Roots of Contemporary African-American Political Ideologies.* Chicago: University of Chicago Press.

D'Souza, G. and J.E. Phelps. 2009. "The Privacy Paradox: The Case of Secondary Disclosure." *Review of Marketing Science* 7: Article 4. Available at: www.bepress.com/romsjournal/vol7/iss1/art4

Evans, D.S. 2009. "The online advertising industry: economics, evolution, and privacy." *Journal of Economic Perspectives* 23.3: 37–60. Available at: http://ssrn.com/abstract=1376607

Forte, M. 2008. "Blackbird: Battles over a Browser." *Open Anthropology.* Available at: http://openanthropology.wordpress.com/2008/12/11/blackbird-battles-over-a-browser/

Fuchs, C. 2009. "Information and Communication Technologies and Society: A Contribution to the Critique of the Political Economy of the Internet." *European Journal of Communication* 24.1: 69–87.

Fulgoni, G. and M. Mörn. 2009. "Whither the Click? How Online Advertising Works." *Journal of Advertising Research* June: 134–142.

Gandy, O.H. 2003a. "Data Mining and Surveillance in the Post-9/11 Environment," in K. Ball and F. Webster, eds, *The Intensification of Surveillance: Crime, Terrorism and Warfare in the Information Age.* London: Pluto Press, 24–61.

——. 2003b. "Public Opinion Surveys and the Formation of Privacy Policy." *Journal of Social Issues* 59.2: 283–299.

——. 2004. "Audiences on Demand," in A. Calabrese and C. Sparks, eds, *Toward a Political Economy of Culture: Capitalism and Communication in the Twenty-First Century.* Lanham, MD: Rowman and Littlefield, 327–341.

——. 2007. "Privatization and Identity: The Formation of a Racial Class," in G. Murdock and J. Wasko, eds, *Media in the Age of Marketization.* Cresskill, NJ: Hampton Press, 109–128.

——. 2009. *Coming to Terms with Chance: Engaging Rational Discrimination and Cumulative Disadvantage.* UK: Ashgate.

——. 2010. "Engaging Rational Discrimination: Exploring Reasons for Placing Regulatory Constraints on Decision Support Systems." *Journal of Ethics and Information Technology* 12.1. Available at: http://www.springerlink.com/content/m55xm7363711361

Gandy, O.H. and K.N. Farrall. 2009. "Metaphoric Reinforcement of the Virtual Fence: Factors Shaping the Political Economy of Property in Cyberspace," in A. Chadwick and P. Howard, eds, *Routledge Handbook of Internet Politics.* New York: Routledge, 349–363.

Gray, H.S. 2005. *Cultural Moves: African-Americans and the Politics of Representation.* Berkeley, CA: University of California Press.

Hagel, J. and M. Singer. 1999. *New Worth: Shaping Markets When Customers Make the Rules.* Boston: Harvard Business School Press.

Haggerty, K.D. 2006. "Tear Down the Walls: On Demolishing the Panopticon," in D. Lyon, ed., *Theorizing Surveillance: The Panopticon and Beyond,* Portland, OR: Willan Publishing, 33–45.

Hoofnagle, C.J. 2009. "Beyond Google and Evil: How Policy Makers, Journalists and Consumers should Talk Differently about Google and Privacy." *First Monday* 14.4. Available at: http://firstmonday.org/htbin/cgiwrap/bin/ojs/index.php/fm/article/viewArticle/2326/2156.

Howe, D. and H. Nissenbaum. 2009. "TrackMeNot: Resisting Surveillance in Web Search," in I. Kerr, C. Lucock and V. Steeves, eds, *Lessons from the Identity Trail: Anonymity, Privacy and Identity in a Networked Society,* New York: Oxford University Press, 418–436.

Kane, B. and B.T. Delange. 2008–2009. "A Tale of Two Internets: Web 2.0 Slices, Dices, and is Privacy Resistant!" *Idaho Law Review* 45: 320–347.

Krishnamurthy, B. and C.E. Wills. 2009. "On the Leakage of Personally Identifiable Information via Online Social Networks." Conference paper, WOSN. Barcelona, Spain, ACM. Available at: http://conferences.sigcomm.org/sigcomm/2009/workshops/wosn/papers/p7.pdf.

Levin, A., M. Foster, B. West, M.J. Nicholson, T. Hernandez and W. Cukier. 2008. *The Next Digital Divide: Online Social Network Privacy.* Toronto: Ryerson University, Privacy and Cyber Crime Institute.

Luke, R. 2002. "habit@online: Web Portals as Purchasing Ideology." *Topia* 8 (Fall): 61–89.

Lyon, D., ed. 2006. *Theorizing Surveillance: The Panopticon and Beyond.* Portland, OR: Willan Publishing.

Marx, G. 2003. "A Tack in the Shoe: Neutralizing and Resisting the New Surveillance." *Journal of Social Issues* 59.2: 369–390.

Micarelli, A., F. Gasparetti, F. Sciarrone, and S. Gauch. 2007. "Personalized Search on the World Wide Web," in P. Brusilovsky, A. Kobsa and W. Nedjl, eds, *The Adaptive Web. Methods and Strategies of Web Personalization.* New York: Springer-Verlag: 195–230.

Millar, J. 2009. "Core Privacy: A Problem for Predictive Data Mining," in I. Kerr, C. Lucock and V. Steeves, eds, *Lessons from the Identity Trail: Anonymity, Privacy and Identity in a Networked Society.* New York: Oxford University Press, 103–119.

Mobasher, B. 2007. "Data Mining for Web Personalization," in P. Brusilovsky, A. Kobsa and W. Nedjl, eds, *The Adaptive Web. Methods and Strategies of Web Personalization.* New York: Springer-Verlag, 90–135.

Mooradian, N. 2009. "The Importance of Privacy Revisited." *Ethics and Information Technology.* Springer. Available at: DOI 10.1007/s10676-009-9201-2

Mossberger, K. 2009. "Toward Digital Citizenship: Addressing Inequality in the Information Age," in A. Chadwick and P. Howard, eds, *Routledge Handbook of Internet Politics.* New York: Routledge, 173–185.

Nakamura, L. 2004. "Interrogating the Digital Divide: The Political Economy of Race and Commerce in New Media," in P. Howard and S. Jones, eds, *Society Online: The Internet in Context.* Thousand Oaks, CA: Sage, 71–83.

Narayan, A. and V. Shmatikov. 2009. "De-anonymizing Social Networks." Paper presented at 30th IEEE Symposium on Security and Privacy. Available at: http://arxiv.org/abs/0903.327v1.

Nissenbaum, H. 2004. "Privacy as Contextual Integrity." *Washington Law Review* 79: 119–157.

Novak, T.P., J. de Leeuw, and B. MacEvoy. 1992. "Richness Curves for Evaluating Market Segmentation." *Journal of Marketing Research* 29.2: 254–267.

Palvia, P. and F. D'Auberterre. 2007. "Examination of Infomediary Roles in B2C e-Commerce." *Journal of Electronic Commerce Research* 8.4: 207–220.

Petty, R., A. Harris, T. Broaddus, and W.M. Boyd III. 2003. "Regulating Target Marketing and Other Race-based Advertising Practices." *Michigan Journal of Race and Law* 8 (Spring): 335–394.

Phillips, D.J. 2004. "Privacy Policy and PETs. The Influence of Policy Regimes on the Development and Social Implications of Privacy Enhancing Technologies." *New Media & Society* 6.6: 671–706.

——. 2009. "Ubiquitous Computing, Spatiality, and the Construction of Identity," in I. Kerr, C. Lucock, and V. Steeves, eds, *Lessons from the Identity Trail: Anonymity, Privacy and Identity in a Networked Society.* New York: Oxford University Press, 303–318.

Powell, A., I.V. Singleton, and L. Corley. (2009). "Process Enablement and Optimization System for Web Advertising Placement and Pricing." United States patent application no. 20090132363.

Raab, C.D. 2009. "Identity: Difference and Categorization," in I. Kerr, C. Lucock, and V. Steeves, eds, *Lessons from the Identity Trail: Anonymity, Privacy and Identity in a Networked Society.* New York: Oxford University Press, 227–244.

Reuter, J. and E. Zitzewitz. 2006. "Do Ads Influence Editors? Advertising and Bias in the Financial Media." *The Quarterly Journal of Economics* 121 (February): 197–227.

Rouvroy, A. 2008. "Privacy, Data Protection, and the Unprecedented Challenges of Ambient Intelligence." *Studies in Ethics, Law, and Technology* 2.1: Article 3. Available at: http://www.bepress.com/selt/vol2/iss1/art3.

Rubin, P.H. and J.M. Shepherd. 2008. "The Demographics of Tort Reform." *Review of Law and Economics* 4.2: 591–620.

Tene, O. 2008. "What Google Knows: Privacy and Internet Search Engines." *Utah Law Review* 4: 1433–1492.

The Angry Black Woman. 2008. "BlackBird Browser—Because the Internet isn't Black Enough." *The Angry Black Woman.* Available at: http://theangryblackwoman.com/2008/12/09/blackbird-browser-because-the-internet-isnt-black-enough/

Turow, J., J. King, C.J. Hoofnagle, A. Bleakley, and M. Hennessy. 2009. "Contrary to what Marketers Say, Americans Reject Tailored Advertising and Three Activities That Enable It." Available at: http://graphics8.nytimes.com/packages/pdf/business/20090929-Tailored_Advertising.pdf

Viswanathan, S., J. Kuruzovich, S. Gosain, and R. Agarwal. 2005. *Online Infomediaries and Price Discrimination: Evidence from the Auto-retailing Sector.* Center for Electronic Markets and Enterprises, University of Maryland. College Park, MD (online, available at: http://ssrn.com/abstract=700384).

Waldfogel, J. 2007. *The Tyranny of the Market: Why You Can't Always Get What You Want.* Cambridge, MA: Harvard University Press.

Zimmer, M. 2008. "The Externalities of Search 2.0: The Emerging Privacy Threats when the Drive for the Perfect Search Engine meets Web 2.0." *First Monday* 13.3. Available at: http://firstmonday.org/htbin/cgiwrap/bin/ojs/index.php/fm/article/viewArticle/2136/1944

7
"Have We Become Postracial Yet?"
Race and Media Technologies in the Age of President Obama

ANNA EVERETT

University of California, Santa Barbara

This study began as an interrogation of the phenomenal new millennial transformations occurring in American electoral politics, in new grassroots activist movements led by politicized and energized youth with a cause, and in a confluence of timely advances in digital technologies that all coincided with the national ambitions of an unlikely contender for the Democratic Party nomination for the 2008 presidential campaign. This unlikely contender, Illinois Senator Barack Hussein Obama, was of mixed race heritage and self-identified as black, and in one audacious campaign season turned traditional political wisdom and practices on their heads. There is little doubt that Candidate Obama could not have achieved his stunning upset of the American political status quo without the stealth-like and completely underestimated force of emergent social media that launched just in time to rival the entrenched powers of establishment politics and the media institutions at their service.

Echoing the revolutionary social change pushed by the dot.com boom of the 1990s, Web 2.0 technologies touting interactivity and 24/7 global connectivity for anyone with a cell phone as well as internet access represented a formidable paradigm shift made possible by such social network systems as MySpace (January 2003), Facebook (February 2004), and the modest February 2005 launch of YouTube, the now premiere video-sharing website. Collectively, these interactive technological formations accelerated the growing erasure and functional dissolve of our familiar and valued boundaries between public and private spheres. The advent of the cable networks' 24/7/365 news cycles, the radical reinvention of cell phones as personal data assistants (Palm Pilots, the BlackBerry, iPhone, etc.) and as new political tools were essential parts of the mix as well.

What these powerful modes of interactive new media production share is the fact that they are driven by and promote a democratizing form of cultural production for the masses known as user-generated content (UGC). UGC contrasts to traditional media cultures and industries, which normally are driven by large media corporations and conglomerates, and the brand of corporate content and messages typified by advertiser-supported broadcast and cable TV network news and entertainment, and mainstream print and radio journalism. So, largely as a result of tech-savvy youth who have driven the popularity and political effectiveness of online social networks and video-sharing websites (which we will combine under the rubric of viral media), a media paradigm shift of major consequence has occurred that cuts two ways, at least for our consideration of new media technologies' alterations of America's contemporary political processes.

First, viral media have enabled media consumers and political activists to become savvy media producers as well as informed consumers, which has made bloggers, and vloggers, major competitors for traditional media companies and powers. Second, traditional media industries have rapidly incorporated viral media tactics into their hegemonic processes (think, for example, about the highly touted CNN/YouTube debates in October 2008). This work recalls the ways that, for example, Howard Dean's and Barack Obama's political fortunes—and misfortunes alike—owe much to young people (college students especially) and the viral media juggernaut they inspired. Also, notable here is the "YouTube effect" and how UGC such as the seminal viral video, *Obama Girl*, and hip-hop music superstar Will.I.AM's "Yes We Can" videos on YouTube signify interesting changes in political discourse and new youth culture's activist practices. In addition, viral media are ushering in what Howard Witt of the *Chicago Tribune* calls the "Viral Civil Rights Movement," a phrase he coined in the wake of the organic Jena 6, and Anti-Immigration Reform Movements. At issue is the question of how viral media and new digital media technologies simultaneously challenge and reinforce the nation's racialized body politic (both manifest and latent), particularly as these technologies exerted growing influence on the crucial 2008 presidential election cycle, and whether or not the shifts and permutations of today's digital media cultures will result in any more of a lasting change as did, say, the Roosevelt era's radio effect (or the Fireside Chats), the Kennedy era's TV effect (from the Nixon–Kennedy television debates), and the Clinton era MTV effect (especially his saxophone-playing appearance on the *Arsenio Hall* TV show).

The Rise of YouTube as Political Player and Obama Rocks the Youth Vote

When Virginia Senator George Allen's 2006 re-election campaign was derailed as a result of what many term his "Macaca" moment (uttering a racist epithet) captured and endlessly circulated on YouTube, issues of race, politics, and ubiquitous media were foregrounded with powerful reverberations that con-tinue to shake mainstream political discourse and structures today. That was nothing compared to the 24/7 televisual inundation of the Reverend Jeremiah Wright sound byte damning America. But, unlike Allen's situation, the hurtful words circulating nationally and internationally, via an endless playback-loop on TV and online, were *not* uttered by Obama. It was Obama's pastor, the Reverend Wright, who bore responsibility in this instance. Still, his were the words that nearly derailed Obama's surprisingly resilient primary campaign run. Drawing upon the media's unparalleled replay of one piece of video footage captured on YouTube, this exploration questions how the volatile mix of race (specifically blackness), history and politics in America still poses a uniquely significant challenge for African American president Barack Obama even at this historic moment and, moving forward. I am interested in the public engagement with and response to YouTube videos targeted at the U.S. electorate, both Obama supporters and detractors. After watching the historical, epochal occurrences of Campaign 2008 closely over the past three years, I find it clear that based on their prominence in high-profile news stories, the maturing social media and the YouTube effect will stay in effect and continue participating in the arbitration of American electoral politics for some time to come.

Now, let us consider briefly how social networks and other digital media technologies were instrumental in mobilizing the collective intelligence (in Pierre Levy's parlance) of America's young people, including African American, Latino/a and other youths of color to effect change in their communities, and in the nation more broadly. Politically active youths are often acknowledged for their centrality in President Obama's electoral victory. However, youth of color too often are not given their due when that credit hinges on digital technology mastery and online activist practices. These concluding remarks and observations will address this lacuna somewhat, and call attention to their digital activism.

Appreciating the import of race and ethnicity matters in discussions and analyses of digital media technologies requires a guarded enthusiasm for the beneficial potential of technological innovations in the everyday lives of youths of color. The enthusiasm here is tempered by a recognition of, but not resignation to, the undeniable consequences of a persistent inequality in the deep structures of our nation's information technology (IT) economy. At the same time, it is difficult not to be optimistic about the myriad ways youths of color today successfully appropriate digital media tools to speak truth to power, to enliven the promises of a digital democracy, and to retrofit what I have been calling "the digital public sphere" to suit their own generational concerns and agendas.

Exemplifying how the digital public sphere operates are three significant events. First is the 2001 use of the web by "conscious" hip-hop artist KRS-One to promote and organize his fourth annual Hip-Hop Appreciation Week in New York City, with a theme of "Charity," and the overarching goal of "decriminalizing" hip-hop's public image. Second, in 2006 there were massive protests against U.S. Representative Sensenbrenner's Immigration Reform Bill HR4437, organized largely by Latino/a, Chicana/o youths using cell phones and the social networking site MySpace, among other media tools, to mobilize hundreds of thousands of people to boycott school and work to take their grievances to such city streets as Los Angeles, Washington, DC, and Detroit, among others. The third and final example is the efforts of activist youths from the MacArthur Foundation-supported Global Kids organization (which has an enormous minority youth constituency) to preserve a dedicated teen space in the popular, 3-D virtual community called Second Life,[1] from the encroachments of adults. And of course the precedent-setting, paradigm-shifting 2004 brigade of fearless Deaniacs whose innovative uses of the internet and the nascent blogosphere, propelled Howard Dean, a little-known medical doctor and governor of Vermont, to the heights of political prominence. Governor Dean became a promising candidate for the Democratic Party largely through their efforts and technological expertise (until the mainstream media derailed his campaign with the infamous "Dean scream" dissembling distraction).

The Deaniacs (as they became known) included a significant online community engaged in erecting in digital space what Hakim Bey would call a temporary autonomous zone or a TAZ, or what Nancy Fraser would identify as a counter public (sphere) for political organizing on behalf of their chosen candidate. Dr Howard Dean's grassroots movement, buoyed by a cadre of tech-savvy youths whom Marc Prensky would term "digital natives," served their candidate well, and laid the blueprint for online, next-gen, political campaign management that Senator Barack Obama took to the next level, and then to the White House.

Of course the exemplars noted above represent a microcosm of the much larger, and more far-reaching phenomenon of activist engagement with digital media technologies, for both good and ill. This benefit/threat dialectic or dualism is at the crux of my concern with digital media activism at this moment, particularly as it challenges and reinforces troubling identity politics in America as the new millennium ossifies, and third- and fourth-generation IT systems take shape. And whether or not we embrace or reject this new information world order from a technophilic perspective or its negating technophobic other, there is no going back to a nostalgic, pre-digital state of political affairs in U.S. politics, a lesson that both Senators John McCain and Hillary Clinton did not fully appreciate until it was too late in the game.

One thing is certain: we have witnessed an amazing historical event and futurist unfolding. At the epicenter of this formidable new information society order are today's youth who, as Don Tapscott puts it, "are growing up digital." At the same time, those of us who might be considered "digital immigrants" according to Marc Prensky's provocative heuristic binarism of "digital natives" (that generation born with digital technologies; see Palfrey and Gasser 2008) vs digital immigrants (learning digital technologies with an analog accent) are not so willing to cede such hard-fought politically progressive ground on the basis of generational location, technological mastery, and perpetual engagement. It was Dean and Obama who understood well and benefited from the necessity of embracing a politics of the big tent (like the internet itself) open to all comers, especially those who come with high-tech gadgets and social networks in tow.

From Obamamania and Obamaphilia to Obamaphobia: Is the Nation Experiencing Voter Remorse?

Since the historic and decisive 2008 election of Barack Obama as the 44th president of the United States, America's national body politic began experiencing an amazing (if not dizzying) about-face regarding the popularity of its first African American president. Undoubtedly none among the mainstream or alternative media punditry, or the politically polarized citizenry at large, expected President Barack Obama's feel-good, putative transracial political capital to endure. Still, the pace of his precipitous decline in approval ratings (after less than two tumultuous years in office) must have been unanticipated even if desired by his fiercest political and ideological foes.[2] After all, any cursory review of extant data on approval ratings for modern U.S. presidents demonstrates that cyclical downturns in popularity must be expected as the daily rough-and-tumble of realpolitik, or political pragmatism, routinely trumps the hopeful ideals and convincing rhetorics of campaign promises. A *Wall Street Journal.Com* (WSJ) statistical comparison of past presidents' ratings over time makes the point, if arguably. In "How the Presidents Stack Up," the WSJ's graphic illustrations chart modern presidential approval ratings from 1945 to 2009 (beginning with Harry Truman and ending with Barack Obama; see Figure 7.1).

Figure 7.1 Charting President Obama's performance ratings, © WallStreetJournal.Com.

Comparatively speaking, then, only President Truman appears to have bested President Obama in falling furthest and fastest from grace. However, given that Truman scores highest of all upon his entry into office (at nearly 90 percent), as opposed to Obama (with scores above 60 percent), it is clear that Truman had farthest to fall.[3] Perhaps his unprecedented plummet was bound up with Truman's fate of occupying the office of the presidency following the death of President Franklin Delano Roosevelt early in his fourth term. It is important to point out at this time that President Obama's early slide in the polls mirrors almost exactly that of President Reagan, and President Reagan's legacy as an effective and popular leader remains secure. Somehow, it does seem that such historical contextualizations are insufficient. What is important is assessing some of the specifics of President Obama's remarkable political fortunes and misfortunes alike, and asking more centrally within the context of revolutionary posthuman digital media culture, "What's race got to do with it?" To begin answering the question requires a sort of discursive detour.

To a large extent, President Barack Obama is a product of one of the most consequential and high stakes wars of our millennial society—not the Iraq War or even the Afghanistan War (although increasingly George Bush's Afghan War is viewed as Obama's War). No. The war responsible for catapulting Obama to the highest elective office in the land is the undeclared, though no less consequential, war between "old" versus "new" media ecologies. I have evoked the metaphor of warring media factions between established and emergent media industries elsewhere.[4] However, the point seems particularly apt in this discussion about competing media technologies pressed into service for highly consequential and epoch-making political gain. And it is precisely to this issue of digital media technologies (especially the internet) impinging on dominant media's hegemonic gatekeeping function that this analysis speaks. If the unanticipated success of the 2008 Obama campaign has revealed anything about how the intersection of race and digital media has altered American political economies and their mediated political discourses forever, it is to underscore how persistent racial divisions are in the U.S. It is true that perpetual structural racism has been challenged quite effectively of late, if not consistently or over the long haul. Still, given his timely and tremendous legislative accomplishments it is difficult to explain President Obama's abysmal ratings in less than two years in office outside of intractable racial politics.

Analyze What? Reifying Fear of a Black President

It is always a challenge and even risky to study a moving target of analysis such as a living president actively carrying out the demands of his office. Clearly, attempting to assess the rapidly proliferating media industries and their unyielding fascination with President Obama, and his fascination with them, complicates this work exponentially. As this project took shape, the goal was modest—a comparative media analysis centered on the newsworthiness of events involving the nation's first so-called "viable" black presidential candidate in mainstream news outlets, print and electronic (i.e. *Time*, *Newsweek*, *The New Yorker*, *Los Angeles Times*, *New York Times*, *Wall Street Journal*, CNN, NBC, ABC, CBS, PBS, MSNBC, Comedy Central, among others), as well as its alternative digital media rivals including such far-flung internet texts as blogs, social media, netroots websites, etc. The project parameters shifted and morphed significantly and well beyond my original intent and temporal scope.[5]

And while addressing the toxic Clinton–Obama campaign dynamics is outside the scope of this chapter, it remains essential to this project as a whole. For our purposes, it is important to consider the likely impact of the media's relentless racialized "body politics" and accompanying "body fictions" (King 2000: vii) to inscribe Obama's public persona and why it matters. *Body Politics and the Fictional Double* (King 2000) is an important volume of essays that help us connect the dots among mainstream and politically Right-wing and Right leaning alternative media's perpetual bombardment of racial and racist master-narratives involving Barack Obama, and their complicity in eroding his already tenuous support among impatient independents and weary Democratic supporters. In her excellent introduction to the volume, Debra Walker King remarks:

> [T]his collection of essays is about the collision between real bodies and an unfriendly informant: a fictional double whose aim is to mask individuality and mute the voice of personal agency. Although this double is created and maintained most often by forces beyond ourselves (television, magazines, cultural mandates and myths), we bear its markers on our bodies, particularly those of age, race and gender. In this way the fictional double is always with us, constantly speaking, telling, misinforming—determining to be heard and heard first . . . Unfortunately the informant they see, and to whom they are willing to listen, lies . . . The lives and relationships affected by the stories that body fictions tell are frequently female and "of color" while the interpreters and empowered authorities are not. (King 2000: vii–viii)

Speaking as an African American professor and scholar, King's observations have merit and are convincing. Moreover, she effectively unmasks the damaging power of racial body fictions that contemporary gatekeepers positioned inside mainstream and other media outlets often deny, disavow, and deploy all at once. To situate the matter more directly in terms of familiar cultural constructs of an essentialized blackness shading Obama, we can consider Maude Hines's interrogation of body language and corporeal semiotics. From the same volume, Hines discusses two separate experiences with white men's storytelling at parties, years apart, and how the word "black" signified on both occasions. She writes:

The night of the first party, I realized that the word "black" in the story had almost nothing to do with pigmentation. To make sense, the word, or the color it represented, had to stand for "huge" and "strong" and "evil" and "misanthropic" and, most of all, "existing primarily to do violence to white men." Although none of these descriptions were used [in one man's story of "five black guys coming toward us. We got in [our car] in time," though], the "five black guys" were clearly not elderly, or peaceful, or small; when these adjectives are substituted, the story doesn't make sense. (Hines 2000: 39)

Hines's point is "to grapple with the silent and unacknowledged language of corporeal semiotics, that system of signification that our [black] bodies represent to others who read them as texts unauthorized by ourselves" (38). If we attend seriously to the incessant discourses of race and blackness (latent or manifest) in media coverage of President Obama, then we are better able to recognize and perhaps resist, as Professor Hines puts it, "the ways in which our bodies *mean* [sic], whether or not we mean them to or not" [original emphasis] (38). And, despite his Herculean efforts to eschew familiar and novel discursive entanglements about race on the campaign trail (to the chagrin, frustration and enmity of some vocal supporters),[6] Senator Obama nonetheless found it necessary to offer up race-specific mea culpas to counter or offset the ever-present specter of the angry black man, "body fictions" that King and Hines effectively demystify. Exemplary in this regard is the media reportage of Jeremiah Wright and the ACORN organizational affiliation episodes, among others, haunting Candidate Obama throughout the 2008 campaign.

Although Candidate Obama maintained his popularity despite being ensnared in some high-profile racial thickets on the campaign trail (most Americans seemed to move past the media hype), the citizenry have not been as tolerant when President Obama inserted himself in such race matters as the July 16, 2009, fracas between black Harvard University Professor Henry Louis (Skip) Gates and white Cambridge Police Sergeant Joseph Crowley, for example. If the 1,544 respondents commenting on the *ABC.Com* story entitled "Obama Called Police Officer Who Arrested Gates, Still Sees 'Overreaction' in Arrest," are any measure, President Obama's patina of post-racial and race-neutral body politics wore thin, at least among most readers invited to comment on this story. In fact, a few bear quoting:

No doubt about it Obama said something stupid. I wonder why he sided with the black guy without hearing the facts first. Could it be that Obama is a racist? Absolutely. Now days if a white guy bothers a black guy in anyway [sic] all the black guy has to do is cry racist! A white guy cuts in line before a black guy. "He's a racist!" Boy, that really takes a lot of intelligence to say racist. I bet my parrot could learn that word in five minutes. Apparently its the main word in Dr Gates, Reverand Wright,

Al Sharptons and Jesse's Jacksons vocabulary [sic]. Hey! aren' these the leaders of Black America today? Well, I guess if I paint my parrot black he could be a leader too. (Posted by rancher61, July 28, 2009)

wow he is so arrogant why wont he just be a man and apologize. (Posted by KF33FK, July 28, 2009)

I think many are missing the big picture. Many of us middle age white men who voted for Obama because he seemed race neutral are looking at him as someone who sided with a "brother" without having the facts. Our viewpoint of him is altered and we no longer see him the same way. (Posted by 4riverroad, July 26, 2009.)

There were, of course, others commenting who agreed with President Obama's position or at least were willing to give him the benefit of the doubt:

Is there anyone out there who wishes they could take back some words? I doubt it. I am sure President Obama wishes he had waited before he replied. I think they were both wrong. Mr Gates may have over-reacted but I never had to teach my son to be careful with cops like black people do. I think he was more offended because of who he is and his feathers got a little ruffled. The cop also over-reacted. He became annoyed when Mr Gates asked him for his name and badge number and decided to make more of this issue than necessary. For a person who studied race relations, he reacted too quickly. So, each one needs to have their feelings soothed and the President is the one to do it. I think having a beer together is a great idea. Nothing fussy . . . just man to man. (Posted by talmag, July 25, 2009.) (Khan *et al.* 2009)

It is not surprising that a majority of the comments take President Obama and Professor Gates to task, with some suspecting Gates of having ulterior motives and seeking publicity, a resumé enhancement, and financial recompense, to mention a few. One poster even questioned why Gates was not tasered for disorderly conduct. A troubling number of respondents articulated concerns about the Gates/Crowly affair being symptomatic of President Obama's cloaked racism against whites finally being revealed. Another asked: "'Is President Obama mad he is half white? why take it out on a white cop and a crazy black professor [sic]. Our nations president 'acted stupidly'" (Khan *et al.* 2009). Most telling about a disconcerting number of comments uploaded to ABC News' online outlet was their frequent leveling of pernicious body fictions at President Obama for nominating Judge Sonia Sotomayor to the Supreme Court. Echoes of Fox News, Rush Limbaugh, and other Right-wing media gatekeepers' talking points disparaging anything associated with President Obama that could be racially tinged or slimed can be seen and heard here.

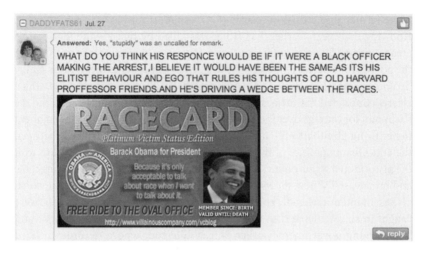

Figure 7.2 Visualizing Obama fatigue as a PhotoShopped credit card simulacrum termed the "Obama Race Card."

President Obama could have—and perhaps should have—avoided weighing in on this racial powder keg while seeking wide support for his controversial legislative agenda. Nonetheless, some of the vitriolic and outright racist commentary and rants unleashed on this ABC News site and elsewhere online speak volumes about President Obama's declining popularity in the polls, especially among white independents and self-proclaimed past supporters. Exacerbating the president's current political misfortunes is a much remarked-upon "enthusiasm gap" among his Democratic base, especially the netroots activists who assisted him in revolutionizing American campaign politics (more about them later in this chapter). As this project nears completion, yet another unnecessary racial imbroglio has heaped further damage upon the Obama Administration's moral authority and progressive credibility vis-à-vis racial healing and transracial political unity. Once again, it is the digital media, specifically the Right-wing blogosphere and Fox News, that lured the Administration and even the National Association for the Advancement of Colored People (NAACP) into an unconscionable reactionary move—fomenting a high-profile, ill-advised transmedia news event to showcase a practice of "zero-tolerance" for racism obtaining at both the NAACP and the Obama-led Department of Agriculture (DOA). Briefly, the fracas involved notorious Right-wing blogger Andrew Breitbart's heavily edited version of a videotaped speech by Shirley Sherrod to an NAACP gathering that, on its face, seemed to reveal this black government worker abusing her position to discriminate against a working-class white farmer. In the controversial video, Sherrod, a black woman, is seen discussing her reluctance to assist an arrogant white farmer (her terms) in securing DOA support for his farming problems. Knowing that, years earlier, her father was killed by racist white men in this area motivated Sherrod's initial response. However, her example of overcoming the politics of racial hate whereby she decided to assist this farmer and his family became the moral of Sherrod's NAACP speech. Breitbart's doctored video, which clearly eliminated the racial healing message of Sherrod's speech, became the flashpoint for outrage over the Obama Administration's DOA rush to judgment in her firing. Breitbart's ill-fated attempt to make a moral equivalence between the anti-Obama politics of the newly constituted Tea Party organization with the historic civil rights politics of the NAACP (as he asserted on numerous cable and broadcast TV new shows) was disingenuous at best, race-baiting at worst.

Best of intentions aside, both organizations (the DOA and the NAACP) were caught in an untenable rush to judgment against this highly sympathetic and long-serving government worker Shirley Sherrod, whose decontextualized remarks about overcoming her own biases and promoting racial cooperation were strategically remixed into a videoclip message espousing the inverse of her regional NAACP speech in April 2010. In her book *Remix: Reading + Composing Culture* (2006), Catherine G, Latterell indicates some key ways this term and its cultural expression function. She writes,

> Popular culture is full of messages that have been reinterpreted and reappropriated. Politicians use catchphrases from television commercials and films in their campaigns . . . we live in a remix culture in which we are not only the readers and listeners but also the writers and designers—the makers of culture . . . behind these artifacts of everyday life are collective assumptions that shape and reveal a culture's thinking. (Latterell 2006: xxxii–xxxiii)

Clearly, Sherrod's remarks were reinterpreted and reappropriated by Breitbart, the Fox News behemoth, and those online and TV viewers ensnared by this particularly destructive brand of remix culture.

Engaging in the very practice they claim to abhor, the Obama Administration and the NAACP hastily condemned Mrs Sherrod and called for her immediate resignation (Gordy 2010). The transmedia firestorm came with the sort of unstoppable alacrity that is currently part and parcel of our new media normal of 24/7 information flows. The stakes and subsequent fallout, as Congressional Black Caucus Chair Congresswoman Barbara Lee makes clear, are that the Obama Administration was seen on an endless media feedback loop not doing "their due diligence, and [reacting] to an unfortunate right-wing attack on a great woman" (quoted in Gordy 2010). One highly damaging, though unintentional, consequence of the Obama Administration's participation in the Sherrod affair was yet again a devastating distraction that overshadowed another of the president's hard-fought legislative victories in a week-long news cycle gone awry.

How these grand narratives cast President Obama and other prominently successful non-whites in government today as the true racists dividing America was eerily, presciently, but not surprisingly pondered by Derik Smith during the height of the 2008 presidential campaign. It appears that desirable postracial politics obtains in America primarily to the extent that black and other people of color do not call out racist practices and utterances occurring in civil society, no matter how egregious. Had President Obama maintained his careful cultivation of a race-neutral or transcendent political persona, as Smith effectively outlines, would his personal approval ratings have remained strong in spite of the black body fictions authorizing the fictional double of blackness in the American cultural imaginary, as discussed above? After all, historic American cultural scripts involving racial politics too often make it difficult to disaggregate fictions about black male violence, outlaw culture, and social danger from the reality of struggling, disempowered black males burdened by a racially biased and unfair legal system that imprisons them disproportionately compared to all other racial and ethnic populations in America.

So, the merit of this question seems evident when we are reminded of some very cogent observations Smith makes in his February 25, 2008, essay "I Am Obama: The American Imagination and the New Black Hero," published online at *PopMatters.Com*. This is a very smart internet review of superstar Will Smith's blockbuster 2007 film entitled *I Am Legend*. Derik Smith draws some incisive corollaries between the nation's embrace (represented by the film's astounding $70 million opening weekend box office gross) of a cinematic black male hero entrusted to save humankind from extinction, and Senator Obama's shocking Iowa Caucus campaign victory "in corn-fed, white bread Iowa," and Smith lays out his assessment of why and how America stood at the precipice of historical political transformation—with a caveat. Beginning with the tongue-in-cheek hyperbolic utterance, "*I Am Legend* swept through theaters like a prophetic, cinematic wind whispering: 'Obama cometh,'" Smith states:

> However, some close analysis of the Obama candidacy and Smith in his *I Am Legend* role also reveals that the viability of the new black hero is dependent upon his ability to carefully regulate his blackness. To satisfy the needs of the national imagination, he must cultivate the patina of blackness while radiating a transcendent racial identity that is not immediately linked to [the] black community, which remains profoundly stigmatized. Because he maintains a prescribed distance from [the] black community, the ascendancy of the new black hero is no way equal to a national desire to redress some of America's most pressing race problems. Ultimately, America's recent fascination with a darker national savior has to be considered in the context of a rich tradition in its narrative in which self-sacrificing men of color offer both salvation and absolution to white protagonists. (Smith 2008)

Almost prophetic, Smith's assertion that Senator Obama seemed to negotiate successfully the politically precarious high wire act of America's racial politics anticipates the cost to a President Obama of becoming mired in the 2009 Gates/Crowley fracas, the 2010 Sherrod fiasco, and the Justice Department's challenge to the racially divisive Arizona Immigration Law. Here is another excerpt from Derik Smith's prescient writing:

> Even as the nation congratulates itself for its historic contemplation of a black president, it mandates that the new black hero avoid strong advocacy for the black community. This is why the symptoms of the nation's most urgent "race issues"—harrowing rates of African-American drug addiction, fratricide, incarceration and economic dereliction— cannot be central talking points in Obama's campaign. The moment he begins to regularly address the unique litany of maladies facing African-Americans (what poet Robert Hayden collated as the "riot squad of statistics"), he runs the risk of being seen as overly-attentive to his ethnic compatriots. However much he may want to, the new black hero cannot ignore the nation's deep skepticism of those who are too closely associated with [the] black community. (Smith 2008)

At this writing, President Obama's job approval ratings plummeted from a strong showing of 66 per cent in January 2009 to a very weak 49 per cent in mid-July 2010, according to Gallup's daily tracking polls. The Right-leaning Rasmussen Daily Presidential Tracking Poll shows similar numbers (Gallup 2010; Rasmussen Reports 2010). That the president's current political malaise cannot be reduced to his real and imagined racial politics goes without saying, and certainly this is not my thesis. While the complexities of American political processes today are varied, largely entrenched, exacerbated by the lack of political will in the national governing bodies, including pointed missteps in judgment by the Democratic Party leadership and the Obama Administration, it is crucial to recognize how central the daily drumbeat of racial intolerance, hysterical hatred of President Obama, and the unrelenting disinformation campaigns being waged by the Right-wing, conservative media industrial complex have been in contributing to the nation's growing fear of its significantly weakened black president.

One particularly disturbing element in President Obama's reversal in popularity has been the rising political power of the Right-wing blogosphere, as the Andrew Breitbart blog, and ABC News online commentary pages discussed above exemplify. Jessie Daniels (2008) has investigated the phenomenon of rising online hate speech in her essay "Race, Civil Rights, and Hate Speech in the Digital Era." In addition to outlining overt white supremacist websites, such as former Ku Klux Klan leader Tom Metzger's *The Insurgent*, she examines a little-known development of covert hate sites she terms "cloaked Web sites." The sites, she writes, "deliberately seek to disguise the racist motives of the Web site's author by using carefully chosen domain names, deceptive graphic user interface (GUI) and language that is less strident than what appears in overt hate speech online" (2008: 138). Her point is that, "Many of the old-school white supremacist groups that were active before the emergence of the digital era have simply moved their rhetoric virtually unaltered from print-based newsletters to Web sites" (2008: 134). Among these cloaked sites she identifies are: www.AmericanCivilRightsReview.com, a site owned by neo-Nazi Frank Weltner; and www.martinlutherking.org, produced by white supremacist Don Black, who also publishes www.Stormfront.org, "one of the earliest and longest continually published Web site of any kind." Black's *Stormfront.org*, Daniels notes, "has been a portal for white supremacist activity since 1999" (2008: 132). While it is not possible to know how much of bashing President Obama is determined by race or by the now legendary rudeness and coarseness of internet flame wars and rants, it is widely accepted that internet anonymity gives cover to and emboldens individuals and groups espousing hate and politically incorrect public discourse.

And if it is the case that Obama-bashing online indicates further that America is experiencing voters' remorse, it is important not to count out President Obama's ability to turn his unfairly wounded presidency around (as his May 2011 capture and killing of Osama bin Laden suggests). God forbid, however, that the hate-filled public airways have not already fomented a climate for and justification of a "Second Amendment Solution" (to quote Tea Party political operative Sharron Angle) to presidential regime change in our increasingly divided nation. In the toxic media environment today, advocacy for a presidential assassination is clearly not off the table, as media stories about "assassinating Obama" ran rampant during the heyday of the 2008 presidential campaign, and continue today as a return of 3,080,000 hits on Google for a keyword search of "assassinate Obama" attests. Also at stake in this discussion is a convincing argument for why we need to attend to the hows and whys of media matters in our emergent digital democracy.

Central to this interventionist approach is a desire to understand especially how digital democracy matters for contemporary race relations, in general, and its visible benefit/threat dialectic in the phenomenal rise of Senator Barack Obama, as the first (and potentially the last, for a long while) African American or black president of the United States of America. It is as though we may be living through a sort of Reconstruction 2.0 contemporary zeitgeist similar to that of our post Civil War past, wherein racially inclusive political power was shared temporarily only to be followed by a horrifically repressive post-Reconstruction era of racial violence and terror of staggering proportions. Defined by a political logic of white supremacy, racially motivated lynchings, voter disenfranchisement, and Apartheid-like Jim Crow racial segregation laws characterized and distorted America democracy until the modern Civil Rights Movement of the 1950s and 1960s.

Reconstructing Democracy and the New Millennial Digital Media Toolkit

At this point, it is necessary to backtrack and discuss certain catalyzing events that led to this research project that originally took as its object a study of the impact of new media technologies (the internet and other digital media) on the historic presidential campaign of Senator Barack Hussein Obama. Expanding on my previous scholarship on race and digital media, this study, as originally configured, was concerned with documenting and assessing the traditional/mainstream ("old") media industries and practices as they influenced Illinois Senator Barack Obama's bid for the 2008 Democratic Party nomination for president. This was to be juxtaposed to the radically transformed media landscape ushered in by the internet, its killer-app (social media networks, i.e. Facebook, MySpace, wikis, Twitter, blogs, and YouTube), and all the other subsequent digital media tools it spawned. To better situate the above reverse chronological exploration of President Obama's most current mediation in terms of "old" and "new" media imperatives, the remaining discussion delineates some key developments that inform this expanded project. These include the rapid diffusion of digital technologies among various consumer/ political demographics, the innovative uses of digital media's transformative technologies, the "old" media strategies of consolidating "new" media under the convergence rubric, and the sole presidential candidate astute enough to harness the new digital media ecology to gain a political advantage during the 2008 campaign season. Most salient is how Obama's digital media strategies became a political game-changer, while helping to reconstruct America's politics of participatory democracy in the process.

In fact, for many Obama's so-called "BlackBerry addiction" made him cool, especially when compared to McCain's self-confessed ignorance of using email, let alone smart phones or PDAs (personal digital assistants). As I discussed elsewhere, "it has been interesting to watch the media's fascination with Obama's technophilia and his penchant for the BlackBerry as his PDA of choice" (Everett 2009a: 200). Airing on November 16, 2008, in anticipation of President-Elect Obama's Inauguration Day, MSNBC's news magazine show *Countdown* featured a segment entitled "Countdown to January 20th," hosted by MSNBC Political Correspondent David Shuster:

> Shuster interviewed political columnist Ana Marie Cox on the necessity for stripping Obama of his beloved BlackBerry . . . Shuster noted: "It is a little shocking that Obama will be the first sitting President to use a laptop, so he's really dragging the Oval Office into the late twentieth century." For Cox, the real question, jokingly was: "Will Obama choose a Mac or PC?" (Everett 2009a: 200)

Taking up the matter also on MSNBC's *Rachel Maddow Show*, Arianna Huffington put the case more directly. She proclaimed that, "Barack Obama's Administration will usher in the first Internet Presidency" (Everett 2009a: 200).

With the ubiquity of old and new media coverage, President Barack Obama became the über-celebrity media text, one capable of testing the limits of new media's digital democracy credibility, while engendering a plethora of racial significations—novel and familiar. It is not insignificant that despite this president's centrist politics and initially inspiring postpartisan and postracial persona cultivated at home, incessant racialized narratives across the old and new media divides began decentering and diminishing his tremendous trans-national appeal and powerful leadership so welcomed abroad. In the post-George W. Bush era, the dominant media's benighted or reactionary coverage of Candidate Obama and later President Obama on the global stage is especially perplexing, and arguably unpatriotic. Too often objective and non-partisan reportage of Obama abroad emanating from respected mainstream news outlets was displaced by framing rhetorics more consistent with Right-wing media's ideological spin.

This seems especially prevalent, as Obama's diplomatic positions on U.S. foreign policy worked to rehabilitate America's global reputation post 9–11, when the unprovoked terrorist attacks had elicited international sympathy and compassion prior to George W. Bush's unprovoked war on Iraq. Framing Obama's ability to draw historic levels of supportive crowds in Germany, France and other nation-states with such denigrating descriptors as "rock star," "appeaser," and "apologist," for example, seemed a diminution of any foreign policy bona fides Obama sought to shore up in comparison to his campaign competitors McCain and Clinton.

Largely, international press coverage of Obama in 2008 was enthusiastic and affirmative, though skepticism about Obama was also palpable in the coverage. Culling from the tabloids, comics, news, and other media representations, *der Spiegel* is revealing. Exemplifying the former, *der Spiegel Online* ran a photo gallery featuring a diverse and representative array of Obama news coverage during his successful visit in Germany. One image gracing the cover of the *Bild* tabloid captures a smiling and waving Obama. Above his visage is a panel of images of German politicians digitally manipulated to look like Obama. The caption reads: "The mass circulation tabloid *Bild* admires the Illinois senator's optimism and beaming smile. The newspaper notes that Germans would like their own Obama" ("Photo Gallery" 2008).

As for the latter or vocal skeptics, German telecom company Deutsche Welle provides reporting of a less celebratory nature. On June 28, 2008, Deutsche Welle's online portal *DW-World.De* posted a story entitled "Germans Disappointed in Obama's Stance on Death Penalty" that discussed German politicians and other observers' strong opposition to Obama's comments in favor of extending the death penalty for child rapists. This reaction came even though, as they reported, Obama "enjoys more popularity [here] than anywhere else in Europe." The 2008 German press coverage of Candidate Obama's European trip is symptomatic of other international press outlets' discursive

Figure 7.3 Obama in the German press.

treatments of his strong appeal and curiosity factor, both online and in more traditional media outlets. In the main, online media headlines from various international news bureaus ranged from the absolutely euphoric to the downright cynical, and positions in between. Primarily, the reception was enthusiastic, especially revisiting the coverage through a Google search of "Candidate Obama in Europe." For example: "Britain Backing Obama by Five to One Majority" (*Evening Standard*, UK, July 14, 2008); "Enter Obama, Pursued by Politicians Desperate to Bask in his Reflected Glory" (*The Independent*, UK, July 26, 2008). Still, today whether or not Obama became a victim more of race than of viral media is a difficult matter to resolve in any case.

In some ways, Obama's exceptionalism as an African American on the global stage suggests a representational excess and dissonant image of black masculinity that American media apparently attempted to contain and explain for their audiences, who claimed to be unsure of just who Barack Obama was and what were his qualifications to be president of the United States. In Lisa Nakamura's influential discussion about how corporate media images manage race, diversity, and discursive transnationality in televisual, print and online commercials about travel and tourism services, one observation suggests a possible rationale for American media's discomfiture with characterizing Obama's transnational appeal more objectively. Nakamura writes: "The continued presence of stable signifiers of otherness in telecommunications advertising guarantees the Western subject that his position, where he may choose to go today, remains privileged" (2000: 17). That Obama was and remains an unstable signifier of black masculine otherness, and one, moreover, who troubles the privileged status of the white Western subject, can account for much in mainstream and other media institutions' often contorted and biased coverage of him.

"Obama" as Prefix

There is an observable Obamaphobia phenomenon that is primarily an anti-Obama rhetoric most readily apprehended by a practice of affixing the name "Obama" onto a series of words often for the purposes of political derision, although the neologism is also deployed for satire, and even pro-Obama sentiments. In terms of the former, some recognizable cases in point are: the Obama Phone, an urban legend that claims President Obama funds free cell phones for poor black and other minority populations. This patent lie has fired up certain adherents in the Right-wing blogosphere featuring some of the vilest racist discussion threads. Other examples (nefarious or otherwise) include more self-explanatory applications such as: Obama Care, Obamanomics, Obamanation, Obama Hood, Obama bucks, and a few others that turn up in a Google search on the phrase "Obama as prefix," for example. One recent keyword search returned 269,000 matches or hits.

For the remainder of this chapter, my discussion shifts to concerns about the critical nexus of pervasive computing and ubiquitous digital media technologies, and Senator Obama and his team's masterful media strategy of tapping the changed national mediascape to advance his historic and successful run for the presidency. We may well lament the compelling nature of America's racial scripts that endure and threaten to undermine what apparently small progressive gains on the postracial front we imagined digital media technologies and a once popular black president might engender.

Conclusion: What's Race and Ethnicity Got to Do With *IT* (Information Technologies)? Are We Postracial Yet?

Until news of the unfortunate racial conflagrations involving Professor Gates and Sergeant Crowley, and government worker Shirley Sherrod blanketed the

Figure 7.4 These images and their anti-Obama thrust can easily be found in the digital ether: (a) Obama bucks; (b) Obama Hood; (c) Obama Care.

mediascape for weeks, rivaling the attention garnered by the YouTube footage of Reverend Wright, it seemed that we wanted, by and large, to believe that America had achieved a remarkable level of postracial harmony. After all, it was only months ago that we elected the first black president in the entire history of our democracy. The ensuing media firestorm attending each occasion seems to have done real damage to President Obama's personal popularity, and perhaps diminished our national desire for working toward an elusive postracist societal ideal. Notwithstanding the apparent glee evinced by some media pundits, bloggers, and website respondents over the rapid dissipation of the national mood celebrating racial healing on Election Day and on President Obama's Inauguration Day, it is crucial that the nation resist the pendulum swing (metaphorically speaking) back to old ways of racist thinking. It may seem odd in this context to invoke Thomas Jefferson, but to paraphrase him, antiracist thinking and actions require constant vigilance.

Returning to the question posed earlier: What's race got to do with it? For those of us who are scholar-skeptics, and enthusiasts for digital technologies as cultural equalizers, we are well advised to heed Jan A.G.M. van Dijk's (2005) warning that, indeed, deepening "divides are byproducts of old inequalities, digital technology is intensifying inequalities, and new inequalities are appearing" (4). That said, it is important to highlight how race and ethnicity get re-presented, remixed, recoded, redeployed, known and understood generally in digital media interactions and transactions, such as in game play, online databases, friendship/social networks, blogs, grassroots community organizing, listservs, IMs or SMS (short message systems), hate speech, etc. This is especially the case where online activism around the phenomenon of the Obama campaign obtained.

Following Sherry Turkle I like to point out the old-school truism operating in the early years of the internet's massification. In the early 1990s, there was a popular cartoon depicting a dog typing on a personal computer with a caption reading "Nobody knows you're a dog on the Internet" (Everett 2009b: 4). Around this same time, the telecom giant MCI produced a compelling TV commercial claiming there is no race, no genders, and no infirmities in the new world of the internet because here "people can communicate mind to mind." These popular examples clearly were symptomatic of the nation's desire to imagine and construct colorblind or hyper-tolerant virtual communities and digital public spheres through the internet's text-driven digital environments during the late 1980s and early 1990s. This gave rise to the widely held perception and apparent wish-fulfillment that imagines America as having arrived at some idyllic race, gender, class neutrality in our civil society. In some important ways we have overcome the divisive identity politics of the past, but in more structural and institutional ways, not so much.

Notes

1 Second Life is described on its website as "a 3-D virtual world entirely built and owned by its residents. Since opening to the public in 2003, it has grown explosively and today is inhabited by more than 6,030,223 people from around the globe." See http://secondlife.com/whatis/.

2 Shortly after President Barack Obama's successful inauguration, Right-wing media personalities voiced their opposition, typified famously by Rush Limbaugh's rush to declare, "I hope Obama fails." And Limbaugh's vocal opposition was not to be outdone as Republican Senator from South Carolina Jim Demint joined the chorus invoking his constituency to make failure of the new president's health care proposal his "Waterloo," terminology tantamount to ensuring irreparable harm to President Obama's legislative agenda and thereby hastening his ultimate political demise. See, for example, Rush Limbaugh's website on January 16, 2009 at: www.rushlimbaugh.com/home/daily/site_011609/content/01125113.guest.html and Ben Smith's "Health Reform Foes Plan Obama's Waterloo," at www.politico.com/blogs/bensmith/0709/Health_reform_foes_plan_Obamas_Waterloo.html

3 See details on U.S. presidents' approval ratings at "How the Presidents Stack Up." *The Wall Street Journal.Com.* Available at: http://online.wsj.com/public/resources/documents/info-presapp0605-31.html.

4 See, for example, my essays: "P.C. (Post-Columbine) Youth Violence: What's the Internet/Video Gaming Got to Do With It?" *Denver University Law Review* 77.4 (2000): 689–698; and "Digitextuality and Click Theory: Theses on Convergence Media in the Digital Age," in Anna Everett and John Caldwell, eds, *New Media: Theories and Practices of Digitextuality* (New York and London: Routledge, 2003), 1–28.

5 Originally, this was going to be a limited project about the media coverage of Illinois Senator Barack Obama's 2008 presidential campaign. Suffice it to say that campaign events made expanding the critical project essential.

6 Derik Smith discusses the backlash Senator Obama generated from journalist Tavis Smiley and Reverend Jesse Jackson because of Obama's carefully cultivated race-neutral persona. See his 2008 post on *PopMatters.Com* at www.popmatters.com/pm/feature/55188/i-am-obama/.

References

Bey, Hakim. 1985, 1991. *The Temporary Autonomous Zone.* Brooklyn, NY: Autonomedia.

Breitbart, Andrew. 2010. "Video Proof: The NAACP Awards Racism—2010." *Breitbart Presents Big Government*, July 19, 2010. Available at: http://biggovernment.com/abreitbart/2010/07/19/video-proof-the-naacp-awards-racism2010/ (accessed August 25, 2010).

Daniels, Jessie. 2008. "Race, Civil Rights, and Hate Speech in the Digital Era," in Anna Everett, ed., *Learning Race and Ethnicity: Youth and Digital Media.* Cambridge, MA: MIT Press.

Everett, Anna. 2009a. *Digital Diaspora: A Race for Cyberspace.* Albany, NY: SUNY Press.

——. 2009b. "Introduction," in Anna Everett, ed., *Learning Race and Ethnicity: Youth and Digital Media.* Cambridge, MA, and London: MIT Press.

Foster, Hal. 1985. *Recodings: Art, Spectacle, Cultural Politics.* Seattle, WA: Bay Press.

Fraser, Nancy. 1990. "Rethinking the Public Sphere: A Contribution to the Critique of Actually Existing Democracy." *Social Text* 25/26: 56–80.

Gallup. 2010. "Gallup Daily: Obama Job Approval." *Gallup.Com Online.* Available at: www.gallup.com/poll/113980/gallup-daily-obama-job-approval.aspx (accessed 24 July 24, 2010).

"Germans Disappointed in Obama's Stance on the Death Penalty." 2008 *DW-Worlde.De*, June 28. Available at: www.dw-world.de/dw/article/0,,3446397,00.html (accessed August 25, 2010).

Gordy, Shirley. 2010. "CBC Chair Speaks on the Shirley Sherrod Fiasco." *Essence.Com*, July 23, 2010. Available at: www.essence.com/news/hot_topics_4/cbc_chair_speaks_on_shirley_sherrod.php (accessed July 24, 2010).

"Hands On with the Obama Phone." *PCMag.Com.* Available at: www.pcmag.com/slideshow_viewer/0,1205,l%253D237228%2526a%253D237230%2526po%253D0,00.asp?p=n (accessed July 18, 2010).

Hines, Maude. 2000. "Body Language: Corporeal Semiotics, Literary Resistance," in Debra Walker King, ed., *Body Politics and the Fictional Double.* Bloomington and Indianapolis: Indiana University Press, 38–55.

"How the Presidents Stack Up." *The Wall Street Journal.Com.* Available at: http://online.wsj.com/public/resources/documents/info-presapp0605-31.html (accessed July 24, 2010).

Israely, Jeff. 2009. "Has Italy's Left Found its Own Obama?" *Time.Com*, February 20. Available at: www.time.com/time/world/article/0,8599,1880979,00.html (accessed May 25, 2010).

Khan, Huma, Michelle McPhee, and Russell Goldman. 2009. "Obama Called Police Officer Who Arrested Gates, Still Sees 'Overreaction' in Arrest." *ABC News/Politics*, July 24. Available at: http://abcnews.go.com/Politics/story?id=8163051&page=1.(accessed May 25, 2010).

King, Debra Walker. 2000. "Introduction: Body Fictions," in Debra Walker King, ed., *Body Politics and the Fictional Double*. Bloomington and Indianapolis: Indiana University Press, vii–xiv.

Latterell, Catherine G. 2006. *Remix: Reading + Composing Culture*. Boston/New York: Bedford/St Martin's.

Limbaugh, Rush. "I Hope Obama Fails." Available at: www.rushlimbaugh.com/home/daily/site_ 011609/content/01125113.guest.html (accessed July 24, 2010).

Miller, Douglas T. 1996. *On Our Own: Americans in the Sixties*. Lexington, Massachusetts and Toronto: D.C. Heath.

Nakamura, Lisa. 2000. "'Where Do You Want to Go Today?' in Beth E. Kolko, Lisa Nakamura, and Gilbert B. Rodman, eds, *Cybernetic Tourism, the Internet, and Transnationality*. New York and London: Routledge, 15–26.

Palfrey, John, and Urs Gasser. 2008. *Born Digital: Understanding the First Generation of Digital Natives*. New York: Basic Books.

Paulus, Paul. 2010. "Obama's File Tax Returns." *johnpaulus.com*, April 15, 2010. Available at: http://johnpaulus.com/blog/2010/04/15/obamas-file-tax-returns/ (accessed July 18, 2010).

"Photo Gallery: Obamania Grips the German Press," July 24, 2008. Available at: www.spiegel.de/fotostrecke/fotostrecke-33622–4.html (accessed 25 August 2010).

Prensky, Marc. 2005. "Computer Games and Learning: Digital Game-Based Learning," in Joost Raessens and Jeffrey Goldstein, eds, *Handbook of Computer Game Studies*. Cambridge, MA, and London: MIT Press, 97–123.

Rasmussen. 2010. "Daily Presidential Tracking Poll." *Rasmussen Reports*, July 28. Available at: www.rasmussenreports.com/public_content/politics/obama_administration/daily_presidential_tracking_poll (accessed July 28, 2010).

Smith, Ben. "Health Reform Foes Plan Obama's Waterloo." Available at: www.politico.com/blogs/bensmith/0709/Health_reform_foes_plan_Obamas_Waterloo.html (accessed July 24, 2010).

Smith, Derik. 2008. "I Am Obama: The American Imagination and the New Black Hero." *PopMatters.Com*, February 25. Available at: www.popmatters.com/pm/feature/55188/i-am-obama/ (accessed May 25, 2010).

Tapscott, Don. 1998. *Growing Up Digital: The Rise of the Net Generation*. New York: McGraw Hill.

Terkel, Amanda. 2008. "Racist GOP Mailing Depicts Obama Surrounded by KFC, Watermelon, and Food Stamps." *Think Progress*, October 16. Available at: http://thinkprogress.org/2008/10/16/obama-bucks/ (accessed October 20, 2008).

Turkle, Sherry. 1995, 1997. *Life on the Screen: Identity in the Age of the Internet*. New York: Touchstone.

Van Dijk, Jan A.G.M. 2005. *The Deepening Divide: Inequality in the Information Society*. Thousand Oaks, London and New Delhi: Sage.

X, Madame. "The Obama Phone." *HubPages.Com*. Online. http://hubpages.com/forum/topic/25409 (accessed July 18, 2010).

8

Connection at Ewiiaapaayp Mountain

Indigenous Internet Infrastructure

CHRISTIAN SANDVIG

University of Illinois, Urbana-Champaign

It's a cloudy spring day in 2004 and Joseph is on top of a mountain on the Santa Ysabel Indian Reservation. He is climbing the tower that provides Internet service to the reservation. Joseph is a teenager and an apprentice network engineer, but it's a job he'll soon give up to become a valet at a nearby casino. As jobs go, it's not much of a comparison: As a casino valet he'll get tips, the chance to drive "some pretty nice cars," and the chance for promotions, while as a network engineer he gets a lower hourly wage and the chance to climb and maintain 80-foot towers with no ladder. The tower he's climbing today isn't normal as towers go—it was already erected and thrown away once (by a cellular telephone company) before Joseph got his hands on it. Joseph's brother Michael bought it in pieces from a salvage yard in El Centro and brought it here. "It was about what, 105 degrees, and we had to pick out all the bolts, the washers, and the nuts out of these 50 gallon drums . . . and count them all," Michael says. The tower adds its 80 feet to the top of this 5,400-foot mountain in the Palomar Mountains, part of the rugged Peninsular Ranges that extend north from Sierra de Juarez. Michael and his colleague Matt didn't just build the tower, they also built the road to get to the mountaintop. On the way there, "the brakes on the trailer started smoking," said Matt, "and we were saying, 'It shouldn't be this heavy.'" They had accidentally bought a steel tower instead of an aluminum one. "We had to get the whole foundation re-engineered," Michael said. Speaking of the broadband Internet system that they both run, Matt added, "We built the network before we knew how it worked exactly."

Back in 2004, Michael and Matt look on as Joseph nimbly scales the support struts to a height equivalent to the roof of a seven-story building. Matt comments, "We didn't get all the safety equipment that comes with these towers . . . like the ladders." Meanwhile, Michael crouches in a nearby plywood shed squinting into a magnifying glass held against the screen of a dusty laptop. For about an hour he rhythmically shouts out signal strength readings in isotropic decibels (dBi). He shouts, ". . . 70 . . . 70 . . . 71 . . . 70 . . . 70 . . ." as

Joseph, clinging to the tower on top of the world, repositions the giant metal bowl-shaped antennas by tiny increments. The monotony is occasionally relieved by Michael's joking and his infectious laugh. Joseph, Michael, and Matt are aiming invisible radio waves of wireless Internet at other distant mountaintops. The shed where Michael crouches is filled wall-to-wall with rows of car batteries connected to a solar array outside. The whole site is surrounded by chain-link to keep out the wild burros—they've roamed here ever since prospectors brought them in the 1850s, and they'll chew anything. Despite its scrapyard provenance, everything is well kept and looks professional, except that to a practiced eye it lacks a certain uniformity: each one of the four antennas bolted to the top of the tall tower came from somewhere else.

The tower is part of the Tribal Digital Village (henceforth, TDV), an innovative and successful solar wireless Internet distribution network that serves Indian lands in Southern California. This mountaintop has faster Internet service than my office at the University of Illinois, and it serves Indian reservations (some without phones, paved roads, or constant electrical power) where many residents now use the Internet every day, although some of them still may not have a phone. Matt, Michael, and Joseph's solar-powered metal towers—the way that the Internet is distributed here—form a system that is very different from one that a telecommunications company like AT&T would build, if they could ever be convinced to build here.

In 2010, the FCC estimated that 65 percent of American households had broadband Internet in the home. That is the proportion of Native Americans with basic telephone service. Statistics about Native broadband are largely unavailable or unreliable, but one unsourced US government estimate puts national broadband penetration on Native lands at well below 10 percent (Genachowski 2010). However, on some reservations served by Joseph, Michael, and Matt of the TDV, broadband penetration is 100 percent and every single resident reports using the Internet daily.[1] This chapter is, first, an attempt to explain the TDV's success and, second, to better understand the difference between the way AT&T might have done things and the way that the TDV has. On the way I will also explain how providing infrastructure on Indian reservations may be such a different problem than supplying it somewhere else. In this I will reflect on indigeneity, infrastructure, user-driven innovation, and appropriation—all discussed in detail later.

On the Reservations of Southern California

The TDV story began in the summer of 2000. At that time the Indian reservations in Southern California had little to no access to the Internet, and this was long after access to the Internet had become normal elsewhere. Although today we would consider it slow, virtually the entire US then had access to the Internet in some form if they chose to subscribe.[2] Almost all American Internet users (90 percent) then used "dial-up" Internet access that required the user to place a call on a telephone line with a modem (NTIA 2000). Dial-up access was available across the US (via a metered telephone call charged by the minute), while more than 96.5 percent of the US population had access to cheaper dial-up Internet service via an unmetered local call (Downes and Greenstein 2002: 1035).[3]

On the reservations, while unmetered dial-up access was available to some places in 2000 (Downes and Greenstein 2002: 1042), on some reservations the poor quality of the telephone lines meant that a modem couldn't connect at all, or it could only connect at a very slow speed that was normal over ten years earlier (9600 bps). On one reservation the telephones themselves would not work when it rained. Other reservations had no telephone service (cellular or landline), and as of this writing they still do not. Some also lack paved roads and electrical power.

The poor state of basic infrastructure on these reservations is not unusual in "Indian Country" (a phrase referring to self-governing Native American lands in the US). By many measures, American Indians are the most economically disadvantaged group in America (Brescia and Daily 2007: 23). Those who self-identified as American Indian in the US Census's American Community Survey in 2007 are the least likely group to be employed, the least likely to hold a professional occupation if they are employed, the least likely to work in a technology-related field,[4] and the most likely to be below the poverty line (US Census Bureau 2008).

In 2000, the tribal governments in San Diego County estimated the overall high school graduation rate on San Diego area reservations at 15 percent and unemployment at 50 percent, and noted that 75 percent of primary school students qualify for free or reduced-cost school lunch programs (a common measure of poverty).[5] Michael, the Network Administrator for the TDV, explains reservations to outsiders using a comparison to the ghetto:

> Life is hard on the reservation; if you're from the inner city, you know what the ghetto is like and life is probably hard in the ghetto. Well, we're rural, but life is just like that on the reservation. You got drugs, you got alcoholism, you got all kinds of different types of abuse, the poverty, I mean, just like the whole thing.

There are few schools on reservation lands. Michael continues,

> When I was in high school, there were 26 of us that started as freshmen. We were bussed 45 minutes off the reservation to go to high school. There were 26 of us when I started, and there were three of us that finished.

The ghetto metaphor and its implicit comparison is probably helpful for Michael because he so often has to defend Native claims to poverty or need to a skeptical non-Native public. For example, online news stories about Native problems that appear on the *North County Times* or the *San Diego*

Union-Tribune Web sites always have their user-contributed comments turned off because the stories will so reliably attract slurs ("squaw," "redskin"). Articles about Native poverty or misfortune attract comments that state that "all Indians are rich" because of exorbitant welfare payments or casino revenues, or that "all Indians are drunk" or "lazy" and therefore deserve any misfortune that befalls them.[6]

Native Americans living in what is now called San Diego County are known as Mission Indians. "Mission" is a reference to place—it refers to groups that were living in the area upon the arrival of the Spanish Franciscans to colonize the region (Research Guide n.d.). In other words, Mission Indians are the people who hold the first known historical connection to the area: they are indigenous. They are often distinguished by language and descent into four groups: Kumeyaay (Diegueño), Cupeño, Luiseño, and Cahuilla (ibid.; see also Hyer 1999). These groups are further distinguished into federally recognized tribes that are sovereign and may hold land in trust. Research on disadvantaged groups that considers race may emphasize appearance, shared culture, or ancestry, but the registration (called "enrollment") in a federally recognized tribal group is a critical identity marker in Indian Country, as is evinced by its frequent discussion and the widespread logo merchandise worn by many enrolled members on every occasion—particularly baseball caps that say the tribe's name.

It would surprise most Californians that San Diego County has more distinct federally recognized Indian reservations than any other county in the United States (Sutton 2006). There are about 350,000 acres of reservation or "trust" lands in Southern California, and about 50,000 Indians living in the San Diego region (Sutton 2006: 75–76). About 8,000 Indians live on these reservations.[7]

Living on a reservation is hard to generalize about. As others have written (Sutton 2003), the details of a tribe's sovereign status and the history of the reservation lands are in each case very particular. Some San Diego area reservations were created after Luiseño leaders advocated for federal reservation status for the lands where they were already living.[8] In contrast, Cupeños from Agua Caliente (Warner's Ranch) were evicted from their homes and relocated by force to a site chosen by the US government, although some resisted and fled (Hyer 1999: 424).

The infamous forced marches from the US policy of Indian removal are usually taught in American History classrooms in units about "Westward expansion," and to the non-Indian (like me) they seem as though they are part of the distant past. (The infamous removal of the Choctaw Nation, for instance, known as the Trail of Tears, occurred in 1831.) But here in the mountains of Southern California the Cupeños were removed in the twentieth century, in 1903. Michael, a Luiseño Indian living on the Rincon reservation, comments:

> My great-great grandmother was a Cupeño—she was thirteen years old when they made the journey down to Rincon. I guess it's not that long

of a hike. I mean, I wouldn't want to do it. But the time they chose for them to do it was really bad, and so a lot of people died.

(The march was about 39 miles over Palomar Mountain.)

As a result of the vicissitudes of history and the fluctuations of Indian policy, some Southern California reservations (such as Pala) are centrally located, reachable by existing roads, and contain arable land and ready access to water. Others are remote and virtually uninhabitable due to their mountainous terrain. Even land within a single reservation (e.g. San Pasqual) may not be contiguous and the individual parcels may not be connected by roads (Srinivasan 2006: 508). As a consequence some reservations are not inhabited, others are subject to land dispute, and some are inhabited seasonally (e.g. Ewiiaapaayp). The only common feature of the reservations in this area may be that they were lands that no one white wanted.

Offline by Design

Both in Southern California and elsewhere in the US, almost all Indian reservations were chosen as prisons. That is, the land was selected in order to isolate Native populations and to remove them from land that might ever be desirable. Today these places lack basic infrastructure like roads, power, and telephones, but ultimately infrastructure is difficult to provide in these areas by design—they are lands chosen to be inhospitable, and the residents were forcibly relocated there by the US government. For this reason, unlike other public policy initiatives that help the underserved and other rationales for telecommunications policy and universal service (see Sawhney 1994), programs like the Federal Indian Telecommunications Initiative and the FCC's Native Nations Broadband Task Force (FCC 2006, 2010) have a very different moral status. They can be conceptualized first as redress and second as a contractual obligation. Subsidizing infrastructure on Native lands is putting back something that the government earlier took away (or made much more difficult) by forced relocation. More broadly, the US government acquired most of its sovereign land area by promising a variety of benefits to Indians, sometimes in perpetuity, and infrastructure investment conceptually fulfills these treaty obligations. This is quite a different perspective than seeing these efforts as either social policy or welfare. For example, the 1851 Treaty of Temecula promises that the US will maintain shops, dwellings, and the services of schoolteachers, a carpenter, blacksmith, and wheelwright on Luiseño reservation lands in perpetuity.[9] Although clearly the technology of infrastructure has changed, the intent was to provision Native infrastructure in exchange for land. The US still has the land, but the reservations lack the promised infrastructure.

Of the eighteen reservations in San Diego County, at this writing only three contain areas that can obtain Internet service via traditional telecommunications companies. While the difficult terrain is one major obstacle, another major problem is the demographics of the reservations themselves which make them uninteresting to corporate providers. As one network technician succinctly put it, "Not enough bodies, too much space in between." (He might have added: not enough money.)

Difficulties are also legal and institutional. As a consequence of the history of warfare between the US and Indian nations, Native sovereignty (the supreme, independent authority over a territory) is one of the most important legal features that define life on reservations. Native sovereignty includes most of telecommunications policy (see FCC 2000) and the details of sovereignty create significant legal and institutional barriers to many of the most basic forms of commercial activity as it is practiced off the reservation (for a review, see Bissell 2004).

The telecommunications industry in the US has evolved away from local efforts, and the accepted standard of service is now integration within a national oligopoly of a few companies (AT&T, Sprint, Verizon, Comcast, and so on). The demographics and geography of the reservations provide no incentive for these companies to engage with the complexities of Native legal exceptionalism. Property ownership is not possible on Native lands and digging may not be permitted—these are major obstacles to the normal approach of carriers like AT&T. A business venture always requires a negotiation with the tribal government, while any non-Native investments on Indian reservations may potentially be expropriated by the tribe. On some tribal lands, even access is forbidden without advance permission. (The reservation is surrounded by a fence, and the gate is locked.) In this institutional environment, only ventures with very high profit potential like casinos can entice non-Native investment into a reservation's collectivist (and mainly non-capitalist) economy.

Native investment by the tribes themselves is difficult because the history of neglect and poor service in telecommunications has been self-reinforcing, as tribal governments often lack technical expertise related to telecommunications. This leaves them both unlikely to succeed at self-provision and also at a serious disadvantage when negotiating with a large telecommunications corporation. One Southern California tribe granted Sprint a lien for the construction of a fiber optic backbone across reservation land, but the tribe did not realize that this was an advantageous negotiating position to ask for telecommunication services. Someone else's Internet thus transits the reservation but for the Indians there is no tap. On the surface just above the buried cable, the Indian telephones don't work.

The dismal state of telecommunications service on reservations has been an increasing source of embarrassment to the US government (US Congress Office of Technology Assessment 1995; FCC 2006, 2010). To improve the economic attractiveness of Indian populations, US subsidies on some reservations allow anyone to subscribe to telephone service for $1 per month if the service is offered, as the federal government will subsidize the rest (FCC 2006). Yet telecommunications infrastructure is still so rudimentary that telephone service (much less Internet service) is not available to many Indian households, regardless of what they would be willing to pay. In the past, even where the telephone was available adoption rates remained remarkably low, suggesting some deeper and so far insoluble obstacles beyond cost.

TDV: The Genesis and Overview

It was in this challenging context that the TDV began and evolved from an experimental university project to an ongoing public service on tribal lands. In this section I will present the origin of the TDV and a sketch of its growth and evolution so that in later sections I can evaluate and generalize from some of TDV's particularities to the evolution of technological infrastructures generally. The TDV began with the serendipitous intervention of research scientist Hans-Werner Braun of the San Diego Supercomputer Center at the University of California, San Diego. A German-born engineer with a long and distinguished career in computer networking, Braun had designed and built Internet backbones as early as the 1980s.[10] When driving through the rural highways of northern San Diego County with his wife he had often noticed the highway signs demarcating Indian reservations. When he wrote a grant proposal to the US National Science Foundation to build a high-speed wireless network connecting remote Southern California academic research centers, he also had Native Americans on his mind.[11] Braun described the genesis by saying,

> Technology like . . . cell phones provides the illusion of reachability. Since you go out in rural areas and you often don't have connectivity, let alone high-speed connectivity. Yet many [research] centers are in very remote areas: out in the desert or on a mountaintop. When I submitted the original . . . grant proposal I wanted astronomy stuff and ecology stuff . . . and the seismic centers were all in the proposal already. Somehow I got the thought, for no good reason, wouldn't it be cool to involve Native Americans? And I put it into the proposal but I had no idea how to do it.

It turned out that the Pala Learning Center already had a grant-funded computer lab, but without broadband Internet connectivity the director has resorted to a sign on the single dial-up connected computer reading "Internet access is limited to 20 minutes." The Pala officials told Hans-Werner that on more distant reservations (like Rincon) school, library, and community center computers gathered dust because no Internet connectivity was available at all.

Thus commenced an almost textbook instance of technology transfer between Hans-Werner's university project and the tribal governments of Southern California. This technology transfer fits what the research policy literature has fittingly called "the mission paradigm" (Bozeman 2000) where government labs pursue topics of national interest with public funds, just as Braun pursued basic and applied research in wireless computing at the San Diego Supercomputer Center. As a policy goal, this public investment aims in part to transfer both process and craft to commercial and educational institutions, ideally particularly benefiting underserved populations. Public money thus funds advanced wireless research at Hans-Werner's university and, eventually, the tribes of Southern California are the beneficiary, creating a spin-off: the TDV.

The TDV network is, at its base, also philanthropic. While initially providing university Internet connectivity to three tribes from his research project free of charge, Hans-Werner asked for installation help from tribal members and told his tribal contacts, "I'm not a service provider." A university/tribal partnership followed and eventually received a $5 million grant from Hewlett-Packard to develop the network on reservation lands, and thus was christened the "Tribal Digital Village" (the title of the grant proposal).[12]

Michael was at that time working at the Rincon Education Center as a youth counselor. When the Center was to be connected to Hans-Werner's university network, Michael participated in the day-long construction of the tower. It was a tricky enough job that each member of the team signed the inside of the radio box with black permanent marker when they finished. From this, a friendship between Hans-Werner and Michael eventually led Michael to the job of Network Administrator for the TDV, despite his lack of formal education in computing. Michael learned about networking on the workbench during visits to Hans-Werner's rural home. Michael reflects,

> we had to put IP addresses into our computers, but I didn't know what an IP address was. [Hans-Werner] just told me the numbers to put in and I put the numbers in. I had NO idea what they were for . . . [Hans-Werner] said, "When you get it set up, try to ping the other side." "Okay," I said, "what is ping?"

Experimentation quickly showed that Michael had a talent for wireless networking, a technical area where he was working with university researchers at near the state of the art. New radios, software, and network designs emerging at the time were invariably finicky, and in order to connect the reservations the TDV had to install equipment in some of the most inhospitable environments possible. Recall that most tower sites lacked power and water, and many were not accessible by road. Indeed, towers were surrounded by hostile thorny vegetation, and were subject to mudslides, rockfalls, washouts and wildfires. (Not to mention the burros.) Winds—the legendary Santa Anas—routinely topped 100 mph on tower sites, playing havoc with the delicate orientation of the antennas and solar panels, or simply blowing down entire structures during storms. Hans-Werner remembers:

> I told him . . . build a network on a bench first, and if you can make that work, you can make it work on a mountaintop. But if you start off on a mountaintop, you're not going to be able to make the network work . . . [When] Michael came online . . . suddenly there was a lot of interaction that resulted in expertise transfer, basically, by us educating them. Then

they educate us as well about some improvements that they've made because they've improved on our design; they made it better. So there was a lot of interaction which ramped down over time as their expertise ramped up . . . initially we did the whole thing and transitioned the technology, transitioned the expertise, and it turned around after a while where we actually were being helped by [start air quotes] them [end air quotes], not only as people but also on the technology side.

The TDV developed by propagating new towers and moving bandwidth away from the university network, then it slowly grew more independent as expertise and funding increased. After three years the bandwidth used for TDV began to be reimbursed via the federal e-Rate program, a universal service initiative which subsidizes services to schools and libraries (for an overview, see Hudson 2004). With e-Rate funding, the TDV eventually stopped relying on university equipment and bandwidth altogether. Graduating from the university network had been a goal from the beginning, and Braun was delighted by this accomplishment. The TDV now exists as a government project of the Southern California Tribal Chairmen's Association, a federation of nineteen tribes.[13]

Although the build-out of TDV was challenging, some of the characteristics that made infrastructure difficult on these reservations made this wireless infrastructure ideal. As Michael says,

You know, we were stuck on Indian reservations in the worst part of the counties. Well, guess what? Haha! We've got all the mountaintops and now we can create this cool wireless network that nobody thought we could do.

The tribes had been banished to the mountaintops, but now the mountaintops were the answer. The tribes controlled ideal tower locations and they also avoided paying rent or purchasing land by avoiding private property (TDV towers were constructed on reservation lands). Construction of these new towers on tribal lands could proceed much faster than off them, as the tribes perform their own environmental assessments. Obtaining permission for new construction is much faster from the tribal council than a building permit would be from the county.

A timeline of milestones for the TDV appears in the Appendix as Table 8.1. Over nine years the TDV grew from a connection to just one computer lab (the Pala Learning Center with the "Internet access is limited . . ." sign) to serve about 1,500 users on seventeen Indian reservations. It began as a way to provide service to government buildings (libraries, schools, fire stations, tribal offices, and community centers), as offering service to a central point in each community is common strategy for many broadband or Internet projects where resources are scarce. The start-up grant from Hewlett-Packard provided end-user equipment (like computers and printers) to jump-start the process. Almost ten years later, a major problem for the network is now that it cannot grow fast enough to accommodate the many demands for new services on reservation lands.

To make all of this possible, Michael, Matt, Joseph, and others constructed twenty-three towers. These range from short rooftop masts to 80-foot steel and aluminum monoliths with elaborate outbuildings and poured concrete bases. As Matt explained it in 2009, TDV operates in a rectangle about 100 miles by 75 miles, spanning the area from the US–Mexico border up into Riverside County. It has 90 miles of backbone (point-to-point) links, and the backbone operates on solar power at 45 Mbit/sec, or about 800 times faster than the dial-up modem it replaced at Pala ten years ago.

This tale of continuous expansion hides important obstacles and strategies that explain infrastructure on Native lands. It also foregrounds a puzzle: How did the TDV succeed when similar initiatives on other tribal lands have not? The obstacles and strategies here concern the network of boxes, wires and waves, but also the residents and network builders. In the next section I will describe the TDV in more detail by considering the Internet users of Mesa Grande. Then in a subsequent section I will investigate the technological evolution of the devices and network engineers. The history of Native American engagement with technology makes the "missionary paradigm" for new technology more fraught than among other populations. That is, technology evangelists can remind San Diego tribal members of other sorts of missionaries.

Tribal Perspectives on the Internet

Without exception the staff of TDV explain its success as a human one. As Matt put it, in the world of tribal politics, just getting this many tribes to do anything together is a capital achievement. The TDV started by offering service to tribal government offices in part so that the first users would be the tribal leaders, who could then act as emissaries for the service to others. At the beginning of the TDV there was already a small population of Internet users on reservation lands using dial-up (as at the Pala Learning Center), and these were usually people with tribal government jobs related to education or administration. The government workers, then, were sometimes the easiest to convince as they were already users. After the TDV provided broadband service to community centers and government buildings the network builders hoped to expand the network to residences. But to do that they needed to encourage Internet use among a population that had little to no experience with Internet use.

Some of the Native perspectives on the Internet and computing generally were difficult for me to grasp because the Internet's promise of connectivity seems manifestly useful—especially in remote areas. There are a few narratives about Internet resistance (Wyatt et al. 2002), but these emphasize that being uninterested in using the Internet is very rare—about 2 percent of the US population was uninterested in 2009 and this is declining (Horrigan 2009). TDV staffers like Matt and Michael and outside collaborators like Hans-Werner enthusiastically share the most optimistic view of the Internet and Internet connectivity. However, while the connotation of "new technology" for most readers will be positive, historically the interface between Native peoples and technology has often been negative (e.g. James 2006).[14] Even free Internet service can be seen as another intrusive government program that follows a stream of misguided past interventions, or as something that is potentially culturally dangerous.

The relatively short history of computing projects on Indian reservations has also produced as many warnings as successes. A project with one meaning off the reservation might find quite a different reception when brought to Indian Country. For example, one of the earliest successful educational computer games produced for use in public schools is "Oregon Trail." It was a blockbuster hit after its release in 1973 and it made the idea of educational computing on personal computers in classrooms mainstream. Although a simple game by today's standards, it is still used in elementary schools around the US. Schoolchildren play the role of white settlers colonizing the West in a manner that is quite alarming to Native users (Bowers et al. 2000: 194). As one instruction manual for a revised version (titled "Westward Ho!") points out dryly, as a player it is a valid move to kill both the hostile and the friendly Indians, but shooting the friendly Indians wastes bullets (Ahl 1986).

In the first blush of enthusiasm for the Internet (particularly in the 1990s) the Internet was celebrated by referring to the possibility of placelessness, or access to information without reference to place, and also to the excitement of anonymity or identity play—in utopian claims about the Internet every user could be equal. The state of indigeneity, in contrast, is a continual assertion of place and an affirmation of identity.

While past research on information and communication technologies has almost always explicitly acknowledged the problems of social justice that plague indigenous peoples, one persistent goal of researchers from this literature is to organize indigenous knowledge for its preservation and broad dissemination (e.g. Neeklmeghan and Chester 2007). But from a Native perspective the interconnection of knowledge is not read as neutral—it is read as extraction of valuable knowledge for use by others without compensation or control. As Howe writes, networked communication "condones equal and immediate access to information by all," but "this is antithetical to the social transmission of morally sanctioned tribal knowledge" (Howe 1998: 23–24).

Government agencies and foundations have promoted the use of computers for the purpose of cultural preservation among indigenous peoples (such as Roy 2006; Srinivasan 2007) and this was one of the justifications for the TDV's founding grant from Hewlett-Packard. Yet the codification of tribal knowledge has not served these nations well in the past, and to have more information available on the Internet can be seen as profoundly ignorant of the practices by which information is organized in these societies. Anthropologists have analyzed today's taken-for-granted technological artifacts such as steel axes (Sharp 1952) and irrigation (Pfaffenberger 1988) and have found them to be implicated in the collapse of indigenous cultures and the impoverishment of Native peoples. Whatever obvious use these technologies seem to be designed for, they have also promoted genocide, forced assimilation, and dependency.

These connections between Internet evangelism and the technologically equipped missionaries of the past have not been missed by commentators: On the Internet, "tribal knowledge is usually treated as secular information with no restrictions on when it is broadcast and received, or who has access to broadcasting and receiving it" (Howe 1998: 24).

> That is, the Internet . . . is not merely the latest "foreign good"—such as cooking pots, firearms, and automobiles—to be adopted into tribal communities . . . until its universalistic and individualistic foundation is restructured to incorporate spatial, spiritual, and experiential dimensions that particularize its application, cyberspace is no place for tribalism. (Howe 1998: 26–27)

Recent Internet projects in the Navajo (Diné) Nation and the Hopi Nation found that those who participated were "concerned about the impact of the Internet on tribal members and tribal cultural knowledge" (Roy 2006: 529). From the perspective of the tribes, a critical challenge is to ensure it is still possible that "[t]ribal elders will act as gatekeepers of traditional knowledge" (Warner 1998: 77). One of the "primary ethical issues around the spread of technology in Indian Country" is "external users' access to a tribe or to an individual . . . and the impact of that interaction" (Warner 1998: 76). In other words, promiscuous connection is the problem, not the goal.

It could be easy to see this concern as exotic (or even as backwards or primitive), but reflecting on other nations quickly shows it to be quite common. France, Hungary, South Korea, Italy, and Spain have also placed legal restrictions on the media to ensure that domestic language and culture are not lost in a sea of imported content. A common approach is the screen quota (or programming quota) and domestic subsidy where a certain percentage of exhibitions are reserved for domestic languages or for domestically produced and subsidized content (Lee and Bae 2004: 164). Public debates about culture and programming quotas remain vibrant in many other countries (for Europe and the UK, see Galperin 2004: 134, 172) and are often an attempt to check or to be heard within the overwhelming flow of media from the US. In this, France and the Native sovereign nations of Southern California may be allies. Today, just as the TDV proposed a tribally separate Internet as a requirement for national sovereignty, the president of the national library of France proposed a similar effort to protect French culture from Google Books (Jeanneney 2006).

The TDV grant proposal went beyond Internet access, promising to fund the digitization of "historical photographs, songs, and spoken language," as well as "digital storytelling," and "Web-based tools for language teaching and preservation" (for a similar project, see Srinivasan 2006, 2007). The grant also proposed a walled garden approach, including a separate e-mail system ("Rez-Mail"), e-greeting card system, and calendar to make "tribal and inter-tribal communication" easier than communication with the outside. But Native populations are not monolithic, and worries about cultural preservation and the dangers of assimilation divide sharply by class. In Eric Michaels's canonical narrative of the introduction of television production among the Warlpiri (Michaels 1994) tribal leaders speaks of the introduction of new media technology in terms of an ongoing cultural and language war between first nations and the dominant culture, and of unique first nations contributions to culture that should be subsidized and supported. But while the tribal leadership sees satellite television as a threat and part of a cultural war, the average Warlpiri television viewer in Michaels's account is thrilled by the chance to see live soccer matches for the first time. Indeed, concerns about assimilation are most often held by the cultural elite, while non-elites can be enthusiastic about new connections and the chance to use tools or see media that are common elsewhere.[15] (The same is true in France.)

Figure 8.1 The TDV services the Adams Drive backbone tower. (2008)

Photo credit: Matt Crain

Figure 8.2 Joseph climbs a backbone tower on the Santa Ysabel Indian
Reservation to the height of a seven-story building. Matt comments,
"We didn't get all the safety equipment that comes with these towers
. . . like the ladders." (2006)

PHOTO CREDIT: Hope Hall

Figure 8.3 Ewiiaapaayp Indian Reservation has high-speed Internet access (from 1 to 45 Mbit/s) but no paved roads, electrical power, or telephones. (2008)

PHOTO CREDIT: Matt Crain

Figure 8.4 "Punky" at home with her laptop on the Mesa Grande Indian Reservation. The reservation has universal broadband adoption. (2008)

PHOTO CREDIT: Hope Hall

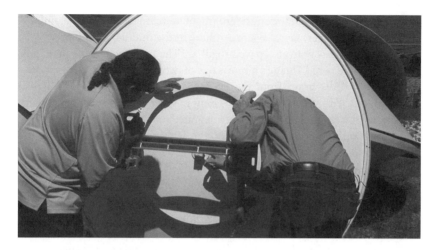

Figure 8.5 Michael and Hans-Werner examine the back of an antenna at the antenna graveyard in rural San Diego County. (2008)

PHOTO CREDIT: Hope Hall

Native Users Are Different; And They Are Required to Be

The TDV project emphasized the profoundly disadvantaged populations on the reservations and proposed the Internet as a tool for cultural preservation because the proposers were savvy about the politics of fundability. That is, funding rationales for the TDV emphasize technology transfer, poverty, and cultural patrimony rather than, say, the essential unfairness of everyone else in the US having the Internet (and telephones, roads, and electrical power) when Indians do not. The grant makes some worrying promises, however, because it implies that success for the TDV will lead to new technological developments, reduce poverty, and preserve culture. This is a serious disconnect between the everyday uses of the Internet and our usual reasons for subsidizing it. This is true for the TDV just as it is in most studies of Internet use in disadvantaged communities elsewhere: people use the Internet in a variety of ways—probably most prominently to entertain themselves and maintain their social connections. These uses conflict with the stridently instrumentalist approach of public policy and philanthropic subsidy. Our public policy assumes that users are working or educating ourselves all the time (e.g. Sandvig 2006). Thus the Internet, widely known to be a great source for pornography and idleness, can be subsidized as an educational and uplifting technological device only by developing a careful blindness about what people actually do with it.

In 2006, TDV expanded service to residential areas with a new connection to the Mesa Grande reservation. When drivers approach Mesa Grande on the only road, it jumps out of the mostly empty landscape as though it were an oasis. Duane, a Mesa Grande resident, night watchman, and former minor-league baseball player, says, "We're out here in the middle of no place. We're 30 minutes either way from a paved road! . . . The milk man, cable man, post man don't come here." Duane's home is one of twenty-two on the reservation—all built by a 1992 grant from the US Department of Housing and Urban Development. The street of homes was built in two phases from generic plans. Architects praise a structure when it is integrated into its site and surroundings: These reservation homes are not. For the visitor, the street produces the distinctly odd effect of a stucco-walled California suburb that has been magically moved far away from its origin: the close-packed houses, streetlights, and the paved road (Hallyeyaaw Drive) start and stop abruptly, as though at a line on an unseen map. Beyond the limit, there is no paving and indeed no man-made structure of any kind. These twenty-two homes and the tribal hall are the only buildings on the reservation, although a nearby parcel is used to keep seventy head of buffalo. When the TDV first began serving residential homes instead of only government buildings (such as schools, libraries, community centers, and tribal offices), the Chairman of the Mesa Grande tribe volunteered this reservation, surely in part due to its extreme isolation.

In 2008 I visited these homes and talked with their occupants about the Internet. When I was invited into their homes I asked them to show me how they normally used it. None of the residents could recall ever attempting to use dial-up Internet, meaning that at the introduction of broadband TDV service in 2006 they went from Internet non-users to daily users. Penetration is 100 percent on the reservation, and all residents reported using the Internet daily. To spur use, residents were given free computers (though relatively simple and slow ones). Even with these incentives, the Internet's sudden popularity wasn't certain. Duane explains:

> When the computers were first given to us, a lot of people down here didn't [want them]. Either [they] weren't computer savvy or they just didn't know what to do with it, you know? Mesa Grande . . . although we're big in number, money-wise, we're probably one of the poorest tribes. And so for a piece of equipment like this to come into some of these houses, it's just a mind-blower. And it almost scares some people. [imitates others] "I don't want to break it." "I don't want somebody to find out I don't know how to use it."

Duane explains that universal adoption—suddenly every home had the Internet and a computer at the same time, and they had the same computer—helped the residents learn to use the Internet together via a mutually supportive experimentation. (Although the TDV did offer formal classes, none of the users we spoke with had taken them.) Duane says,

> I'm not the smartest bird in the world, but I can figure most things out. So I can get on a computer and send my [e-mail] and go through it.

In fact, I can figure almost anything out. How long [it takes] is a whole different story!

All of the users of the TDV were at great pains to demonstrate the Internet's benefits for education and employment use, as this was the most readily accessible framing that would justify the existence of the network to me—and they knew the network was unusual. The moral burden of receiving free computers and not paying monthly charges meant that a frenzy of instrumental language was always deployed when I arrived, along with effusive praise of the TDV staff and government providers. The Internet was "educational," "for the children," "for the kids," "for homework," "for training," "for jobs," "for work," and "improves our opportunities." It was "a help." As Duane says, "The bottom line is it was a big help. And once people found out that it was help and not, you know, a hinder, I think, I don't think nobody down here disagrees with us being able to get it."

Of course the Internet is educational, but it is other things as well. After spending more time with the Internet users of Mesa Grande, it is clearer that they use the Internet mostly in the same way that anyone else would. Candice, a Mesa Grande teenager and casino worker nicknamed Punky, starts out with the justifications that were so familiar: "Lots of people, like, use the Internet to look into college and, you know, like, things you can do in the future. You know, and, how you can better yourself." After a longer interview, Punky admits that Mesa Grande teens use the network mostly as we would expect them to. She says,

> Oh yeah. Everybody does [use the Internet] here. Actually, you know, like, MySpace [laughs]. Lots of people down here have MySpace and talk to each other over the MySpace, chat, things like that [laughs] . . . Yeah, well, um, my cousin who I, um, I went to high school with I didn't see for a long time. And I went on her MySpace thing and found out she was pregnant, and so I congratulated her and, it's good to see that. And she had a baby, and it's a beautiful baby boy, so . . . I got to see that, and . . . she did [put the pictures online].

Again, undoubtedly Punky is right when she says that the Internet is used to "better yourself," but what is fascinating here is the moral burden—the requirement for utility—that subsidized Internet has put on Indian users. As mentioned above, providing Internet access here is one of the most difficult challenges in Internet provision anywhere. To justify their expensive and heavily subsidized use of the Internet they must perform difference—they must act like disadvantaged Indians who seek uplift and the preservation of their culture, despite the fact that (just as it was in Michaels's account of the Warlpiri), they may be more interested in MySpace or soccer games.

Duane uses the Internet for hours on almost every work day, and he was very clear about its place after he comes home from work.

For me, I use it more as a toy than as a tool. I love the computer as far as just being able to get on it and just, uh, play on it; like I said, I mainly use it as a toy. That's my biggest thing: I'm not afraid to relax and enjoy things. I'm not one of them guys, or one of them people that have to go out and just [motions] . . . So I'll come home, eat something, and I'll come straight to my hole here [gestures at desk] and I'll turn on the TV. And the TV is nothing but noise most of the time; the computer is my main attraction. I'll turn on the TV or radio for the news and play—most the time—[online] poker, or a video baseball game [for] three or four hours at a time. You can buy a [CD-ROM game] . . ., but you buy a disc and it's just not live, you know? You play it once or twice, it's old news. Every time you get on the Internet it seems to be new, you know?

Duane also mentions keeping in touch with an old friend who travels avidly by receiving his e-mails from Amsterdam and New Mexico.

The difficulty of using public money to subsidize uses like Duane's has a long history in US policy. With the telephone, American legislators have long tried to separate the "useless" and "useful" and only subsidize the latter. For example, federal "Lifeline" subsidies have been designed to encourage telephone adoption so that the ability to call 9-1-1 would be universally available—potentially saving entire communities via the early reporting of fires before they spread. Yet this subsidy has often been structured so that the government cannot be accused of paying for talking on the phone for pleasure: by far the dominant actual use of the phone.[16]

Just as the TDV users are hesitant to admit they use subsidized MySpace and video baseball, the back-and-forth between what a technology "is designed for" vs "is used for" is obviously loaded and prescriptive in many settings. In the late 1980s French international aid agencies developed a solar-powered lighting kit for charitable export to rural Côte d'Ivoire (Ivory Coast) and other "less developed countries" (Akrich 1992). A lighting kit was chosen for charitable export because providing light is an uncontroversial use of charity. Indeed, the lighting kit itself was painstakingly designed to prevent its users from adapting it for any use other than lighting. In part the French designers restricted the system because they assumed that electricians in Côte d'Ivoire were not skilled enough to repair or modify it. (They would only break it.) Although the kit was "hardened" with non-standard plugs and wiring, in the end local electricians managed to successfully modify it to allow the solar panels to power television sets. (In international aid circles this use of charitably provided power systems is sometimes called "the television problem."[17]) Watching television was the use that the recipients of the kit most preferred, but that the designers and funders of the kit least preferred (Akrich 1992).

The TDV has avoided most controversy about the uses of these subsidies because they justifiably feel, when pressed about it, that they should be able to use the Internet "just like everyone else." While other wireless Internet Service

Providers that I have studied were justified by either straightforward profit on the one hand or transformative utopian claims on the other, the TDV was the only network that I've encountered whose most consistent internal justification is equality. While the users justify themselves by claiming educational benefits, the producers say things like "level playing field," "equality," "fairness," "getting what everybody else has." As Matt says, "It's not a money-maker. Nobody's gonna get rich." Michael makes a claim to entitlement: "It's what the people deserve."

As a provocative addendum, while the TDV may aspire to equality, the continuing mismatch of infrastructure development on reservations does make for some Internet uses that are quite unusual off Native lands, and it does provide circumstances where the TDV user is unlikely to look like anyone else. One of the earliest home users of the TDV, whom I'll call Chairman X, lived in an area without electrical power.[18] After the TDV service was installed, his new morning routine included going outside to start up his gasoline-powered generator so that he could check his e-mail. On the remote Ewiiaapaayp reservation, where there is no electricity or telephone service, communication with the outside required hiking on a footpath up a mountain to hope for a chancy cell phone signal, or a 20-minute drive to old Highway 80. The most important Internet use spoken about there was wildfire reporting and making calls to emergency services. Now Desi, an Environmental Program Manager for this Kumeyaay tribal government, has personally evolved a very distinctive communication system. He uses a solar-charged car battery to boot his laptop from the tribal hall. He then connects to the Internet via the TDV. In 2008 he had no phone service on the reservation but he was not (yet) familiar with Skype or Internet telephone services. He had a way around the problem. Once online, he bookmarked an SMS gateway Web page that allows him to send SMS (text) messages to cellular phones from the Web for free. When something comes up at Ewiiaapaayp he texts down the mountain. His texts always say, "CHECK YOUR E-MAIL."

Cloudy Days and Hard-Won Knowledge

Technologically, the challenges facing Matt and Michael differed from those of the university research network where the TDV started. The university network's backbone consisted of powered sites and used existing telecommunications towers, but the lands available for the TDV backbone were remote and often at high elevation—and they often had no infrastructure at all.

Even with $5 million in start-up funding it was clear that a traditional approach to infrastructure construction would still be too expensive. Contracting with a cellular tower construction crew that worked for Pacific Bell, for example, would quickly exhaust their budget and provide only a few installations. Matt and Michael needed to locate towers in locations where a new road or trail would have to be created for the occasion, and this created impressive new obstacles even while it might save money on rent. Michael had the idea of enlisting his family members to carry bags of dry concrete mix and jugs of water in backpacks up steep hiking trails in order to stabilize the foundation of towers where no road could reach. Part of the unorthodoxy of Michael and Matt's approach was often the degree of risk that they were comfortable with. At one point, Michael built a tower by strapping the components onto the chassis of an ATV and driving it up the steep, rocky hillside. ("I thought [Michael] was insane," remembered Hans-Werner. "I got to the top!" replied Michael.) A later strategy of borrowing backhoes and building their own access roads was equally perilous. This is an area where a light rain can quickly turn the soil into impassable mud; the tight switchbacks and steep grades led to at least one Ready Mix Concrete Truck (bringing concrete for the tower foundation) sitting on the homemade road only to slowly lean over, with one wheel spinning in the air over a precipice. After these road-building adventures, a particularly difficult tower was constructed by dropping the equipment onto the mountaintop from a rented helicopter.

While one might think of the corporate engineers that developed and sold these towers, antennas, and radios as the experts on them, in fact the user of a device who is intimately familiar with its operation in their local context often has far more information about its performance characteristics and uses (von Hippel 1998, 2005). In this sense the TDV staff are users of the apparatus of wireless networking provided elsewhere.[19] In their construction of the TDV backbone network, Matt and Michael developed expertise with radios and antennas that made visits or phone calls with their vendors seem as though the chairs had been reversed. Matt and Michael could dictate the real performance characteristics of a given antenna or radio out of their long familiarity and the TDV's extreme conditions. To achieve connectivity in mountains across the North County and beyond, Michael and Matt often pushed beyond the limits (particularly range) listed on the specification sheets produced for their devices. In 2007, for instance, the San Diego wildfires destroyed two towers and came near a third tower at Adams Drive. The heat caused a pressure difference that exploded the glass membranes from all of the solar panels. The formerly drum-shaped, formerly airtight radio enclosures were left looking like sagging grey deflated balloons. The TDV was a kind of rugged technology sorting function: some devices continued to operate even when subjected to these terrific strains; others did not.

Matt and Michael readily acknowledge that they didn't know what they were doing, particularly in the early days. Michael jokes about their early network planning process by saying that they would get up on a mountain with a telescope and say,

"That's the direction. Can you see this [other] mountain?" And we'd look, and we'd walk around, and we'd get under trees so we could find the way. "Yeah, we see that mountain. Okay, that's a good point." Now we'd walk over to the other side to the vantage point: "Now, can you see that mountain over there?" "No." "Well, let's go over here. Can you see it?" "Yeah."

Their approach provided some innovative engineering because they didn't know what kinds of configurations were off-limits or outlandish. It led to wasted efforts, to be sure, such as their foray into satellite-fed broadband backhaul (where the latency and asymmetry proved intolerable) that was later abandoned, or the network topography experiments that led to the later removal of four towers and the re-routing of the backbone itself. Yet they also gradually demonstrated the way to run a very high-speed wireless backbone completely on solar power, surprising their mentor Hans-Werner and later leading him to consult them on solar installations. During their first attempts, atypical strings of cloudy days over a few key relay towers would abruptly cut off all Internet access to most of the network. But in what economists have called learning-by-using (Rosenberg 1982: 122), recurring cycles of use, evaluation, and modification improved and then stabilized the TDV's use of solar power. As Hans-Werner said, "It's green. It's all solar powered in [TDV's] backbone. And I find that very impressive." They are now experimenting with wind.

The TDV embarked on what the business literature has called a series of "innovate-or-buy" decisions. In other words: Build my own custom wireless network infrastructure or hire consultants to do it for me. As mentioned above, the decisions seemed straightforward and were decided on cost—professional customization was too expensive. The tribes spent liberally from their initially unskilled labor instead of contracting for expensive outside expertise. But even if more funding had been available, this innovate-or-buy calculus is not always straightforward. As von Hippel writes,

> Some individual users . . . may decide to innovate for themselves rather than buy even if a traditional accounting evaluation would show that they had made a major investment in time and materials for an apparently minor reward in product functionality. The reason is that individual users may gain major rewards from the process of innovating, in addition to the rewards from the product. (2005: 61)

Von Hippel emphasizes "control over my own work" (2005: 61) as a psychological reason that individuals might invest huge sums in an innovation process rather than buying something, even something custom-made for them. However, the analog to "control over my own work" in the TDV case is tribal sovereignty, a collective overriding social goal and not a psychological one. Indeed, the technology transfer literature and public policy in this area assumes at least the learning rewards from innovation as given, and may assume that great sums should be spent on minor customizations in the hope of transferring tacit knowledge, skills, and social connections.

In this case the technology transfer rationale has carried the day, transforming Michael from an afterschool tutor to a skilled network administrator with extensive professional connections across the forefront of wireless networking research and practice. The tribes themselves were transformed from users to producers: they now self-provide telecommunications services via TDV. In the process they have pioneered new configurations and assemblies of equipment and protocol stacks that are innovative among their peers, and copied. It is remarkable, then, that the academic rationale about the rewards of learning and control holds little weight with the people who lived through it.

Even though each struggle and setback was a chance to acquire new expertise, those involved in the project are now ready to give up their hard-won skills in exchange for normalcy. If we had the chance to do it again, they say, we wouldn't do it this way. Instead, they speak of spending their time writing more grants or raising more money to hire contractors who are already expert. Rather than delight in learning about tower construction, the expertise is a reminder that they had to do it themselves, and they didn't have the money or the status to have the same infrastructure as everyone else.

One extended foray with experimental mesh networking technology left a particularly bad taste behind. While the TDV received a grant to experiment with truly cutting-edge mesh protocols at Mesa Grande in the hope that meshing could reduce the overall system cost, they found the experimental equipment too temperamental, and soon abandoned the effort. While a successful new mesh deployment could pilot an innovative protocol suite for others, the TDV reasoned about this morally. Their users didn't deserve to be the guinea pigs of the networking world, and they aspired to "just plain Internet." Matt put it plainly: "No more experiments." Again, it's true that each trial by fire taught them something, but each piece of hard-won knowledge was still a reminder of their unusual status. Innovation, in this context, is both liberating and oppressive at the same time.

Joseph's tower climb at the beginning of this chapter provides a further example. Even though his work with Matt and Michael on the TDV surely taught him all about network engineering, the knowledge he gained was not sufficient for Joseph to pursue a high-tech, white-collar career in computing. Although he would be employable in such a job, no jobs like that exist anywhere near the reservations. (For example, almost all of the Mesa Grande reservation residents work for either casinos or the tribal government.) For Joseph, the technology transfer is a success (it developed his skills) but it doesn't take him anywhere worth going. Work in the casinos as a valet is the bottom rung of a defined career path. In contrast, a computing job is a dead end.

Appropriation Toward Parity: Understanding Difference in Technology

All of the differences between TDV and AT&T elaborated so far fit under the broad umbrella of the word "appropriation," one of the most intriguing concepts in the study of technology. Pronounced with a long second "a," to appropriate a technology literally means to possess it without permission—it denotes ownership, control, and the ability to modify. People are generally fascinated by stories where a technology was intended to do one thing but then it was forcefully re-made in order to do something else, just as old cellular telephone towers, new wireless signals, car batteries and more were re-made to provide Internet service by TDV. Appropriation is almost never portrayed as a boring step in the development of technology–instead it is couched as a kind of noble resistance, a daring assault launched by an underdog on the powerful. (Michael: "haha! . . . nobody thought we could.") Accounting for appropriation is useful because it can free us from the assumption that technologies always unfold in the ways they are intended to, or that a particular technology necessarily produces particular consequences (technological determinism).

In cases like this one it is not helpful to think about technology as a single monolithic object (like "the Internet" or "electrical power") that diffuses (Rogers 2003) through cultures and societies. Instead the technology itself is always changing—it exists as a complicated network of interested parties who all work to achieve their own interests with and through it, changing it at every turn (Latour 2005). These changes to the technology are central in the study of appropriation. This is about more than making sense of a new technology (sometimes called domestication) and it is more than changing your life to fit a new technology into your habits and practices (sometimes called articulation). Appropriation appears in technology stories as the engine of difference (see Eglash *et al.* 2004): it's a concept that connotes virtuous inventors, hackers, tinkerers, phreaks, and colorful technical virtuosos who strive to change the sterile status quo by imprinting their countercultural ethos into the machines that they modify. Information and communication technologies are topics of special importance in the study of appropriation because they may be more easily designed to allow or forbid their own transformation and therefore appropriation (Hess [1995] terms this "flexibility," more recently Zittrain [2008] discusses this as "generativity"). Appropriation is also taken to be a significant source of innovation and creativity in the trajectory of technological design (von Hippel 1998).

I hoped, in the preceding text, to provide an introduction to the unusual challenges of infrastructure on Indian reservations, and an introduction to the unusual successes of the TDV. Yet this story has much larger implications. Like any appropriation story, the story of the Tribal Digital Village has underdogs and daring, but in the end I find it speaks for a very different perspective on appropriation than what has often been written: a perspective that I will call "appropriation toward parity." Rather than an engine of difference, in the case of the TDV it is clearer that some kinds of appropriation can be engines of *similarity* in the development of technological infrastructures, and that this asks us to reconsider the role of aspiration in the design of new technologies. In the scholarship of technology this aspirational component has largely been left out because appropriation is shown as an innovation—it leads to a technology that is culturally or technically a better fit with its users.

To recap, the TDV is a novel wireless Internet distribution network that provides Internet access to remote indigenous communities in Southern California. It was developed mainly by people with no experience in wireless technology or providing Internet service. While it is a technologically innovative system in many ways, the communities concerned would really rather have a more normal system—ideally provided by a more usual Internet provider. Matt, Michael, and everyone involved are justly proud of TDV's many achievements —it might be said it has succeeded against all odds, and although there are other efforts at tribal self-provision there is no clear competitor to TDV in terms of its technological daring, speedy rise, and universal adoption and use on some of its lands. Yet all of these achievements are also reminders of the odds and the obstacles. Matt, recall, would rather have had enough money to "just hire someone." The regrets of these reluctant innovators make their way into the design choices about the wireless system that they developed. Since ultimately their goal is to have the same Internet service as everyone else, this aspiration toward parity makes them cover up some of the novel features of their system, and (along with Native American identity and the funding models involved here) it provokes dissonance when their users need to be both exceptional and normal. Writing about appropriation has emphasized that different cultural (and geographic, and other) circumstances will produce different technological systems, just as the tribes of the Southern California mountains produced an Internet service that does not look like AT&T. Rather than celebrating the difference, it is worth noting that their different system may be striking and unusual only as a necessary step toward the ultimate goal of assimilation. (I mean assimilation both in a good and a bad sense—both as "fairness" and "sameness.") That is, appropriators may or may not produce difference by intent. The TDV is a wholly unusual distribution network elaborately built at great effort and expense using unorthodox means so that Punky can be an ordinary teenager. In circumstances of appropriation toward parity, you will design a system that is as different as it has to be so that you can be the same.

Technology tends to start with the powerful and then flows "downhill" to everyone else (see Eglash *et al.* 2004). Skilled technology designers are usually the ones who get to design and modify technology with permission, so most appropriation work involves users or otherwise non-traditional technology designers. If a relatively powerless or a marginal user is the one who ends up changing or controlling a widespread technological system this is seen by many writers as an opportunity for investigation and even celebration. Many of the most well-known writing about appropriation in the study of technology takes this template to heart as a way of understanding the forgotten or suppressed histories of technological innovation. If not handled delicately it can sound fatally patronizing, but handled well it gives students of technology and social justice a chance for celebration and optimism in a circumstance where these are rarely found. A popular current example of the genre is the blog Afrigadget (www.afrigadget.com/), where each entry chronicles examples of African ingenuity and most of the ingenuity on display (but not all of it) involves duplicating a technological effect, function, or consequence with inferior materials. The more sophisticated researchers in this area are always keenly aware of the injustice that turns appropriation work a sour color if you look at it closely. As Eglash writes, "insofar as appropriation is a response to marginalization, we should work at obviating the need for it by empowering the marginalized" (Eglash *et al.* 2004: xvii). The TDV story shows us that there is a danger in cherishing the adaptability of the oppressed, who must adapt by necessity because they have no other choice.

In the standard view of user-driven innovation it is clear that appropriation is innovation-positive. The different user situations of the marginal and oppressed (or really, almost any diversity among users) can produce new designs and modifications, some of which may prove broadly valuable. In this view the TDV's evolution of its solar tower wireless Internet distribution system is potentially a model with wide application. The shortcuts and expediencies pioneered by TDV could be copied by other similarly constrained network builders. This view of appropriation invites us to consider the TDV as a site of innovation and perhaps a "best practice," as then-FCC Chairman Michael Powell did when he visited the TDV for a tour. However the particularities of the TDV case show that it is not a model for self-starting entrepreneurship or for a social policy.

While Powell toured Native lands to promote Native self-provision of telecommunications services and celebrate their promise and successes, he also advocated an overall do-it-yourself, entrepreneurial approach that mistakes the genesis of TDV, a project of massive subsidy. This was a well-justified subsidy, because it is not clear how an unsubsidized network would ever be viable in these areas with this population. While self-provision succeeded here, it did so because of the proximity of a major research university (a University of California campus), therefore this is not a model that can be duplicated across Indian Country. Indeed, traversing the history of TDV as we have done doesn't lead to a checklist of practices that will aid another provider to surmount the same challenges. Instead, it leads to a keen appreciation for the unique personalities, institutional factors, and luck that enabled the TDV to succeed with such an ambitious provision project. Indeed, the lesson of TDV for me has been the expensive and systemic attention that must be paid to Indian Country in order to reverse decades of neglect.

Recent research about computing and mobile phones demonstrates that there are many distinct strategies of appropriation. From Latin American culture, one is cannibalism, or appropriation through absorption and transformation. "We will swallow what they give us" and produce something else (Bar *et al.* 2007: 17). In contrast to cannibalism, another tactic is baroque infiltration, where new invasive forms of new technology are surrounded by exuberant contrasts and substitutes in order to render the new technology less effective or change the way it is used—a tactic pioneered by European Catholics to resist the culture of the Protestant reformation (20). I mean "appropriation toward parity" as a goal and not a tactic per se, but it resonates most keenly where there is a specific history of injustice. It is impossible to know from one case study whether appropriation toward parity is a particularly Native American form. (I doubt it.) Yet in asking how appropriators like the TDV conceptualize difference in themselves and in their technology it provides us with a new way to think about technological change and human identity. It reminds us that having the Internet here at Mesa Grande or Ewiiaapaayp Mountain means something quite different than it does in the affluent suburbs of San Diego.

Appendix A: Note on Method

This chapter is an attempt at what Star (1999) has called an ethnography of infrastructure. Unlike other infrastructure studies (Jackson *et al.* 2007), learning from and with Indians is a serious challenge with unique problems and obligations (see Smith 2006). As Frank writes,

> At its deepest, the reticence by tribal . . . communities to allow non-members to undertake studies that document the issues and complexities of contemporary life combines the memory of the historical denigration of Native Americans through objectification and subjugation, often at the hands of "researchers." (Frank 2005: 13)

As a result, the research project as a whole was planned in partnership with the TDV organization, and grant funding for the project was jointly applied for and paid to the partnership. My goal as a researcher was to learn about the TDV, while the TDV's goal was to learn about itself.

Although I followed news of the TDV from 2002, I substantively engaged with TDV starting in 2003 when, along with graduate students, I interviewed the TDV directors at a variety of annual conferences and professional meetings (these interviews have continued through 2007). I also took four trips to California, one in 2004 (for one day), 2007 (two days), 2008 (for seven days), and 2009 (one day). Our interviews included tribal government staff, TDV staff, TDV users, and TDV collaborators. I have interviewed thirty-six people, some of them multiple times. At this writing I have studied the TDV for seven years (2003–2010) and amassed 380 recordings and over 1,000 photographs.

This study is then what Yin has called a longitudinal, embedded, single-case design selected for atypicality (Yin 2003: ch. 2). The method is primarily the ethnographic interview, with a variety of sources of documentation, including still photography, HD video recording, audio recording, and the collection of TDV documents intended for internal and external distribution (similar to Miller & Slater 2001). All recorded interviews were transcribed. I have also benefited from a cooperative agreement with another, related research project that has conducted other interviews independently of ours.[20]

I circulated a draft of this chapter to the community for comment (a process that ethnographers sometimes call participant validation). As our fieldwork was conducted cooperatively, our interlocutors also received copies of all of the photography, recordings, and transcripts that we produced. The response to the draft was uniformly positive. The only point of disagreement turned out to be the reasons behind the TDV's success when so many other similar projects have failed. This question "What's different about the TDV?" animated our research project, and in the end our interlocutors were as curious about it as we were. Several people who responded had different ideas and these also differed from my draft. This chapter was revised to incorporate these suggestions without altering the central argument.

AppendixB: Tables

Table 8.1 A Timeline of the Tribal Digital Village

2000	National Science Foundation awards Braun $2.3m via the University of California at San Diego to construct an experimental high-performance wireless research and education network First Indian site (Pala) added to university network
2001	Braun serves three Indian reservations and about twenty users Tribes receive $5m grant from Hewlett-Packard to expand network TDV founded by tribal governments TDV first offers service to tribal offices, libraries, and schools
2002	TDV begins experiments with solar power on mountaintops
2003	TDV bandwidth first subsidized by Federal e-Rate Program Chairman Powell of the US FCC visits to tour TDV
2004	TDV is first independent from university bandwidth
2006	TDV offers first widespread service to homes at Mesa Grande TDV begins experiments with mesh routing
2007	San Diego wildfires damage three TDV towers
2008	TDV rebuilds two damaged towers
2009	TDV serves seventeen Indian reservations and about 1,500 users

Table 8.2 Towers and Installations of the Tribal Digital Village

Year	Tower Name	Function	Note
–	Mt Whitney	Relay	
–	Mt Woodson	Relay	
–	Mt Laguna Observatory	Relay	University-owned Initially a telephone pole
2000	Pala	Feed	On the TDV office roof
2001	Adams Drive	Relay	Reprovisioned 2004 Melted by wildfire 2007 (but still working)
2001	San Pasqual	End	
2002	Pauma Valley	End	
2002	Rincon Reservation	End	
2002	Palomar Mountain	Relay	Wooden tower Route deprecated Tower now defunct
2002	Chairman's House	Relay	Route deprecated; defunct
2002	Los Coyotes	Relay	Route deprecated; defunct
2002	Santa Ysabel #1	Relay	Route deprecated; defunct
2002	La Jolla (a.k.a. Vallecitos Intermediate)	Relay	Previously university-owned Destroyed by wildfire 2007, rebuilt 2008

continued . . .

Table 8.2 Towers and Installations of the Tribal Digital Village . . . *continued*

Year	Tower Name	Function	Note
2002	Santa Ysabel Reservation	End	
2003	La Posta Intermediate	Relay	
2003	La Posta Reservation	End	
2003	Manzanita	End	
2003	Campo	End	
2004	Santa Ysabel Tract 2	Relay	
2004	Santa Ysabel Tract 3	Relay	
2005	Los Coyotes	End	
2005	Ewiiaapaayp Mountain	Relay	Infested by wasps
2006	Mesa Grande	Relay	Experimental mesh routing destroyed by wildfire 2007, rebuilt 2008
2007	Barona Library	End	
2007	Campo Intermediate	Relay	
2009	La Posta Intermediate	Relay	
TBD	Jamul	End	Planned expansion
TBD	Viejas	End	Planned expansion

Acknowledgements

The author would like to thank Matthew R. Rantanen and Michael Peralta and the other producers and users of the Tribal Digital Village who were willing to spend time with me. In addition, Matt Crain, Hope Hall, Emily Shaw, and Ross Frank provided invaluable research assistance and consultation. Katie Kuppler, Lindsay Hinkle, Siddhartha Raja, and Jeff Kolar provided crucial assistance in the transcription of interviews and the editing of video footage. This material is based on work supported by the National Science Foundation under Grant No. IIS-0546409. This research project was also kindly supported by the Social Science Research Council of New York and the Community Informatics Initiative at the University of Illinois at Urbana-Champaign. The author would like to thank Caroline Haythornthwaite for comments on an early draft. An earlier version of the chapter concerning the history of the TDV was presented to the 59th annual meeting of the International Communication Association. An earlier version of this chapter concerning the material on appropriation was presented to the 34th annual meeting of the Society for the Social Studies of Science.

Notes

1 Mesa Grande, the reservation that first received broadband to the home from TDV.
2 About 44 percent of the US population used the Internet in 2000 (NTIA 2000).
3 This figure is from 1997 and would surely have been higher by 2000.
4 When Pacific Islanders and American Indians are both measured together.

5   These figures are taken from SCTCA grant application materials.
6   For example, "S.D. Indian Reservations Damaged by Wildfires," at: http://legacy.signonsandiego.com/news/metro/20071023-1752-bn23indian.html.
7   This estimate is from SCTCA documents submitted to the Hewlett-Packard Foundation in 2000 in the request for funding for the Tribal Digital Village Project.
8   These reservations represent a subset of the traditional lands historically associated with the Luiseño. Hyer (1999) argues that the tribally initiated creation of a reservation that included the lands that were already occupied by the tribe was attempted as an unusual strategy to prevent further white encroachment (188–189).
9   Southern California reservations were established by executive order, not by treaty. Although treaties promising compensation were negotiated and signed by the tribes and Indian agents, they were later disavowed by the US Senate and kept secret (Heizer and Elsasser 1980: 231–234). Some compensation has since been paid in the courts.
10 Actually, the NSFNET backbone. Braun was co-Principal Investigator for the NSFNET—the US National Science Foundation-funded network that succeeded ARPANET and was privatized to evolve into the broader public Internet in 1995.
11 This network became the UCSD High Performance Wireless Research and Education Network. See: http://hpwren.ucsd.edu/.
12 Half of the Hewlett-Packard grant consisted of Hewlett-Packard equipment, not cash.
13 Barona, Cahuilla, Campo, Chemehuevi, Ewiiaapaayp, Inaja, Jamul, La Jolla, La Posta, Los Coyotes, Manzanita, Mesa Grande, Pala, Pauma, Rincon, San Pasqual, Santa Ysabel, Sycuan, and Viejas.
14 In a small study of tribal high school and college students in South Dakota and Washington State, identification with American Indian identity was negatively associated with the idea that technology is a positive force.
15 Eric Michaels has since become a figure of controversy (O'Regan 1990, Ginsburg et al. 2002, Hinkson 2002, Deger 2006).
16 One of California's federally funded telephone LifeLine subsidies provides welfare recipients with a phone at home for $3.66 per month, but they may only make sixty local calls. For more information, see the California Public Utility Commission rate schedules: www.cpuc.ca.gov/PUC/Telco/Public+Programs/lifelinedetails.htm#discounts.
17 Thanks to Ethan Zuckerman for alerting me to this phrase.
18 Since this anecdote was narrated to me by others I do not have permission to use Chairman X's real name.
19 Both Hans-Werner and TDV mostly use commodity networking equipment, although TDV assembles its own towers and everyone involved experiments with software and configuration.
20 I would like to thank Ross Frank for his continuing assistance in this project.

References

Ahl, D. 1986. *Basic Computer Adventures*. Redmond, WA: Microsoft Press.
Akrich, M. 1992. "The De-Scription of Technical Objects," in W.E. Bijker and J. Law, eds, *Shaping Technology/Building Society: Studies in Sociotechnical Change*. Cambridge: MIT Press, 205–224.
Anonymous. (n.d.). 1852 California Treaty of Temecula (Unratified). Available at: https://eee.uci.edu/clients/tcthorne/Hist15/Treaties.html.
Bar, F., F. Pisani, and M. Weber. 2007. "Mobile Technology Appropriation in a Distant Mirror: Baroque Infiltration, Creolization, and Cannibalism." Paper presented to the Seminario sobre Desarollo Económico, Desarrollo Social y Comunicaciones Móviles en América Latina. Buenos Aires, Argentina. Available at: http://arnic.info/Papers/Bar_Pisani_Weber_appropriation-April07.pdf.
Bissell, T. 2004. "The Digital Divide Dilemma: Preserving Native American Culture While Increasing Access to Information Technology on Reservations." *Journal of Law, Technology, and Policy* 4.1: 129–151.
Bowers, C.A., M. Vasquez, and M. Roaf. 2000. "Native People and the Challenge of Computers: Reservation Schools, Individualism and Consumerism." *American Indian Quarterly* 24.2: 182–199.
Bozeman, B. 2000. "Technology Transfer and Public Policy: A Review of Research and Theory." *Research Policy* 29: 627–655.

Brescia, W. and T. Daily. 2007. "Economic Development and Technology–Skill Needs on American Indian Reservations." *American Indian Quarterly* 31.1: 23–43.

Deger, J. 2006. *Shimmering Screens: Making Media in an Aboriginal Community.* Minneapolis: University of Minnesota Press.

Downes, T. and S. Greenstein. 2002. "Universal Access and Local Internet Markets in the US." *Research Policy* 31: 1035–1052.

Eglash, R., J. L. Croissant, G. Di Chiro, and R. Fouché, eds. 2004. *Appropriating Technology: Vernacular Science and Social Power.* Minneapolis: University of Minnesota Press.

FCC (Federal Communications Commission). 2000. "Statement of Policy on Establishing a Government-to-Government Relationship with Indian Tribes." Docket 00–207. Washington, DC: Federal Communications Commission. Available at: www.fcc.gov/Bureaus/OGC/Orders/2000/fcc00207.doc

——. 2006. "Expanding Telecommunications Access in Indian Country." Consumer and Governmental Affairs Bureau Publication. Washington, DC: Federal Communications Commission. Available at: www.fcc.gov/indians/itibooklet.pdf

——. 2010. "FCC Establishes FCC–Native Nations Broadband Task Force." Washington, DC: Federal Communications Commission. Available at: http://hraunfoss.fcc.gov/edocs_public/attachmatch/DA-10-1008A1.pdf

Fouché, R. 2006. "Say It Loud, I'm Black and I'm Proud: African Americans, American Artifactual Culture, and Black Vernacular Technological Creativity." *American Quarterly* 58.3: 639–661.

Frank, R. 2005. "Historians in Tribal Projects: Traditions in Translation." Paper presented to the 45th Annual Meeting of the Western History Association, Scottsdale, AZ.

Galperin, H. 2004. *New Television, Old Politics: The Transition to Digital TV in the United States and Britain.* Cambridge: Cambridge University Press.

Genachowski, J. 2010 (March 2). "Prepared Remarks of FCC Chairman Julius Genachowski to the National Congress of American Indians. Winter Session, National Congress of American Indians." Washington, DC. Available at: http://hraunfoss.fcc.gov/edocs_public/attachmatch/DOC-296645A1.pdf

Ginsburg, F., L. Abu-Lughod, and B. Larkin, eds. 2002. *Media Worlds: Anthropology on New Terrain.* Berkeley, CA: University of California Press.

Heizer, R.F. and A.B. Elsasser. 1980. *The Natural World of the California Indians.* Berkeley: University of California Press.

Hess, D. 1995. *Science and Technology in a Multicultural World.* New York: Columbia University Press.

Hinkson, M. 2002. "New Media Projects at Yuendumu: Inter-Cultural Engagement and Self-Determination in an Era of Accelerated Globalization." *Continuum: The Australian Journal of Media & Cultural Studies* 16.2: 201–220.

Horrigan, J. 2009. *Home Broadband Adoption 2009.* Washington, DC: Pew Internet & American Life Project. Available at: www.pewinternet.org/Reports/2009/10-Home-Broadband-Adoption-2009.aspx

Howe, C. 1998. "Cyberspace is No Place for Tribalism." *Wicazo sa Review* 13.2: 17–27.

Hudson, H.E. 2004. "Universal Access: What Have We Learned from the e-Rate?" *Telecommunications Policy* 28: 309–321.

Hyer, J.R. 1999. "'We Are Not Savages': Native Americans in Southern California and the Pala Reservation, 1840–1920." Doctoral dissertation, University of California, Riverside. Retrieved from UMI Proquest Digital Dissertations (UMI No. 9944675).

Jackson, S.J., P.N. Edwards, G.C. Bowker, and C.P. Knobel. 2007. "Understanding Infrastructure: History, Heuristics, and Cyberinfrastructure Policy." *First Monday* 12.6. Available at: http://firstmonday.org/issues/issue12_6/jackson/index.html

James, K. 2006. "Identity, Cultural Values, and American Indians' Perceptions of Science and Technology." *American Indian Culture and Research Journal* 30.3: 45–58.

Jasanoff, S. (2004). "The Idiom of Co-production," in S. Jasanoff, ed., *States of Knowledge: The Co-Production of Science and the Social Order.* London: Routledge, 1–12.

Jeanneney, J.-N. 2006. *Google and the Myth of Universal Knowledge: A View from Europe*, trans. T.L. Fagan. Chicago: University of Chicago Press.

Latour, B. 2005. *Reassembling the Social: An Introduction to Actor–Network Theory.* Oxford: Oxford University Press.

Lee, B. and H.-S. Bae. 2004. "The Effect of Screen Quotas on the Self-sufficiency Ratio in Recent Domestic Film Markets." *Journal of Media Economics* 17.3: 163–176.

Michaels, E. 1994. *Bad Aboriginal Art: Tradition, Media, and Technological Horizons.* Minneapolis: University of Minnesota Press.

Miller, D. and D. Slater. 2001. *The Internet: An Ethnographic Approach.* Oxford: Berg.

Miller, J.C. and C.P. Guzelian. 2003. "A Spectrum Revolution: Deploying Ultrawideband Technology on Native American Lands." *CommLaw Conspectus* 11.2: 277–307.

Neeklmeghan, A. and G. Chester. 2007. "Knowledge Management in Relation to Indigenous and Marginalized Communities in the Digital Era." *Information Studies* 13.2: 73–106.

NTIA (National Telecommunications and Information Administration). 2000. *Falling Through the Net: Toward Digital Inclusion.* Washington, DC: GPO. Available at: www.ntia.doc.gov/reports/anol/index.html

O'Regan, T., ed. 1990. "Communication and Tradition: Essays After Eric Michaels." *Continuum: The Australian Journal of Media and Culture* 3.2. Available at: www.mcc.murdoch.edu.au/ReadingRoom/3.2/3.2.html

Pfaffenberger, B. 1988. "Fetishized Objects and Humanized Nature: Towards an Anthropology of Technology." *Man* 23.2: 236–252.

Research Guide. n.d. "Research Guide: The Indians of San Diego County and Baja California." *San Diego State University Library Research Guides.* San Diego, CA: San Diego State University. Available at: http://infodome.sdsu.edu/research/guides/calindians/insdcnty.shtml

Rogers, E. 2003. *The Diffusion of Innovations,* fifth edn. Glencoe, IL: Free Press.

Rosenberg, Nathan. 1982. *Inside the Black Box: Technology and Economics.* Cambridge: Cambridge University Press.

Roy, L. 2006. "Building Tribal Community Support for Technology Access." *The Electronic Library* 24.4: 517–529.

Sandvig, C. 2006. "The Internet at Play: Child Users of Public Internet Connections." *Journal of Computer-Mediated Communication* 11.4. Available at: http://jcmc.indiana.edu/vol11/issue4/sandvig.html

Sawhney, H. 1994. "Universal Service: Prosaic Motives and Great Ideals." *Journal of Broadcasting and Electronic Media* 38.4: 375–395.

Sharp, L. 1952. "Steel Axes for Stone-Age Australians." *Human Organization* 11.1: 17–22.

Smith, L.T. 2006. *Decolonizing Methodologies: Research and Indigenous Peoples.* London: Zed Books.

Srinivasan, R. 2006. "Indigenous, Ethnic and Cultural Articulations of New Media." *International Journal of Cultural Studies* 9.4: 497–518.

——. 2007. "Ethnomethodological Architectures: Information Systems Driven by Cultural and Community Visions." *Journal of the American Society for Information Science and Technology* 58.4: 723–733.

Star, S.L. (1999). "The Ethnography of Infrastructure." *American Behavioral Scientist* 43.3: 377–391.

Sutton, I. 2003. *American Indian Territoriality: An Online Research Guide,* revised edn. University of Oklahoma Law Center. Norman, OK: University of Oklahoma. Available at: http://thorpe.ou.edu/treatises.html

——. 2006. "Researching Indigenous Indians in Southern California." *American Indian Culture and Research Journal* 30.3: 75–127.

US Census Bureau. 2008. *2005–2007 American Community Survey.* Available at: www.census.gov/prod/2008pubs/acs-09.pdf

US Congress Office of Technology Assessment. 1995. "Telecommunications Technology and Native Americans: Opportunities and Challenges." TA-ITC-621. Washington, DC: US Government Printing Office. Available at: www.princeton.edu/~ota/disk1/1995/9542/9542.PDF

Warner, L.S. 1998. "Technology Issues in Indian Country Today." *Wicazo sa Review* 13.2: 71–81.

von Hippel, Eric. 1998. *The Sources of Innovation.* Oxford: Oxford University Press.

——. 2005. *Democratizing Innovation.* Cambridge, MA: MIT Press.

Wyatt, Sally, G. Thomas, and T. Terranova. 2002. "They Came, They Saw, They Went Back to the Beach: Conceptualizing Use and Non-Use of the Internet," in S. Woolgar, ed., *Virtual Society: Technology, Cyberbole, Reality.* Oxford: Oxford University Press, 23–40.

Yin, R.K. 2003. *Case Study Research: Design and Methods,* third edn. Thousand Oaks: Sage.

Zittrain, J. 2008. *The Future of the Internet and How to Stop It.* New Haven: Yale University Press.

III
Digital Segregations

9
White Flight in Networked Publics?

How Race and Class Shaped American Teen Engagement with MySpace and Facebook

DANAH BOYD[1]

Microsoft Research and Harvard Berkman

Center for Internet and Society

In a historic small town outside Boston, I interviewed a group of teens at a small charter school that included middle-class students seeking an alternative to the public school and poorer students who were struggling in traditional schools. There, I met Kat, a white 14-year-old from a comfortable background. We were talking about the social media practices of her classmates when I asked her why most of her friends were moving from MySpace to Facebook. Kat grew noticeably uncomfortable. She began simply, noting that "*MySpace is just old now and it's boring.*" But then she paused, looked down at the table, and continued.

> It's not really racist, but I guess you could say that. I'm not really into racism, but I think that MySpace now is more like ghetto or whatever. (Kat)

On that spring day in 2007, Kat helped me finally understand a pattern that I had been noticing throughout that school year. Teen preference for MySpace or Facebook went beyond simple consumer choice; it reflected a reproduction of social categories that exist in schools throughout the United States. Because race, ethnicity, and socio-economic status shape social categories (Eckert 1989), the choice between MySpace and Facebook became racialized. This got reinforced as teens chose to self-segregate across the two sites, just as they do in schools.

After Kat told me that MySpace was "*like ghetto,*" I asked her if people at her school were still using MySpace and she hesitantly said yes. Her discomfort in discussing the topic was palpable and it became clear that she didn't know how to talk about race or the social divisions she recognized in her school.

> The people who use MySpace—again, not in a racist way—but are usually more like ghetto and hip-hop rap lovers group. (Kat)

an earlier social network site that was notably popular among 20- to 30-
something urban dwellers in major urban U.S. cities. Although individual
teenagers joined MySpace early on, teens became a visible demographic on the
site in 2004. Most early adopter teens learned about MySpace through one of
two paths: bands or older family members.

Teens who learned of MySpace through bands primarily followed indie rock
music or hip-hop, the two genres most popular on MySpace early on. MySpace
allowed teens to connect with and follow their favorite bands. Early adopter
teens who were not into music primarily learned about the site from a revered
older sibling or cousin who was active in late-night culture. For these teens,
MySpace was cool because cool elders thought so.

Teenagers who joined MySpace began proselytizing the site to their friends.
Given its popularity among musicians and late-night socialites, joining MySpace
became a form of (sub)cultural capital. Teens, especially those in urban settings,
tend to look to the 20- to 30-something crowd for practices that they can
emulate. MySpace's early popularity among teens was tightly entwined with its
symbolic reference to maturity, status, and freedom in the manner espoused
by urban late-night culture. While teens often revere the risky practices of a
slightly older cohort, many adults work to actively dissuade them from doing
so. By propagating and glorifying 20-something urban cultural practices and
values, MySpace managed to alienate parents early on.

With little mass media coverage of MySpace before News Corporation
acquired the company in mid-2005, many teens learned of the site through
word-of-mouth networks, namely friends at school, church, activities, and
summer camp, as well as from older family members. Given its inception in
the Los Angeles region, West Coast teens found MySpace before East Coast
teens, and urban teens joined before suburban or rural teens. The media
coverage that followed the acquisition further escalated growth among teens.

Immediately after News Corporation bought MySpace, much of the media
coverage focused on the bands. After adults began realizing how popular
MySpace was with teens, news media became obsessed with teen participation
and the potential dangers they faced (Marwick 2008). This media coverage was
both a blessing and a curse for MySpace. On one hand, some teens joined the
site because media sold it as both fashionable among teens and despised by
parents. On the other hand, some teens avoided joining because of the perceived
risks and parents began publicly demonizing the site.

As MySpace simultaneously appealed to and scared off U.S. teens, other social
network sites started gaining traction with different demographics. Most did
not appeal to teenagers en masse, although niche groups of teens did join many
different sites. In 2004, Facebook launched, targeting college students.
Originally, access to Facebook was intentionally limited. Facebook started as a
Harvard-only social network site before expanding to support all Ivy League
schools and then top-tier colleges and then a wider array of colleges. Because

of its background, some saw Facebook as an "elite" social network site. The "highbrow" aura of Facebook appealed to some potential participants while repelling others.

The college-centered nature of Facebook quickly appealed to those teenagers who saw college, and thus Facebook access, as a rite of passage. They were aware of the site through older family members and friends who had already graduated high school and gone off to college. Before access became readily available, college-bound teens began coveting entrance. For many, access to the social world of college became a marker of status and maturity. Even those who had MySpace accounts relished the opportunity to gain access to the college-only Facebook as a rite of passage.

In September 2005, Facebook began slowly supporting high schools. While this gave some teens access, the processes in place for teens to join and be validated were challenging, creating a barrier to entry for many potential participants. Those who managed to join were often from wealthier schools where the validation process was more solidified or quite motivated—typically because they wanted to communicate with close friends in college.

Facebook finally opened access to all in September 2006. Sparking a wave of teen adoption, this is the origin point of teens self-sorting into MySpace and Facebook. The segment of teens that initially flocked to Facebook was quite different from those who were early adopters of MySpace. Yet, in both cases, the older early adopters shaped early teen engagement, both in terms of influencing adoption and defining the norms. As teens engaged, they developed their own norms stemming from those set forth by the people they already knew on the site.

While plenty of teens chose to participate on both sites, I began noticing that those teens who chose one or the other appeared to come from different backgrounds. Subculturally identified teens appeared more frequently drawn to MySpace while more mainstream teens tended towards Facebook. Teens from less-privileged backgrounds seemed likely to be drawn to MySpace while those headed towards elite universities appeared to be headed towards Facebook. Racial and ethnic divisions looked messier, tied strongly to socio-economic factors, but I observed that black and Latino teens appeared to preference MySpace while white and Asian teens seemed to privilege Facebook.

In observing these patterns in multiple communities in the U.S., I found myself uncertain as to whether or not they could be generalized. Certainly, there were exceptions to each pattern. Still, I felt the pattern was significant. This prompted me to write an essay on my blog where I mapped out what I observed (boyd 2007a). Thanks to coverage from the BBC and many popular bloggers, my essay went viral, sparking debate, outrage, and controversy. It also sparked researchers who were seeing similar patterns to approach me to share their unpublished findings.

Analysts at two unnamed marketing research firms contacted me to say that they witnessed similar patterns with youth at a national level but were unable to publicly discuss or publish their finding, but scholars and bloggers were more willing to share their findings. In a parallel study, Eszter Hargittai (2007) found that parental education as well as race and ethnicity were significant predictors of social network site choice when analyzing survey data collected from a freshman class at a diverse Midwest college. White and Asian students as well as those whose parents had higher levels of education were overrepresented on Facebook while Hispanic students and those whose parents did not have a high school degree were more likely to use MySpace. African-American college students were not more likely to use Facebook or MySpace. While Hargittai's findings with college freshmen reflect a similar trend to my observations with high school-age teens, it is important to note that college participation itself is shaped by racial and socio-economic inequalities and that Facebook was initially a tool for college students. Thus, Facebook may well be overrepresented in Hargittai's data and college-age populations not attending college may have different preferences. Taking a different approach, blogger Chuck Lam (2007a, 2007b) examined the social network site habits of students from 15 schools in San Francisco based on their rating at GreatSchools, finding that students from higher-ranked schools were more active on Facebook while those from lower-ranked schools were more active on MySpace.

Two years later, marketing research firm Nielsen Claritas reported that wealthy individuals are 25 percent more likely to use Facebook while less affluent individuals are 37 percent more likely to be on MySpace (Hare 2009). In the same year, S. Craig Watkins (2009) published his qualitative and survey data with college students, revealing a racial and ethnic division in preference as well as anti-MySpace attitudes by collegiate Facebook users that parallel those of high school students. While there is no definitive longitudinal statistical data tracking the division amongst teens, these studies provide a valuable backdrop to the perceptions teens have about the sites and their users.

The Organization of Teen Friendship

There's an old saying that "birds of a feather flock together." Personal networks tend to be rather homogeneous, as people are more likely to befriend those like them. Sociologists refer to the practice of connecting with like-minded individuals as "homophily." Studies have accounted for homophily in sex and gender, age, religion, education level, occupation, and social class, but nowhere is homophily more strongly visible in the U.S. than in the divides along racial and ethnic lines (McPherson *et al.* 2001). The reasons behind the practice of homophily and the resultant social divisions are complex, rooted in a history of inequality, bigotry, and oppression and stemming from the complexity of the political economy and structural constraints in American life.

Youth often self-segregate by race, even in diverse schools (Moody 2001; Thorne 2008). While it is easy to lament racial segregation in friendships, there are also social and psychological benefits to racial and ethnic clustering. Tatum (1997) argues that self-segregation is a logical response to the systematized costs of racism; connecting along lines of race and ethnicity can help youth feel a sense of belonging, enhance identity development, and help youth navigate systematic racism. Still, as Bonilla-Silva (2003) has highlighted, people's willingness to accept and, thus expect, self-segregation may have problematic roots and contribute to ongoing racial inequality.

When I asked teens why race defines their friendships, they typically shrugged and told me that it's just the way it is. As Traviesa, a Hispanic 15-year-old from Los Angeles, explained,

If it comes down to it, we have to supposedly stick with our own races . . . That's just the unwritten code of high school nowadays. (Traviesa)

Race was not an issue only in major metropolitan communities. Heather, a white 16-year-old in Iowa, told me that her school was not segregated, but then she went on to mark people by race, noting that "*the black kids are such troublemakers.*" This conflicting message—refusing to talk about race explicitly while employing racial language in conversation—was common in my interviews as well as those of other scholars (Pollock 2005). While there was no formal segregation in Heather's school, like the de facto residential segregation that continues to operate in many American cities, the black teens in her predominantly white school stuck together socially and were stereotyped by the white teens.

Another way of looking at teen friendships is through the lens of social categories and group labels. Many of the teens I interviewed had language to demarcate outcasts (e.g. "*gothics,*" "*nerds,*" "*Dirty Kids,*" etc.) and identify groups of peers by shared activity (e.g. "*band kids,*" "*art kids,*" "*cheerleaders,*" etc.). Often, labels come with a set of stereotypes. For example, Heather explained:

You've got the pretties, which are the girls that tan all the time. They put on excessive makeup. They wear the short skirts, the revealing shirts, that kind of things. Then you've got the guys who are kind of like that, dumb as rocks by the way. (Heather)

Youth subcultures can be seen as an extension of social categories; what differentiates them typically concerns identification. While teens often identify with particular subcultures, social categories are more frequently marked by others.

Social categories serve to mark groups and individuals based on shared identities. In her seminal text on the topic, Penelope Eckert (1989) highlighted that membership in social groups is not random. Social categories develop in ways that reproduce social distinctions. While Eckert focuses her analysis on the class distinctions embedded in the labels "jocks" and "burnouts," work on children and youth in schools also reveals that racial divisions in schools are also marked through labels and social categories (Thorne 2008). Unlike class, race and ethnicity are often made visible—albeit, blurred—in the labels youth use. In my fieldwork, I found that clearly dominant racial groups went unmarked, but labels like *"the blacks," "the Chinese people," "the Hispanics," "the Mexicans," "the white people,"* and so forth were regularly employed to define social groupings. In other cases, and in part because they are aware that using such categories could be perceived as racist, teens used substitutes that more implicitly mark race- and class-based difference. For example, the word *"urban"* signals *"black"* when referring to a set of tastes or practices. Similarly, some of the labels teens use have racial implications, such as *"Dirty Kids," "gangstas,"* and *"terrorists."* While not all Dirty Kids are white, not all gangstas are black, and not all terrorists are of Middle Eastern descent, they are overwhelmingly linked in teens' minds. Race and class are also often blurred, especially in situations where the logic of stratification may not be understood by teens but appears visible through skin color.

As much of the literature on youth in educational contexts has revealed (Thorne, 1993; Eckert 1989; Perry, 2002), social categories and race-based labels are also used to mark physical turf in the lunchroom and beyond. Often, this becomes a way in which youth self-segregate. Keke, a 16-year-old black girl in Los Angeles, described in detail where students in her racially diverse school physically gathered during lunch and between classes:

> The hallways is full of the Indians, and the people of Middle Eastern decent. They in the hallways and by the classrooms. The Latinos, they all lined up on this side. The blacks is by the cafeteria and the quad . . . Then the outcasts, like the uncool Latinos or uncool Indians, the uncool whites, they scattered. (Keke)

Each ethnic and racial group had its gathering spot, but only one had a name: *"Disneyland"* is an area in the public yard where *"the white people"* gathered. While Keke is probably unaware that Disneyland is, as Avila (2004: 3) puts it, "the archetypical example of a postwar suburban order," the notion that students in an urban Los Angeles school label the turf where white people gather by referencing the Orange County suburban theme park known for its racial and ethnic caricatures is nonetheless poignant.

Like the school yard, online environments are often organized by identity and social categories. In some cases, this is explicit. Social network sites like BlackPlanet, AsianAvenue, and MiGente explicitly target audiences based on race and ethnicity. Many who participate in these communities struggle with what it means to be in a public space driven by race, what boundaries should exist, how to manage racism, and other race- and ethnicity-driven dialogues

(Byrne 2008). While neither MySpace nor Facebook is explicitly defined in terms of race, they too are organized by race. Most participants self-segregate when connecting with their pre-existing networks without been fully aware of the social divisions that unfold. Yet, when teens are asked explicitly about who participates where, racial terms emerge.

The Network Effects of MySpace and Facebook Adoption

Like school lunchrooms and malls, social network sites are another space where youth gather to socialize with peers (boyd 2007b). Teens joined social network sites to be with their friends. Given social divisions in both friendship patterns and social spaces, it is unsurprising that online communities reflect everyday social divisions. Yet, unlike prior genres where teens collectively used similar tools but segmented their interactions, their engagement with social network sites spanned two sites—MySpace and Facebook.

Teens provide a variety of different explanations for why they chose MySpace or Facebook. Some argued that it was a matter of personal preference having to do with the features or functionality. For example, Jordan, a biracial Mexican-white 15-year-old from Austin prefers Facebook because it allows unlimited photos. Conversely, Anindita, an Indian-American 17-year-old from Los Angeles, values MySpace's creative features:

Facebook's easier than MySpace but MySpace is more complex... You can add music, make backgrounds and layouts, but Facebook is just plain white and that's it. (Anindita)

Teens also talked about their perception of the two sites in relation to their values and goals. Cachi, an 18-year-old Puerto Rican girl from Iowa, uses both MySpace and Facebook, but she sees them differently:

Facebook is less competitive than MySpace. It doesn't have the Top 8 thing or anything like that, or the background thing. (Cachi)

Safety—or rather the perception of safety—also emerged as a central factor in teen preference. While teens believed Facebook was safer, they struggled to explain why. Tara, a Vietnamese-American 16-year-old from Michigan, said,

[Facebook] kind of seemed safer, but I don't know like what would make it safer, like what main thing. But like, I don't know, it just seems like everything that people say, it seems safer. (Tara)

Teens' fear of MySpace as "unsafe" undoubtedly stems from the image portrayed by the media, but it also suggests a fear of the "other."

By far the most prominent explanation teens gave for choosing one or the other is the presence of their friends. Teens choose to use the social network site that their friends use. Kevin, a white 15-year-old in Seattle, explains:

I'm not big on Facebook; I'm a MySpace guy. I have a Facebook and I have some friends on it, but most of my friends don't check it that often so I don't check it that often. (Kevin)

When teens choose to adopt both, what distinguishes one from the other often reflects distinct segments of their social network. For example, Red, a white 17-year-old from Iowa, has a profile on both sites, but

the only reason I still have my MySpace is because my brother's on there. (Red)

Even teens who prefer the features and functionality of one site use the other when that's where their friends are. Connor, a white 17-year-old from Atlanta, says that he personally prefers MySpace because there's *"too much going on"* on Facebook.

It's like hug me and poke me . . . what does that even mean? (Connor)

Yet, Connor signs into Facebook much more frequently than MySpace *"because everybody's on Facebook."*

Social network site adoption took the form of a social contagion spreading through pre-existing peer networks. For some teens, the presence of just one friend was enough of an incentive to participate; others only joined once many of their friends were present. Once inside, teens encouraged their friends to participate. MySpace and Facebook have network effects: they are more valuable when more friends participate. Some teens went so far as to create accounts for resistant friends in order to move the process along (boyd 2008). As word of each site spread, adoption hopped from social group to social group through pre-existing networks for teens. In choosing to go where their friends were, teens began to self-segregate along the same lines that shape their social relations more broadly: race and ethnicity, socio-economic status, education goals, lifestyle, subcultural affiliation, social categories, etc.

Tastes, Aesthetics, and Social Status

For many teens, embracing MySpace or Facebook is seen as a social necessity. Which site is "cool" depends on one's cohort. Milo, an Egyptian 15-year-old from Los Angeles, joined MySpace because it was *"the thing"* in his peer group, but another girl from the same school, Korean 17-year-old Seong, told me that Facebook was the preferred site among her friends.

What is socially acceptable and desirable differs across social groups. One's values and norms are strongly linked with one's identity membership. When working-class individuals eschew middle-class norms in preference for the norms and expectations of their community, they reproduce social class (Willis 1981; Gaines 1998). The idea that working-class individuals should adopt middle-class norms is fundamentally a middle-class notion; for many working-class individuals, the community and its support trump potential upwards mobility. Norms also differ across racial and ethnic groups and are reinforced as people of color seek to identify with their racial and ethnic background (Tatum 1997).

While what is seen as cool can be differentiated by group, there is also a faddish nature to the process. Seong preferred Facebook because it was *"exclusive."* She moved from Xanga to MySpace to Facebook as each new site emerged, preferring to adopt what was new rather than stay on a site as it became widely embraced. Conversely, white 15-year-old Summer from Michigan rejected the idea of switching to Facebook simply because it was new. She preferred to be where her peers were, but she noted that the *"designer class of people"* in her school joined Facebook because they felt the need to have *"the latest thing."* In this way, subcultural capital influenced the early adoption of Facebook; it was fashionable to some simply because of its newness.

The construction of "cool" is fundamentally about social status among youth (Milner 2004). Teenagers both distinguish themselves through practices of consumption, fashion, and attitudes and assess others through these markers (Hebdige 1979; Shankar 2008). Yet, neither tastes nor attitudes nor cultural consumption practices are adopted randomly. Race and class shape practices and the social agendas around race and class also drive them (Crane 2000). Taste also serves as a mechanism and marker of distinction, and people's tastes are rooted in class distinctions (Bourdieu 1984).

While both Bourdieu and Hebdige argue that those from lower social positions are defining their tastes in opposition to hegemonic structures, what constitutes "cool" is also localized, differing across social categories, geography, and groups. Consumption practices and fashion that denote high status in some groups may be meaningless elsewhere. In this way, teens often traffic in what Sarah Thornton (1995) calls "subcultural capital" even when they themselves are not subculturally identified. Markers of status can be locally defined and may have more to do with information access or media consumption than consumption of physical goods. Furthermore, discussions of and connection to those with access to valued consumer objects may also be valuable in and of itself, resulting with what Shankar (2008) calls "metaconsumption." Online, status markers take on new form but in ways that are reminiscent of offline practices. For example, the public articulation of connections on social network sites is a way of visibly marking oneself in relation to others and their status (Donath and boyd 2004).

In an environment where profiles serve as "digital bodies" (boyd 2008), profile personalization can be seen as a form of digital fashion. Teens' Facebook and MySpace profiles reflect their taste, identity, and values (Donath 2007). Through the use of imagery and textual self-expressions, teens make race, class, and other identity markers visible. As Nakamura (2008) has argued, even in the most constrained online environments, participants will use what's available to them

214 • danah boyd

to reveal identity information in ways that make race and other identity elements visible.

In describing what was desirable about the specific sites, teens often turned to talk about aesthetics and profile personalization. Teens' aesthetics shaped their attitudes towards each site. In essence, the *"glitter"* produced by those who *"pimp out"* their MySpaces is seen by some in a positive light while others see it as *"gaudy," "tacky,"* and *"cluttered."* While Facebook fans loved the site's aesthetic minimalism, others viewed this tone as *"boring," "lame,"* and *"elitist."* Catalina, a white 15-year-old from Austin, told me that Facebook is better because

Facebook just seems more clean to me. (Catalina)

What Catalina sees as cleanliness, Indian-American 17-year-old Anindita from Los Angeles labels simplicity; she recognizes the value of simplicity, but she prefers the *"bling"* of MySpace because it allows her to express herself.

The extensive options for self-expression are precisely what annoy some teens. Craig Pelletier, a 17-year-old from California, complained that,

these tools gave MySpacers the freedom to annoy as much as they pleased. Facebook was nice because it stymied such annoyance, by limiting individuality. Everyone's page looked pretty much the same, but you could still look at pictures of each other. The MySpace crowd felt caged and held back because they weren't able to make their page unique. (Craig)

Craig believes the desire to personalize contributed to his peers' division between MySpace and Facebook.

In choosing how to express themselves, teens must account for what they wish to signal. Teens are drawn to styles that signal their identities and social groups. Due to a technical glitch, MySpace enabled users to radically shape the look and feel of their profiles while Facebook enforced a strict minimalism. To the degree that each site supports profile personalization in different ways, identity and self-presentation are affected. While some are drawn to the ability to radically shape their profiles to their liking, others prefer an enforced cleanness.

Teens who preferred MySpace lamented the limited opportunities for creative self-expression on Facebook, but those who preferred Facebook were much more derogatory about the style of profiles in MySpace. Not only did Facebook users not find MySpace profiles attractive, they argued that the styles produced by MySpace users were universally ugly. While Facebook's minimalism is not inherently better, conscientious restraint has been one marker of bourgeois fashion (Arnold 2001). On the contrary, the flashy style that is popular on MySpace is often marked in relation to "bling-bling," a style of conspicuous consumption that is associated with urban black culture and hip-hop. To some, bling and flashy MySpace profiles are beautiful and creative;

to others, these styles are garish. While style preference is not inherently about race and class, the specific styles referenced have racial overtones and socio-economic implications. In essence, although teens are talking about style, they are functionally navigating race and class.

Taste is also performed directly through profiles; an analysis of "taste statements" in MySpace combined with the friend network reveals that distinctions are visible there (Liu 2007). The importance of music to MySpace made it a visible vector of taste culture. Youth listed their musical tastes on their profiles and attached songs to their pages. While many genres of music were present on MySpace, hip-hop stood out, both because of its salience amongst youth and because of its racial connotations. Although youth of all races and ethnicities listen to hip-hop, it is most commonly seen as a genre that stems from black culture inside urban settings. Narratives of the ghetto and black life dominate the lyrics of hip-hop and the genre also serves as a source of pride and authenticity in communities that are struggling for agency in American society (Forman 2002). For some, participating in this taste culture is a point of pride; for others, this genre and the perceived attitudes that go with it are viewed as offensive. Although MySpace was never about hip-hop, its mere presence became one way in which detractors marked the site.

Taste and aesthetics are not universal, but deeply linked to identity and values. The choice of certain cultural signals or aesthetics appeals to some while repelling others. Often, these taste distinctions are shaped by class and race and, thus, the choice to mark Facebook and MySpace through the language of taste and aesthetics reflects race and class.

A Networked Exodus

After the posting of my controversial blog essay about the distinction between MySpace and Facebook, teens began to contact me with their own stories. Anastasia, a 17-year-old from New York, emailed me to explain that it wasn't simply a matter of choice between the two sites; many of her peers simply moved from MySpace to Facebook. Until now, I have focused on the choice that teens make to adopt MySpace or Facebook. But Anastasia's right: there is also movement as teens choose to leave one social network site and go to the other. By and large, teens did not leave Facebook and go to MySpace. Rather, a subset of teens left MySpace to go to Facebook. This can be partially explained as an issue of fads, with teens leaving MySpace to go to the "new" thing. But even if this alone could explain the transition, it does not explain why some teens were more likely to switch than others. Anastasia argues that, at least in her school, who participated can be understood in terms of social categories:

My school is divided into the "honors kids" (I think that is self-explanatory), the "good not-so-honors kids," "wangstas" (they pretend to be tough and black but when you live in a suburb in Westchester you can't claim much hood), the "latinos/hispanics" (they tend to band together even though they could fit into any other groups) and the "emo kids" (whose lives are alllllways filled with woe). We were all in MySpace with our own little social networks but when Facebook opened its doors to high schoolers, guess who moved and guess who stayed behind . . . The first two groups were the first to go and then the "wangstas" split with half of them on Facebook and the rest on MySpace . . . I shifted with the rest of my school to Facebook and it became the place where the "honors kids" got together and discussed how they were procrastinating over their next AP English essay. (Anastasia)

The social categories Anastasia uses reflect racial, ethnic, and class divisions in her school. Anastasia's description highlights how structural divisions in her school define what plays out on MySpace and Facebook. Movement from MySpace to Facebook further magnifies already existing distinctions. In California, 17-year-old Craig blogged about the movement in his school, using the language of taste, class, and hierarchy.

The higher castes of high school moved to Facebook. It was more cultured, and less cheesy. The lower class usually were content to stick to MySpace. Any high school student who has a Facebook will tell you that MySpace users are more likely to be barely educated and obnoxious. Like Peet's is more cultured than Starbucks, and Jazz is more cultured than bubblegum pop, and like Macs are more cultured than PCs, Facebook is of a cooler caliber than MySpace. (Craig)

In his description, Craig distinguishes between what he sees as highbrow and lowbrow cultural tastes, using consumption patterns to differentiate classes of people and describe them in terms of a hierarchy. By employing the term "caste," Craig uses a multicultural metaphor with ethnic and racial connotations that runs counter to the supposed class mobility available in U.S. society. In doing so, he's locating his peers in immutable categories and tying tastes to them. While Craig may not have intended to imply this, his choice of the term "caste" is nonetheless interesting.

These two accounts provide insight into who left, but they don't account for why. To get at why, we must start by considering how MySpace's cultural position shifted during this period. The following is a descriptive portrait of a series of relevant events that contributed to teen departure. It is an over-simplified account based on my fieldnotes during that period.

MySpace was once a cultural center for youth culture. As it grew increasingly popular, a moral panic emerged over the potential risks of sexual predators (Marwick 2008). While the risks were overblown (Shrock and boyd 2009), fear spread. Involved parents—typically from more educated and wealthier communities—began looking closer and they didn't like what they saw. While my examination of MySpace profiles revealed that more teens referenced God,

Jesus, Bible quotes, and other religious symbols than uploaded scantily clad self-images, parents typically assumed that the latter dominated MySpace and this upset them. Furthermore, these parents were often horrified by the practices of the urban 20-somethings, especially those from different cultural backgrounds who appeared to have different moral codes. The media helped produced a techno-panic, often by leveraging adult fears of urban black signals such as bling and hip-hop.

Even though most teens were primarily socializing with their peers, some parents feared that the presence of and potential exposure to different and, presumably, deviant practices might corrupt their children. In short, they did not see MySpace as "safe" and they did not want their children communing with people they would not approve of them associating with elsewhere. Fear drove some parents to banish MySpace. Teens who were forced to leave were more likely to come from households where their parents were involved in monitoring their kids' online behaviors but were not themselves on MySpace. They were less likely to have siblings, cousins, and other family members present in MySpace. In short, the teens who were forced to leave tended to come from more privileged backgrounds. Their disappearance fractured their friends' networks, reducing the value of MySpace.

Amidst this, MySpace failed to address the problems presented by spammers and scammers. Teens started receiving an onslaught of friend requests from scammers and their accounts started getting hacked due to security flaws introduced when users started copying and pasting layout code into profile forms. Given their penchant for vibrant profiles and willingness to track down code, youth were especially vulnerable. Because of the widespread technopanic, many of the teens I interviewed who left MySpace read these security attacks as proof of the presence of sexual predators and other "creepy" people. Those whose friend networks on MySpace were already fractured were most inclined to leave.

The emergence of Facebook hastened this process. Many parents saw Facebook as a "safe" alternative to MySpace, primarily because it was not possible to make a profile truly public. (Arguably, making a profile visible to everyone in a geographic region is akin to being public.) Adults did not see the same signals on Facebook that frightened them. Many reinforced the spatial and racial distinctions by demonizing MySpace and embracing Facebook. Countless teens who were not allowed on MySpace were permitted to join Facebook. Teens who had friends in college were especially quick to join. With an alternative in place, many who were doubtful of MySpace or whose friends had departed switched.

Concerns about MySpace and safety were widespread, but how people responded varied. Many teens made their profiles private or friends-only, but others left or were forced to leave because of the fear. As they departed, their friends were more likely to go as well because of the importance of social cohesion. Many of those who left joined Facebook. The same network effects that motivated teens to join MySpace hastened their departure. The early departers were not evenly distributed across the network. The factors that prompted or forced some teens to leave and the factors that minimized their incentives to stay affected certain groups of teens more than others. In short, teens from privileged backgrounds were more likely to defect. This helped create the impressions that Anastasia and Craig described.

MySpace: A Digital Ghetto?

One provocative way of reflecting on the networked movement from MySpace to Facebook is through the lens of "white flight." The term "white flight" refers to the exodus of white people from urban American centers to the suburbs during the twentieth century. This simplistic definition obscures the racial motivations of those who left, the institutionalized discrimination that restricted others from leaving, and the ramifications for cities and race relations (Kruse 2005). Many who left did so to avoid racial integration in communities and schools. Not everyone could leave. Although the suburbs were touted as part of the "American Dream," families of color were often barred explicitly by ethnically exclusive restrictions on housing developments or indirectly by discriminatory lending practices (Massey and Denton 1998). Suburbs were zoned to limit low-income housing and rentals, thereby limiting who could afford to move there. What followed was urban decay. Governmental agencies reduced investments in urban communities, depopulation lowered property values and shrunk tax bases, and unemployment rose as jobs moved to the suburbs. The resultant cities were left in disrepair and the power of street gangs increased. Through "white flight," racial identities were reworked as spaces were reconfigured (Massey and Denton 1998; Avila 2004; Harris 2007).

Given the formalized racism and institutionalized restrictions involved in urban white flight, labeling teen movement from MySpace to Facebook as "digital white flight" may appear to be a problematic overstatement. My goal is not to dismiss or devalue the historic tragedy that white racism brought to many cities, but to offer a stark framework for seeing the reproduction of social divisions in a society still shaped by racism.

Consider the parallels. In some senses, the first teens to move to the "suburbs" were those who bought into a Teen Dream of collegiate maturity, namely those who were expressly headed towards dorm-based universities and colleges. They were the elite who were given land in the new suburbs before plots were broadly available. The suburbs of Facebook signaled more mature living, complete with digital fences to keep out strangers. The narrative that these digital suburbs were safer than the city enhanced its desirability, particularly for those who had no interest in interacting with people who were different. Some teens were moved because of the policies of their parents. Early settlers incentivized their friends to join them.

While formal restrictions on who could move lifted in September 2006, the more subtle network-based disincentives did not. Those teens whose family and friends were deeply enmeshed in the city of MySpace were less inclined to leave for the suburbs. Those who left the city often left their profiles untended and they often fell into disrepair, covered in spam, a form of digital graffiti. This contributed to a sense of eeriness, but also hastened the departure of their neighbors. As MySpace failed to address these issues, spammers took over like street gangs. What resulted can be understood as a digital ghetto.

Needless to say, the frame of "white flight" only partially works, but the metaphor provides a fertile backdrop to address the kinds of language I heard used by youth. It also provides a fruitful framework for thinking of the fear and moral panic surrounding MySpace. Fear of risk and perception of safety are salient in discussions of ghettos. Many whites fled the city, believing it crime-ridden, immoral, and generally unsafe. While outsiders are rarely targets of violence in the inner city, the perception of danger is widespread and the suburbs are commonly narrated as the safe alternative. The same holds for MySpace. Fears concerning risks on MySpace are overstated at best and more often outright misunderstood. Yet, they are undoubtedly widespread. In contrast, Facebook's origin as a gated community and parents' belief that the site is private and highly monitored reflect the same values signaled by the suburbs.

The network segmentation implied by a "digital white flight" also helps explain why, two years later, news media behaved as though MySpace was dead. Quite simply, white middle-class journalists didn't know anyone who still used MySpace. On May 4, 2009, *The New York Times* ran a story showing that MySpace and Facebook usage in the U.S. had nearly converged (with Facebook lagging slightly behind MySpace); the title for this article was "Do You Know Anyone Still on MySpace?" Although the article clearly stated that the unique visitors were roughly equal, the headline signaled the cultural divide. The *New York Times* staff were on Facebook and assumed their readers were too. This article generated 154 comments from presumably adult readers. Some defended MySpace, primarily by pointing to its features, the opportunity for connecting, and the cultural relevance of musicians and bands. Many more condemned MySpace, bemoaning its user interface, spam, and outdatedness. Yet, while only two MySpace fans used condescending language to describe Facebook (*"Facebook is very childish"* and *"Facebook is for those who live in the past"*), dozens of MySpace critics demeaned MySpace and its users. Some focused on the perception that MySpace was filled with risky behavior:

> MySpace become synonymous with hyper-sexual, out of control teens, wild partying 20-somethings, 30- to 40-somethings craving attention, sexual predators on the hunt, and generally un-cool personal behavior from a relatively small, but highly visible number of users.

Others used labels, stereotypes, and dismissive language to other those who preferred MySpace, often suggesting a class-based distinction:

My impression is that MySpace is for the riffraff and Facebook is for the landed gentry.

Compared to Facebook, MySpace just seems like the other side of the tracks—I'll go there for fun, but I wouldn't want to live there.

My impression is [MySpace is] for tweens, high school kids that write emo poetry, and the proletariat. once the younger demo goes to college, they shift to Facebook. the proletariat? everyone knows they never go to college!

Just as those who moved to the suburbs looked down upon those who remained in the cities, so too did Facebook users demean those on MySpace. This can be seen in the attitudes of teens I interviewed, the words of these commenters, and the adjectives used by the college students Watkins (2009) interviewed. The language used in these remarks resembles the same language used throughout the 1980s to describe city dwellers: dysfunctional families, perverts and deviants, freaks and outcasts, thieves, and the working class. Implied in this is that no decent person could possibly have a reason to dwell in the city or on MySpace. While some who didn't use MySpace were harshly critical of the site, others simply forgot that it existed. They thought it to be irrelevant, believing that no one lived there anymore simply because no one they knew did.

To the degree that some viewed MySpace as a digital ghetto or as being home to the cultural practices that are labeled as ghetto, the same fear and racism that underpinned much of white flight in urban settings is also present in the perception of MySpace. The fact that many teens who left MySpace for Facebook explained their departure as being about features, aesthetics, or friendship networks does not disconnect their departure from issues of race and class. Rather, their attitude towards specific aesthetic markers and features is shaped by their experiences with race and class. Likewise, friendship networks certainly drove the self-segmentation, but these too are shaped by race such that departure logically played out along race lines. The explanations teens gave for their decisions may not be explicitly about race, ethnicity, or class, but they cannot be untangled from them, just as fear-based narratives about the "ghetto" cannot be considered without also accounting for race, ethnicity, and class.

In some senses, the division in the perception and use of MySpace and Facebook seems obvious given that we know that online environments are a reflection of everyday life. Yet, the fact that such statements are controversial highlights a widespread techno-utopian belief that the internet will once and for all eradicate inequality and social divisions. What unfolded as teens adopted MySpace and Facebook suggests that this is not the case. Neither social media nor its users are colorblind simply because technology is present. The internet mirrors and magnifies everyday life, making visible many of the issues we hoped would disappear, including race and class-based social divisions in American society.

Note

1 www.danah.org/.

References

Arnold, Rebecca. 2001. *Fashion, Desire and Anxiety: Image and Morality in the 20th Century*. Rutgers, NJ: Rutgers University Press.

Avila, Eric. 2004. "Popular Culture in the Age of White Flight: Film Noir, Disneyland, and the Cold War (Sub)Urban Imaginary." *Journal of Urban History* 31.1: 3–22.

Bonilla-Silva, Eduardo. 2003. *Racism Without Racists: Color-blind Racism and the Persistence of Racial Inequality in the United States*. Lanham, MD: Rowman and Littlefield.

Bourdieu, Pierre. 1984. *Distinction: A Social Critique of the Judgment of Taste*. Cambridge, MA: Harvard University Press.

boyd, danah. 2007a. "Viewing American Class Divisions Through Facebook and MySpace." *Apophenia*, June 24. Available at: www.danah.org/papers/essays/ClassDivisions.html

——. 2007b. "Why Youth (Heart) Social Network Sites: The Role of Networked Publics in Teenage Social Life," in David Buckingham, ed., *MacArthur Foundation Series on Digital Learning—Youth, Identity, and Digital Media Volume*. Cambridge, MA: MIT Press, 119–142.

——. 2008. *Taken Out of Context: American Teen Sociality in Networked Publics*. PhD dissertation, University of California-Berkeley.

——. and Nicole Ellison. 2007. "Social Network Sites: Definition, History, and Scholarship." *Journal of Computer-Mediated Communication* 13.1: article 11. Available at: http://jcmc.indiana.edu/vol13/issue1/boyd.ellison.html

Byrne, Dara. 2008. "The Future of (the) 'Race': Identity, Discourse, and the Rise of Computer-mediated Public Spheres," in Anna Everett, ed., *MacArthur Foundation Series on Digital Learning—Learning Race and Ethnicity Volume*. Cambridge, MA: MIT Press, 15–38.

Crane, Diana. 2000. *Fashion and Its Social Agendas: Class, Gender, and Identity in Clothing*. Chicago, IL: University of Chicago Press.

Donath, Judith. 2007. "Signals in Social Supernets." *Journal of Computer-Mediated Communication* 13.1: article 12. Available at: http://jcmc.indiana.edu/vol13/issue1/donath.html

Donath, Judith and danah boyd. 2004. "Public Displays of Connection." *BT Technology Journal* 22.4: 71–82.

Eckert, Penelope. 1989. *Jocks and Burnouts: Social Categories and Identity in the High School*. New York: Teacher College Press.

Forman, Murray. 2002. *The 'Hood Comes First: Race, Space, and Place in Rap and Hip-Hop*. Middleton, CT: Wesleyan University Press.

Gaines, Donna. 1998. *Teenage Wasteland: Suburbia's Dead End Kids*. Chicago, IL: University of Chicago Press.

Hare, Breanna. 2009. "Does Class Decide Online Social Networks?" *CNN* October 24. Available at www.cnn.com/2009/TECH/10/24/tech.networking.class/

Hargittai, Eszter. 2007. "Whose Space? Differences among Users and Non-users of Social Network Sites." *Journal of Computer-Mediated Communication* 13.1: article 14. Available at: http://jcmc.indiana.edu/vol13/issue1/hargittai.html

Harris, Dianne. 2007. "Clean and White and Everyone White," in Dianne Harris and D. Fairchild Ruggles, eds, *Sites Unseen: Landscape and Vision*. Pittsburgh, PA: University of Pittsburgh Press.

Hebdige, Dick. 1979. *Subculture: The Meaning of Style*. London: Routledge.

Kruse, Kevin. 2005. *White Flight: Atlanta and the Making of Modern Conservativism*. Princeton, NY: Princeton University Press.

Lam, Chuck. 2007a. "Analyzing Facebook Usage by High School Demographic." *Data Strategy*, September 14. Available at: http://datastrategy.wordpress.com/2007/09/14/analyzing-facebook-usage-by-high-school-demographic/

——. 2007b. "Examining MySpace Usage by High School." *Data Strategy* September 19. Available at: http://datastrategy.wordpress.com/2007/09/19/examining-myspace-usage-by-high-school/

Liu, Hugo. 2007. "Social Network Profiles as Taste Performances." *Journal of Computer-Mediated Communication* 13.1: article 13. Available at http://jcmc.indiana.edu/vol13/issue1/liu.html

McPherson, Miller, Lynn Smith-Lovin, and James Cook. 2001. "Birds of a Feather: Homophily in Social Networks." *Annual Review of Sociology* 27: 415–444.

Marwick, Alice. 2008. "To Catch a Predator? The MySpace Moral Panic." *First Monday* 13.6: article 3.

Massey, Douglas and Nancy Denton. 1998. *American Apartheid: Segregation and the Making of the Underclass*. Cambridge, MA: Harvard University Press.

Milner, Murray, Jr. 2004. *Freaks, Geeks, and Cool Kids: American Teenagers, Schools, and the Culture of Consumption*. New York: Routledge.

Moody, James. 2001. "Race, School Integration, and Friendship Segregation in America." *American Journal of Sociology* 107.3: 679–716.

Nakamura, Lisa. 2008. *Digitizing Race: Visual Cultures of the Internet*. Minneapolis: University of Minnesota Press.

Perry, Pamela. 2002. *Shades of White: White Kids and Racial Identities in High School*. Durham, NC: Duke University Press.

Pollock, Mica. 2005. "Race Bending: 'Mixed' Youth Practicing Strategic Racialization in California," in Sunaina Maira and Elisabeth Soep, eds, *YouthScapes: The Popular, the National, the Global*. Philadelphia, PA: University of Pennsylvania Press.

Shankar, Shalini. 2008. *Desi Land: Teen Culture, Class, and Success in Silicon Valley*. Durham, NC: Duke University Press.

Shrock, Andrew and danah boyd. 2009. "Online Threats to Youth: Solicitation, Harassment, and Problematic Content," in John Palfrey, Dena Sacco, and danah boyd, eds, *Enhancing Child Safety & Online Technologies*. Durham, NC: Carolina Academic Press.

Tatum, Beverly. 1997. *"Why Are All the Black Kids Sitting Together in the Cafeteria?" and other Conversations About Race*. New York: Basic Books.

Thorne, Barrie. 1993. *Gender Play: Girls and Boys in School*. New Brunswick, NJ: Rutgers University Press.

——. 2008. "'The Chinese Girls' and 'The Pokémon Kids': Children Negotiating Differences in Urban California," in J. Cole and D. Durham, eds, *Figuring the Future: Globalization and the Temporalities of Children and Youth*. Santa Fe, NM: SAR Press.

Thornton, Sarah. 1995. *Club Cultures: Music, Media, and Subcultural Capital*. Cambridge: Polity Press.

Wacquant, Loic J.D. 1997. "Three Pernicious Premises in the Study of the American Ghetto." *International Journal of Urban and Regional Research* 21.2: 341–353.

Watkins, S. Craig. 2009. *The Young and the Digital: What the Migration to Social-Network Sites, Games, and Anytime, Anywhere Media Means for Our Future*. Boston, MA: Beacon Press.

Willis, Paul. 1981. *Learning to Labor: How Working Class Kids Get Working Class Jobs*. New York: Columbia University Press.

10

Open Doors, Closed Spaces?
Differentiated Adoption of Social Network Sites by User Background

ESZTER HARGITTAI

Northwestern University

Introduction

Social network sites (SNS) have become some of the most popular online destinations. According to site ranking statistics available on the Web site ranking.com, MySpace was the 11th most popular destination on the Web in August, 2007, while Facebook was 45th at the time. Those are already impressive positions on the popularity scale, but the sites climbed even higher on the list by November, 2009, when, according to the same source, MySpace was the eighth most popular destination on the Web while Facebook was the third. Not surprisingly, this level of popularity has led to much coverage of such sites in the popular press as well as academic research on their social implications. For example, a search of the major American and global newspapers yields thousands of articles on related topics while academic papers now number in the hundreds, having grown exponentially toward the end of the twenty-first century's first decade.[1] Interestingly, while lots of work has focused on the implications of using such sites, a significant antecedent question of who is most likely to adopt them in the first place has seen little investigation. That question is the central focus of this chapter. Are there systematic differences in who does and does not become a user of social network sites? Moreover, are people equally likely to join the various sites in this domain, e.g. Facebook and MySpace, or do we observe systematic differences in who spends time on one versus other such sites?

Why should we care about who uses social network sites and whether different types of groups adopt them at similar rates? As sites gain in popularity, assumptions start mounting about the extent to which everybody has integrated them into their everyday lives, assumptions that may not be correct and that may be biasing against certain populations. For example, if a college professor wrongly assumes that all of her students are Facebook users and thus integrates the service into her teaching, then she may be biasing against students who have never used the site, who spend little time on it or who are less familiar with it. Moreover, if usage is based on some type of user characteristic such as race or ethnicity, then this bias may occur along such lines and would not randomly affect different types of students—rather, would bias systematically against certain types of students. Similarly, if a government or nonprofit agency thinks it can spread important public service announcements to its constituents by putting out messages on such sites, then that has problematic implications if not all segments of the population are, indeed, spending time on these services and thus would be excluded from receiving the disseminated message. This argument can be extended to the domain of business ventures as well. If companies wrongly assume that everybody is on these sites while some people are significantly less likely to use them then, again, certain population segments may be systematically excluded from gaining access to certain types of information and services. Accordingly, it is important to investigate whether various population segments are turning to different social network sites at similar levels.

In addition to the substantive contributions of looking at which specific SNSs people use, this chapter makes methodological contributions to the literature as well. As the results show, disaggregating with which specific site one is engaged is important, because people do not randomly select into their uses and aggregate analyses of SNS usage may suppress important trends. This suggests that one should tread lightly when generalizing from studies about the use of one SNS to the use of other such services. While these sites do share commonalities, they also have distinct features—whether at the level of site design or the particular communities that comprise their user base—that may encourage different types of activities and may attract different populations. Thus, a look at SNS use both on the aggregate and with respect to specific sites is important if we are to gain a better understanding of how use of such sites is spreading across various population segments and the social implications of these trends.

Differentiating Types of Internet Uses

The now-classic *New Yorker* cartoon proclaimed in 1993 that "On the Internet nobody knows that you are a dog" (Steiner 1993) suggesting that one's identity was so hidden on the Web that opportunities would be widely open to all regardless of background characteristics that may have traditionally disadvantaged some people over others. The idea that people would be on an equal footing once having adopted use of the medium assumes that offline characteristics are not mirrored in people's online pursuits. However, work over the last several years has found this not to be the case. Already in the early 2000s people suggested that despite initial impressions and arguments about how users shed their offline identities in online interactions (Turkle 1995), offline identities very much carry over to online behavior (Smith and Kollock 1999; boyd 2001). This suggests that the Internet is not necessarily leveling the playing field the way that the famous *New Yorker* cartoon would have us believe. Rather, constraints or benefits people experience in their offline lives are often mirrored in their online actions and interactions.

Indeed, work looking at how different people use the Internet in their everyday lives has found systematic differences across types of users. For example, even while women caught up with men in some countries (e.g. the United States) concerning basic connectivity, their uses continued to differ whereby men spent more time online and claimed higher-level skills than women (Bimber 2000; Jackson *et al.* 2001; Ono and Zavodny 2003; Hargittai and Shafer 2006) consistent with earlier literature on gender differences in technology use more generally speaking (Hall and Cooper 1991; Livingstone 1992; Herring 1994; e.g. Frissen 1995). Other factors such as socioeconomic status have also been shown to predict types of Internet uses (Howard *et al.* 2001; Madden 2003; Livingstone and Helsper 2007). For example, so-called "capital-enhancing" activities (DiMaggio and Hargittai 2001) such as looking for financial, political, or government information online are associated with socioeconomic status whereby those from privileged backgrounds engage in such online pursuits more than their less privileged counterparts (Howard *et al.* 2001; Hargittai and Hinnant 2008). Moreover, the circumstances under which people use the medium such as their autonomy (Hassani 2006) and experience of use (Howard *et al.* 2001) are also related to the purposes to which they put the medium with more locations of access points and more time spent online associated with more diverse types of uses (Hargittai and Hinnant 2008; e.g. Hargittai 2010).

Research has also shown that even when controlling for other factors such as income and education, people from different racial and ethnic backgrounds engage in online activities at different levels. For example, Howard *et al.* (2001) found that African American Internet users were more likely to check sports scores, play a game, look for jobs or seek religious information online than Whites, while they were less likely to participate in auctions or buy products online. Hispanic respondents were less likely to get financial information on the Web than Whites. Asian Americans were more likely to seek news about politics online than Whites and were especially more likely to buy and sell stocks and bonds on the Web. Analyzing one of the data sets upon which the present chapter is based (the 2007 portion), Hargittai (2010) observed that African American and Hispanic young adults visited fewer types of sites than Whites and Asian Americans. That paper also found that African American and Hispanic students exhibited considerably lower levels of understanding of Internet-related terms than Whites and Asian Americans (Hargittai 2010: 102).

Given that various background characteristics of people as well as the context of their Internet uses and their level of experience have all been shown to influence types of online pursuits in general, it is worth considering whether they may also relate to social network site usage in particular. That is, given earlier work on differentiated Internet uses among people from different backgrounds, there is no reason that we should assume equal adoption of SNSs across population segments. In fact, the little work that has been done in this domain (boyd 2007; Hargittai 2007; boyd this volume) has suggested variations by race and ethnicity in SNS usage. Work that solely focuses on users of social network sites excludes, by definition, people who are non-users. Insofar as these people are systematically different from those who embrace these services, it behooves us not to know anything about them since thereby we ignore entire groups of people from our discussions without realizing or recognizing that we may be doing so.

An important reason for the scarcity of work predicting SNS usage is the lack of appropriate data necessary to address such questions. Despite the evolution in the focus of Internet user studies on particular online behavior (Wellman and Haythornthwaite 2002; Howard and Jones 2003), categorizations of online activities have remained relatively broad, making it difficult to understand who does what online, why, and how this influences various domains of people's lives. Additionally, because the popularity of SNSs is relatively recent, initial data collection efforts about Web uses did not focus on them. On more general surveys of Internet uses, it is more customary to ask about the topics one encounters on Web sites (e.g. Internet use for the purposes of gathering information about political or health topics) than to inquire in detail about specific sites and communities on which people may be accessing information or connecting with their friends, family and colleagues. Perhaps it is in part due to such methodological issues that few appropriate data sets exist to address basic adoption of different SNSs.

Data limitations may explain why many studies about SNSs often focus on just one such site like Facebook (e.g. Steinfield *et al.* 2008; Ross *et al.* 2009) or MySpace (Pfeil *et al.* 2009) making it impossible to compare adoption rates across services. Some studies (e.g. Lewis *et al.* 2008) take as their sampling frame users of these sites, thereby automatically excluding those who are not on them in the first place (e.g. conducting a census of certain profiles on one SNS would have such a limitation). By excluding non-users, the resulting sample lacks the necessary variance on basic usage to investigate variation in adoption rates. On the rare occasion when data have been available on non-users in addition to users, the focus of the research has been elsewhere. For example, Pasek *et al.* (2007) do have disaggregated data by site and variance on their usage, but they look at the predictive power of SNS use on civic engagement rather than exploring what explains SNS usage in the first place. Tufekci (2008) has information about people maintaining profiles on both MySpace and Facebook, but when looking at predictors of using such a site at all, she only considers data about people's privacy concerns, which is the main focus of her investigation. Her paper does not, however, look at what basic demographic characteristics may distinguish users and non-users. Given the focus of existing work, then, there is a need for more research that looks at basic SNS use as the outcome of interest (i.e. the dependent variable) and considers what factors explain the adoption of such sites in the first place.

American college students offer an ideal population to study differences in particular types of digital media uses given their high—often 100 percent—connectivity levels and frequent uses of the medium. Regarding SNS adoption in particular, young people were the main initial users of the most popular such sites (boyd and Ellison 2007) and even today are more likely to be on them than others from older age groups (Lenhart *et al.* 2010), suggesting that focus on adolescents and young adults is especially important if we are to gain a better understanding of how such sites are being incorporated into people's lives. Moreover, because young adults tend to be more wired than their older counterparts (Jones and Fox 2009), it can be beneficial to focus studies on this population if the goal is to understand who may or may not be using specific online services rather than concentrating on basic access statistics. The next section introduces the unique data sets available here to address these questions followed by an examination of social network site adoption by different population groups.

Data and Methods

I draw on data about two diverse groups of young adults to answer the questions raised above. The data represent two cohorts of first-year students at the University of Illinois, Chicago.[2] The first data set was collected in February–March, 2007; the second was gathered two years later in February–April, 2009, on a different group of students. A paper–pencil survey was administered in the one course on this urban campus that is required for everybody, the First-Year Writing Program. By working with this course, the project avoids biasing against people who may be less likely to take certain classes since this one is required of everybody on campus. In the 2006–2007 academic year, there were 87 sections offered as part of this course of which 85 participated in the study; in the 2008–2009 academic year there were 92 course sections of which 86 took part in the project. Overall, counting all students who were enrolled in the course in the two years, the 2007 study yielded an 81.9 percent response rate while the 2009 study had a response rate of 80.5 percent. The analyses presented in this paper draw on the 1,060 first-year students in the 2007 sample and the 1,115 first-year students in the 2009 sample.[3]

The survey was administered on paper rather than on the Web so as not to bias against those students who are online less frequently or who are less inclined to fill out online forms for whatever reason (e.g. lack of enough private time spent on the Web). Since having ample time online to engage in various activities is linked to the questions of interest in this study, it was important not to use a data-collection method that might be related to it.

Measures: Demographics

Table 10.1 presents the demographic make-up of the two samples. Although both genders are well represented, slightly more women than men participated in the study in both years. Students were asked their year of birth to calculate their age. The majority of the sample (97 percent in the 2007 sample; close to 99 percent in the 2009 sample) are either 18 or 19 years of age so that variable is nearly constant in the sample and is not included in the analyses. For measure of race and ethnicity, in line with U.S. Census conventions, students were first asked if they were Hispanic or of Latino origin and about a fifth (18.8 percent) in 2007 and about a quarter (24.0 percent) in 2009 indicated to be so. Then students were asked their race including the following categories: (a) White/Anglo/Caucasian/Middle Eastern; (b) Black/African American; (c) Asian; (d) American Indian or Alaskan Native; (e) Other. Most respondents in the "Other" category indicated Hispanic origin and were coded accordingly. The resulting race and ethnicity categorization of participants is as follows: Hispanic, non-Hispanic African American, non-Hispanic Asian American, non-Hispanic Native American, and non-Hispanic White. As the figures in Table 10.1 indicate, less than half of both samples are White and there are a considerable number of both Hispanic students and Asian Americans in both groups. There are fewer African Americans although they still make up almost 8 percent of

Table 10.1 Background of Study Participants

	Percent	
	2007	*2009*
Women	55.8	58.7
Age		
18	64.8	66.2
19	32.2	32.6
20–29	3.0	1.2
Race and Ethnicity		
African American, non-Hispanic	7.7	10.6
Asian American, non-Hispanic	29.6	22.2
Hispanic	18.8	24.0
Native American, non-Hispanic	1.2	0.5
White, non-Hispanic	42.7	40.8
Parents' Highest Level of Education		
Less than high school	7.4	7.2
High school	19.0	15.9
Some college	20.1	23.7
College	34.4	34.6
Graduate degree	19.1	18.7
Lives with parents	53.1	49.6

the 2007 group and just over 10 percent of the 2009 sample. There are just a handful (17 or 1.6 percent in 2007 and 5 or 0.5 percent in 2009) of Native Americans in the group. These numbers are so small as to make separate statistical analyses of this group unworkable and these respondents have thus been excluded from the analyses that consider respondents' race/ethnicity.

I collected data about parental education as a proxy for socioeconomic status. Respondents were asked to report the level of education of both their mother and father using the following categories: (a) less than high school degree; (b) high school degree; (c) some college; (d) college degree (for example: B.A., B.S., B.S.E); (e) advanced graduate (for example: master's, professional, Ph.D., M.D., Ed.D.). Based on information from these two questions, I created a parental education variable that is assigned the value of the highest education by either parent, e.g. if a student has a mother with a high school degree and a father with a college degree then the parental education variable for that student is coded as "college degree". Table 10.1 shows that there is considerable diversity in both samples regarding the educational background of students' parents. In both groups, close to a quarter of students come from families in which neither parent has more than a high school education. In both samples, just below a fifth of participants have at least one parent who has a graduate degree.

As evidenced by these descriptives, while the samples are homogenous when it comes to age and education level (everybody is in the first year of college), there is considerable diversity regarding race/ethnicity and parental educational background. In fact, this campus consistently ranks among the most ethnically diverse universities in the United States (U.S. News and World Report 2009), an important reason why it was chosen as the site of the research project upon which this paper draws.

Measures: Social Context of Use

The use of digital media does not happen in social isolation and thus measuring context of usage is important for a more nuanced understanding of what explains differentiated uses. Accordingly, the survey included a measure of whether the student could go online at a friend or family member's house and whether the student lives with his/her parents or elsewhere (e.g. alone in a dorm or with roommates). As the last row in Table 10.1 indicates, about half of the sample lives with parents while the other half lives either alone or with roommates. The figures on the first row of Table 10.2 show that while the majority of students have access to the Internet at a friend or a family member's house, 10 percent in both years do not, suggesting lower levels of autonomy for a tenth of respondents when it comes to using the Internet in various locations and at various times.

Measures: Internet Experiences

Although all respondents are Internet users, they may not be identical when it comes to their online experiences. I use two measures to assess experience with

Table 10.2 Internet Use Context and Experiences

	2007		2009	
	Mean	*St. Dev.*	*Mean*	*St. Dev.*
Has access to the Internet at a friend or family member's house	0.9	(0.3)	0.9	(0.3)
Number of use years	6.3	(2.0)	5.7	(2.3)
Hours spent on the Web weekly	15.5	(10.0)	17.4	(10.0)

the Internet: number of use years and hours spent on the Web weekly. The former measure is calculated using information from survey questions that ask about the stage in one's academic career when the student first became an Internet user (i.e. in elementary school or earlier, in middle school, in high school before senior year, senior year of high school or during college). Because slightly different questions asked about this variable on the two surveys, the coefficients in the regression analyses are not directly comparable. User years were capped at 10 for the 2007 sample (19.9 percent of the sample fell into this category) and at 9 for the 2009 sample (22.5 percent of that group had this value). This measure is logged in the analyses given that there are likely diminishing returns to additional years of having been a user as the number of years increases. Time spent on the Web weekly (excluding email, chat and voice services) is derived from answers to two questions asking about hours spent on the Web on an average day; one inquiring about weekdays, the other about an average Saturday or Sunday. This measure ranges from 0 to 42 hours and is also logged in the analyses for reasons similar to logging number of use years. On average, students report spending 15.5 hours in 2007 and 17.4 hours in 2009 (standard deviation: 10.0 in both cases) on the Web weekly with the bottom 10 percent spending less than an hour on the Web daily compared to the top 10 percent reporting 4–5 hours of daily usage.

These figures illustrate that while there is certainly some amount of variation in access and use, there are no basic barriers standing in the way of these young adults in accessing the Internet. Limits may be put on their uses due to other factors (e.g. the need to share resources at home, time taken up with a job or commuting), but everybody in the two samples has basic access. This suggests that traditional concerns about the so-called digital divide do not apply to the study participants concerning availability of the Internet and so looking at such a wired group of users allows us to control for basic Web access and focus on differences in details of use instead.

Measures: Social Network Site Usage

Both surveys included questions about respondents' knowledge of and experiences with six social network sites. In the 2007 study, the following sites were included, based on the general popularity of these sites at the time: Bebo, Facebook, Friendster, MySpace, Orkut and Xanga. Because four of these (see Table 10.3) were used by a very small portion of the sample (7 percent or much less) and did not appear to gain in popularity among this demographic in the following two years, they were replaced by four other SNSs in the 2009 survey, namely: AsianAve, BlackPlanet, Glee and MiGente.

For each site, respondents were first asked to report whether they had ever heard of it. Next, they were asked to indicate their experiences with it by choosing one of the following options: (a) have never used it; (b) tried it once, but have not used it since; (c) have used it in the past, but do not use it nowadays; (d) currently use it sometimes; (e) currently use it often. To calculate usage figures for each SNS, participants who responded by choosing the (d) or (e) option were given the value of 1, signaling usage of the particular site. From information about the use of each separate SNS, I constructed an overall social network site usage variable that gets a value of 1 if the respondent uses any of the six SNSs on the survey and a 0 if the respondent does not report using any of them.

Methods of Analysis

I start by presenting basic information about respondents' familiarity and experiences with various social network sites (Table 10.3). Then, I use logistic regression analyses to consider what explains the adoption of any SNSs (Table 10.4). Given that the outcome variable is dichotomous—that is, someone either uses SNSs or not—this is the relevant statistical technique (Pampel 2000). The results reported are odds ratios, meaning that any figure above 1 constitutes a higher propensity to engage in SNS usage, whereas a figure lower than 1 suggests that that type of characteristic lowers the likelihood of social network site usage. Next, I present basic frequencies (Table 10.5) regarding the use of Facebook and MySpace, separately, by user background characteristics (i.e. gender, race and ethnicity, and parental education). Finally, I employ logistic regression analyses again, this time to explore predictors of specifically using Facebook and MySpace, respectively (Table 10.6).

Male is the base gender category in the models. Dummy variables are used for race and ethnicity with White as the base. Dummy variables are also used for parental education with some college education (but no college degree) as the omitted category. Both the question of living at home with parents and the question of having access to the Internet at a friend or family member's house are included as a dummy variable where 1 signals yes to that question and 0 stands for no. The models presented in the first column labeled "Background only" consider solely the core background characteristics of the user (gender, race and ethnicity, and parental education), whereas the columns labeled "Full model" also contain information about Internet use context and experiences.

Table 10.3 Familiarity and Experience with Social Network Sites among Study Participants

Site	Year	Uses it*	Has heard of it	Has never used it	Tried it once, but no more	Used to use it, no longer
Facebook	2007	78.8 (62.8)	99.4	14.2	3.6	3.4
	2009	87.2 (75.0)	99.7	6.4	3.0	3.4
MySpace	2007	54.6 (38.4)	99.5	20.8	9.4	15.2
	2009	40.0 (15.9)	99.5	15.4	8.0	40.6
Bebo	2007	0.6 (0.0)	9.6	95.4	2.8	1.2
Friendster	2007	3.3 (1.0)	43.3	84.7	5.6	6.4
Orkut	2007	1.6 (0.6)	5.8	97.1	0.5	0.8
Xanga	2007	6.2 (1.9)	76.4	61.7	11.8	20.3
AsianAve	2009	0.1 (0.0)	7.0	95.4	2.3	2.2
BlackPlanet	2009	0.5 (0.2)	15.7	94.0	3.3	2.2
Glee	2009	0.1 (0.0)	3.4	98.9	0.7	0.3
MiGente	2009	0.4 (0.1)	13.9	92.3	5.1	2.2

* These figures summarize the percentage of students who use the site currently "sometimes" and "often". Figures for those reporting to use the site *often* are in parentheses.

Any SNS Usage

In the 2007 sample, 87.7 percent of respondents used at least one social network site (Hargittai 2007) while in the 2009 sample 91.2 percent reported spending time on at least one such site. Are some people not using these sites because perhaps they have never heard of them? As the figures in the column labeled "Has heard of it" in Table 10.3 indicate, that is not the case. In both years, virtually everybody had heard of at least Facebook and MySpace. Consequently, non-use is not a result of not being familiar with these services. Rather, despite knowing about such sites, in 2007 over 12 percent and in 2009 close to 9 percent of the sample chose not to spend time on SNSs. Are these students systematically different from users?

Table 10.4 reports the results of logistic regression analyses looking at what user background characteristics explain whether a student uses any social network sites. Consistent across the two years is that women are more likely to use at least one social network site than men. Overall, there is no difference in social network site adoption by race and ethnicity and almost none by parental education. The only exception is the result of the background-only model in 2009 where students whose parents have less than a high school education are considerably less likely to use any SNS. However, once we control for social context of use and Internet experiences, this relationship is no longer statistically significant. Rather, what seem to matter in both years are living context and how much time students spend online. Those living with their parents are less likely to use SNSs and those who spend more time on the Web are more likely to be users, perhaps not surprisingly since time spent on SNSs itself constitutes time spent online.

Based on these findings, we may be inclined to conclude that other than gender, user background characteristics such as race and ethnicity are not related to social network site usage. However, these aggregated statistics about *any* SNS usage may be masking findings that pertain to the use of *specific* social network sites. After all, these sites have different histories and affordances and thus may attract different types of users. Accordingly, if the data allow such disaggregation, as the data set here does, it is important to examine predictors of individual site usage.

Specific SNS Usage

Table 10.3 shows basic usage statistics for each of the ten sites included in the two surveys. The figures suggest that Facebook and MySpace are by far the most popular sites from the six listed on each survey. Facebook was the most popular in 2007, with close to 79 percent of the sample reporting at least some use of it. The site remained the most popular in 2009, with an even larger portion of the then first-year students reporting use at 87 percent. In 2007, over half of respondents used MySpace, popularity that declined by the time the 2009 first-year cohort took the survey, as only 40 percent of them reported using this site.

The other four sites in both years (Xanga, Friendster, Orkut and Bebo in 2007; AsianAve, BlackPlanet, Glee and MiGente in 2009) were significantly less widespread in this group.

Table 10.5 reports the level of Facebook and MySpace popularity by type of user attribute. The statistics are broken down by gender, race and ethnicity, and parental education for samples of both years. We find significant differences by type of user. In 2007, women were more likely to use MySpace than men, but there were no differences for Facebook use. This changed for the 2009 cohort as we observe gender differences for both sites. Women were more likely than men to use both, with an especially large gender difference in MySpace usage.

Table 10.4 Results of Logistic Regression Analyses Explaining the Use of Any Social Network Site (of six) (Standard Errors in Parentheses)

	2007		2009	
	Background only	*Full model*	*Background only*	*Full model*
Gender	**1.60***	**1.70****	**2.26*****	**2.47*****
(Female = 1)	(0.32)	(0.34)	(0.50)	(0.58)
Hispanic	0.80	0.90	0.82	1.05
	(0.22)	(0.25)	(24)	(0.32)
African American	0.60	0.62	1.49	1.23
	(0.21)	(0.23)	(0.68)	(0.58)
Asian/Asian	0.95	0.99	1.18	1.09
American	(0.22)	(0.24)	(0.18)	(0.18)
Parents' edu:	1.30	1.80	**0.42***	0.51
Less than high school	(0.55)	(0.82)	(0.17)	(0.21)
Parents' edu:	0.85	0.90	0.79	0.90
High school	(0.24)	(0.26)	(0.27)	(0.31)
Parents' edu:	1.50	1.40	1.18	1.19
College degree	(0.41)	(0.39)	(0.37)	(0.38)
Parents' edu:	1.25	1.10	0.95	0.87
Graduate degree	(0.38)	(0.34)	(0.33)	(0.32)
Living with parents		**0.63***		**0.31*****
		(0.13)		(0.08)
Has Net access at friends'/		**2.05****		1.57
family members'		(0.54)		(0.48)
Hours on Web/week		**1.41***		**1.52***
(logged)		(0.20)		(0.26)
Years online		0.92		1.40
(logged)		(0.31)		(0.36)
N	1,032	1,014	1,078	1,052
Chi^2	12.31	31.78	27.18	59.36
Pseudo R^2	0.01	0.04	0.04	0.09

* $p<0.05$, ** $p<0.01$, *** $p<0.001$

Table 10.5 Percentage of Different Groups of People who Use Facebook and MySpace (Use Defined as "Use Sometimes" or "Use Often")

	2007		2009	
	Facebook	MySpace	Facebook	MySpace
Gender				
Male	78	49***	84**	29***
Female	80	59***	89**	41***
Race and ethnicity				
White, non-Hispanic	83**	57	90*	30**
Hispanic	60***	73***	75***	58***
African American, NH	80	58	91	51***
Asian American, NH	84**	39***	93**	16***
Parental education				
Less than high school	64***	73***	70***	56***
High school	73*	57	83*	45*
Some college	74*	57	88	41*
College	86***	55	92**	30**
Graduate degree	83	41***	89	26**

* $p<0.1$, ** $p<0.01$, *** $p<0.001$

Regarding race and ethnicity, the most pronounced and consistent findings across the two samples concern students of Hispanic and Asian origin. Hispanic students are significantly less likely to use Facebook in both years, whereas they are much more likely than others to use MySpace. In contrast, Asian and Asian American students are more likely to use Facebook than others (as are Whites), but are significantly less likely to use MySpace. In 2007, just over a third of Asian American participants reported using MySpace compared to over half of Whites and African Americans and almost three-quarters of Hispanic students. In 2009, while use of MySpace declined across the board, marked differences remain by race and ethnicity. Namely, just 16 percent of Asian Americans report using it, as compared to less than a third of Whites, while more than half of African Americans and Hispanic students were on the site. See Figure 10.1 for a graphical representation of how racial and ethnic background relates to Facebook and MySpace use in the samples for the two years.

We also find significant differences by socioeconomic background measured here as parents' level of education. The most pronounced finding in this regard is that students whose parents have less than a high school education are significantly less likely to be on Facebook in both years, while they are significantly more likely to be MySpace users in both samples. In contrast, those who have at least one parent with a college education are significantly more likely to be Facebook users, while those who have at least one parent with a graduate degree

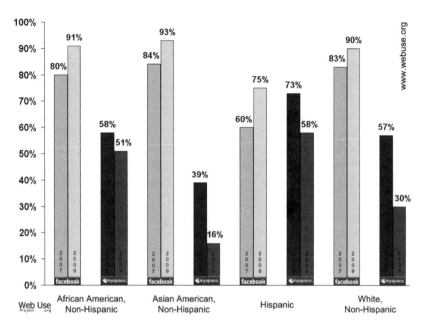

Figure 10.1 Percentage of Students using Facebook versus MySpace in 2007 and 2009 by racial and ethnic background

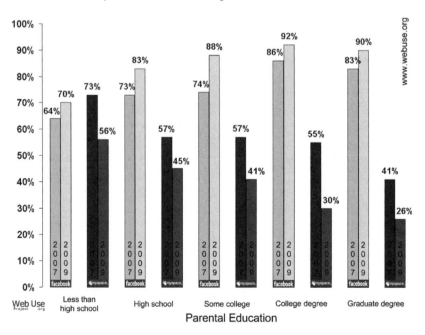

Figure 10.2 Percentage of students using Facebook versus MySpace in 2007 and 2009 by level of parental education

are considerably less likely to use MySpace. Again, these findings hold across both samples. See Figure 10.2 for a graphical representation of these patterns.

Because there is a relationship between parental education and a student's race and ethnicity, it is best also to look at these associations using more advanced statistical techniques that allow us to control for other factors while examining the relationship of the various background variables to the outcomes of interest (i.e. Facebook use and MySpace use). I use logistic regression analyses to consider the relationship of several factors and specific SNS usage concurrently.[4] The independent variables in the models are the same as those described above concerning the analyses examining any SNS usage.

Findings presented in Table 10.6 suggest that the predictors of specific social network site usage are not uniform across different services. Many of the relationships observed in the bivariate analyses are robust even when we hold other factors constant. Regarding gender, women's likelihood to use both Facebook and MySpace is higher than that of men, suggesting that the figures in Table 10.5 remain significant.

Bivariate analyses presented earlier showed that race and ethnicity relates to social network sites students decide to adopt. Now we can consider whether these findings are robust when we hold other factors constant. The figures in Table 10.6 indicate that they are. Hispanic students are much less likely to use Facebook in both years than Whites (the omitted category). In contrast, they are considerably more likely to use MySpace, again findings consistent in both 2007 and 2009 samples. If anything, this association between Hispanic origin and MySpace use has only become more pronounced over time. Thus, even when we control for students' socioeconomic background, their Internet use context and experiences, we find significant differences in whether those of Hispanic origin use Facebook and whether they use MySpace compared to White students not of Hispanic origin. The other students showing significantly different behavior compared to Whites are Asians/Asian Americans. They are significantly less likely than White students to use MySpace, a finding that is similar in both 2007 and 2009.

We also find a statistically significant relationship between the parental education of students and their choice of social network sites in the case of some services although these associations have decreased comparing the 2007 sample to the 2009 group. In 2007, while controlling for other factors, students with more highly educated parents were more likely to use Facebook than those with lower-educated parents and less likely to use MySpace. In contrast, in 2009 this relationship is no longer significant. However, we do find that in 2009 students whose parents have less than a high school education are much less likely to be on Facebook than those whose parents have some college education (the omitted category) even when we control for other factors. Considering the figures in Table 10.5 in light of these findings suggests that some of the differential usage rates by parental education are likely driven by racial/ethnic background.

Table 10.6 Explaining Use of Facebook and MySpace (Standard Errors in Parentheses)

	2007				2009			
	Facebook use		MySpace use		Facebook use		MySpace use	
	Background only	Full model	Background only	Full model	Background only	Full model	Background only	Full model
Gender	1.30	1.37#	1.38*	1.53**	1.9**	2.0**	1.65***	1.69***
(Female = 1)	(0.21)	(0.23)	(0.18)	(0.21)	(0.36)	(0.41)	(0.23)	(0.25)
Hispanic	0.35**	0.38***	1.66*	1.80**	0.42***	0.58*	2.80***	2.71***
	(0.07)	(0.08)	(0.33)	(0.37)	(0.10)	(0.15)	(0.51)	(0.51)
African American	0.83	0.78	0.89	0.95	0.94	0.77	2.12***	1.90**
	(0.26)	(0.26)	(0.22)	(0.25)	(0.34)	(0.29)	(0.48)	(0.43)
Asian/Asian American	1.01	1.01	0.46***	0.45***	1.22	1.16	0.67***	0.64***
	(0.21)	(0.21)	(0.07)	(0.07)	(0.18)	(0.18)	(0.07)	(0.07)
Parents' edu: Less than high school	0.97	1.30	1.64	1.97*	0.42*	0.50*	1.14	1.05
	(0.30)	(0.42)	(0.51)	(0.65)	(0.14)	(0.17)	(0.33)	(0.31)
Parents' edu: High school	1.00	1.11	0.94	0.93	0.71	0.84	1.18	1.15
	(0.23)	(0.27)	(0.20)	(0.20)	(0.20)	(0.25)	(0.25)	(0.25)

Parents' edu: College degree	1.97**	1.81*	1.11	1.05	1.16	1.22	0.89	0.92
	(0.45)	(0.42)	(0.21)	(0.20)	(0.32)	(0.35)	(0.16)	(0.17)
Parents' edu: Graduate degree	1.45	1.22	0.62*	0.60*	0.89	0.82	0.70	0.71
	(0.37)	(0.32)	(0.13)	(0.13)	(0.27)	(0.26)	(0.15)	(0.16)
Living with parents		0.48***		0.95		0.26***		1.22
		(0.09)		(0.13)		(0.06)		(0.18)
Has Net access @ friends'/family members'		1.65*		1.93**		1.55		0.94
		(0.39)		(0.43)		(0.42)		(0.21)
Hours on Web/week (logged)		1.65***		1.54***		1.40*		1.38**
		(0.19)		(0.16)		(0.21)		(0.15)
Years online (logged)		0.97		1.33		1.50		0.77
		(0.27)		(0.32)		(0.33)		(0.13)
N	1,027	1,009	1,025	1,007	1,076	1,050	1,072	1,046
Chi^2	59.43	99.86	79.42	110.65	58.50	104.63	134.83	144.35
Pseudo R^2	0.06	0.09	0.056	0.08	0.07	0.13	0.10	0.11

* # $p<0.1$, * $p<0.05$, ** $p<0.01$, *** $p<0.001$

Turning to the social context of use, we see that in both years, students who live with their parents (about half of each sample) are statistically significantly less likely to use Facebook than others, although we find no such relationship with MySpace in either year. As to having access to the Internet at a friend or family member's house, while such autonomy of use mattered to both Facebook and MySpace use in 2007, there does not seem to be a relationship between this variable and SNS usage in 2009.

Finally, when it comes to experience with the Internet and how that relates to Facebook and MySpace adoption, it looks as though being a veteran user does not make a difference. However, more time spent online does, as those who spend time on the Web more are more likely to use both services. Of course, this is not necessarily surprising since the mere fact that students use these services would lead them to spend more time online.

Summarizing these findings in light of the results presented in the previous section, it is clear that while an aggregate look at SNS use does not show much systematic relationship between a student's demographic characteristics and SNS experiences, disaggregating the analyses by site tells a very different story. Students' race and ethnicity is strongly related to which social network sites they use, a finding that has remained constant even after two years from the initial study claiming such a relationship (Hargittai 2007).

The Reasons for and Implications of Differential SNS Usage

As noted above, students who live at home are less likely to use Facebook than those who live with roommates or on their own. This could be due to different factors. One reason for this relationship may be that parents have rules about their children's Internet uses in the home, limiting what students can do online. Another possibility is that having to share machines with others in the household leads to fewer opportunities for the kind of private browsing that would allow for exploring social network sites. A completely different reason for these results may be that students who live at home are in tight social communities and are thus less likely to seek out opportunities to connect with people online. However, because this finding only holds for Facebook adoption and not MySpace use, the explanation has to be more site-specific. In particular, students may be most likely to use Facebook for keeping in touch with their college peers; however, by spending less time on campus, students who live with their parents know fewer of their peers and less about them, thus perhaps having less of a desire to keep in touch with them at the level afforded by a site like Facebook. Unfortunately, a possible consequence is that a tool that could help keep these students in touch with their college peers despite not living among them may lead to increased isolation by not following details of college life offline or online. Without more nuanced data, whether qualitative or quantitative, it is hard to speculate about non-adoption of certain sites.

When trying to explain the different rates of uptake among respondents of these sites, it is important to remember that respondents in these two studies are all on the same campus. Given that much of what users do on these sites concerns the maintenance of relationships they already had with others before joining the site (Ellison *et al.* 2007), it is important to consider site practices in the context of people's overall social networks. The available data do not allow for probing deeper into how a student's preference for one social network site over another is influenced by his or her friends' SNS preferences. Nonetheless, based on what we know about the types of connections people maintain on such sites (Ellison *et al.* 2007), it is fair to assume that one's existing offline network influences which sites one joins. Since we know that people tend to socialize and spend time with others like them (Marsden 1987), it is reasonable to expect that students from similar backgrounds might migrate toward the same services. Indeed, research on MySpace in particular has found that, once on the site, users tend to communicate with others like them (Thelwall 2009).

The findings may also be related to the different histories of these systems. Initially, Facebook was only available to students at certain elite colleges followed by an expansion to students at all American universities (boyd and Ellison 2007). These initial restrictions shaped the types of people the site attracted. Although by the time of these studies Facebook had opened up membership to everybody, a year before the first data collection period it was still restricted, requiring affiliation with an educational institution. In contrast, any Internet user could create an account on MySpace. While the restrictions may not have influenced the options available to respondents directly, if they had friends who had not gone on to college then those are people they may not have been able to connect with on Facebook, thereby disincentivizing its use.

What is especially intriguing is that these differences have persisted over time. The Internet is often thought of as a rapidly changing medium and, indeed, new services appear constantly. Regardless of such constant technological innovations, however, the findings presented here suggest that certain social aspects change less quickly. Users take a while to adopt services and once they develop patterns of uses, these may get perpetuated across people's networks influencing uses over time.

Forming relationships with members of one's cohort is an important part of the college experience. As Ellison and colleagues (2007) have found, Facebook use is indeed related to the formation and maintenance of social capital among a group of college students. What is potentially troubling based on the findings in this study is that those who live at home with their parents, i.e. students who are already less likely to be on campus to build relationships with their peers, are precisely the ones who are also less likely to use online services that facilitate additional interactions with other students. This then implies that it is the students for whom use of social network sites may make the most difference that are the ones missing out. That is, if those who are already interacting less with others in person are also the ones in contact with their peers less online, then that has the potential to result in a two-tiered social system where some people are able to cultivate lots of connections in college while others benefit from this part of the experience considerably less.

Conclusion

Using two unique data sets with unprecedented granularity about the adoption of different social network sites, coupled with detailed demographic background about students, this chapter has looked at what types of user characteristics—from among two diverse groups of first-year students at an urban public university—are most likely to be linked to the use of Facebook, MySpace and other SNSs. In particular, this study has considered how people's demographic characteristics and the social surroundings of their uses might relate to the particular social network sites they embrace. When looking at SNS user statistics on the aggregate, we only find a relationship of gender to such site usage in addition to the importance of context of use and experiences with the medium. However, once we focus on the use of specific sites, we also find statistically significant relationships between other variables and SNS usage as well.

One of the most striking findings of this study—also addressed by boyd in this volume—is the significant variation in social network site usage by race and ethnicity. In particular, Hispanic students are statistically significantly less likely to use Facebook and more likely to use MySpace than Whites in the sample. In contrast, Asian and Asian American students are much less likely to use MySpace than Whites. These findings do not show up in the aggregated SNS use model (Table 10.4), highlighting the importance of not collapsing SNS usage depending on the research questions of interest. That is, if we were only looking at SNS usage overall, we would not perceive any relationship between race and ethnicity and social network site usage, even though clearly such relationships exist and do so across time. Overall, the data suggest that from 2007 to 2009, the popularity of Facebook increased among all segments of participants and the prevalence of MySpace use declined for each group. Nonetheless, different levels of use among racial and ethnic groups persisted from one time period to the next.

The goal of this chapter has been to compare SNS users and non-users and to consider whether adoption of different social network sites is related to user background. The findings suggest some systematic differences in who chooses to spend time on such sites and who does not. Importantly, findings also suggest that different population segments select into the uses of different services, posing a challenge to research that tends to collapse use of all social network sites. Most studies that look at SNS uses focus on one service only. The findings presented in this paper suggest caution when trying to generalize findings from the use of one site to the use of other related services. A significant finding of the study is that aggregated SNS use statistics hide important differences among usage preferences among a diverse sample of users by specific site. Simply looking at, for example, whether race and ethnicity is related to SNS use suggests that there are no differences across groups. However, once we disaggregate specific site usage in the analyses, we find significant divergences. In so far as use of Facebook is qualitatively different from use of MySpace and these in turn are different from other such sites, recognizing and critically considering these differences is important for the domain of SNS use research regardless of the methods of analysis.

In addition to addressing methodological and substantive questions about SNS uses, this chapter also contributes to issues addressed by digital inequality scholars. The fact that students select into the use of different services based on their racial and ethnic background in addition to their parents' level of education suggests that there is less intermixing of users from varying socioeconomic backgrounds on such sites than the supposed freedom of online interactions may suggest. That is, while at first glance it may seem that on the Internet nobody knows who you are (Steiner 1993), in reality the membership of certain online communities mirrors people's social networks in their physical world so online actions and interactions cannot be seen as independent of people's background characteristics. Rather, constraints one experiences in everyday life are reflected in online behavior, thereby possibly limiting the extent to which students from various backgrounds may interact with others not like them. This then may result in fewer opportunities from online interactions for some as compared to others.

Acknowledgment

The author is grateful to the John D. and Catherine T. MacArthur Foundation for supporting this research.

Notes

1   Social media scholar danah boyd maintains a bibliography of academic work on social network sites at www.danah.org/researchBibs/sns.html.
2   The author of this piece is not now nor has ever been affiliated with this school beyond the scope of this project. This campus was chosen due to the diverse composition of its student body and the importance of that factor to the questions of interest in the overall study.
3   The questionnaire in both cases included an item to verify students' attentiveness to the survey. A small portion of students (3.4 percent in 2007; 4.5 percent in 2009) responded incorrectly to this verification question, suggesting that they were checking off responses randomly instead of replying to the substance of the questions. These students have been excluded from the data and analyses presented here in order to minimize error introduced through such respondents. The 1,060 and 1,115 students all answered the verification question correctly.
4   As noted earlier, students of Native American background have been excluded from these analyses due to their small numbers.

References

Bimber, B. 2000. "The Gender Gap on the Internet." *Social Science Quarterly* 81.3: 868–876.
boyd, d. 2001. "Sexing the Internet: Reflections on the Role of Identification in Online Communities." Paper presented at Sexualities, Medias, Technologies, University of Surrey, 21–22 June.

———. 2007. "Viewing American Class Divisions through Facebook and MySpace." Apophenia blog essay. Available at www.zephoria.org/thoughts/

———. 2011. "White Flight in Networked Publics? How Race and Class Shaped American Teen Engagement with MySpace and Facebook," in L. Nakamura and P. Chow-White, eds, *Digital Race Anthology*. London: Routledge.

boyd, d. and N.B. Ellison. 2007. "Social Network Sites: Definition, History, and Scholarship." *Journal of Computer-Mediated Communication* 13.1: 210–230.

DiMaggio, P. and E. Hargittai. 2001. "From the 'Digital Divide' to 'Digital Inequality': Studying Internet Use as Penetration Increases." Princeton, Center for Arts and Cultural Policy Studies, Woodrow Wilson School, Princeton University.

Ellison, N.B., C. Steinfeld, and C. Lampe. 2007. "The Benefits of Facebook 'Friends': Social Capital and College Students' Use of Online Social Network Sites." *Journal of Computer-Mediated Communication* 12.4: Article 1.

Frissen, V. 1995. "Gender is Calling: Some Reflections on Past, Present and Future Uses of the Telephone," in K. Grint and R. Gill, eds, *The Gender–Technology Relation: Contemporary Theory and Research*. Bristol, PA: Taylor and Francis, 79–94.

Hall, J. and J. Cooper. 1991. "Gender, Experience and Attributions to the Computer." *Journal of Educational Computing Research* 7.1: 51–60.

Hargittai, E. 2007. "Whose Space? Differences Among Users and Non-Users of Social Network Sites." *Journal of Computer-Mediated Communication* 13.1: 276–297.

———. 2010. "Digital Na(t)ives? Variation in Internet Skills and Uses among Members of the 'Net Generation'." *Sociological Inquiry* 80.1: 92–113.

Hargittai, E. and A. Hinnant. 2008. "Digital Inequality: Differences in Young Adults' Use of the Internet." *Communication Research* 35.5: 602–621.

Hargittai, E. and S. Shafer. 2006. "Differences in Actual and Perceived Online Skills: The Role of Gender." *Social Science Quarterly* 87.2: 432–448.

Hassani, S.N. 2006. "Locating Digital Divides at Home, Work, and Everywhere Else." *Poetics* 34: 250–272.

Herring, S. 1994. "Gender Differences in Computer-Mediated Communication: Bringing Familiar Baggage to the New Frontier." Paper presented at Making the Net*Work*: Is There a Z39.50 in Gender Communication?, American Library Association Annual Convention, Miami.

Howard, P.E.N. and S. Jones. 2003. *Society Online*. Thousand Oaks, CA: Sage.

Howard, P.E.N., L. Rainie, and S. Jones. 2001. "Days and Nights on the Internet: The Impact of a Diffusing Technology." *American Behavioral Scientist* 45.3: 383–404.

Jackson, L.A., K.S. Ervin, P. Gradner, and N. Schmitt. 2001. "Gender and the Internet: Women Communicating and Men Searching." *Sex Roles* 44.5/6: 363–379.

Jones, S. and S. Fox. 2009. *Generations Online in 2009*. Washington, DC: Pew Internet and American Life Project.

Lenhart, A., K. Purcell, A. Smith, and K. Zickuhr. 2010. *Social Media and Young Adults*. Washington, DC: Pew Internet and American Life Project.

Lewis, K., J. Kaufman, M. Gonzalez, A. Wimmer, and N.A. Christakis. 2008. "Tastes, Ties, and Time: A New Social Network Dataset using Facebook.com." *Social Networks* 30.4: 330–342.

Livingstone, S. 1992. "The Meaning of Domestic Technologies: A Personal Construct Analysis of Familial Gender Relations," in R. Silverstone and E. Hirsch eds, *Consuming Technologies*. New York: Routledge, 113–130.

Livingstone, S. and E. Helsper. 2007. "Gradations in Digital Inclusion: Children, Young People, and the Digital Divide." *New Media and Society* 9: 671–696.

Madden, M. 2003. *America's Online Pursuits*. Washington, DC: Pew Internet and American Life Project.

Marsden, P.V. 1987. "Core Discussion Networks of Americans." *American Sociological Review* 52: 122–131.

Ono, H. and M. Zavodny. 2003. "Gender and the Internet." *Social Science Quarterly* 84.1: 111–121.

Pampel, F.C. 2000. *Logistic Regression: A Primer*. Thousand Oaks, CA: Sage.

Pasek, J., E. More, and D. Romer. 2007. "Realizing the Social Internet? Online Social Networking Meets Offline Civic Engagement." Unpublished manuscript.

Pfeil, U., R. Arjan, and P. Zaphiris. 2009. "Age Differences in Online Social Networking—a Study of User Profiles and the Social Capital Divide among Teenagers and Older Users in MySpace." *Computers in Human Behavior* 25.3: 643–654.

Ross, C., E.S. Orr, J. Sisic, M. Simmering, and R. Orr. 2009. "Personality and Motivations Associated with Facebook Use." *Computers in Human Behavior* 25.2: 578–586.

Smith, M. and P. Kollock, eds. 1999. *Communities in Cyberspace.* London: Routledge.

Steiner, P. 1993. "On the Internet, Nobody Knows You're a Dog." *New Yorker* 69: 61.

Steinfield, C., N.B. Ellison, and C. Lampe. 2008. "Social Capital, Self-esteem, and Use of Online Social Network Sites: A Longitudinal Analysis." *Journal of Applied Developmental Psychology* 29.6: 434–445.

Thelwall, M. 2009. "Homophily in MySpace." *Journal of the American Society for Information Science and Technology* 60.2: 219–231.

Tufekci, Z. 2008. "Can You See Me Now? Audience and Disclosure Regulation in Online Social Network Sites." *Bulletin of Science, Technology and Society* 28: 20–36.

Turkle, S. 1995. *Life on the Screen: Identity in the Age of the Internet.* New York: Simon and Schuster.

U.S. News and World Report (2009). "America's Best Colleges 2010."

Wellman, B. and C. Haythornthwaite. 2002. *The Internet in Everyday Life.* Oxford: Blackwell.

11
New Voices on the Net?*
The Digital Journalism Divide and the Costs of Network Exclusion

ERNEST J. WILSON III

University of Southern California

SASHA COSTANZA-CHOCK

MIT

Introduction

In the information society, diverse communities' capacity to tell their own stories is especially critical. The transformation of the Internet into the key platform for communication and journalism has created the illusion that barriers long faced by people of color in print and broadcast media will melt away. At the same time, the election of Obama has created, for some, the illusion that the United States of America has entered a new, "post-racial" era. However, having a Black man in the White House, however important a sign of progress, cannot alone erase the fact that race, class, and gender all continue to unjustly structure Americans' opportunities in every sphere of life. Race-based exclusion from full access to and participation in both old and new information and communications technologies (ICTs) remains entrenched.

Consider the most recent available U.S. Economic Census data on business ownership: at the time it was conducted, the overall U.S. population was about 13 percent Black, 13 percent Latino, 4 percent Asian and Pacific Islander, 1 percent American Indian, and 69 percent non-Hispanic White. However, non-Hispanic Whites owned 90 percent of businesses in nearly every category, including the "information industries": radio stations, TV stations, and newspaper publishing (U.S. Census Bureau 2006; and see Appendix, Table 11.1). Whites continue to own 90 percent of all businesses, despite the fact that America will be majority "minority" within a single generation (in 2042, according to the latest projections by the U.S. Census Bureau 2009). Although the lack of diversity in media ownership reflects a wider pattern across all business sectors, the information industries are qualitatively different and, arguably, more important, because of the central role they play in our democracy.

---

* The Costs of Network Exclusion argument presented in this chapter owes a great deal to Dr. Rahul Tongia, who is co-author of these thoughts.

The media are the soil in which civic discourse takes root, but the media also perpetuate inequality via a lack of representation—or a skewed and inaccurate representation—of the public.

In a provocative article for *The Nation*, written in 2008, Amy Alexander pointed to the continuing weight of race in the practices of American media, at a moment when new digital platforms were burgeoning yet the economy was hitting rock bottom. She wrote that "traditional news-delivery systems, while far from perfect, did provide access and influence to thousands of journalists of color. Yet the massive staff cuts at these traditional media outlets are disproportionately diminishing the ranks of journalists of color" (Alexander 2008). She described, with cautious optimism, the growth of participation by people of color in the world of online media. We agree that this is a moment of considerable opportunity for people of color to tell their own stories and the stories of their communities, and to be included in the wider discourses of American life. Yet, the continued momentum of institutionally entrenched racism, crashing against the current realities of economic recession, creates serious tensions inside today's media institutions. There are inclusionary and exclusionary pressures in play, and it is not at all clear which trend will win out. It is clear, however, that the outcome will have deep consequences for the democratic character of American society in the years ahead.

In this chapter, we review data that documents the long-term and persistent exclusion of people of color in the U.S. from ownership of and employment in the news media. We find that people of color are chronically underrepresented as owners and professional journalists in every major communications platform: newspapers, commercial TV, commercial radio, public TV, public radio, and online. We then turn to the debates over the digital divide, and argue that the ability to participate in content production and distribution is increasingly a question of network access. In this light, we conclude with a reformulation of traditional paradigms for thinking about the "digital divide," reversing "Metcalfe's Law" to concentrate not on the benefits of inclusion, but on the societal costs of consistent network exclusion along race (or other) lines.

Race, Ownership, and Employment in the U.S. Media Industries

We begin with the by now well-supported claim that where people of color own media firms and are employed by them as content producers inside an industry sector or network (network in the broadest sense, not in the narrower sense of a broadcast "network" like ABC), they are likely to produce more and better content about their communities (Cottle 2000). Journalists and editors play a special role in such networks—they are not simply members or participants, but they also act as network brokers or intermediaries between the dominant culture and the subaltern or minority culture, as mediated through the networks in which they participate. If people of color do not participate actively or in numbers roughly proportional to their geographic community's demographics (both as individuals, and as sometime brokers or representatives of their communities of racial and ethnic origin), then they, their communities, the quality of public discourse, and the broader public will all suffer. Let us be clear in our assumptions: it is certainly true that good content about diverse communities can be made by talented people of any background (think of the protean writer, director and producer Norman Lear). Nor do we wish to endorse an essentialist view of racial or ethnic identities as fixed, singular, homogenous, or static. Yet it is also true that stories told by those who have lived them carry an unmatched power to enlighten and inform. While there is no iron-clad rule that only Black writers write well about Black experiences, nor that minority ownership automatically translates into particular kinds of representation, it remains the case that scholarly research reveals strong correlations between media ownership, hiring practices, and content: media outlets owned or controlled by people of color are more likely to hire a greater number of people of color, and newsrooms with more people of color tend to run more stories about communities of color (Gandy 1998; Jacobs 2000).

The extent of minority media power varies across the different media industries and platforms—print, commercial broadcast, public broadcast, and online. In this section, we will explore the ways that ownership and employment of people of color differ between the leading American media institutions. For example, we imagine that people of color should be better represented, in terms of station control and employment, in public broadcasting than in print or in commercial broadcasting, since public broadcasting by nature has greater political oversight and, indeed, has a mandate to reflect racial diversity. We also expect online media to be the most diverse of all.

Just how underrepresented are people of color across the American media? What do the data say about their exclusion from networked communication? And what does this mean for American democracy?

Print

The exclusion of people of color from the field of print journalism can only be described as chronic. With rare exceptions, both the numbers and proportions of print journalists of color are declining, while people of color own just a handful of daily newspapers. Under these conditions, it should not be surprising that mass market newspapers in the United States have never given fair, accurate, or proportional coverage to people of color and their communities (Cottle 2000; Jacobs 2000; Wilson 2000).

The best source of information on minority employment in the newspaper industry is the American Society of Newspaper Editors (ASNE), which has surveyed all U.S. newspapers about the number of women and people of color they employ, and in what jobs, since 1978 (see Appendix, Table 11.2). ASNE's 2009 annual report tells us that, while in a more nearly equitable United States, minorities would be over 30 percent of the newspaper workforce, they currently comprise just 13 percent, and this percentage continues to decrease (ASNE 2009a). A look inside "total minority employment" at the separate figures for Asian American, African American, Latino, and Native American newsroom employees tells an even more disturbing tale. There was a slightly rising percentage of Asian American journalists from 2.37 percent in 2002 to 3.22 percent in 2008, but this number has now begun to fall (to 3.18 percent in 2009). Meanwhile, the total number of Asian American newsroom employees peaked in 2007 at 1,764 and by 2009 dropped to 1,466 (out of a total of 46,670 newsroom employees). Black and Native American journalists are declining both in absolute numbers and in terms of their share of newsroom positions: the number of Black newsroom staff fell from a peak of 2,985 in 2005 to 2,412 in 2009, and dropped from 5.51 percent to 5.17 percent of all newsroom employees. Native American news staff fell from a peak of 313 in 2004 to 293 in 2009 (or just 0.63 percent of the total). Latino newsroom employees peaked in 2006 at 2,409, then fell to 2,087 (4.47 percent of the total) in 2009.

Perhaps the situation looks bad in this moment of crisis, but is improving over time. Over the long run, the percent minority employment is indeed trending upward, from about 4 percent in 1978 to about 13.5 percent today. However, long term, incremental gains in minority newspaper employment took 30 years to move just 10 percent, or about 3.3 percent per decade. It also must be noted that minority newspaper employment rates have begun to slip *downward* since their peak in 2006. The U.S. Census reports that "minorities, now roughly one-third of the U.S. population, are expected to become the majority in 2042, with the nation projected to be 54 percent minority in 2050" (U.S. Census 2008). If the current rates of change hold, then by 2040 the newspaper workforce will barely reach 25 percent minority employment against a 50 percent minority general population. ASNE President Charlotte Hall put it best: "The loss of journalists is a loss for democracy. The loss of people of color from our newsrooms is especially disturbing because our future depends on our ability to serve multicultural audiences" (ASNE 2009b).

In terms of ownership, the most complete source of national statistics on newspaper publishers, the U.S. Economic Census, tells us that 93.5 percent of newspaper owners are White, 3.2 percent Asian, 2.4 percent Black, 1.6 percent Hispanic, and 1 percent American Indian (Beresteanu and Ellickson 2007). Sadly, against a general background of declining newspaper circulation, revenue, and employment, racial and gender diversity remain a distant ideal in the newspaper world.

It might be expected that the Old Boys' networks dominate print, the oldest form of media. How do commercial broadcast television and radio compare?

Commercial Broadcasters

Our aim here is not to delve into the complex analysis of how commercial broadcast media appropriate representations of people of color and circulate them transnationally (Gray 2005). We assign ourselves the much more mundane task of examining race-based inequality in ownership of and employment in commercial radio and TV. A recent study of Federal Communications Commission (FCC) data commissioned by the media policy advocacy group Free Press reveals that while people of color make up more than a third of the U.S. population, they own less than 8 percent of radio stations and only about 3 percent of TV stations (Turner and Cooper 2007). Another study by one of the same authors notes that minority ownership of full-power commercial broadcast stations, both radio and television, was all but eliminated following the 1996 Telecommunication Act, which relaxed media consolidation limits (Turner 2007). They also found that between 2006 and 2007, "African American-owned full power commercial TV stations decreased by nearly 60 percent, from 19 to 8, or from 1.4 percent to 0.6 percent of all stations," and that "Latinos comprise 15 percent of the entire U.S. population, but only own a total of 17 stations, or 1.25 percent of all stations" (Turner and Cooper 2007).

Another study, commissioned by the FCC, examined ownership data from 2002 to 2005. The authors found that, in 2005, minorities owned just 379 out of 14,015 radio stations and just 17 out of 1,778 television stations. In other words, the study found that people of color owned less than 3 percent of radio and less than 1 percent of TV broadcast licenses (Beresteanu and Ellickson 2007; and see Appendix, Table 11.3). National Telecommunications and Information Administration (NTIA) reports between 1990 and 1999 demonstrate that, over the long run, ownership has stagnated: minorities held 2.9 percent of broadcast licenses in 1990, 3.0 percent in 1994, and 2.9 percent in 1998 (NTIA 2000a). The Census Bureau's 2002 Survey of Business Owners found that, of 20,093 non-Internet broadcasting firms, 16,698 were White-owned, 1,219 were Hispanic- or Latino-owned, 1,207 were Black-owned, 677 were Asian-owned, just 123 were American Indian- or Alaska Native-owned, and *none* were owned by a Native Hawaiian or Other Pacific Islander (U.S. Census Bureau 2006).

Employment diversity in commercial broadcasting is much closer to parity than ownership, but still lacking. Data from the Radio-Television News Directors Association (RTNDA) show a slow increase from a 17 percent minority TV workforce in 1995 to about 24 percent in 2008, but during the same time period a decline in the radio workforce from 15 percent to 12 percent people of color (Papper 2008). If we zoom out to a longer view, once again we find that the employment rates for people of color in commercial broadcasting do not even keep pace with changing demographics (Papper 2008; and see Appendix, Table 11.4). In sum, commercial broadcasters are certainly more diverse than newspapers, but they continue to systematically exclude people of color.

What of public broadcasters? Surely we can expect to find minority station control and employment diversity in public radio and television. After all, these are the media institutions explicitly charged with the mandate to inform, educate, and reflect the full diversity of ideas of the American people.

Public Broadcasters

The Corporation for Public Broadcasting (CPB) designates a station "minority-controlled" if "at least 50 percent of its full-time employees and 50 percent of its governing board are members of minority racial or ethnic groups" (CPB 2007). Although it is a simplification, here we will take minority station control to be analogous to ownership in the commercial sector. In 2008, public radio had 71 minority controlled stations: 29 African American, 28 Native American, 10 Hispanic, and 4 Multicultural, out of about 700 public radio stations. This means that roughly 10 percent of public radio stations were minority controlled, far more than in the commercial radio sector but far less than demographic parity. Public TV, meanwhile, had just 6 minority-controlled stations (1 African American, 1 Hispanic, 1 Asian Pacific Islander, and 3 Multicultural) out of a total of 356, or about 1.7 percent. As we expected, people of color have a greater ownership stake in our public broadcasting system than in commercial broadcasting, but there is still a long way to go.

The CPB has collected data on minority employment in public radio and television since 1978. These records mostly show a slow and steady increase in minority employment from 1978 (12.6 percent in radio, 13.9 percent in TV) to about 1998 (19.6 percent in radio, 18.8 percent in TV). This was followed by stagnation for most of the last decade, with the 2008 CPB report finding public radio minority employment at 19.8 percent and public TV minority employment at 19.4 percent (see Appendix, Table 11.5). Inside the national public broadcasting organizations (CPB, PBS, and NPR), minorities are 29.8 percent of employees, a proportion that comes closer to parity with the general population than in any other sector of the media system (CPB 2009).

Overall, then, public radio and TV stations do a better job of employee diversity than newspapers or commercial radio broadcasters, and are more or less on par with commercial television broadcasters. Nationwide, the management of the public broadcasting system better reflects the diversity of the American people than any other part of the media sector. However, people of color occupy only two-thirds of the positions in local public broadcasting stations that they would were these stations to reflect the general population. If public broadcasters do not begin to increase minority employment and retention rates, they will fall further and further behind the nation's changing demographics. Given the ownership and employment situation, it is little surprise that public media content, while improving, still fails to reflect diverse racial and ethnic experiences and attract diverse audiences.

Now we turn to the innovative field of online media. If the boosters of digital diversity are correct, then the explosion of online content should take us beyond the outdated limitations of minority ownership and employment in legacy media. Since anyone can start their own blog, the old problems of scarcity—limited spectrum, limited channels—should be over, and everyone's voice should have an equal chance to be heard.

Digital Diversity?

The first challenge to understanding diversity in online journalism is simply to describe what is happening with a fast-moving target like "online journalism." Of course, the Internet is more accessible than any other medium, in the sense that the barriers to entry (setting up a blog or web page) are very low and anyone can "broadcast" whatever they like (we will return to questions of general internet access inequality in the following section). However, if we continue to focus on questions of ownership and employment diversity—for example, on who owns online publishing and broadcasting firms, or who makes a living creating online content—the evidence brings us back to the reality of racial disparity. The forces of structural racism that work to keep people of color underrepresented as owners and employees in the print, commercial broadcasting, and public media sectors, unsurprisingly, continue to operate in the relatively new field of online journalism.

That is not to say that new online media and journalism outlets provide no opportunities for people of color. Quite the contrary: the 2009 ASNE report, for example, counted online journalists employed by newspapers and found that nearly 19.6 percent were people of color (ASNE 2009a). By that measure, there is greater employment diversity in full-time online journalism than in print, but less than in broadcast TV. Another indicator of potential diversity among budding online journalists can be found in research revealing that people of color who are online are more likely to blog, have their own website, and have a digital video camera than non-Hispanic Whites, across all age groups (Korzenny and Korzenny 2008). On the other hand, few would argue with the statement that online news is presently dominated by White, male, middle-class voices. We do not have a gold standard data source for Internet news diversity, but anecdotal evidence abounds: what proportion of "A-list" political bloggers are people of color? Women of color? Or check http:// technorati.com/pop/blogs; how many of the top 100 are not written by White males?

Several empirical studies support this anecdotal evidence; for example, a 2004 Pew survey noted that 77 percent of online content creators were White (Lenhart *et al.* 2004). The U.S. Census Bureau (2006) found that people of color owned only 1,243 out of 12,158 (about 10.2 percent) of firms categorized as "Internet publishing and broadcasting." The vast majority of these were single-person businesses (reporting no employees); of the 1,770 Internet publishing and broadcasting firms reporting employees, Whites owned 1,369 while people of color owned 125, or just 7 percent (U.S. Census Bureau 2006). The same report found about 40,000 employees of Internet publishing and broadcasting, with fewer than 660 employed at minority-owned firms. Whites also owned 39,160 out of 46,859 firms categorized as "Internet service providers, web search portals, and data processing services." The American Community Survey

(2007) examines more recent employee data and also finds an almost two to one gender disparity in this sector.

We have demonstrated long-term racial inequality in ownership and employment across every major media platform. Although ownership and employment in professional online journalism remains understudied, available evidence strongly suggests that the diversity metrics in this area are much like those in public radio: better than most of the media industry, but still far from parity with the nation's population. People of color are severely underrepresented as owners of and paid reporters for online news firms. If the long-term rate of change in this sector mirrors that of any other part of our media system, online journalism will never reach full racial parity without a major intervention that breaks the norms of business as usual.

However, we would be remiss to conclude our discussion of online journalism here. Focusing only on incorporated firms and professional (employed) online journalists would fail to engage one of the most important transformations of the media sector: the explosion of popular participation in the production and circulation of online news. Whether framed as citizens' media (Rodriguez 2001), citizen journalism (Outing 2005; Burns 2008; Rosen 2008), grassroots media (Gillmor 2006), participatory news (Deuze *et al.* 2007), mass self-communication (Castells 2007), user-generated content (Thurman 2008; van Dijck 2009), free labor for the cultural economy (Terranova 2004), or in any other terms, it is undeniable that nonprofessionals are participating on a vast scale in the production of online news and journalism. This activity, and its potential as a site for a radical shift toward the inclusion of voices of people of color, cannot be captured by statistics based on formal business ownership or paid employment. Instead, we must return to the debates over who, exactly, gets to participate in digital networks.

The Digital Divide and the Cost of Network Exclusion

In the early years of the information revolution, Internet access inequality was framed by policymakers in terms of a growing digital divide, both domestically and internationally (NTIA 1998, 1999). During this time, a few scholars focused attention on the relationship between race and internet access (Hoffman and Novak 1998). However, the debate was largely drowned out by what appeared, at first blush, to be the steady diffusion of networked communication technology to all populations across lines of race, class, gender, and geography. Undeniably, the Internet and mobile phones gained massive uptake in the first decade of the new millennium. In developed countries (OECD 2009), for example, higher penetration rates have shifted the Internet user base from a highly educated, mostly male and young demographic, to one that now includes the majority of the population of the G-8 countries. A majority (greater than 50 percent) of women and people of color in all advanced economies became Internet users.

What looked like a closing gap between information haves and have-nots in the advanced economies found its parallel in transnational comparative perspective as computer use in developing countries soared. Indeed, Internet use in developing countries accelerated so rapidly that some believed the North–South gap might be closing as well. For example, in China the internet usage rate jumped from 1.7 percent to 19.0 percent between 2000 and 2008; in Brazil, the same rate climbed from 2.9 percent in 2000 to 35.2 percent in 2008 (ITU 2008). The unprecedented rate of diffusion of mobile phones also raised hopes for an additional path to equitable network connectivity. For example, India jumped from 1.2 percent mobile penetration in 2002 to 20 percent in 2007 and is now adding between 7 and 9 million new subscriptions per month (ITU 2008), and most African countries—long plagued by the lowest levels of ICT connectivity in the world—also displayed robust mobile growth.

Furthermore, the near-simultaneous collapse of the computer industry and the telecommunications industry at the start of the decade drowned a great deal of analytical attention to and policy regarding the topic. To non-experts in government and among funding agencies, the subject of the digital divide seemed to become less pressing than before. The domestic debate over the divide was further buried when the Bush Administration replaced the term "digital divide" with "digital inclusion," published reports emphasizing how many Americans were online rather than how many were excluded, cut funds for programs aiming to increase Internet access among underserved populations, slashed community technology center funding, and even deactivated the website digitaldivide.gov (Jaeger et al. 2005). Sensing the shift in the wind, industry support for digital divide research dried up, and innovations in industry increasingly focused on skimming the cream from wealthier markets and specialized products. This is not to say that moves away from the term were entirely ideologically driven. During the same time period, scholarly work emerged that questioned the original concept of a binary "divide," emphasized the multidimensional nature of ICT access, appropriation, and use, and argued that the notion of "divide" was inherently misleading (DiMaggio and Hargittai 2001). Scholars emphasized the need to reframe the digital divide as a complex phenomenon in which access to hardware and applications play an important role, but so do access to financial resources, knowledge, social networks, and formal Internet training (Norris 2001; Warschauer 2004; Wilson et al. 2005). In light of these shifts, techno-determinist arguments were resurgent. Much of the popular press, and many policymakers, either ignored digital access inequality or assumed that the market left to its own devices would, in time, provide universal Internet access across the country and around the globe.

Access Inequality, Remixed?

With the historic election of Obama to the presidency, coupled with the global financial collapse, a paradoxical paradigm shift took place. On the one hand, some imagined that Obama's election ushered in a new, post-racial polity; at the same time, the massive failure of the financial markets and their regulators signaled a new willingness to discuss the possibility that markets, left to their own devices, do not necessarily produce optimal outcomes. In this context, it has become possible to ask again, as a matter of public policy, how people of color might be disproportionally impacted by the lack of oversight in areas like housing, health, and even Internet access. In the academy and beyond, the broader question of global equality and inequality has once again returned full force. Issues of global wealth inequality, raised most dramatically at the turn of the millennium by the global justice movement, have been taken up by authors like Joseph Stiglitz (2002), David Held and Ayse Kaya (2007), who point to evidence of growing inequality both within and between countries. Once-socialist economies like India and China have seen tremendous growth in GDP as they sprint up the capitalist road, but at the cost of spiraling income inequality where wealth distribution was formerly more egalitarian. Other scholars point to inter-country inequality, as between Africa at one extreme and North America on the other. These claims have been met by counterclaims that use other metrics to find decreasing inequality, or little change at all (Dowrick and Akmal 2005). The point is that economic asymmetries are again, appropriately, on the intellectual and policy agenda. As before, it remains an empirical question to what extent these gaps are fed by ICTs—and to what extent they in turn feed ICT access gaps.

In the U.S., the most recent and extensive survey by the National Telecommunications and Information Administration (NTIA 2010) finds continued growth in broadband access for all groups, with 68.7 percent of all households having computers and internet connections, and 63.5 percent with broadband connections at home. However, broadband access continues to be stratified by race, with 66 percent of White (non-Hispanic) and 67 percent of Asian persons reporting broadband at home, compared to 46 percent of Black, 43 percent of American Indian, and 40 percent of Hispanic persons (see Appendix, Figure 11.1). The study also found that 84 percent of college-educated people above the age of 25 had broadband in the home, compared to just 28 percent of those with no high school diploma. The widest gap was based on family income: persons in households making under $15,000 per year (in other words, homes supported by those with minimum wage or less-than-minimum wage jobs, the underemployed, or the unemployed) reported just 29 percent broadband at home, compared to 70 percent of households making above $50,000, 85 percent of those making above $100,000, and 89 percent of those with incomes above $150,000. In other words, middle-class and upper middle-class households are twice or even three times as likely to have broadband access as working poor households (Horrigan 2008; NTIA 2010).

Global figures of Internet inequality are much more stark. In 2008, the number of Internet users increased to about 1.5 billion, but this is still only about a quarter of the world's population. International Telecommunications Union (ITU) data show just 5.3 percent of the world's population with broadband subscriptions, and in 2007 "just over 10 percent of the world's population in developing countries were using the Internet, compared to close to 60 percent in the developed world" (ITU 2008). Unsurprisingly, broadband Internet is concentrated almost exclusively in the world's wealthiest countries, or in the hands of local elites in major urban areas in middle-income and poor countries. For example, the African continent has just 0.2 broadband subscribers per 100 people, compared to 3.4 in Asia, 4.2 in Brazil, 14 in the EU, and 21 in the USA (ibid.). Developed countries are not immune to concerns about global network disparity: even the U.S. laments its steady fall in OECD measures of broadband access, from 4th to 15th in the world (OECD 2009).

In addition, while basic access to computers and the Internet is widespread, if unequal, people's degree and kind of usage continues to be structured along existing lines of social inequality. Upper middle-class kids tend to feel more empowered to engage in discourse and debate, and we know that race, class, and gender shape young people's use of the Internet in important ways (Hargittai 2007; and see chapters by boyd and by Hargittai, this volume). Many have come to refer to these differences as the *participation gap* (Jenkins 2006). The evidence is fairly clear that basic access to a digital platform does not automatically result in one's becoming a content producer. We also know that corporate and state actors use complex data mining techniques to "race" web users (Gandy, this volume). In the field of digital news, this "informational-ization of race" (Chow-White 2008) may modify web users' Internet experience, as sites feed them different stories, advertisements, and links based on the location they have been assigned in a presumptive identity matrix. In addition, terms like "access" and "participation" are a constantly moving frontier because of technological innovation. At the turn of the last century, few imagined that having a telephone in the home was an essential public service. By 1950, household access to a telephone was considered a necessity for modern living, and the definition of "access" changed accordingly. Public service commissions for cities, states and countries promulgated new regulations to make this once-new technological device commonplace. Today, the meaning of an "essential service" is still defined in part by the technological frontier, and more and more voices insist that to be truly connected today, consumers and citizens must have "access" to broadband. Since that is hardly the case in many parts of the world, the matter of network inclusion and exclusion again comes to the fore, in a kind of continuing fugue of technology and human "necessity."

In sum, then, the new digital media, while in many ways far more open than print and broadcast media, also continue to reflect structural access inequalities and to be marked by systematic network exclusion as well as by participation gaps along race, class, and gender lines, both domestically and internationally. What does pervasive network exclusion along race (or any other) lines mean for the future of U.S. democracy? In the following section, we draw on work by Wilson and Tongia in order to reframe the discussion about the "digital divide" in terms of the formal costs of network exclusion.

Wilson–Tongia Formulation

The cost of excluding people of color from both legacy and new media networks can be evaluated by both inclusion- and exclusion-based models. Scholarly work on network structure and value tends to focus on the positive values associated with network inclusion. Perhaps the greatest, most cited example of a model of network inclusion is Metcalfe's Law. In contemporary discourse on the value of communication networks, Metcalfe's Law has become synonymous with connectivity, stating that as more people join a network, the value they add to the network increases exponentially, i.e. the value of the network is proportional to the square number of users. The underlying mathematics for Metcalfe's Law is based on pairwise connections (e.g. telephony). If there are four people with telephones in a network, there could be a total of 3 + 2 + 1 = 6 links. The full math for Metcalfe's reasoning leads to the sum of all possible pairings between nodes, so the value of the network size n is

$$\frac{(n)(n-1)}{2}$$

which is often simplified as approaching n^2. With this model, one can evaluate the per-person value of inclusion in a network.

If we know the value of a network as per Metcalfe's Law, assuming each member is equal (a simplification that is likely to be untrue, but that is a matter for another text), we can calculate the value of inclusion per person. But what of the excluded? Intuitively, as a network grows in size and value, those outside the network face growing disparities. How do we measure these disparities? Using an inclusion-based model, one might decide that the cost of exclusion is simply the difference between the outsiders' value (= 0) and the per-person value of those included. For example, if Metcalfe's Law has a value approximating n^2, the per person value of inclusion simply approaches $(n^2)/n$ = n. Thus, exclusion would lead to a disparity of n based on the size of the network, which is the difference between the per-person value of those inside (= n) and those outside (= 0).

What inclusion-based models fail to capture, however, is that any network is of a finite size—if not in theory, then in practice. For example, if we state that our network size is 19, Metcalfe's Law finds a value proportional to 19^2 = 361, and a per-person included value of ~19. Thus, the cost of exclusion from our network with n = 19 is also 19 (the difference between 19 and 0, which is the value assigned to those not in the network). This formulation for calculating the cost of exclusion indicates the same cost regardless of whether the applicable population universe is 20 people or 200 people. However, the cost of exclusion should certainly be different if we have only one excluded person or 181! Therefore, we posit that the cost of exclusion should depend on the number (and/or proportion) of people excluded as well as the size of the network.

And so, we refer to the Wilson–Tongia formulation (Figure 11.2), which makes the costs of exclusion endogenous by taking the number of people excluded into account.

If we compare the inclusion-based framing to the exclusion-based framing, the ratio of these two formulations is the same for any network law, and equal to

$$\frac{n}{N-n}$$

where n is the people in the network, and N is the total applicable population size. We can recognize that this ratio is growing, and inclusion and exclusion formulations crossover (are equal) only at $n = (0.5)(N)$. This means that the costs as calculated by exclusion-based formulations become higher as a network (e.g. technology adoption) reaches half of the population (Tongia and Wilson, 2011).

In other words, the greater the proportion of people in a population included within and enjoying the benefits of a network, the more quickly the costs of exclusion grow for those excluded from that network. The costs to those who are already in the network of excluding others from the network can also be calculated in this way. A critical issue before us is under what conditions, or in what sequence, do the costs of exclusion become most severe to the excluded (and how might we demonstrate the costs to the included)?

Wilson and Tongia have shown that the severity of exclusion costs shifts depending in part on the proportion of the population included and excluded; on the differential quality of the "new" network; and on the availability and relative quality of other networks (Tongia and Wilson, 2011). Inclusion- and exclusion-based framings are similar in value up to a point—

Equation 1: Inclusion-based Framing	Existing Exclusion Cost (ie, disparity) formulations = per person included value	*[Network Value as per any Law]*
		Members in the Network (= n)
Equation 2: Exclusion-based Framing	Proposed Exclusion Cost Formulation = total network value divided by number of people excluded	*[Network Value as per any Law]*
		Members outside the Network (= N – n)

Figure 11.2 Wilson–Tongia Formulation

roughly half the population. *It is precisely when only a minority of the population is not in the network that the costs of exclusion rise dramatically.* When only a few people are members of a network, the exclusion is spread out among the majority of the population but the *advantage* is held by only a few. Once a network includes the majority of the population, the *disadvantage* is held by only a few. In logical terms, for $n < 0.5N$, the included have an advantage they share, while for $n > 0.5N$, the excluded have a disadvantage they share. In such a formulation, the lowest disparity between frameworks is when $n = 0.5N$. When only a small fraction of the population is in the network, the median person in the population is excluded. Hence, inclusion is the exception, and not the norm. When the majority of the population is in the network, exclusion is the exception, and not the norm (Tongia and Wilson, 2011).

This has profound implications for how we understand diversity and race-based exclusion in both legacy and new media networks. Globally, twice as many people on earth are excluded from the Internet as are included: 4+ billion versus 2 billion. Thus, worldwide, Internet access is an advantage held by a few. Domestically, however, Internet penetration has reached 70–75 percent, with broadband Internet penetration above 60 percent (NTIA 2010). Internet access, and specifically broadband connectivity in the home, has thus moved from a competitive advantage to a competitive necessity. Furthermore, as more and more people move from dial-up to broadband, websites increasingly incorporate rich media content; data transfer during a given browsing session thus increases dramatically. Dial-up users have to wait longer and longer for page loads, rendering them worse off in an absolute sense, not just a relative sense, compared to broadband users (Tongia and Wilson, 2011). The costs of network exclusion—the disadvantages already faced by those excluded from the network (primarily people of color and low-income people)—will only continue to rise.

We have tried, briefly, to reframe the question of the digital divide around a new model of the costs of network exclusion within a single network scenario. In reality, network inclusion and exclusion is far more complex. Manuel Castells, in his latest book, draws our attention to the power that privileged information intermediaries wield in the network society, either by operating within a single network or as agents who switch network flows (including news or other information) between complementary networks (Castells 2009). Our aim has simply been to frame the issues of racial exclusion, diversity, and the digital divide in network terms; we believe in this way they gain analytic depth and introduce a set of concepts and theories not typically included in these discussions. This is a small step in trying to open up the discourse. We encourage scholars, policymakers, and activists to focus greater attention on how all forms of network exclusion impose increasing costs both on the excluded and on those inside the network.

Conclusions

We began this chapter by examining the undeniable evidence that people of color remain excluded from ownership and employment across all aspects of our media system. Our key findings are summarized in Table 11.6. In terms of media ownership diversity, we found that both commercial and public television have the lowest rates of control by people of color (1 percent and 2 percent, respectively), while print (8 percent) and public radio (10 percent) have the highest rates, with inconclusive data about online media (but online news ownership by people of color may be similar to public radio at 7–10 percent). Employment figures showed the national public broadcasting organizations substantially ahead of everyone else (29 percent), followed by commercial TV (24 percent), public radio (20 percent), and public TV (19 percent). Online media employment metrics are spotty, but one indicator suggests that about 20 percent of online news employees are people of color, while print (13 percent) and commercial radio (8 percent) are last in line. Thus, despite slow, long-term progress, our media system remains largely unreflective of the diversity of our body politic. To put it bluntly: America will be majority

Table 11.6 Media Ownership and Employment Diversity Across Platforms

Platform	Ownership (% people of color)
Online	? (10.2% all firms/7.1% firms with employees)[1]
Public radio	10%[2]
Print	8.3%[1]
Commercial radio	2.7%[3]
Public TV	1.7%[2]
Commercial TV	0.96%[3]

Platform	Employment (% people of color)
National public broadcasting	28.9%[2]
Commercial TV	23.6%[4]
Public radio	19.8%[2]
Online	? (19.6% of online newspaper staff)[1]
Public TV	19.4%[2]
Print	13.4%[5]
Commercial radio	11.8%[4]

Sources: 1 U.S. Census Bureau 2006; 2 CPB 2009; 3 FCC (in Beresteanu and Ellickson 2007); 4 RTNDA (in Papper 2008); 5 ASNE 2009a

"minority" within a generation, but at this rate the American mediascape will never look like the American public.

We have a plethora of new media platforms and endlessly proliferating applications, but the hard fact remains: an increasingly multiracial and multicultural society requires not only multiple channels, but truly diverse ownership, employment, participation, and content. The new media tools are full of potential for diverse voices to be heard, but the realization of this potential will be neither easy nor automatic. Access inequalities still prohibit many sectors of the population from participating, including many people of color. Information industry insiders are tempted to rely on their existing social networks to recruit talent, and outsiders are likely to become cynical or discouraged. To be fully connected increasingly requires broadband access, and therefore disparities in broadband network access will become increasingly problematic in the U.S. as penetration passes 50 percent in most parts of the country. As the Wilson–Tongia formulation demonstrates, the costs of network exclusion increase as networks grow to include more than 50 percent of the population. These costs are not trivial, and they continue to rise as more and more essential services for citizenship—including the tools for media discourse—migrate from the traditional world of "brick and mortar" to the online universe.

To realize the promises and reap the benefits of a deepened democracy hinted at in Obama's election, we badly need to transform our media system to better reflect the diversity of our society and polity. We need an "information revolution" that is not merely technical and commercial, but that also brings more and more people greater opportunities to create their own stories and gain access to the information they need to lead fuller, more meaningful and productive lives as citizens of multiple communities. One can easily embrace the slogan "change we can believe in," but how can we believe in a media system that so consistently fails to reflect the changes in who we really are as a people? The costs of continued exclusion will be borne most heavily by the excluded, who are most likely to be people of color and low-income people. Yet all of us suffer if the stories of the least powerful and the least visible of our citizens are excluded from the national discourse. American democracy can only reach its full potential when all people have their voices heard and their full creativity acknowledged.

Appendix

Table 11.1 Business Ownership by Race and Ethnicity

NAIC	Name	Percent				
		Hispanic	White	Black	AmInd	Asian
22	Utilities	0.85	96.79	1.13	0.89	1.44
23	Construction	3.57	97.15	1.24	0.68	1.04
31–33	Manufacturing	3.57	94.57	0.72	0.48	4.09
42	Wholesale trade	3.84	91.40	0.60	0.25	7.57
44–45	Retail trade	3.60	89.55	1.22	0.42	8.58
48–49	Transportation and warehousing	5.60	94.07	2.99	0.54	2.10
51	Information	2.82	93.04	2.07	0.40	4.33
515112	Radio stations	3.71	93.29	4.35	0.17	2.27
515120	TV stations	6.04	89.11	4.89	0.00	6.03
511110	Newspaper publishers	1.58	93.50	2.44	1.00	3.24
52	Finance and insurance	3.03	95.39	1.70	0.38	2.54
53	Real estate, rental, leasing	2.40	94.90	1.04	0.26	3.56
54	Prof., scientific, tech. services	2.77	93.57	1.57	0.47	4.29
55	Mgmt of companies	1.36	95.74	1.03	0.38	2.76
56	Admin. support and waste mgmt and remedial services	5.50	93.27	3.38	0.63	2.61
61	Educational services	3.55	90.60	3.10	0.65	5.25
62	Health care and social assist.	4.14	85.88	4.14	0.44	9.20
71	Arts, entertainment, recreation	2.13	95.13	2.33	0.34	2.069
81	Other services (except public)	5.11	89.07	2.28	0.45	8.16
All non-farm businesses		3.85	91.32	1.82	0.47	6.21

Source: 2002 U.S. Economic Census, cited in Beresteanu and Ellickson 2007.

Table 11.2 Minority Employment in Daily Newspapers, 1978–2009.

Year	Total Workforce	Minorities in Workforce	% Minorities in Workforce
1978	43,000	1,700	3.95
1979	45,000	1,900	4.22
1980	47,000	2,300	4.89
1981	45,500	2,400	5.27
1982	49,000	2,700	5.51
1983	50,000	2,800	5.6
1984	50,400	2,900	5.75
1985	53,800	3,100	5.76
1986	54,000	3,400	6.3
1987	54,700	3,600	6.56
1988	55,300	3,900	7.02
1989	56,200	4,200	7.54
1990	56,900	4,500	7.86
1991	55,700	4,900	8.72
1992	54,500	5,100	9.39
1993	53,600	5,500	10.25
1994	53,700	5,600	10.49
1995	53,800	5,900	10.91
1996	55,000	6,100	11.02
1997	54,000	6,100	11.35
1998	54,700	6,300	11.46
1999	55,100	6,400	11.55
2000	56,200	6,700	11.85
2001	56,400	6,600	11.64
2002	54,400	6,600	12.07
2003	54,700	6,900	12.53
2004	54,200	7,000	12.95
2005	54,100	7,300	13.42
2006	53,600	7,400	13.73
2007	55,000	7,400	13.43
2008	52,600	7,100	13.52
2009	46,700	6,300	13.41
2010	41,500	5,500	13.26

Source: ASNE 2010.

Table 11.3 Media Ownership by Race and Gender (FCC Data)

Year	Platform	Number of stations	Female owned	Minority owned	% Female owned	% Minority owned
2002	Radio	13,662	407	377	2.98	2.76
	TV	1,739	27	20	1.55	1.15
2003	Radio	13,696	382	391	2.79	2.85
	TV	1,749	28	16	1.60	0.91
2004	Radio	13,696	393	372	2.87	2.72
	TV	1,758	27	17	1.54	0.97
2005	Radio	14,015	384	379	2.74	2.70
	TV	1,778	27	17	1.52	0.96

Source: FCC data, cited in Beresteanu and Ellickson 2007.

Table 11.4 Broadcast News Workforce, 1995–2008

% Television Employees	2008	2007	2006	2005	2000	1995
Caucasian	76.3	78.5	77.8	78.8	79.0	82.9
African American	10.1	10.1	9.5	10.3	11.0	10.1
Hispanic	10.3	8.7	9.6	8.7	7.0	4.2
Asian American	2.7	2.3	2.7	1.9	3.0	2.2
Native American	0.5	0.4	0.5	0.3	<1.0	0.6

% Radio Employees	2008	2007	2006	2005	2000	1995
Caucasian	88.2	93.8	93.6	92.1	90.0	85.3
African American	7.8	3.3	2.5	0.7	5.0	5.7
Hispanic	3.6	0.7	1.9	6	3.0	7.5
Asian American	0.4	1.1	1.8	0.7	1.0	0.6
Native American	0	1.1	0.2	0.5	1.0	1.0

Source: Papper 2008.

Table 11.5 Public Broadcaster Station Employment 1978–2008

Year	Percent Public Radio Minority Employment	Percent Public TV Minority Employment
1978	12.6	13.9
1998	19.6	18.8
2006	20.4	18.7
2007	19.9	19.2
2008	19.8	19.4

Source: CPB reports to Congress 1978–2008.

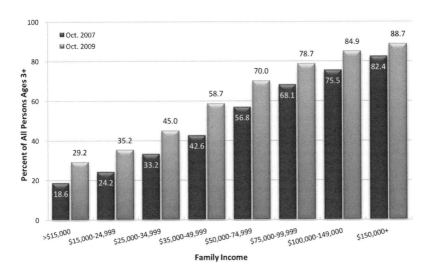

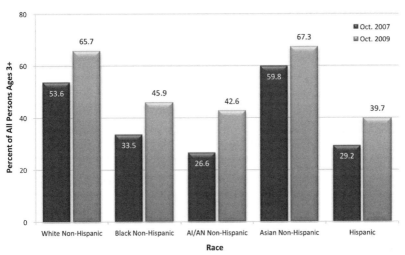

Figure 11.1 Persons using broadband in the home, 2007–2009

Source: NTIA 2010.

266 • E.J. Wilson III and S. Costanza-Chock

References

Alexander, Amy. 2008. "The Color Line Online." *The Nation*, August 4. Available at: www.thenation.com/doc/20080804/alexander (accessed March 20, 2009).

American Community Survey. 2007. "Civilian Employed Population 16 Years and Over: Information; Internet Publishing and Internet Service Providers." *American Community Survey 1-Year Estimates*. ACS. Available at: http://tinyurl.com/62bqke (accessed March 10, 2009).

ASNE (American Society of Newspaper Editors). 2009a. *Newsroom Employment Census*. ASNE. Available at: http://asne.org/key_initiatives/diversity/newsroom_census.aspx (accessed March 30, 2010).

——. 2009b. "U.S. Newsroom Employment Declines." ASNE. Available at: http://asne.org/article_view/articleid/12/u-s-newsroom-employment-declines-12.aspx (accessed March 31, 2010).

Beresteanu, Arie and Paul B. Ellickson. 2007. *Minority and Female Ownership in Media Enterprises*. Washington, DC: Federal Communications Commission. Available at: http://fjallfoss.fcc.gov/edocs_public/attachmatch/DA-07-3470A8.pdf (accessed November 3, 2007).

Burns, A. 2008. "Select Issues with New Media Theories of Citizen Journalism." *M/C Journal* 11.1. Available at: www.journal.media-culture.org.au/index.php/mcjournal/article/viewArticle/30/0 (accessed March 10, 2010).

Castells, M. 2007. "Communication, Power and Counter-power in the Network Society." *International Journal of Communication*, February 8, 1:1. Available at: http://ijoc.org/ojs/index.php/ijoc/article/view/46/35

——. 2009. *Communication Power*. New York: Oxford University Press.

Chow-White, P.A. 2008. "The Informationalization of Race: Communication Technologies and the Human Genome in the Digital Age." *International Journal of Communication* 2: 1168–1194.

Cottle, Simon. 2000. "Media Research and Ethnic Minorities: Mapping the Field," in S. Cottle, ed., *Ethnic Minorities and the Media*. Buckingham and Philadelphia: Open University Press, 1–30.

CPB (Corporation for Public Broadcasting). 2007. *CPB Annual Report to Congress*. CPB. Available at: www.cpb.org/aboutcpb/reports (accessed December 20, 2008).

——. 2009. *Public Broadcasting's Services to Minorities and Diverse Audiences*. CPB. Available at: www.cpb.org/aboutcpb/reports/diversity (accessed August 8, 2009).

Deuze, M., A. Bruns, and C. Neuberger. 2007. "Preparing for an Age of Participatory News." *Journalism Practice* 1.3: 322–338.

DiMaggio, Paul and Eszter Hargittai. 2001. "From the 'Digital Divide' to 'Digital Inequality': Studying Internet Use as Penetration Increases." Working Paper #15, Summer. Princeton: Center for Arts and Cultural Policy Studies. Available at: www.princeton.edu/culturalpolicy/workpap15.html (accessed March 10, 2010).

Dowrick, S. and M. Akmal. 2005. "Contradictory Trends in Global Income Inequality: A Tale of Two Biases." *Review of Income and Wealth* 51.2: 201–229.

Gandy, Oscar H. 1998. *Communication and Race: A Structural Perspective*. New York: Oxford University Press.

Gillmor, D. 2006. *We the Media: Grassroots Journalism by the People, for the People*. Cambridge, MA: O'Reilly Media.

Gray, Herman. 2005. *Cultural Moves: African Americans and the Politics of Representation*. Berkeley and Los Angeles: University of California Press.

Hargittai, Eszter. 2007. "Whose Space? Differences among Users and Non-users of Social Network Sites." *Journal of Computer-Mediated Communication* 13.1: article 14. Available at: http://jcmc.indiana.edu/vol13/issue1/hargittai.html (accessed April 2, 2009).

Held, D. and A. Kaya. 2007. *Global Inequality*. Cambridge: Polity Press.

Hoffman, D.L. and T.P. Novak. 1998. "Bridging the Racial Divide on the Internet." *Science* 280 (April 17): 390–391.

Horrigan, John. 2008. "Home Broadband Adoption 2008." Pew Internet and American Life Project. Available at: www.pewinternet.org/pdfs/PIP_Broadband_2008.pdf (accessed August 27, 2008).

ITU (International Telecommunications Union). 2008. "Global ICT Developments." ITU-D Market Information and Statistics. Available at: www.itu.int/ITU-D/ict/statistics/ict/index.html (accessed October 10, 2008).

Jacobs, Ronald N. 2000. *Race, Media, and the Crisis of Civil Society: From Watts to Rodney King*. Cambridge: Cambridge University Press.

Jaeger, P.T., J.C. Bertot, C.R. McLure, and L.A. Langa. 2006. "The Policy Implications of Internet Connectivity in Public Libraries." *Government Information Quarterly* 23.1: 123–141. http://dx.doi.org/10.1016/j.giq.2005.10.002.

Jenkins, Henry. 2006. *Convergence Culture: Where Old and New Media Collide.* New York: New York University Press.

Korzenny, Felipe and Betty Ann Korzenny. 2008. "Online Technology Ownership." *Multicultural Marketing Equation Study 2007, Report #2.* Center for Hispanic Marketing Communication at Florida State University. Available at: http://hmc.comm.fsu.edu/Publications/Reports (accessed February 14, 2009).

Lehrman, Sally. 2005. *News in a New America.* Miami: Knight Foundation. Available at: www.justicejournalism.org/projects/lehrman_sally/KF_News-in-a-New-America_web.pdf (accessed March 10, 2009).

Lenhart, Amanda, John Horrigan, and Deborah Fallows. 2004. *Content Creation Online.* Pew Internet and American Life Project. Available at: www.pewinternet.org/pdfs/PIP_Content_Creation_Report.pdf (accessed March 15, 2009).

Norris, P. 2001. *Digital Divide: Civic Engagement, Information Poverty, and the Internet Worldwide.* Cambridge: Cambridge University Press.

NTIA (National Telecommunications and Information Administration). 1998. *Falling Through the Net II: New Data on the Digital Divide.* July. Washington, DC: National Telecommunications and Information Administration.

——. 1999. *Falling Through the Net: Defining the Digital Divide.* November. Washington, DC: National Telecommunications and Information Administration.

——. 2000a. *Changes, Challenges, and Charting New Courses: Minority Commercial Broadcast Ownership in the United States.* U.S. Dept. of Commerce, NTIA Minority Telecommunications Development Program. Available at: www.ntia.doc.gov/opadhome/mtdpweb/01minrept/Front00.htm (accessed March 1, 2008).

——. 2000b. *Falling Through the Net: Toward Digital Inclusion.* October. Washington, DC: National Telecommunications and Information Administration.

——. 2010. *Digital Nation: 21st Century America's Progress Toward Universal Broadband Access.* February. Washington, DC: National Telecommunications and Information Administration. Available at: www.ntia.doc.gov/reports/2010/NTIA_internet_use_report_Feb2010.pdf (accessed March 10, 2010).

OECD. 2009. "OECD Broadband Subscribers per 100 Inhabitants, by Technology, June 2009." *OECD Broadband Statistics.* Available at: www.oecd.org/document/23/0,3343,en_2649_34225_33987543_1_1_1_1,00.html (accessed April 2, 2010).

Outing, S. 2005. "The 11 Layers of Citizen Journalism." *Poynter Online.* Available at: www.poynter.org/content/content_view.asp?id=83126 (accessed March 23, 2010).

Papper, Bob. 2008. *2008 Women and Minorities Survey.* RTNDA/Hofstra University. Available at: www.rtdna.org/pages/media_items/cover-story-2008-women-and-minorities-survey1472.php (accessed May 7, 2009).

Rodriguez, Clemencia. 2001. *Fissures in the Mediascape: An International Study of Citizens' Media.* Cresskill, NJ: Hampton Press.

Rosen, J. 2008. "A Most Useful Definition of Citizen Journalism." *PressThink.* Available at: http://journalism.nyu.edu/pubzone/weblogs/pressthink/2008/07/14/a_most_useful_d.html (accessed March 11, 2010).

Stiglitz, J.E. 2002. *Globalization and its Discontents.* New York: W.W. Norton.

Terranova, T. 2004. *Network Culture: Politics for the Information Age.* London: Pluto Press.

Thurman, N. 2008. "Forum for Citizen Journalists? Adoption of User Generated Content Initiatives by Online News Media." *New Media & Society* 10: 139–157.

Tongia, R. and E.J. Wilson III. 2011. "Network Theory | The Flip Side of Metcalfe's Law: Multiple and Growing Costs of Network Exclusion." *International Journal of Communication* [Online] 5:0. Available at: http://ijoc.org/ojs/index.php/ijoc/article/view/873/549.

Turner, S. Derek. 2007. "Off the Dial: Female and Minority Radio Station Ownership in the United States." Free Press, June 16. Available at: www.freepress.net/files/off_the_dial_summary.pdf (accessed May 6, 2008).

Turner, S. Derek and Mark Cooper. 2007. "Out of The Picture 2007: Minority and Female TV Station Ownership in the United States." Free Press. Available at: www.freepress.net/files/otp2007.pdf (accessed May 6, 2008).

U.S. Census Bureau. 2006. *2002 Survey of Business Owners.* Washington, DC: U.S. Department of Commerce, Economics and Statistics Administration, U.S. Census Bureau. Available at: http://www2.census.gov/econ/sbo/02/sb0200cscosumt.pdf (accessed March 29, 2010).

——. 2008. "An Older and More Diverse Nation by Midcentury." *U.S. Census Bureau News,* August 14. Available at: www.census.gov/Press-Release/www/releases/archives/population/012496.html (accessed January 20, 2009).

——. 2009. *2009 National Population Projections (Supplemental).* Washington, DC: U.S. Department of Commerce, Economics and Statistics Administration, U.S. Census Bureau. Available at: www.census.gov/population/www/projections/2009projections.html (accessed March 28, 2010).

van Dijck, J. 2009. "Users Like You? Theorizing Agency in User-Generated Content." *Media, Culture & Society* 31.1: 41.

Warschauer, M. 2004. *Technology and Social Inclusion: Rethinking the Digital Divide.* Cambridge, MA: MIT Press.

Wilson, Clint C. 2000. "The Paradox of African American Journalists," in S. Cottle, ed., *Ethnic Minorities and the Media.* Buckingham and Philadelphia: Open University Press, 1–30.

Wilson, E.J., III, M.L. Best, and D. Kleine. 2005. "Moving Beyond 'The Real Digital Divide.'" *Information Technologies and International Development* 2.3: iii–v.

IV
Biotechnology and Race as Information

12

Roots and Revelation

Genetic Ancestry Testing and the YouTube Generation

ALONDRA NELSON

Columbia University

JEONG WON HWANG

> Just wanted to take ya'll through the steps of me doing my paternal African roots . . . I'm going to send you all on a trip with me. And, hopefully . . . ya'll will have positive feedback about my results . . . Give me questions, give me comments, share this video with your friends and family, because I want ya'll to do this, too.
>
> (*yeamie*, genetic genealogist on YouTube)[1]

As is widely acknowledged, parallel developments in computing and molecular biology precipitated the genomics era. A noteworthy extension of this interdependence of bytes and genes is the budding role played by social network sites (SNS) on the terrain of consumer genetics.[2] The Google-backed personal genomics company 23andMe that sells consumers genetic inferences about their "health, disease and ancestry," for example, was launched in 2007 as an e-business with a social networking component.[3] As envisioned, this feature allows 23andMe's clients to tap into the wisdom of the crowd by sharing and aggregating data about their respective genetic analyses. Virtual communities have also risen up more organically around other types of direct-to-consumer (DTC) genetic testing in the form of listservs and blogs through which users disclose and discuss the SNPs ("snips"), Y-chromosome DNA (Y-DNA), mitochondrial DNA (mt-DNA) and haplotype group results they purchased from various enterprises toward the end of conjecturing identity, familial origins or disease predisposition.[4] In this essay, we examine another iteration of the interplay between on-line community and DTC genetics—the use of the video-sharing SNS *YouTube (Broadcast Yourself)*™ by African American genealogists, who have purchased DNA testing to learn about their ancestry. With this phenomenon, the authoritative "imprimatur" of genetic science and the practice of genealogy are married to the media cultures of Web 2.0 and reality television.[5] These broadcasts that predominantly feature men and women in their twenties and thirties suggest the centrality of social networking to community formation among young adults. This phenomenon also suggests the broadening demographic appeal of genetic root-seeking; interest in genealogy, a practice that has long been the provenance of older adults and retirees, may be growing in a younger generation, owing in part to the recent technological mediation of root-seeking.

SNSs such as Facebook, Twitter, Flickr and YouTube capture the public's imagination because of their capacity to facilitate the creation of community. These sites share Web 2.0 features such as information sharing, interaction and customization. But YouTube, established in February 2005, is unique among SNSs for the ease with which it can be used to upload and circulate videos. In just a few years' time, YouTube has become the most important virtual space for the sharing of music videos and songs; news segments and current events; memorable moments from movies and television shows; how-to demon- strations and homemade viewer videos, as well as opinions about this posted material. The prominence of this SNS is reflected in the ability of its videos to rapidly draw the eyes of millions of viewers: that is, in the language of social media, "to go viral."

The founding of YouTube followed by just a few years the emergence of DTC genetics. Recently a genre of broadcasts that we describe as *roots revelations* has emerged on this SNS. With these videos, genealogists use YouTube's functions to disseminate and court reactions to their root-seeking journeys.[6] In these tightly shot, almost confessional videos, genealogists describe the genetic ancestry testing process and their reactions to it. They try on genetically derived identities. Using image, sound and text, they perform the new or elaborated selves made available to them through genetic ancestry testing.

The practice of genealogy was popularized in the late 1970s after the publication of Alex Haley's book *Roots: The Saga of an American Family* and, soon after, the debut of the eponymous television mini-series.[7] The roots journey involves the reconstruction of family history, principally through the use of archival documentation dutifully assembled by the root-seeker over many years or decades. More recently, a spate of genealogy-themed, unscripted (or "reality") television shows, such as prominent Harvard University academic Henry Louis "Skip" Gates Jr's successful *African American Lives* franchise, have highlighted the ease and immediacy with which the roots endeavor can currently be undertaken, be it carried out for a root-seeker by another individual (e.g. a certified genealogist) or a company (such as Gates' African DNA that sells traditional and genetic ancestry tracing). On this novel family history landscape, the apex of the roots journey is "the reveal"—to borrow a concept from reality television—the revelation of new or surprising information, often based upon genetic test results, to a subject who expresses astonishment or elation or both before an audience. Thus, in the post-Haley era, the practice of root-seeking might be said to now require not simply the reconstruction of a familial narrative or excavation, but also the performance of one's response to this genealogical account, as well as the presence of an audience to observe it. Broadcasting oneself on YouTube is one means to these ends.

Moreover, as an SNS, YouTube is inherently a vehicle through which the audience can express its opinions about roots revelations back to the videos' creators. These broadcasts provide not only a way for genealogists to circulate their genetic test results, but also an audience with whom to share their experiences and, potentially, with whom to develop affiliations. In the words of *yeamie*, from the epigram that begins this essay, genetic genealogists use the site, in part, to generate "positive feedback about [their] results." A diverse array of viewers differently bears witness to the roots journey: Viewers' reactions indeed include "positive" responses. Audience members claiming ties to the ethnic groups or countries to which a root-seeker has been associated by a testing service, for example, may enthusiastically receive (and thus authenticate) a broadcaster's results. At the same time, some in the audience may reflect skepticism about genetic ancestry testing and, implicitly, also about the presuppositions about kinship and community that undergird it. In both instances, the circulation of roots revelations offers a small window on public perception of the growing use of genetic ancestry testing.

As Nelson has described previously, "affiliative self-fashioning"—the constitution of individual identity, through and toward the goal of association with others, including ancestors and DNA "kin"—is a significant aspiration for consumers of genetic ancestry testing.[8] As we detail here, roots revelations are one manner in which this affiliative identification and interchange is achieved. The videos thus serve not only as a forum for the evaluation of new selves by a multifaceted social network, but also a vehicle of self-making. In other words, although prompted by the consumption of genetic ancestry testing, our root-seekers and their viewers interrogate and assess identity and community membership via social network interaction. More specifically, drawing on the work of the anthropologist John L. Jackson, roots revelations might be understood as enactments of "racial sincerity"—that is, a race-based yet non-essentialist form of negotiated, interactional identity.[9]

Genes and Bytes

DTC genetic genealogy testing has burgeoned over the last several years. This commercial enterprise evolved from techniques developed in molecular genetics, human population genetics, and biological anthropology.[10] With this form of analysis, a consumer's ancestry or family history is inferred from the comparison of his or her DNA with a company's proprietary database of genetic samples.[11] Several types of tests are offered by the growing number of purveyors of DNA analysis for genealogical purposes:[12] "Racio-ethnic composite" testing—such as the *Ancestry Painting* evaluation sold by 23andMe —yields to a customer percentages of African, Asian and European ancestry.

A second type of testing, haplogroup analysis, of which the Genographic Project is paradigmatic, informs a consumer of distant ancestry, typically thousands or tens of thousands of years in the past.[13]

A third common category of genetic genealogy is "ethnic lineage" testing— analysis of Y-chromosome DNA and mitochondrial DNA (mt-DNA). Y-DNA is passed inter-generationally from fathers to sons. Through examination of these sex-linked genes, a direct line of male ancestors (patrilineage) can be traced. mtDNA, the energy mechanism of cells, is inherited by sons and daughters from their mothers; it contains characteristic "hypervariable" regions that can be assayed to discern genetic matrilineage. A hypothetical ethnic lineage result, based on analysis purchased from the African Ancestry company, might suggest that a root-seeker's Y-DNA traced to the Yoruba people, who reside in many countries in contemporary West Africa. Or, using the Oxford Ancestors service, it might be inferred that a client's mtDNA showed commonality with residents of Central and Western Eurasia.[14] For genealogists, part of the appeal of ethnic lineage testing is that it intimates "mothers" and "fathers" and generates a specific contemporary region, nation-state or community to which a consumer can trace origins (rather than, say, an association with a historically and/or temporally distant population). This third type of testing might be said to be the form of genetic analysis that best approximates the narrative arc of Haley's *Roots*, in which "lost" national and racio-ethnic identity and kin were recovered.

Haley's family tree was refashioned from the author's own (and subsequently somewhat controversial) research. Twenty-first-century genealogy, on the other hand, relies largely on technical developments that make the practice accessible to the general public as a product. Both the digitization of documents necessary to root-seeking practice via websites such as Ancestry.com and the cottage industry of DTC genetic testing companies that promise to uncover family history with DNA analysis have contributed to growing interest in genealogy. In the process, the reduction of genealogical labor for individual root-seekers—relative to the more arduous *Roots* example—has also become possible.

Reveal Yourself

Traditional, digital and genetic methods of ancestry tracing are prominent in the recent spate of genealogy-themed, reality television shows. "The reveal" is an essential element of genealogy programs such as *Motherland: A Genetic Journey* (2003), *Motherland: Moving On* (2006) and *Who Do You Think You Are?* (2004—) on Britain's BBC and, in the U.S., celebrity-driven shows such as PBS's *African American Lives* (2006), *Oprah's Roots* (2007), *African American Lives II* (2008), and *Faces of America* (2010), and NBC's *Who Do You Think You Are?* (2010—).[15] Media studies scholar June Deery writes that "the reveal" functions "both to uncover and to display. . . to a dual audience of subject and TV viewers."[16] With televised genealogy shows, furthermore, what is uncovered or displayed—most often to a root-seeker via a host—is information about a notable predecessor, a significant historical event, or unexpected affiliations. The poignancy of these televised reveals is manifested by our root-seekers as heightened emotion or with the flat affect of shock. For example, in *African American Lives*, a show that featured the genealogy of prominent blacks, genetic genealogy results destabilized long and dearly held ideas about ancestry and identity: Social scientist Sara Lawrence-Lightfoot, who self-identifies as African American and American Indian, was stunned when host Skip Gates disclosed that racio-ethnic composite testing suggests she has "no Native American" ancestry whatsoever. Astronaut Mae Jemison, the first black woman to travel to space, on the other hand, was pleasantly surprised to learn that her composite includes an inference of 13 percent "East Asian" ancestry. Similarly, during a striking moment in *African American Lives II*, the comedian Chris Rock was brought to the brink of tears when he learned from host Skip Gates that a previously unknown forebear bootstrapped his way up from slavery to two stints in the South Carolina legislature.[17]

In the post-Haley era, genealogical labor can thus be at a remove from the interested root-seeker. Genealogists may accordingly take on a new role: No longer solely family history archeologists engaged in the lonely pursuit of excavating vital records and census documents, they can become performers whose job it is to react to genealogical information that is revealed to them. Perhaps unsurprisingly then, less prominent root-seekers than those featured on televised genealogy programs have taken to YouTube to perform and broadcast their reveals and to disseminate their reflections on the genetic genealogy testing experience. Below we describe and analyze several of these roots revelations.

As of October 2010, a search for the terms "genealogy," "genetics" and "DNA" resulted in several hundred videos. Many of these can be described as "roots revelations" videos because they feature some aspect of the genetic genealogy trajectory from the collection of the DNA sample to the results reveal. Here we focus on a small subset of black genealogists because we are specifically interested in genetic ancestry testing and African diasporic identity.[18] We accordingly employed purposive sampling and sought out videos that conveyed blacks' experiences with genetic genealogy.[19] (Our sample is therefore and purposely not representative of all genealogy videos on YouTube or of all African American root-seeking practice; moreover, our discussion of the roots revelation phenomenon is impressionistic and our conclusions are necessarily provisional.)

We arrived at this sample by searching the YouTube site for combinations of the keywords or search terms "African," "ancestry," "roots," and "black" in addition to "genetics," "DNA," and "genealogy." Of more than 500 videos, twenty-two met our criteria. However, nine of these were explicitly promotional: that is, they were intended to advertise the services of one or more genetic ancestry testing companies. Here, we examine thirteen roots revelations uploaded to the SNS by ten root-seekers between 2007 and 2009.[20] The videos spanned from five to ten minutes in length. We viewed each of these videos several times and also transcribed them. We then coded these transcripts as well as the associated "comments" sections (i.e. the social network audience's written responses to the videos). The "tags" that root-seekers assigned to their videos were also recorded; as we note below, tagging is one strategy that YouTube users employ to shape the audience for their videos. As well, we made note of the broadcasters' descriptions of their videos; these brief writings offered additional perspective on why our root-seekers purchased genetic genealogy testing.

Five of the root-seekers are women and five are men. They are all young adults. Although we do not know any of the broadcasters personally, all appear to be under forty years of age; the majority are younger than thirty. Because genealogy has typically been time- and resource-intensive, it has traditionally been the provenance of older adults or retirees with leisure time. But genealogy's intersections with cutting-edge DTC genetic testing and social network technologies have helped to increase its popularity among a younger demographic. Although it is considered a hobby, ancestry tracing can be a serious undertaking for this new generation of genealogists. One root-seeker, an African American male, who appeared to be in his late teens and used the name *NurturingOurRoots101*, stressed in his video that genealogy was no mere recreational pursuit for him. The goal of his broadcast, he stated, was to help other "students to see where they come from in Africa, to know their ancestors and genealogy." He continued,

> some . . . [ask] about genealogy being a hobby. It's not a hobby, definitely not a hobby, because a hobby is something you do for relaxation and pleasure. But we do not do [it] for pleasure . . . Genealogy . . . is a necessity [for] knowing who you are and everything you hope to be.[21]

Notably many had also been tagged with terms that signaled the history and politics of black experience like "racism" and "slavery." Discussing public and private spheres on YouTube, media studies scholar Patricia Lange explains that broadcasters may deliberately "calibrate access to their videos" and "create larger or smaller media circuits by using technical features such as . . . strategic tagging."[22] Tagging refers to designating keywords for videos. Tags may serve to hail viewers based upon common language or shared racial, sexual, religious, or national identities; in turn, tagging may help to foster the formation of affinity groups and feelings of community between broadcasters and the audience.

Another way that these root-seekers shaped their audience was by placing their videos into YouTube's "Education" category (rather than in the more expected "People & Blogs" category). This was true of *vegasview77*, who assigned "education" as both a category and a tag to his reveal. In a written statement appended to his video, this root-seeker declared: "Always remember that DNA has memory . . . I'm so pleased my results came back as 100% certain, yeah that's right 100%!"[23] This categorization was likely utilized by this root seeker to impute gravitas and validity to both the root-seeking journey and genetic genealogy testing.

Roots Revelations

Roots revelations depict genealogists' receipt of genetic information about their ancestry. Although we found considerable variation among the videos, they share several qualities. Most broadcasts suggest why root-seekers embark upon genetic genealogical testing and why they were prompted to create their videos. Videos may feature detailed step-by-step descriptions of the genetic genealogy testing process, from purchase to results. *yeamie*, for example, filmed himself collecting the DNA sample that he would send to the African Ancestry company for analysis:

> These are the test kit instructions right here for the "premium ancestry kit." [He holds a piece of paper containing instructions up to the camera.] I'll just read them to you. "Number one, fill out the specimen information form . . ." Check . . . I'm gonna swab my cheeks right now with these swabs. But, first, I wanna get some water to rinse my mouth. [Rinses his mouth and spits the water out.] [Again, reading directions.] "Remove cotton swab from package. Swab firmly along the inside of each of your cheeks, approximately 20 times per cheek." [Counts 1, 2, 3, 4, etc., as he wipes the inside of each cheek.][24]

A few of the other roots revelations we documented also include display or discussion of the collection of DNA samples. However, the broadcasts more often than not center on the moment of "the reveal" and the genealogists' reactions to this new genetically derived information.

The Reveal

Roots revelations customarily involve the public disclosure of one's often previously unknown genetic affiliation (i.e. racial composite, ethnicity, haplotype group, etc.). Although a few of the genealogists we followed performed or recalled their reveals post hoc, most allowed the audience to witness the climactic moment when their genetic ancestry test results were opened. The root revelations we examined appear to be self-filmed with the exception of that of *Jasmynecannick*, who had her reveal documented by a friend with whom she converses in her video. Whether or not the results are revealed "live" on camera, the root-seekers consistently share their results with theatrical flair.

Figure 12.1a jasmynecannick's reveal filmed by a friend

Figure 12.1b In a celebratory gesture, *jasmynecannick* holds up the map and
certificate of ancestry that she received from African Ancestry.
These documents indicate her inferred African ethnicity.

yeamie, who identifies as a black man, filmed himself opening the envelope containing the results of the Y-DNA test he purchased from African Ancestry. Before the camera, he slowly reads from the letter containing his results: "The Y chromosome that we determined from your sample has European ancestry ... We understand this information may be diffi—" At this point, *yeamie* interjects, "No, it's not. That's what they say, but I already know I got white in me." Carrying on reading the results letter where he left off, he says, ". . . difficult to accept, especially if you are not aware of any European men on your paternal line . . ." Again, *yeamie* inserts his perspective between the lines of the company's result letter: "That I know; that's why I did my father's [the paternal line]." Towards the end of his broadcast, the root-seeker endeavors to demonstrate to the audience that the results were anticipated: "I am not surprised . . . I'm not shocked to get any results because I pretty much know my make-up already." Wrapping up, he musters the following statement of bittersweet fulfillment: "I'm very proud to know what I am. I am European and proud of it. So, all the Europeans out there and my Europeans in YouTube land, I'll check you out later. Peace! Black power!"[25]

With *yeamie*'s broadcast, viewers witness the very moment when he learns his test results and discovers, furthermore, that his Y-DNA traces to Europe rather than Africa. Proclaiming his prior awareness of and, moreover, his satisfaction with this news of European ancestry, *yeamie* seeks to downplay the fact that his results may have been surprising. The exclamation of "Black power!" after his expression of European pride is perhaps intended to be ironic. It may also be a subtle negation of the test results, evidence of *yeamie*'s recognition that "European DNA" does not make him a white person.

Figure 12.2 yeamie's reveal. Here he displays the map of Europe that was included in his results package. In keeping with his Y-DNA result, the map is titled "Europe" (the continent of Asia also appears prominently on this map)

A broadcaster going by the name of *cocopuff236* also permitted the YouTube audience to observe him as he read for the first time the results of a genetic genealogy test he had purchased.

> I'm just going to jump into it . . . These are the results of my mother's maternal lineage from AfricanAncestry.com. And, the results are . . . "It's a great pleasure that our report on the Matriclan analysis had identified your maternal genetic ancestry. The sequence that we determined from your sample is of Middle Eastern ancestry. The sequence belonged to the haplo-group N1C, a non-African lineage."[26]

He continues, describing elements of his results package: "There is a map that says haplo-group N1 is most commonly found among the Ashkenazi Jewish population in Central and Eastern Europe."[27]

In contrast to *yeamie*, who tried to minimize the extent to which his shock was apparent to the social network audience by repeatedly interrupting the narrative flow of African Ancestry's results letter, *cocopuff236*'s reveal is more a straightforward reckoning with unanticipated information. Nevertheless, *cocopuff236* almost immediately follows his reveal with qualification: "Now, like they say further in the letter, it doesn't mean that we're not African American. That's just . . . one side of the family, one portion."[28] He surmises that "it goes to show that you can't always go by hearing from your family members, because in our family we were told that we were mixed with Native Americans. But I guess the DNA test shows otherwise."[29]

Born Again

The "Certificate of Ancestry" that African Ancestry gives to its clients as part of their results packages is featured prominently in several of the roots revelations we analyzed. This document, signed by the company's chief executive officer, Gina Paige, and its chief science officer, Rick Kittles, illustrates a customer's genetic ancestry designation in attractive detail. African Ancestry's "certification" is of symbolic importance to root-seekers like *Jasmynecannick*, who declared that she felt "complete" after receiving documentation that affiliated her with both the Bubi people in Bioko Island, Equatorial Guinea, and the Tikar tribe and Fulani people of Cameroon.[30] The power of the certificate was also evident in a video posted by a root-seeker named *CameroonStar*, who articulated the certificate's influence in this way, "I'm extremely excited because I've known this for years 'inside,' but to actually have it on paper, coming from your DNA . . .!"

African Ancestry contributes to the valorization of its ancestry certificates by advising root-seekers to put the documents on show in their homes. *yeamie*, reading from his results letter, conveyed the company's recommendation in his video: "We have also enclosed a certificate of ancestry *authenticating* that your polymorphisms match with people living in Europe. You can display it among other important family documents."[31] Indeed, in several videos, genealogists announced their intention to frame their certificates, store them with other cherished possessions or exhibit them in a prominent place. One root-seeker stated, for example, "I'm going to get a frame for it! But not before I scan and send it to everybody in the family!"[32]

For some, these documents authoritatively confer identity. *KILLcolorstruck*'s reveal included quotes from his Certificate of Ancestry: "'African Ancestry hereby certifies that Johnson Martin shares maternal genetic ancestry with the Mafa, Hide and Tikar people living in Cameroon.' And it's signed by the person who did this thing." Holding up this document and looking into the camera, *KILLcolorstruck* continued, declaring somberly, "This is my African-ness." Root-seekers clearly placed high value on documentation of their genetic ancestry results. One person regarded her certificate not only as a mark of identity but furthermore as analogous to an official vital record. During her roots revelation, *Jasmynecannick* exclaimed, "*I have a new birth certificate!* . . . Now, when people ask me where I'm from, I can say, '[Do you mean] pre- or post- Middle Passage?'"[33] Reacting to this roots revelation, YouTube viewer *xbkzfineztx* wrote,

> Congratulations on finally knowing YOU. I did [my genetic ancestry testing] recently, which prompted me to look at [your video] . . . I want to take one more test by a different company, which will be African Ancestry. *I want my birth certificate too, shoot!*[34]

Results kit artifacts become props in roots revelation videos. Indexical to the root-seeker's own DNA, this documentation also stands in for YouTube genealogists' "true" origins.

Roots Commentariat

> Tell me what you guys think.
> (*cocopuff236*)[35]

As the above dialogue between *Jasmynecannick* and *xbkzfineztx* suggests, interactions between root-seekers and their audience are a key facet of roots revelations. Transmission of these videos on YouTube enable genetic genealogists' association with an expansive network of persons, both unknown and known. On the one hand, like genealogy-themed television shows, the audience for these videos may be amorphous and wide-ranging. On the other, the SNS's features allow video-makers to prescribe their viewership or to categorize their videos in ways that will attract the most desired audience.[36]

In turn, the social network audience, which may be strategically cultivated, offers root-seekers feedback about their reveals. Each of the videos we analyzed elicited audience commentary. Recall from this chapter's epigram that root-seeker *yeamie* hoped for "positive" reactions to his reveal broadcast. Expressions of affirmation and support were the overwhelming reaction to *yeamie*'s two videos. Positive observations were additionally the most common response to the other roots revelations we considered.

However, as *yeamie*'s case also exemplifies, the audience had a wider range of reactions too. Acknowledging that *yeamie* seemed visibly shocked by his genetic ancestry results despite assertions to the contrary, his viewers also extended commiseration. *TevyeWill* replied, "Yeah, Id've [*sic*] been disappointed . . . very interesting my Black European friend, just goes to show how little DNA matters/relates to our physical differences." Similarly, a viewer named *skylabx2000* offered, "I salute your bravery brother, don't let it bug you." Another with the moniker *CVGodfather* remarked, "It[']s not really bad news cuz I know you were kind of expecting this. It's obvious that your African traits dominate your [E]uropean traits. lol." *lerinhar*, who was both a root-seeker and a commenter in our sample, replied: "interesting video bro! I[']m sorry you got those results but at least you know your paternal ancestry."[37]

Audience and Diaspora

SNSs encourage a sense of proximity between broadcasters and commenters, in spite of the temporal and spatial distance characteristic of virtual exchange. On YouTube this familiarity is partly achieved through filming technique and style: Close-angle views and *sotto voce* tones are employed on roots revelations that approximate the "confessional" interludes on reality TV shows such as *The Real World* and *Survivor*. These videos create intimacy despite the fact that they can be grainy and poorly lit. Media scholar Patricia Lange explains that on YouTube interaction may be privileged over aesthetics. She suggests that "quality is not necessarily the determining factor in terms of how videos affect social networks."[38] Rather, Lange suggests, broadcasters "creat[e] and circulat[e] video" in order to "enact social relationships between those who make [them] and those who view" them.[39]

Building from Lange's observation, in addition, the SNS-enabled social interactions we observed could have a specifically diasporic valence because the audience for black American root-seekers' videos was comprised in part of viewers who professed African nationality (and residence on the continent or abroad). Audience members claiming affiliation with the group, ethnicity or nation to which a root-seeker was matched by DNA often celebrated the identities unfurled on the videos. After viewing *Jasmynecannick*'s reveal, in which the genealogist learned that her matrilineage traced to contemporary West Africa, commenter *Crisjones77* replied, "BE PROUD OF UR HERITAGE AND DON'T FORGET TO GO TO CAMEROON[.] I[']m from Congo[,] by the way[.]"[40] *lerinhar* received a similarly agreeable response to his roots revelation from *Akok98*, who wrote, "Although I'm not American[,] I understand the struggles of all African diaspora nations. I'm from Sudan. But nonetheless I see how that bridge . . . with ancestry was broken during slavery . . . I'm proud of you and others."[41]

Members of the social network audience claiming African ethnicity or nationality also warmly received root-seekers into motherland identities and communities. *vegasview77*'s genetic ancestry results suggested a link to the Akan group. In reply to this video, viewer *termanology85* wrote: "my mother is Akan (Guan ppl.). big ups and welcome." In response to *CameroonStar*'s reveal that made public her genetic assignment to Cameroon, *Estorpai* noted, "Welcome home. You are from a great country," while *LeClubMJJ* similarly greeted her by writing, "I'm from Cameroon, from the Bamileke tribe. I live in California . . . Congratulations to Afro-Americans interested in their roots. Welcome HOME sisters and brothers."

In a recent meditation on heritage tourism in Ghana, cultural theorist Saidiya Hartman proposes that salutations and familial invocations between West Africans and black Americans—underpinned as they are by "redemptive narratives," "promises of filiation," "fantasies of origin" and even economic interests—may be instrumental or insincere.[42] Unlike the case of Ghanaian tourism, exchanges that take place around roots revelations many not produce tangible benefits for "African" commenters. Affective benefits can accrue to genealogists, however, through social network interactions with viewers who sanction their genetic ancestry results from a privileged "African" vantage point.[43] In this way, roots revelations may condition "affiliative self-fashioning," constituting genetic genealogists' identities through technology, sentiment and sociality.[44]

On the other hand, "African" audience members also challenged root-seekers' claims of affiliation—ancestry certificates and performative reveals notwithstanding. In the comments that accompanied *Jasmynecannick*'s roots revelation, a debate ensued about African American root-seeking. A viewer using the Nguni name *bongiwe* expressed deep skepticism of black Americans' genealogical aspirations and was dismissive of the measures to which they were willing to go in pursuit of African ancestry. *bongiwe* complained,

> [a]s an African I find it sad and forever tragic the legacy of slavery and the impact it has left on Black Americans. Constantly in search of an identity. There are endless salesmen and business [sic] willing to sell you an identity if you are desperate enough and willing to buy it.[45]

Another commenter argued that affiliation with Africa had to be established through action, rather than inferred through DNA analysis. *Shoshaloza1*, whose moniker described a genre of South African call-and-response folksongs and was thus especially fitting for this debate, retorted:

> African American? No, no, no, no, no, no. It's American black! The only Africans in America are the ones who were born in Africa! If they consider themselves so African, they should come to Africa and use their

talents here to strengthen the reputation of Africa! Instead, they . . . strengthen the reputation of America! . . . Now it is time for American blacks to come back to help Africa. Otherwise, they shouldn't even call themselves African![46]

Somewhat in agreement, *9revolta* contended that an "African American is someone who has come from Africa, and has gained citizenship in America."[47] On the surface, the discussion that transpired in reaction to this video appeared to be a dispute over nomenclature. Yet it was also a contest over the stakes of black Americans' claims to African identity. For *Shoshaloza1*, in particular, there was recognition that genetic genealogy testing, for all its feel-good potential for U.S. blacks, was an asymmetrical exchange, offering little material gain for this viewer and other self-declared "Africans" in the social network.

Other doubts conveyed by viewers about roots revelations were related to the accuracy of genetic analysis. *cocopuff236*'s reservations paradoxically led him to consider *additional* testing. This root-seeker received results that associated him with Northern Europe. But *cocopuff236* "was not happy about" this because he had hoped that the test would reveal his "African tribe."[48] In the comments section below his video, he wrote that he planned to get "another test from a different company to see if my haplogroup is African."[49] *cocopuff236* was not distrustful of genetic genealogy technology; rather, he was dissatisfied because the genealogical aspiration that prompted his purchase of a DNA test—i.e. evidence of his African ancestry—remained unfulfilled. However, some commenters did highlight the potential limitations of genetic genealogy. *philgdev* recommended to *cocopuff236* that he should not regard his results as conclusive because "just one branch of your family" was tested.[50] *TRUTHTEACHER2007* had little faith in DTC testing purveyors. In response to *yeamie*'s roots revelation, this viewer carped, "I have a big problem with these companies because they are not telling the truth. DNA can't tell you your total lineage."[51]

Skepticism about genetic genealogy was sometimes couched in a discourse of value. Responding to roots revelations, viewers frequently asked our root-seekers about the cost of the tests. In reply to one such query, *vegasview77* wrote that "the cost is about $350[,] but the database is HUGE." The genealogist clearly intended to communicate that the expense he incurred was justified by the accuracy of the results demonstrated by the company's extensive reference database of DNA samples. Given that price information about genetic genealogy testing is readily available to internet-savvy YouTube viewers via a basic search engine inquiry, the persistence of the question "How much did it cost?" should also be regarded as a question of value beyond strictly economic concerns. "How much does it cost?" might be understood to also mean "Is it worth it?" This latter question exceeds a cost–benefit analysis and points to consideration of the emotional or moral value of the pursuit of roots through consumption. This question about price could also suggest that acquiescence to a genetic view of kinship brought with it both benefits and sacrifices (that is, "costs" of another type).

This second sense of the potential costs of genetic genealogy was on display during a poignant episode in *Jasmynecannick*'s roots revelation. Immediately following her reveal, she is filmed excitedly calling her grandmother to share her results. In response to the news that their family may have West African ancestry, *Jasmynecannick*'s grandmother intoned, "We're from South Carolina." The granddaughter root-seeker countered,

> Our family is from Equatorial Guinea and Cameroon . . . and not South Carolina! [She faces her friend who is videotaping her reveal.] Grandma is saying that she has "been fine" for 87 years not knowing where she comes from and is saying that . . . "those genetic genealogy test companies can tell people anything."[52]

With notable exasperation and in the hopes that documentation of the results might quell her grandmother's suspicions, *Jasmynecannick* says, "I'll show you the certificate [of Ancestry] when I come over tomorrow."

Broadcast Your (Racial) Self

> Sincerity demands its performance.
> (John L. Jackson, *Real Black*)[53]

In 2008, Access DNA was founded.[54] This internet-based company does not sell genetic testing; rather, it provides genetics education and genetic counseling to members of the public interested in better understanding the results they have received via DTC DNA testing services. A company offering such information is only necessary—and potentially profitable—in a context in which there are few opportunities for consumers to get feedback about their test results, because federal regulations require such consultation only in medical settings.

In part, roots revelations reflect and fill a similar need for comment and counsel following "recreational" genetic testing. Using YouTube, genealogists disseminate videos and receive audience feedback about their experiences. Viewers' responses range from emotional reaction to technical considerations. While the "positive" responses sought by *yeamie* and other root-seekers were prevalent in our sample, such reactions are not guaranteed in the interactive space of the social network site. Reception to the videos included celebration, endorsement, commiseration and outright skepticism. Although contention is characteristic of SNS (e.g. the "trolling" phenomenon), critical responses to roots revelations suggest that the veracity and significance of genetic genealogy testing may come under particular scrutiny, sometimes arising from both broadcasters' and viewers' evident discomfort with scientific analysis as the arbiter of identity. In other instances, reservations emerge from viewers' knowledge of the technological limitations of the analysis. Reveals may also be contested by the putative symbolic communities in which these African American root-seekers seek membership.

Such critiques notwithstanding, affirming interactions with the social network audience may help these root-seekers to fulfill their genealogical aspiration of establishing novel genetically derived, historically denied identities. Developments in computer science and molecular biology offer new avenues for the construction and performance of racial identity. Roots revelations videos suggest that African American genealogists' identities can be drawn not only from genetic ancestry results but also from the networked interaction that occurs between broadcasters and their audiences. Like heritage tourism, YouTube facilitated our root-seekers' association with others from their new genetic "family" or community.

These interactions might be regarded as enactments of what John Jackson describes as "racial sincerity."[55] "Racial authenticity," its opposite, is a process of subjectification in which one's identity is shaped from without by "social phenotypes" and rigid expectations—including genetic determinism—that "delimit individuals' social options."[56] The concept of racial sincerity, on the contrary, captures a more dynamic process in which a subject is an agent in his or her racial self-making, negotiating and evaluating external cues—including, for example, the identificatory call-and-response available via YouTube— instead of being shaped absolutely by them. As Jackson notes further, unlike the subject–object relation of "authenticity" in which racialized persons are fastened to and by stereotypes, sincerity is "a liaison *between subjects*," between "*social interlocutors*."[57] Expanding a continuum of African diasporic cultural politics, roots revelations, we argue, are an instantiation of this type of racial sincerity, conveyed through the divulgence and performance of genetic ancestry results and subsequent interaction with a social network audience. Additionally, sincerity, in its most literal meaning, underscores the earnestness on display in many of these YouTube broadcasts as these root-seekers search for answers to one of life's most imperative questions—"Who am I?"[58]

Acknowledgments

The authors acknowledge research support from the Office of the Provost at Yale University and the Office of the Provost at Columbia University in the City of New York. Jessie Daniels, Catherine Lee, Ann Morning and Wendy Roth offered thoughtful feedback that helped us to clarify the ideas presented here. Nelson thanks Valerie Idehen and Talibah Newman for their invaluable research assistance and Stephanie Greenlea, Alexis Hill, David Licata, C.A. Miranda, Joan H. Robinson, Ronald Gregg, Rebecca Herzig, and Michael Yarbrough for enlightening discussions in the course of writing this essay.

Notes

1 www.youtube.com/watch?v=kpoygNwIEUQ&feature=video_response (accessed February 11, 2010).

2 Some important examinations of the imbrication of SNS and genetics include Sandra Soo-Jin Lee and LaVera Crawley, "Research 2.0: Social Networking and Direct-to-Consumer (DTC) Genomics," *The American Journal of Bioethics* 9 (2009): 35–44; Lynette Reid, "Networking Genetics, Populations, and Race," *The American Journal of Bioethics* 9 (2009): 50–52; and Ainsley J. Newsom, "Personal Genomics as an Interactive Web Broadcast," *The American Journal of Bioethics* 9 (2009): 27–29, as well as several other contributors to this recent, personal genomics-focused issue of *AJB*. With the exception of Newsom, these authors do not address the subject of this chapter—the use of the SNS YouTube by consumers of DTC genetic testing services.

3 www.23andme.com. See also Lee and Crawley, "Research 2.0."

4 For one example of the proliferation of blogs dedicated to ancestry tracing, see Maureen A. Taylor, "Fab Forty: 40 Best Genealogy Blogs," *Family Tree Magazine*, May (2010): 42–47.

   Single nucleotide polymorphisms (SNPs or "snips") are sites in the DNA where common variations occur: that is, where the bases that comprise chromosomes may differ. SNPs are coded onto computer chips (SNP chips) to facilitate ready comparison of individual genomes. Haplotype groups are sets of SNPs on a region of a single chromosome that are typically inherited together; these groupings can be used to map population migration and, it is hoped, disease risk.

5 Troy Duster, *Backdoor to Eugenics*, second edition (New York: Routledge, 2003 [1990]), 156.

6 Nelson thanks C.A. Miranda for bringing the presence of the AfricanAncestry.com channel and root-seekers videos on YouTube to her attention. Although we focus on the broadcasts of African American root-seekers, this phenomenon is broadly common on the SNS.

7 Alex Haley, *Roots: The Saga of an American Family* (New York: Dell, 1976).

8 The idea of "affiliative self-fashioning" is introduced in Alondra Nelson, "Bio Science: Genetic Genealogy Testing and the Pursuit of African Ancestry," *Social Studies of Science* 38 (2008): 771–774 and Nelson, "The Factness of Diaspora: The Social Sources of Genetic Genealogy," in B. Koenig, S. Lee, and S. Richardson, eds, *Rethinking Race in a Genomic Era* (New Brunswick, NJ: Rutgers University Press), 258–259.

9 John L. Jackson, Jr. *Real Black: Adventures in Racial Sincerity* (Chicago: University of Chicago Press, 2005).

10 See, for example, Luigi Cavalli-Sforza, Paolo Menozzi and Alberto Piazza, *The History and Geography of Human Genes* (Princeton, NJ: Princeton University Press, 1994); Mark Jobling and Chris Tyler-Smith. "Fathers and Sons: The Y Chromosome and Human Evolution," *Trends in Genetics* 11.11: 449–55.

11 For a discussion of types of genetic genealogy testing from the perspective of what social possibilities they yield for consumers, see Nelson, "Bio Science," 765–767.

12 Racio-ethnic composite testing involves analysis of one's full nuclear DNA in order to make claims about ancestry. A subject's genetic sample is compared with panels of proprietary, "ancestry informative" SNPs. The end result is an "admixture" of three of four statistically constituted categories—African, Native American, East Asian, and European—based on the presence of genetic markers said to be predominant among each of these "original" populations. Notably, these markers are present across the *spectrum* of human groups. A hypothetical customer might learn his racio-ethnic composite to be 60 percent East Asian, 32 percent African and 8 percent Native American. This form of analysis was developed by the now defunct DNAPrint Genomics company. However, it is still in use by genetic genealogy companies, including 23andMe.

13 https://genographic.nationalgeographic.com/genographic/index.html (accessed March 20, 2010).

14 See the Oxford Ancestors website on its "MatriLine DNA Service": www.oxfordancestors.com/component/page,shop.product_details/flypage,flypage/product_id,17/category_id,6/option,com_virtuemart/Itemid,67/ (accessed March 19, 2010). On the African Ancestry company's "African Lineage Database," see: www.africanancestry.com/database.html (accessed March 19, 2010). The ethnic lineage testing offered by Oxford Ancestors is popular among persons of European descent because this company guarantees customers who fit this profile a match to one of the mitochondrial "daughters of Eve" with 95 percent certainty. Similarly, African Ancestry is popular among persons of African descent, in part because this black-owned company boasts the largest reference database of African DNA.

15 The *Motherland* series also aired on cable television in the U.S on the Sundance Channel.

16 June Deery, "Interior Design: Commodifying Self and Place in 'Extreme Makeover,' 'Extreme Makeover: Home Edition,' and 'The Swan,'" in Dana Alice Heller, ed., *The Great American Makeover: Television, History, Nation* (New York: Macmillan, 2006), 169. On the history and affective significance of "the reveal" in television, see Anna McCarthy, "'Stanley Milgram, Allen Funt, and Me': Postwar Social Science and the 'First Wave' of Reality TV," in Laurie Ouellette and Susan Murray, eds, *Reality TV: Remaking Television Culture* (New York: New York University Press, 2004) 19–39.

17 Lawrence-Lightfoot and Jemison appear in *African American Lives*, producers Henry Louis Gates, Jr, Williams R. Grant, and Peter W. Kunhardt. DVD. Public Broadcasting Service, 2005. Chris Rock's family genealogy is featured in *African American Lives II*, producers Henry Louis Gates, Jr, Williams R. Grant, Peter W. Kunhardt, and Dyllan McGee. DVD. Public Broadcasting Service, 2007.

18 Nelson is presently at work on a book about the circulation of genetic ancestry testing in African diasporic culture.

19 Michael Patton, *Qualitative Research and Evaluation Methods*, third edition (Thousand Oaks, CA: Sage, 2002), 238–239.

20 In analyzing the data, we decided to discard the data for one of the video clips we gathered, which was an interview of a male root-seeker posted by AfricanAncestry.com on YouTube. We have come to a consensus that the formation of the video clip could have been controlled to a great extent as it may serve an indirect advertisement purpose to encourage a specific group of viewers to take the genetic genealogy test from African Ancestry.com. Therefore, it was concluded that the specific video clip might impede an accurate assessment of the YouTube video's impact on the responses to genetic genealogy tests. Indeed, AfricanAncestry.com has its own YouTube channel; this suggests that roots revelation videos might also endeavor to re-create the narrative arc of the "testimonials" about genetic genealogy constructed by the company.

21 http://www.youtube.com/watch?v=aYf4J9Ga—U (accessed February 11, 2010).

22 Patricia G. Lange, "Publicly Private and Privately Public: Social Networking on YouTube," *Journal of Computer-Mediated Communication* 13.1 (2007): article 18. Available at: http://jcmc.indiana.edu/vol13/issue1/lange.html (accessed November 12, 2009).

23 www.youtube.com/watch?v=x-4TPC5NMQ4

24 www.youtube.com/watch?v=kpoygNwIEUQ&feature=video_response (accessed February 11, 2010).

25 www.youtube.com/watch?v=8OiiNdlxxvo.

26 www.youtube.com/watch?v=putwL69UNpY&feature=related.

27 www.youtube.com/watch?v=putwL69UNpY&feature=related.

28 www.youtube.com/watch?v=putwL69UNpY&feature=related.

29 www.youtube.com/watch?v=putwL69UNpY&feature=related.

30 www.youtube.com/watch?v=hZzQU3dT9DA&feature=related.

31 www.youtube.com/watch?v=8OiiNdlxxvo (emphasis added).

32 www.youtube.com/watch?v=hZzQU3dT9DA&feature=related.

33 www.youtube.com/watch?v=hZzQU3dT9DA&feature=related (emphasis added).

34 Ibid. (emphasis added).

35 www.youtube.com/watch?v=putwL69UNpY&feature=related.

36 Patricia G. Lange, "Publicly Private and Privately Public: Social Networking on YouTube," *Journal of Computer-Mediated Communication* 13.1: article 18. Available at: http://jcmc.indiana.edu/vol13/issue1/lange.html (accessed November 12, 2009).

37 All comments are in response to this video: www.youtube.com/watch?v=8OiiNdlxxvo. *lerinhar* is both a root-seeker and a commentator.

38 Lange, "Publicly Private and Privately Public," 11.

39 Lange, "Publicly Private and Privately Public," 11.

40 www.youtube.com/watch?v=hZzQU3dT9DA&feature=related.

41 www.youtube.com/watch?v=8OiiNdlxxvo.

42 Saidiya Hartman, "The Time of Slavery," *South Atlantic Quarterly* 101.4 (Fall 2002): 759.

43 For a comprehensive, critical discussion of recent scholarship on race, racism and technology, see Jessie Daniels, "Race and Racism in Internet Studies: A Review and Critique," unpublished manuscript. The rich imbrication of diaspora and technology is explored in Emily Noelle Ignacio's *Building Diaspora: Filipino Cultural Community Formation on the Internet* (New Brunswick, NJ: Rutgers University Press, 2005). We follow her argument that new media and

the internet can both solidify, create and reconstitute the definition and meaning of diasporic community.

44 The idea of "affiliative self-fashioning" is discussed in Alondra Nelson, "Bio Science: Genetic Genealogy Testing and the Pursuit of African Ancestry," *Social Studies of Science* 38 (2008): 771–774 and Nelson, "The Factness of Diaspora," 258–259.
45 www.youtube.com/watch?v=hZzQU3dT9DA&feature=related. Thanks to Michael Yarbrough for helping to illuminate the meaning of the name "bongiwe."
46 www.youtube.com/watch?v=hZzQU3dT9DA&feature=related.
47 www.youtube.com/watch?v=hZzQU3dT9DA&feature=related.
48 www.youtube.com/watch?v=putwL69UNpY&feature=related.
49 www.youtube.com/watch?v=putwL69UNpY&feature=related.
50 www.youtube.com/watch?v=putwL69UNpY&feature=related.
51 www.youtube.com/watch?v=kpoygNwIEUQ&feature=video_response (accessed February 11, 2010).
52 www.youtube.com/watch?v=hZzQU3dT9DA&feature=related.
53 Jackson, *Real Black*, 14.
54 www.accessdna.com/useraccount/default.aspx.
55 Jackson, *Real Black*.
56 Ibid. 13, 227.
57 Ibid. 15 (emphasis added).
58 Keith Wailoo, "Who Am I? Genetics and the Crisis of Historical Identity," in Keith Wailoo, Alondra Nelson, Catherine Lee, eds, *Genetics and the Unsettled Past: The Collision of DNA, Race, and History* (New Brunswick, NJ: Rutgers University Press, 2012).

References

Boyd, David and Nicole Ellison. 2007. "Social Network Sites: Definition, History and Scholarship." *Journal of Computer-Mediated Communication* 13.1: article 11, p. 1.
Cavalli-Sforza, Luigi, Paolo Menozzi and Alberto Piazza. 1994. *The History and Geography of Human Genes*. Princeton, NJ: Princeton University Press.
Daniels, Jessie. 2010. "Race and Racism in Internet Studies: A Review and Critique". Unpublished manuscript.
Deery, June. 2006. "Interior Design: Commodifying Self and Place in 'Extreme Makeover,' 'Extreme Makeover: Home Edition,' and 'The Swan,'" in Dana Alice Heller, ed., *The Great American Makeover: Television, History, Nation*. New York: Macmillan, 159–174.
Duster, Troy. 2003. *Backdoor to Eugenics*, second edition. New York: Routledge.
Haley, Alex. 1976. *Roots: The Saga of an American Family*. New York: Dell.
Hammer, Michael F. 1995. "A Recent Common Ancestry for Human Y Chromosomes." *Nature* 378.6555: 376–378.
Hartman, Saidiya. 2002. "The Time of Slavery." *South Atlantic Quarterly* 101.4 (Fall 2002): 757–777.
Ignacio, Emily Noelle. 2005. *Building Diaspora: Filipino Cultural Community Formation on the Internet*. New Brunswick, NJ: Rutgers University Press.
Jackson, John L., Jr. 2005. *Real Black: Adventures in Racial Sincerity*. Chicago: University of Chicago Press.
Jobling, Mark A. and Chris Tyler-Smith. 1995. "Fathers and Sons: The Y Chromosome and Human Evolution." *Trends in Genetics* 11.11: 449–455.
Lange, Patricia G. 2007. "Publicly Private and Privately Public: Social Networking on YouTube." *Journal of Computer-Mediated Communication* 13.1: article 18. Available at http://jcmc. indiana.edu/vol13/issue1/lange.html (accessed November 12, 2009).
Lee, Sandra Soo-Jin Lee and LaVera Crawley. 2009. "Research 2.0: Social Networking and Direct-to-Consumer (DTC) Genomics." *The American Journal of Bioethics* 9: 35–44.
McCarthy, Anna. 2004. "'Stanley Milgram, Allen Funt, and Me': Postwar Social Science and the 'First Wave' of Reality TV," in Laurie Ouellette and Susan Murray, eds, *Reality TV: Remaking Television Culture*. New York: New York University Press, 19–39.
Nelson, Alondra. 2008. "The Factness of Diaspora: The Social Sources of Genetic Genealogy," in B. Koenig, S. Lee and S. Richardson, eds, *Rethinking Race in a Genomic Era*. New Brunswick, NJ: Rutgers University Press, 253–268.
——. 2008. "Bio Science: Genetic Genealogy Testing and the Pursuit of African Ancestry." *Social Studies of Science* 38.5: 759–783.

Newsom, Ainsley J. 2009. "Personal Genomics as an Interactive Web Broadcast." *The American Journal of Bioethics* 9: 27–29.

Patton, Michael Quinn. 2002. *Qualitative Research and Evaluation Methods,* third edition. Thousand Oaks, CA: Sage.

Reid, Lynette. 2009. "Networking Genetics, Populations, and Race." *The American Journal of Bioethics* 9: 50–52.

Taylor, Maureen A. 2010. "40 Best Genealogy Blogs." *Family Tree Magazine,* March 1. Available at www.familytreemagazine.com/article/fab-forty (accessed March 7, 2010).

13
Genomic Databases and an Emerging Digital Divide in Biotechnology

PETER A. CHOW-WHITE

Simon Fraser University

To use this flood of knowledge, which will pour across the computer networks of the world, biologists not only must become computer-literate, but also change their approach to the problem of understanding life. The next tenfold increase in the amount of information in the databases will divide the world into haves and have-nots, unless each of us connects to that information and learns how to sift through it for the parts we need.
(Walter Gilbert)[1]

In the mid-1990s, a group of American and British scientists met at a seaside resort in the Caribbean to discuss ownership of the DNA data they were generating from the Human Genome Project (HGP). They felt that the information from this emerging technology was too valuable for any one person or organization to own and decided genome data should be treated as a public good. This was a laudable goal and a revolutionary one in terms of scientific norms regarding information access. Traditionally, scientists keep data close to the lab and share with colleagues they work with or through close friendship networks. In interviews I conducted from 2005 to 2009 with stakeholders in genomic research, a geneticist explained that the principle of open access scientists agreed to in the Bermuda meetings was part of a larger social movement in science.

Genomics exemplifies a shift in the cultural practices of science from the protection of data to the sharing of it. A geneticist I interviewed referred to this change in practice among scientists as "democratizing the data" where data sets would be available to researchers on an international scale and, as he says "open, as in belonging to the public." The most important technologies to apply what the scientists called the Bermuda Accord (also known as the Bermuda Principles) are the Internet and digital databases to facilitate global access to genome data sets. As the Nobel laureate and genetic scientist Walter Gilbert predicts in the epigraph above, at stake would be the potential of a global digital divide in genomic information. For genome scientists, creating a culture of science that is socially responsible and ethical meant borrowing the model of open access to digital information from Internet pioneers and computer hackers.

Policy makers, scholars, and activists made similar arguments about the Internet and the emerging digital divide between rich and poor, men and women, whites and minority groups about the same time as the Bermuda meeting. "Access" was supposed to be the key to creating a more equitable society, they argued. However, as the digital divide discourse evolved in the 2000s, scholars found that access to the Internet and digital information is only the starting point in addressing the digital divide (Mehra 2004; Servon 2002) and turned to issues of quality of access, such as dial up versus broadband adoption (Dailey et al. 2010; Gant et al. 2010), and the nature of digital information, such as racial representation online (Nakamura 2008) and the informationalization of race (Chow-White 2008).

In the 1990s, scientists and policy makers echoed techno-utopian discourses about the Internet in claims about the potential scientific and social implications for the completion of the Human Genome Project. Leading scientists envisioned an opportunity in this emerging technology to level the (digital) global playing field in scientific research and make positive contributions to society in science and health. For example, project leader Francis Collins and his colleagues explained in Science the HGP was the most important project in the history of biology and medicine and would have "unprecedented impact and long-lasting value for basic biology, biomedical research, biotechnology, and health care" (Collins et al. 1998: 682). As scholars and policy makers pushed questions of the digital divide beyond access to consider the inclusiveness of the Internet and racial representation in digital culture, discussions in genomics followed a different trajectory. One of the most significant findings from the HGP is that humanity is 99.9 percent the same at the molecular level. With this evidence, many constituencies within and beyond the academy trumpeted the end of biological notions of race and the scientific validation of race as a social construction.

Discussions about access turned to the racial representation of genome information as stakeholders from the social sciences and humanities, policy circles, private enterprise, and advocacy groups joined scientists (Bamshad 2005; Bamshad et al. 2004; Fausto-Sterling 2004; Lee and Koenig 2003; Schwartz 2001). Many individuals in and outside of the institution of science interpreted the results of the HGP as confirmation of a common humanity. However, not everyone was convinced. Scientists turned from sameness to mapping differences between individuals from Africa, Asia, and Europe in the next major genome project launched shortly after the HGP, the International HapMap Project. Many debates about the biological vs social nature of race, the role of race in scientific research, and the validity of race as a biological variable took place in scientific and medical journals such as Science, Nature, and the Journal *of the American Medical Association* and at academic and state-sponsored meetings. Many raised concerns that a new form of racial realism[2] was emerging from the deluge of DNA data and genome association studies (Braun *et al.* 2007; Chow-White 2009; Duster 2005; Ossorio 2005).

While debates about the politics of racial representation in genomics ensued during the 2000s, the flow of genome information into digital databases that began as a trickle in the late 1990s became a torrent. Stakeholders paid less attention to the relations of representation in terms of which social groups were being included in genome databases and in studies about the genetic origins of human disease. Lee (2009) suggests that there is a shortage of DNA samples from people of African, Asian, Hispanic, and North American ancestries. Tang (2006) also argues that there is a dearth of epidemiological studies on non-white populations.

In this chapter, I extend the concept of the digital divide into genome science. I argue that, despite a global proliferation of DNA databases and genome scientists adopting discursive ethos of democracy, inclusion, and global diversity in regards to genomic resources, there is a global digital divide in genomic data. This form of digital information inequality has consequences for database representation and for the production of scientific and health knowledge. In the first section, I draw on extensive interviews I conducted with scientists, humanists, social scientists, policy makers, and advocacy groups working on the International HapMap Project to explore how genome scientists borrowed an open source model and inclusive forms of community engagement to democratize scientific knowledge and research. In the second section, I discuss the recent global boom in DNA databases and how scientists and medical researchers have used this information to understand genetic variation and human health. At the same time, however, they pursued this aim through the lens of biological notions of racial difference. In the third section, I analyze genome population studies published in scientific journals and show how the digital DNA contents of genome databases are skewed in the direction of whiteness. Despite the turn to difference in genomics, individuals of Asian and African ancestries are underrepresented and there are even fewer DNA samples from Hispanic and Aboriginal peoples used in the production of knowledge about genome variation, medical conditions, and human health. I conclude the chapter with a discussion of theoretical and empirical implications of the findings for race, representation, technology, and science.

Democratizing the Data and Informational Inclusion: Open Access, Techno-Consent, and Community Engagement

One of the most significant developments in the history of the Internet is the competition between models of access and ownership of digital information between advocates of copyright and the open source, copyleft movement. Advocates of the latter based their agenda on practices of sharing source codes for software so anyone can revise them and return the updated version back into the public cyber-domain. Like other battles over intellectual property and copyright in the digital age, such as the downloading of bittorrent files or mp3 music files in the case of Napster, the copyleft approach to genomic "source code" is not without controversy in biology. Genome scientists' open access model, the Bermuda Principles, represents a political movement and a cultural shift in the academic and public sector scientific community. The Internet provides the means for the Bermuda Principles to be carried out. This type of approach goes against the traditional practice of scientists in keeping their data private until publication and the proprietary nature of the biotechnology industry (Collins 2006). In the HapMap planning meetings in 2001, however, scientists engaged in heated discussions about the open access mandate and the ability to patent the genetic information (Interview 2017). Across the interviews, HapMap members were particularly enthusiastic and principled about this practice as human DNA has virtually unlimited opportunities for developments of cures for disease:

> If you look at some of the databases now that are open to all researchers that constitute international resources, the collaboration used to be one on one in terms of disease or in terms of friendship even between different scientists. Now we have international databases that are curated, annotated, put up to date where people can share. So in terms of making science really international and making science open in the humanistic, old sense of science, open as in belonging to the public, I think it's been absolutely tremendous. (Interview 2008)

Marturano (2003) suggests that adopting the open source philosophy follows many computer hackers where the source codes are shared, modified, and redistributed. Scientists become "hackers of human data," thus strengthening the scientific community by shifting the emerging patent-and-perish culture to a gift economy where status among peers comes from the sharing of know-ledge, which is already part of the practice of scientists. For the interviewees, the open source model is critical for a more robust and collaborative science as well as more responsible to a global public.

> I think it's an opportunity for the West and the industrialized economies to efficiently transfer the intellectual benefits of wealth and investment and this technology to the developing world. There's no reason that South Africa has to re-sequence the human genome to study the parts that are relevant to urban disease there, they can leverage off of what we've done internationally. So, I think that's a fantastic opportunity for international science and humanities as a whole. I think science can bridge boundaries in a way that other cultural enterprises can't do. (Interview 1016)

This population geneticist expresses enthusiasm and optimism for the potential of genome information produced by developed countries to benefit the global south through a traditional model of development and technology transfer. A number of the members of the HapMap Project thought the data from genome projects based in the global north could overcome a digital divide in DNA information. However, the focus of this geneticist and others tended to be on delivery of sequence data, a genomic ICT4D,[3] instead of structural disparities such as the scientific knowledge economy and technological capacities for genome technology in the global south, which are critical capacity building projects for connecting to global scientific networks.

A number of the participants of the project referred to the open source practice as "democratizing the data." There are a number of features to open access. The information needs to be accessible through files that can be downloaded from a public website. Of course, the user needs to have access to the Internet and, ideally, a broadband or better connection, as well as the facilities to store the data. In the case of HapMap, the project's homepage serves as the portal to the project databases. Simple queries that return responses and graphical interfaces for browsing data are critical to the sharing of data. One respondent felt that, in the long run, this approach will have a

> great and profound impact on the way biomedical science is being done because it's a very infectious idea and it's not an idea that existed in biomedicine before. (Interview 1001)

Biomedical research has been a process of doing one's own experiment, writing the result in a notebook, which sits there until the publication of the results that may share only parts of the primary data. Prior to the Internet, the data would be held locally as there was no pressure, technologically or in the scientific research culture, to freely distribute it, as "researchers enjoyed a luxury of primary access and unique access to their data" (Interview 1016). Normally, a scientist would only share the information with colleagues by presenting the work at a conference or writing a paper that goes through peer review.

Either way, the end result is a highly extracted and interpreted diversion of an experiment. Now, many journals require submission to a database such as Genbank (I discuss this database further in the next section) before authors can submit articles for review. That paradigm is evolving due to research like genomics and the use of ICTs.

> When you collect the data using a more objective device that sort of collects the raw data and then you share it over the Internet the next person can come along and do a different interpretation of that data. And that is totally, that is dependent on technologies for collecting data. But it's, it's most fundamentally about archiving and distributing data, which is based on the Internet. (Interview 1001)

Democratizing the data depends on the network capacity of databases and the Internet as well as a social movement from within the biomedical sciences. It appears to directly confront private models of the biotechnology industry where the keeping of trade secrets in closed labs is considered crucial to competing in the marketplace.

Organizers of HapMap are not against the practice of patenting. The HapMap "Data Release Policy" states:

All data generated by the Project will be released into the public domain. The participants in the Project believe that patents should not be issued for a SNP or haplotype for which a "specific utility"—as defined in patent law—has not been generated. However, if a specific utility can be demonstrated for a SNP or haplotype, any group, whether associated with the Project or not, should be able to apply for a patent, as long as this action does not prevent others from obtaining access to data from the Project.[4]

Democratizing the data may work in terms of access. However, one HapMap member pointed out the limitations of this approach in terms of the quality of data. Differing from the copyleft movement and open source, where the codes can be redesigned and released into cyberspace, HapMap data has curators to monitor data quality. The job of curator takes place at the National Center for Biotechnology Information at the NIH's National Library of Medicine and works as a kind of gatekeeper of the information, in terms not of access but of the actual content.

The problem with data is that in a democracy not all voices of reason should have an equal opportunity to be voted and heard. There is a tension in science between having all possible voices heard and in running the risk of some of those are not accurate, meaning that you know we do need a way of establishing standards of quality and content and then being you know, either saying you know the stuff we distribute is known to be of high quality and we don't need to individually measure the quality of every datum as it moves through a plate. Or we need a transport mechanism that accepts everything but allows a user to filter easily for high or low quality at every step. You see that redundancy is good when everything's being measured well, but a project that just introduces a lot of noise and low quality data into a system could probably be, everyone's worse off, it's a tragedy of the commons kind of effect. (Interview 1016)

Scientists' desire to incorporate democratic notions into their institutional practices did not only emerge from within the academic and policy circles. The social movements of the 1960s and 1970s challenged existing norms about the order of society and, primarily, the subordinate positions of racial minorities, women, and gay men and lesbians. Feminist and gay liberation movements challenged the biomedical sciences to be more participatory and responsible to community constituencies and the larger (global) society. Science and medicine had long kept a distance from the public with legitimacy, credibility, and expertise exercised from within. Scientists and doctors talked and everyday people listened with a sense of awe and trust. Radical critiques of the medical–industrial complex in the 1960s were joined by women working to regain control over their own bodies in the 1970s, which was built on by AIDS activists working with and inside biomedical institutions in the 1980s (Epstein 1996). Issues such as patient or subject participation and trust moved from being assumed though the authority of the doctor or scientists to informed consent being earned through ethical regulations and conversation between the two parties. Everyday people have become much more involved in the health process in understanding their personal health issues (Rice and Katz 2006) as information about health and scientific studies has become much more accessible over the Internet. A consistent trend in rankings of top Internet usages since the mid-1990s has been for finding health information (Cline and Haynes 2001; Cole 2004; Leaffer 2006; Pew Internet & American Life Project *et al.* 2003, 2005). Individuals commonly use the information to ask new questions or a second opinion (Heaton 2010; Rice and Katz 2001; Williams-Jones 2003).

A bioethicist who works for a global health organization referred to the emerging institutional shift in science and medicine as a "choice model" and linked its development to the rise of information technologies.

This transition is clearly happening in every society around the world at different speeds, different rates, and different ways . . . information technology is behind that. The development of personal computers, access to the Internet, new forms of communication . . . I think even new parts of personal identity is represented in information technology, is clear for people, they spend increasing amounts of their daily life involved in communication, on mobile telephones, email, and other forms of communication. (Interview 2011)

This bioethicist argued that the older, paternalistic models do not work in the information age. This is largely due to the social movements described by Epstein, but also due to the diffusion of ICTs. In top-down approaches to scientific research, science researchers often took samples from individuals without properly informing them of the risks or outcomes. The HeLA cell line is a classic example, where a doctor took cancerous cells from Henrietta Lacks, an African-American woman, without consent in the 1950s. The researcher grew the biological material and sold them for research around the world without returning economic benefit to Henrietta Lack (Gilroy 2004; Landecker 2000; Skloot 2010). Research communities no longer find these practices ethically acceptable, as subjects must give their consent through an informed process.

In genomics, scientists negotiate informed consent at both the community and individual levels. For example, the HapMap Project engaged the four participating populations in community consent, which differs from traditional consent models in two key ways. First, consent must be gained at the local level through representative community groups. Second, the terms of consent are not simply presented by researchers and signed by individuals. Consent is negotiated between the researchers and community representatives. This is in part a response to lessons learned in the 1990s when the organizers of the Human Genome Diversity Project (HGDP) encountered massive resistance from numerous indigenous groups when approached using the traditional top-down approach. The HGDP was nicknamed the "Vampire Project" as community groups recalled a history of mistreatment by Western scientists and protested the seeking of the blood of indigenous people with no clear outcome of improved health (Reardon 2005). Native American representatives from Indigenous Peoples Against Biocolonialism attended the initial HapMap meetings in the summer of 2001 and declined to participate until the research showed that their inclusion was necessary for scientific reasons (Interview 1022).

Tavani (2003) argues that the same technologies that have made it possible to find genes that cause certain diseases, thus speeding up the process of discovering cures, are undermining the principle of informed consent in research by threatening an individual's privacy. Hunting for disease genes produces huge amounts of data that is stored in databases. This data is sorted through and analyzed using data-mining techniques which "discover" hidden patterns, properties, and statistical correlations. New aggregates of groups or categories can be produced in the process. These types of community formation "make up new citizens" through biomedical and biological languages and practices combined with everyday people organizing along lines of disease knowledge and prevention (Rose and Novas 2004: 445). When individuals contribute their DNA to health research, they are unwittingly contributing to this process. Scholars have also raised questions about the reproduction of traditional group notions of race. DNA databases have expanded at an increasing rate since the completion of the HGP and science has largely turned to mapping difference between racialized groups, raising concerns about the reification of race in science.

DNA Databases, Global Genome Projects, and Race

In 1982, the National Institutes of Health launched Genbank, the first DNA database to collect and annotate all publicly available DNA sequences. DNA sequencing was very slow during the initial years and scientists were able to bank 680,000 bases in the database. That number grew to almost 10 million by 1986 (Moody 2004: 26). Sequencing technology has sped up rapidly over the last twenty years and Genbank held approximately 60 billion bases in 2006 and 85 billion in 2008. By the middle of 2009, Genbank contained almost 150 billion bases from over 260,000 species with human DNA as the highest percentage per group (Genbank 2009). Other genome databases include the DNA Polymorphism Discovery Resource (National Human Genome Research Institute) and Pharmgkb, the pharmacogenetics and pharmacogenomics knowledge base, developed at Stanford University and funded by the NIH.

Scientists study DNA to understand the genetic origin of complex diseases, common points of variation in sequences, and clues to the evolutionary history of humanity. One of the most significant claims of the Human Genome Project is that humans are 99.9 percent the same at the genetic level. We all share the same genetic makeup and are much more alike than different. This claim dates back to the work of biologist Richard Lewontin and his colleagues in the 1970s.[5] However, the mapping of the human genome by the public/private ventures of the National Institutes of Health and Celera Genomics, headed by Francis Collins and Craig Venter respectively, has given the claim scientific validity and symbolic veracity. While the HGP found that human groups are all the same, the next HGP, the International HapMap Project, turned to differences between racialized groups.

After announcing the completed draft sequence of the HGP in 2000, Francis Collins began planning the next large-scale mapping project. The following year, an international and interdisciplinary consortium met in Bethesda to organize the HapMap Project. When genome scientists began poring through mounds of DNA data, they noticed patterns of lengthy stretches in sequences. Instead of the genome being a completely unique order of bases and pairs for each individual, it is organized into blocks of DNA patterns, sort of neighborhoods of DNA in genes. Those neighborhoods can be identified by a single variation called a SNP (pronounced "snip").[6] "Tag" SNPs identify haplotypes, like the one house on a block that is a different color than the others, making it easier for scientists to locate genes involved in medical conditions. The HapMap Project aimed to identify and catalog these haplotypes in a database called dbSNP. The project sampling strategy included 270 individuals from "populations with ancestry from parts of Africa, Asia, and Europe" (International HapMap Consortium 2003: 789). Interviews with participants at the initial planning meeting in 2001 indicated that scientists seemed to prefer racial names for the groups. Others pushed for colorblind language. A bioethicist and social scientist made this observation:

it's been an educational process for some, especially the genetic scientists, but also for the people involved in all aspects. Some scientists were using . . . East Asian or even Asian as a name for the Japanese and Han-Chinese sample. We insisted that this is inappropriate as Asia includes too many different groups, I mean thousands of different groups. China itself includes fifty groups and you can't call people like this. Therefore we adopted the name JPT, and it was a long discussion and I think everyone had a kind of contention on this in the end. I think the question of concern about racial discrimination and racial discrimination and classifying these

HapMap samples in that way was a serious concern for everyone involved.
(Interview 2011)

The organizing committee labeled the samples according to geographical origin rather than overtly racial signifiers: CEU for the American/Mormon samples, YRI for the Yoruba samples from Nigeria, JPT for the samples from Tokyo, and CHB for the samples from Beijing. I was told by a number of interviewees who attended the preliminary HapMap meetings held in the summer of 2001 that the discussions were very open about the politics of genomics and race. A bioethicist in attendance commented that it was "in the fabric of the meeting." However, another attendee described the discussions of race and community as at an elementary level. Some left the meeting without adopting the colorblind terminology. When I interviewed a white statistician, he said the sample populations represented *"the three sort of major continental groups or racial groups or whatever your preferred term is"* (Interview 1002)

His response indicates that even though the organizers picked labels in an attempt at race-neutrality, the historical discourses of racial science are difficult to shake. The HapMap sample populations are from different continents that fall into the main racial categories in the U.S. census and that are commonly used in biomedical research. Risch *et al.* (2002) and Petsko (2004) are examples of scientists who advocate for using the racial categories set out by the Office of Management and Budget in 1977 for the U.S. census. The geographic distance among the sample groups accentuates any gross genomic differences in the organization and frequency of SNPs between groups. Using historically more proximate groups may have shown more gradual differences that "might uproot conventional notions of racial boundaries and inspire new trajectories of research that dispense with age-old notions of racial difference" (Lee 2005: 2135). Instead of creating an opportunity in genomics to diverge from historical practices of racial science, the resulting maps of genome variation reinforce what Kim refers to as the racial triangulation of Asians, whites, and blacks (Kim 1999). Despite the presumption that there is no genetic basis for race, which scientists and social scientists largely agree on, racial type categories continue to be used in mapping projects and genome-wide association studies that identify and compare genetic differences between groups.

Some of the scientists I interviewed claimed that there was an increase in what they called "black–white–Asian studies" that compared the genetic differences between these trivariate racialized groups and threatened to increase the validity of biological notions of race (Interview 1016). This increase would be consistent with the turn to difference in genomics post-HGP. However, as the databases expanded, and biomedical, public health, and scientific journals published an increasing amount of population studies in the past decade, the debates about the validity of race as a variable in scientific research over-shadowed a more fundamental problem that was emerging.

An Expanding Global Informational Divide in Genomics

In a number of the more recent interviews I conducted, the interviewees indicated that more studies were being conducted on white sample groups than other groups. While collecting data for another study in 2008, I noticed this trend over the past decade. Other scholars noticed emerging disparities as well (Lee 2009; Tang 2006). This is an interesting and troublesome development despite the increase in comparison studies and global genome diversity projects such as HapMap and its current successor, the 1000 Genomes Project.[7] I investigated this trend in two ways. First, I re-analyze the findings from a meta-analysis published in the scientific journal *Nature* conducted by Ioannidis and colleagues on genetic disease and population studies. Second, I gathered genome comparison studies from 1998 to 2007 in major scientific and biomedical journals to find out what racial groups are being studied by scientists (Table 13.1).[8]

Ioannidis and colleagues conducted an analysis of 43 meta-analyses published from 1996 to 2004 to determine the validity of racial differences in genetic risk for complex diseases (Ioannidis *et al.* 2004). Out of the 697 individual studies that made up the 43 meta-analyses, 69 percent included European sample groups, 20 percent Asian, 7 percent African, and 5 percent "Other" groups, which included an array of ethnic, national, and religious identifications, such as "Hawaiian," "Native American," and "Hindu." There are also disparities across the meta-analyses. European samples were included in all 43 of the meta-analyses while Asian samples were included in 80 percent of them. Almost half of the meta-analyses did not include any African samples. In the ones that did include samples from individuals of African descent, none had large sample sizes of 1,000 individuals or more (Tang 2006). Only eighteen studies included samples from any other population. The deepest disparities in the meta-analysis data collected in the Ioannidis study are in the sample databases. Figure 13.1 shows the total number of available DNA samples for each group across all of the 697 studies included in the meta-analysis. European samples far outweigh all of the other groups *combined* by a ratio of over 4:1.

Table 13.1 Sampled Journals

Sample Sets (N = 403)	Journals Sampled
General Science	*Nature*
	Science
Genetic	*Nature Genetics*
	Genome Research
	Genome Biology
Clinical	*New England Journal of Medicine*
	JAMA
	British Medical Journal

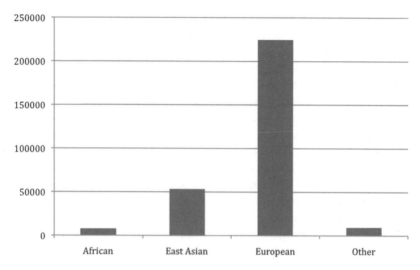

Figure 13.1 Total Available DNA Samples

African samples account for 3 percent of the total DNA database, Asian 18 percent, all "Other" 3 percent, and European 76 percent.

The Ioannidis study was not meant to measure levels of inclusion in genetic studies of health. In fact, the authors conducted the analysis to counter the rising racial realism in genome comparison studies (Chow-White 2009). Ioannidis and colleagues' use of the trouble quotes around the word "race" ("'Racial' differences in genetic effects for complex diseases") is unusual in the scientific literature, especially in a research article. Treating "race" as an unstable and problematic term harks back to the 1980s and 1990s when critical scholars in the social sciences and humanities regularly deployed the trouble quotes to signal the socially constructed nature of the concept. Generally, scientists rarely explain why identified populations are being used in research studies, how populations are labeled, or define race or ethnicity, even though a number of journals have adopted editorial policies that outline these procedures as basic practices (Sankar *et al.* 2007). Even though the authors of the meta-study chose to indicate the problematic nature of the construct of race, they only go as far as to state in the first sentence of the article, "'Race' is difficult to define and inconsistently reported in the literature" (Ioannidis *et al.*: 1312). The authors did not collect the data set in order to investigate the digital divide in genomics, which limits the extent to which the findings can be generalized. Also, the researchers' criteria excluded an additional 91 meta-studies from their initial data set. The most notable criterion for inclusion was that the meta-study had to show statistically significant results. That is, they chose studies that showed the *strongest* findings for genetic differences between racial groups. The overall disparities in available samples may actually be sharper in a more comprehensive investigation of the larger data set. Another limitation is the data is not time ordered, even though the studies were published over a period of nine years.

In order to further investigate the qualitative findings from the interviews, I conducted a visual–graphical quantitative analysis to see if I could confirm the existence of a digital divide and examine the trends in amount of studies and distribution of sample groups. The samples included groups of individuals that were coded as having origins from Africa, Asia, Europe, the Middle East, and being identified as Hispanic, Aboriginal, and Other. Figure 13.2 shows the distribution of total study populations per year. Out of all the sample groups, European origin samples tended to be the most studied population in all years. The next significant groups were of African and Asian descent. The other sample populations constituted a fraction of the overall study populations across the years. Also, the gross number of population studies increases over the time period, especially after 2005, which is the same year the first publication from the International HapMap Project appeared in *Nature*. When I transposed the data into trend lines for each population group over time, three developments stand out (see Figure 13.3). One, the average number of studies based on Middle East, Hispanic, Aboriginal, and Other groups remains constant over time. Two, while the averages for Africa and Asia are similar from 2000 to 2004, they diverge and Africa leads in the latter part of the time period. Three, the average European samples are consistently the highest, almost doubling the averages of the next two groups, Africa and Asia. This gap decreases moderately after 2005 as the averages increase for each of the top three groups. Overall, Figure 13.2 shows a major increase in the total amount of genetic population studies after 2005. However, the running three-year averages in Figure 13.3

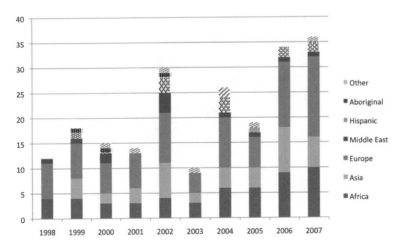

Figure 13.2 Total Study Populations Per Year, 1998–2007

reveal that all groups do not share the increase. The top three groups (Africa, Asia, Europe), increase at an increasing rate after 2005, while the averages from the remaining groups remain constant over time. The sharpest increase is in the Europe averages.

Next, I visually analyzed the totals for each group over time. The first pie chart (Figure 13.4) measures the distribution of the total number of samples for each group.

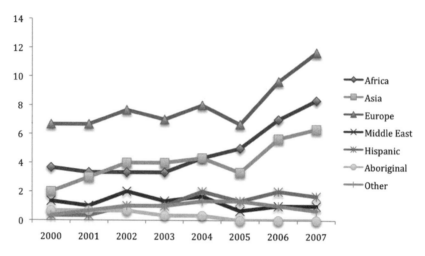

Figure 13.3 Average Study Populations Per Year, 2000–2007 (Running Three-Year Average)

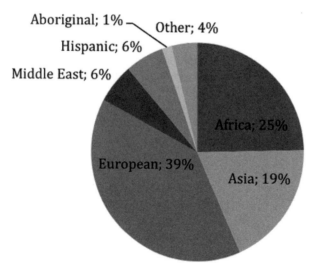

Figure 13.4 Total Study Groups, 1998–2007 (Percentage)

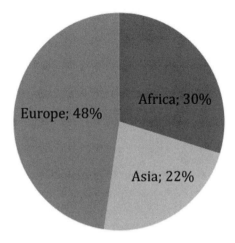

Figure 13.5 Africa, Asia, Europe Study Groups, 1998–2007

European study groups make up 39 percent of the total, followed by African 25 percent, and Asian 19 percent. Middle East, Hispanic, Aboriginal, and Other had a combined total of just over 20 percent of the groups included in all studies. Over time, African, Asian, and European samples are the most studied groups. Among these three groups, European samples constitute almost half of the entire study populations over the last decade (Figure 13.5).

The findings of the primary data collected from some of the most prestigious, high impact, and widely read journals in the sciences confirm the existence of a digital divide in genomics. There are more European samples used in genetic studies than any other group. Also, the analysis shows disparities between non-white populations, with African and Asian samples being included far more than Hispanic, Middle Eastern, Aboriginal groups. Further, the time order analysis reveals that this trend is increasing over time. Global diversity is severely underrepresented in genetic studies and this imbalance appears to be deepening.[9]

Conclusion

In the information age, the dominant organizing principle is the network where power operates through the space of flows. Network exclusion can have far-reaching consequences for the disconnected (see Wilson and Costanza-Chock, this volume). As Walter Gilbert so aptly predicted in the quote that opens this chapter, the proliferation of genome databases could create a digital divide. Over the last decade, an increasing torrent of genome data has been expanding databases at an accelerating rate. For example, from 2006 to 2008 the Genbank database grew 41 percent and from 2008 to 2009 it increased by 76 percent. From 2002 to 2009, its holdings jumped almost 700 percent (Genbank 2009;

Moody 2004). Publicly held genomic data tends to be available through open access protocols as many scientists and policy makers view genome information as a public good. Access to genome information alone, however, does not overcome a genomic digital divide. By examining the nature of the data and considering questions of representation, I found additional challenges to "democratizing the data" such as a bias in genome databases towards whiteness in the raw number of DNA samples and genetic disease association and epidemiology studies.

Media theorist Lev Manovich aptly theorizes databases as a "new symbolic form of the information age" (2002). Like the old media forms of the twentieth century, such as television and film, new media databases are the digital materials for storytelling and knowledge production. Data and code are the sites of struggle over the politics of representation in genomics. Interviews with scientists and bioethicists indicated that unproblematic biological notions of race and human differences structure the organization of databases and individual research designs. There are competing discourses within science that argue for the social nature of racialized populations that seek to debunk racial realism in favor of notions of a common genomic humanity. It is only by addressing these two fronts that the informational divide can be diminished.

Appendix: Code for Interviews

Interview 1001	Geneticist
Interview 1002	Geneticist
Interview 1016	Geneticist
Interview 1022	Geneticist and bioethicist
Interview 2008	Bioethicist
Interview 2011	Bioethicist
Interview 2017	Bioethicist

Notes

1 Lenoir 1998: 61. Walter Gilbert pioneered the development of methods to sequence DNA in the 1970s. Along with Fred Sanger and Paul Berg, he was awarded a Nobel Prize in 1980.
2 I borrow this term from the legal scholar and critical race theorist Derrick Bell (1992, 1995). In the late 1980s and early 1990s, he was concerned that the neo-conservative movement was eroding gains made by civil rights policies under the guise of so-called innate differences between racial groups. He called the underlying ideology of conservatives racial realism. See also Chow-White 2008 and 2009.
3 ICT4D (Information and communication technologies for development) is a term that encapsulates different development models for underdeveloped countries that focuses on technological interventions for social and economic progress, such as the One Laptop Per Child program.
4 www.hapmap.org/datareleasepolicy.html.
5 While Lewontin has been credited with the 99.9 percent figure (Gannett 2001), the discursive move to sameness was a prominent feature of the post-WWII UNESCO Statements on Race (see Reardon 2005).
6 Single Nucleotide Polymorphism.
7 www.1000genomes.org.

8   The findings are based on a time-ordered sample of the data set. In total, 204 articles were collected and every other article was included in the coding data set, starting with the second earliest study. The starting point was chosen at random between the first and second articles in the data set.

9   Historically, women and racial minority groups have been largely excluded from biomedical studies except as examples of deviance and, thus, have marginal representation in the databases that have provided the evidence and the narratives for normative medical practices and policies. To counter this structural disparity, President Bill Clinton signed the 1993 NIH Revitalization Act to provide a mandate for the inclusion of women and minorities in publicly funded research. In order to qualify for funding, researchers would have to show how women and minority groups would be included in the research design as study participants. The U.S. Congress followed seven years later with the Minority Health and Health Disparities Research and Education Act of 2000. These two policy initiatives are another form of democratizing the data. Access to data is crucial but is a limited step if there are disparities of representation in DNA databases. Coupled with the global growth in the genome databases and the increasing numbers of large-scale studies of genome variation (such as HapMap) and genetic origins of disease after the Human Genome Project, these policy initiatives would govern the increased representation of people of color in DNA databases.

References

Bamshad, M. 2005. "Genetic Influences on Health: Does Race Matter?" *Journal of the American Medical Association* 294.8: 937–946.

Bamshad, M., S. Wooding, B.A. Salisbury, and J.C. Stephens. 2004. "Deconstructing the Relationship between Genetics and Race." *Nature Genetics Reviews* 5.8: 598–609.

Bell, Derrick. 1992. "Racial Realism." *Connecticut Law Review* 24: 363.

——. 1995. "Racial Realism—After We're Gone: Prudent Speculations on America in a Post-Racial Epoch," in Richard Delgado, ed., *Critical Race Theory: The Cutting Edge*. Philadelphia: Temple University Press.

Braun, L., A. Fausto-Sterling, D. Fullwiley, E.M. Hammonds, A. Nelson, W. Quivers, S.M. Reverby, and A.E. Shields. 2007. "Racial Categories in Medical Practice: How Useful Are They?" *PLoS Medicine* 4.9: 1423–1428.

Castells, M. 2000. *The Rise of the Network Society*, second edition. Oxford: Blackwell.

——. 2009. *Communication Power*. Oxford: Oxford University Press.

Chow-White, P.A. 2008. "The Informationalization of Race: Communication Technologies and the Human Genome in the Digital Age." *International Journal of Communication* 2: 1168–1194.

——. 2009. "Data, Code, and Discourses of Difference in Genomics." *Communication Theory* 19.3: 219–247.

Cline, R.J.W. and K.M. Haynes. 2001. "Consumer Health Information Seeking on the Internet: The State of the Art." *Health Education Research* 16.6: 671–692.

Cole, J.I., M. Suman, P. Schramm, R. Lunn, J.-S. Aquino, D. Fortier, *et al.* 2004. *World Internet Project: Surveying the Digital Future, Year Four*. Los Angeles: The Digital Future Report, USC Annenberg School Center for the Digital Future.

Collins, Francis. 2006. "The Heritage of Humanity." *Nature Human Genome* S1: 9–12.

Collins, Francis, Ari Patrinos, Elke Jordan, Aravinda Chakravarti, Raymond Gesteland, LeRoy Walters, and and the members of the DOE and NIH planning groups. 1998. "New Goals for the U.S. Human Genome Project: 1998–2003." *Science* 282: 682–89.

Dailey, Dharma, Amelia Bryne, Alison Powell, Joe Karaganis, and Jaewon Chung. 2010. *Broadband Adoption in Low-Income Communities*, Report 103. Washington, DC: Social Science Research Council.

Duster, T. 2005. "Race and Reification in Science." *Science* 307.5712: 1050–1051.

Epstein, S. 1996. *Impure Science: Aids, Activism, and the Politics of Knowledge*. Berkeley, CA: University of California Press.

Fausto-Sterling, A. 2004. "Refashioning Race: DNA and the Politics of Health Care." *Differences* 15.3: 1–37.

Gannett, Lisa. 2001. "Racism and Human Genome Diversity Research: The Ethical Limits of 'Population Thinking'." *Philosophy of Science* 68.3: S479–S92.

Gant, Jon P., Nicol E. Turner-Lee, Ying Li, and Joseph S. Miller. 2010. *National Minority Broadband Adoption: Comparative Trends in Adoption, Acceptance and Use*. Washington, DC: Joint Center for Political and Economic Studies.

Genbank. 2006. "International Sequence Databases Exceed 100 Gigabases." Available at: www.ncbi.nlm.nih.gov/Genbank/ (accessed June 15, 2006).

Genbank. 2009. *Genbank Overview.* Available at: www.ncbi.nlm.nih.gov/Genbank/

Gilroy, P. 2004. *Between Camps: Nations, Cultures and the Allure of Race.* London: Routledge.

Heaton, L. 2010. "Internet and Health Communication," in R. Burnett, M. Consalvo and C. Ess, eds, *The Handbook of Internet Studies.* Malden, MA: Blackwell.

International HapMap Consortium. 2003. "The International HapMap Project." *Nature* 426.18: 789–796.

Ioannidis, John P.A., Evangelia E. Ntzani, and Thomas A. Trikalinos. 2004. "'Racial' Differences in Genetic Effects for Complex Diseases." *Nature Genetics* 36.12: 1312–1318.

Kim, C.J. 1999. "The Racial Triangulation of Asian Americans." *Politics & Society* 27.1: 105–138.

Landecker, H. 2000. "Immortality, in Vitro: A History of the HeLa Cell Line," in P. Brodwin, ed., *Biotechnology and Culture: Bodies, Anxieties, Ethics.* Bloomington: Indiana University Press.

Leaffer, T. 2006. "The Digital Health-Care Revolution: Empowering Health Consumers." *The Futurist* 40.3: 53–57.

Lee, S.-J. 2005. "Racializing Drug Design: Implications for Pharmacogenomics for Health Disparities." *American Journal of Public Health* 95.12: 2133–2138.

——. 2009. "Race, Risk and Odds Ratios: The Relevance of Personal Genomics for the Non-European." Paper presented at The Age of Personal Genomics: 5th International DNA Sampling Conference, Banff, Canada, September 16–18.

Lee, S. and B. Koenig. 2003. "Racial Profiling of DNA Samples: Will it Affect Scientific Knowledge about Human Genetic Variation?" in B. Knoppers, ed., *Populations and Genetics: Legal and Socio-ethical Perspectives.* Leiden, Netherlands: Martinus Nijhoff, 231–245.

Lenoir, Timothy. 1998. "Shaping Biomedicine as an Information Science." Paper presented at the Conference on the History and Heritage of Science Information Systems (Information Today, Inc.).

Manovich, L. 2002. *The Language of New Media.* Cambridge, MA: MIT Press.

Marturano, A. 2003. "Molecular Biologists as Hackers of Human Data: Rethinking IRP for Bioinformatics Research." *Journal of Information, Communication and Ethics in Society* 1.4: 207–216.

Mehra, Bharat, Cecelia Merkel, and Peterson Bishop. 2004. "The Internet for Empowerment of Minority and Marginalized Users." *New Media and Society* 6.6: 781–802.

Moody, G. 2004. *Digital Code of Life: How Bioinformatics is Revolutionizing, Science, Medicine, and Business.* Hoboken, NJ: John Wiley and Sons.

Nakamura, L. 2008. *Digitizing Race: Visual Cultures of the Internet.* Minnesota: University of Minnesota Press.

Ossorio, P. 2005. "Race, Genetic Variation, and the Haplotype Mapping Project." *Louisiana Law Review* 66 (Special Issue): 131–143.

Petsko, G.A. 2004. "Color Blind." *Genome Biology* 5.12: 199.191–199.193.

Pew Internet & American Life Project, S. Fox, and D. Fallows. 2003. *Internet Health Resources.* Washington, DC: Pew Internet and American Life Project.

Pew Internet & American Life Project, S. Fox, and L. Raine. 2005. *The Online Health Care Revolution: How the Web Helps Americans Take Better Care of Themselves.* Available at: www.pewinternet.org

Reardon, J. 2005. *Race to the Finish: Identity and Governance in the Age of Genomics.* Princeton and Oxford: Princeton University Press.

Rice, R.E. and J.E. Katz, eds. 2001. *The Internet and Health Communication: Experiences and Expectations.* Thousand Oaks, CA: Sage.

——. 2006. "Internet Use in Physician Practice and Patient Interaction," in M. Murero and R.E. Rice, eds, *The Internet and Healthcare: Theory, Research, Practice.* Mahwah, NJ: Lawrence Erlbaum.

Risch, N., E. Burchard, E. Ziv, and H. Tang. 2002. "Categorization of Humans in Biomedical Research: Genes, Race, and Disease." *Genome Biology* 3.7: comment2007.2001–comment2007.2012.

Rose, N. and C. Novas. 2004. "Biological Citizenship," in A. Ong and S.J. Collier, eds, *Global Assemblages: Technology, Politics, and Ethics as Anthropological Problems.* Malden, MA: Blackwell, 439–463.

Sankar, P., M.K. Cho, and J. Mountain. 2007. "Race and Ethnicity in Genetic Research." *American Journal of Medical Genetics* Part A.143A: 961–970.

Schwartz, R.S. 2001. "Racial Profiling in Medical Research." *New England Journal of Medicine* 344.18: 1392–1393.

Servon, Lisa. 2002. *Bridging the Digital Divide: Technology, Community, and Public Policy.* New York: Blackwell.

Shreeve, J. 2004. *The Genome War: How Craig Venter Tried to Capture the Code of Life and Save the World.* New York: Alfred A. Knopf.

Skloot, R. 2010. *The Immortal Life of Henrietta Lacks.* New York: Crown.

Tang, Hua. 2006. "Confronting Ethnicity-Specific Disease Risk." *Nature Genetics* 38.1: 15.

Tavani, H.T. 2003. "Genomic Research and Data-mining Technology: Implications for Personal Privacy and Informed Consent." *Ethics and Information Technology* 6.1: 15–28.

Williams-Jones, Bryn. 2003. "Where There's a Web, There's a Way: Commercial Genetic Testing and the Internet." *Community Genetics* 6: 46–57.

14

The Combustible Intersection
Genomics, Forensics, and Race

TROY DUSTER

New York University, University of California, Berkeley

Every Sunday night, at the California Attorney General's DNA lab in Richmond (CA) an automated matching program sorts through more than 1 million DNA profiles of known felons[1] to find possible fits (*"cold hits"*) with unidentified crime-scene samples (Humes 2009). The next morning, when analysts arrive at work, they will find up to about fifty possible matches. In an ordinary week, about ten of those will be found as "definitive." So begins Edward Humes' extraordinary account of how this technology would—on one Monday morning in 2005—link a 71-year-old Stockton man, John Puckett, to the 1972 rape and murder of Diana Sylvester, a young nurse in San Francisco. Whether that link is more problematic than "definitive" is at the heart of an increasingly heated debate among forensic scientists, prosecutors and defense attorneys—with the judiciary caught umpiring a contest where the rules of the game are in constant flux. But before we turn to the debate, we need to set the stage and frame the boundaries of the playing field—and in order to do that, we must begin with an explanation of "the cold hit."

The reason why the technology that pinpointed Puckett (some three decades after the crime) is called a "cold hit" is because Puckett was never implicated until database-matching software kicked out his name. "No witnesses, confession, no footprints or fingerprints tied Puckett to the crime." As far as the police are concerned, Puckett may indeed have left a *fingerprint* of sorts, albeit one that has come to be known as a *DNA fingerprint*. Regarding the matter of certitude, the expert for the prosecution said that the chance for a coincidental match was one in 1.1 million—dubbed a *Random Match Probability*. "What the jurors did not know, and what the judge didn't think they needed to know, is that there is another way to run the numbers [and by this alternative math] the odds of a coincidental match in Puckett's case are a whopping one in three" (Humes 2009).

Part of this story examines prosecutorial claims trumpeting DNA fingerprinting as unassailable, definitive evidence. A recent book by Lynch *et al.* (2008), and new research by Kahn (2009) and Murphy (2007, 2008) each provide historical accounts of how these claims developed. But another part of the story has to do with the age-old balancing act between security and freedom—the "special needs" of government to protect its citizens versus the individual's right to privacy. For example, there are constitutional limits that prevent the government from entering your home and searching your belongings without demonstration of good reason (warrant). Yet the government can and does search your DNA—as we shall see—without any "cause" save arbitrary social and political forces happened to turn you up in a DNA database. Over the last three decades, our nation's prison population has dramatically increased, more than doubling to now hold over 2 million of its citizens (Austin *et al.* 2007). Many end up incarcerated because they happen to live in communities where police systematically practice "buy and bust" drug operations. It will come as a surprise to many that these operations are rare in white neighborhoods, where drug use is *relatively higher* than in African American and Latino communities (Levine and Small 2008). As more and more arrestees are locked into national DNA forensic databases, we will see an increasingly volatile intersection of race and ethnicity and the "certainty" of DNA forensics. This brings us to the necessity to address a common misconception about the use of DNA evidence to exonerate versus convict. Erin Murphy has a graphic analogy that explains why the two strategies involve very different levels of certitude:

the use of DNA typing to inculpate a person—by which I mean to say that a suspect is the likely source of a sample—fundamentally differs from its use to exculpate. The simplest analogy is to blood typing. Imagine a murder scene at which police find a blood sample certain to belong to a killer. Crime scene technicians test the blood sample and show that it is type O. Later, the police find and draw blood from two suspects. One suspect is type AB; the other is type O. We can, with unreserved confidence, say that the first person is not the killer, but regarding the second suspect, we can only say that she is included within a class of people that includes the killer. The probability that she is the actual killer turns on how many other people have that blood type, along with any other evidence that we might be able to adduce. (Murphy 2008: 493)

The Inadvertent Molecular Reinscription of Race[2]

One of the deeply consequential spin-offs of the mapping and sequencing of the entire human genome has been the use of new and constantly evolving technologies to identify individuals at the level of the micro-chip. This capacity for identification of millions, even billions across the globe is going to have "spin-offs" that may ultimately dwarf the original intentionality of the early advocates of a genome map. The first of those spin-offs is just now emerging—the subtle, sometimes inadvertent re-inscribing of race at the molecular level. A second development—the use of markers for individual identification, and for claims to "authenticity" for group membership—has substantially penetrated the criminal justice system with forensic uses. This includes the use of DNA in post-conviction cases to determine whether there has been a wrongful conviction, the kind of situation that would help to free the innocent. Another use is the collection of DNA from suspects or arrestees in pretrial circumstances to increase the DNA database, which in turn is designed to help law enforcement determine whether there are matches between the DNA samples of those suspects or arrestees and tissue samples left at some unsolved crime: the net to catch the guilty. This is a long way from the original purpose for mapping the genome.

The rationale behind the Human Genome Project, and for the Haplotype Map Project which followed, has always been the search for ways to improve our health. In the last five years, there has been a peculiar and fateful irony in the convergence of the desire (and pressure) to use genetics to improve our health, and the decision by the Congress to require that the National Institutes of Health record data and engage in research to lessen the health disparities between racial and ethnic groups. In 2000, Congress passed the Minority Health and Health Disparities Research and Education Act of 2000 #106–525, which mandated the National Institutes of Health to support research on health disparities between groups categorized by race and ethnicity.

As a direct consequence, the last few years have seen a sharp increase in articles that report health disparities between members of the majority white population and the various groups racially and ethnically designated. That was to be expected. Moreover, since the National Human Genome Research Institute is a branch of the National Institutes of Health, it would follow that research on human genetics would enter the fray, with scientists poised and ready to assert the unique contribution of molecular genetic differences to an explanation of these health disparities. For example, because the rate of prostate cancer in African Americans is more than double that of white Americans, it was inevitable that some would attempt to explain this through the lens of genetics. This in turn would lead down the path that would serve to rescue old racial taxonomies and their relationship to genetic profiles and genetic conditions. It was not expected that, in so doing, this strategy would inadvertently resuscitate the idea that genetic differences between those we place in racial categories might well explain different health outcomes. This is territory fraught with minefields for obvious reasons, dating back to the eugenics movement in the United States and its promulgation and extension into Nazi Germany (Reilly 1991; Kühl 1994; Proctor 1999). But now we return to the forensic issues that currently animate so much of contemporary concerns about certitude claims for DNA uses.

Some Clarification about "Fingerprint" Identification[3]

The conventional wisdom is that DNA fingerprinting is just a better way of getting an identifying marker. That is wrong. The traditional physical imprint of your finger or thumb provides only that specific identifying mark, and for many decades was widely believed to be unique for each individual.[4] Quite unlike the actual fingerprint, the DNA contains information about many other aspects than simply a marker for identification. It contains information about potential or existing genetic diseases or genetic susceptibilities, and it also contains information about your family. The relevance of this to forensic science will become clear when we turn to a new technology called "familial searching." These can involve data of interest to one's employer and of course, to insurance companies. For these reasons, law enforcement officials claim that they are only interested in that part of the DNA that will permit them to provide identifying markers that are not in coding regions.[5] While the FBI and local and state law enforcement officials tell us that they are only looking at genetic markers in the non-coding region of the DNA, as early as 2000 twenty-nine states already required that tissue samples with the far more general information be retained in their DNA data banks after profiling is complete (Kimmelman 2000: 211).

Only one state, Wisconsin, requires the destruction of tissue samples once profiling is complete. The states are the primary venues for the prosecution of violations of the criminal law, and their autonomy has generated considerable variation in the use of DNA databanks and storage. Even as late as the mid-1980s, most states were only collecting DNA samples on sexual offenders. The times have changed quite rapidly. All fifty states now contribute to the FBI's Combined DNA Index System (CODIS). Moreover, there has been rapid change in the inter-linking of state databases. In just two years, the database went from a total of nine states cross-linking "a little over 100,00 offender profiles and 5,000 forensic profiles" to thirty-two states, the FBI, and the U.S. Army linking "nearly 400,000 offender profiles, and close to 20,000 forensic profiles" (Gavel 2000). States are now uploading an average of 3,000 offender profiles every month. If this sounds daunting, computer technology is increasingly efficient and extraordinarily fast. It takes only 500 microseconds to search a database of 100,000 profiles.

Crime Scene Investigation and DNA Forensic Databanks

In the DNA databanks used by criminal justice authorities, biological samples are collected from crime scenes—just as popularized by the television series *CSI*. These are called "forensic samples." A second kind of data collection is from persons who are known to the police, mainly because they have been convicted of a crime or, more recently, merely arrested. These are called variably "known samples" or "offender samples." As of August 2010, the U.S. National DNA database contained 8,649,605 offender profiles and 328,067 forensic profiles.[6] When someone who has been arrested has his or her DNA profile uploaded into the CODIS database, it can be compared to the scores of thousands of crime-scene samples in the CODIS forensic database.

Back to the Puckett Case and "One in a Million" Claims

Now we return to the case of John Puckett, whose sample was in the batch of "known samples." Why did the criminal justice system conclude that his DNA sufficiently matched that in their forensic database to accuse him of a thirty-year-old murder? A forensic sample is a digitalized description of twenty-six specific points of the DNA molecule.[7] These twenty-six points were chosen because they are thought to be sufficiently distinctive from other segments of the DNA. This actually translates to mean thirteen loci, but since the DNA is a double-helix, there are thus twenty-six points.

> If enough of the loci from the suspect's DNA line up with those from the DNA found at the crime scene (and if none are found to be different), a match is declared. Once that happens, a statistic is generated that shows how rare (or common) the matched genetic profile is in the general population. Statisticians call this "random match probability" and it is often a very small number, which can be very helpful to a prosecutor trying to win a conviction. (Humes 2009: 2)

In cold-hit cases, the task is to try to obtain a match at a set of as many as possible of the thirteen loci. However, when starting with a database of hundreds of thousands of DNA profiles *instead of that of a specific suspect*, statisticians are in general agreement that Random Match Probability is the wrong statistic. The appropriate question to be answered is the likelihood that the technology will mistakenly identify an innocent person.

In the fall of 2006, the U.S. Congress passed legislation authorizing a thorough study of forensic science—to be conducted by the National Academy of Sciences. The report, *Strengthening Forensic Science in the United States: A Path Forward*, was released in early 2009 and raised serious questions about how the science was being neglected, even blocked out, in claims-making by prosecution experts.[8] "There is no uniformity in the certification of forensic practitioners, or in the accreditation of crime laboratories" (National Research Council 2009: 6).

Indeed, here is what twenty-five leading statisticians signed on to in a letter to the California Supreme Court in *People v. Johnson* [139 Cal. App. 4th 1135 (2006)]:

> The fact that a suspect is first identified by searching a database unquestionably changes the likelihood of the matching being coincidental . . . We all agree that the fact that the suspect was first identified in a DNA database search must be taken into account (i.e. when asserting probabilities about chances for a coincidental match).

This has important bearing on all cold-hit cases, but especially ones in which this is the solitary evidence. It is therefore fascinating that Puckett was convicted in 2008, by a jury, even though his DNA matched on only five-and-a-half loci (Moore 2009). Just as in the above account of how John Puckett was identified, there is another case that throws some fascinating if disturbing light back on the Puckett situation. John Davis is a California state prisoner who had been linked by a "cold hit" to a 1985 rape–murder in San Francisco. Davis had been arrested for robbery, and thus his DNA had been collected and was entered into the state's database.

> The only evidence against him was the DNA [match], plus the fact that he'd lived in the area at the time—the . . . match occurred after DNA was eventually extracted from semen found on the body of the murder victim. The cold-hit match held good across 13 different sections, or loci . . . [and] a 13-locus match seemed unassailable. (Jefferson 2008)

However, Davis' defense attorney, Bicka Barlow, is not only a lawyer, she also holds an advanced degree in genetics. Barlow had read about an interesting case in Arizona, where two people matched at nine loci. Conventional and prevailing statistical wisdom says that the odds of a random match at nine loci would be one in a billion. She filed a subpoena seeking more data on this case, and learned in November, 2005, that Arizona's offender database contained genetic profiles of 65,493 offenders, and "within that pool, 122 pairs of people had DNA that matched at nine loci—and 20 pairs had profiles that matched at 10 loci" (Jefferson 2008: 32).

Now the story turns into an interesting melodrama about the search for truth versus the organizational imperatives of the FBI and prosecuting attorneys' interest in protecting the image of DNA cold-hit technology as definitive. Barlow posted her results on a website in order to alert other public defenders of her findings. Then she subpoenaed California's Department of Justice to compel the state's crime lab to analyze how common such unexpected pair matches were in the California offender database. "The FBI sent out a nation-wide alert [to state crime labs] saying, 'Notify us if you get any requests like this,'" she says, and "the Arizona Attorney General faxed me a letter from CODIS that said basically, 'If you don't take this [Barlow's web posting] down, we'll bar your state from participation in the national database" (Jefferson 2008: 33). A San Francisco judge refused to permit her to probe California's database.

Forensic Science vs Science

Barlow is not alone in her skepticism about DNA cold-hit technology. In a recent law review article, Erin Murphy (2007) has raised similar issues of the limits of asserting just how definitive DNA matches can be in "cold-hit" cases. Yet, this is a world in which the "*CSI* effect" has captured the public imagination, and where DNA evidence has come to be seen as nearly infallible (Willig 2004).

We know African Americans are being arrested at a rate of at least five times greater than whites for minor violations such as marijuana possession, even though the best available evidence suggests that whites are more likely than blacks to use (and thus possess) marijuana at every age level (Levine and Small 2008). The DNA of arrestees is being collected more and more routinely (twelve states now collect DNA from those merely arrested), and thus we are witnessing a new kind of convergence with portents for even greater racial disparities in convictions and rates of incarceration. The vast majority of persons convicted of crimes plead guilty, without their case ever going to trial. The reason is simple. The prosecuting attorney engages in a "plea bargain" in which the accused agrees to a lesser sentence in return for pleading guilty to a lesser crime.

It has been known for more than three decades that approximately 90 percent (or more in some jurisdictions) of defendants plead guilty to a crime rather than take their case to a jury (Heumann 1978; Altschuler 1979). This saves the state the problem of convening a jury and going through a lengthy trial. Indeed, if even a third of those in prison requested jury trials, the system would be clogged up for decades. So, the plea bargain is a Faustian bargain of sorts—and everyone in the criminal justice system knows it. The segment of the society that is surprised by the ubiquitous nature of the plea bargain is— everybody else, i.e. the general public. Mesmerized by decades of radio and then television portrayals of criminal court jury proceedings, from *Perry Mason* to *Law and Order*, from *Closer* and *Cold Case* to the *Crime Scene Investigation* series, the public is more likely to think that juries play a decisive role in the determination of guilt or innocence. Indeed, the so-called "*CSI* effect"—the idea that the prosecution needs to come up with DNA evidence—has made some penetration into jury selection and jury membership (Willig 2004).

This has two direct kinds of relevance to racialized dragnets and racialized databases. First, we have data that show that defendants confronted with the "information" that there is DNA evidence against them are far more likely to see this as "definitive evidence"—and thus more likely to accept a less advantageous plea bargain (Prainsack and Kitzberger 2008). Murphy (2007) and others have noted the successful "creep" of the *CSI* effect on the general public. But Prainsack and Kitzberger (2008) have discovered that defendants are perhaps even more susceptible to the *CSI* effect, i.e. the tendency to believe that DNA evidence is sufficient to secure a conviction. Their work with prosecutors and interviews with defendants in the United Kingdom document just how much the technology of the *DNA Mystique* (Nelkin and Lindee 2004) has become a part of the taken-for-granted features of the *zeitgeist*. Since prosecutors have become increasingly aware of this, they can and do tell those arrested and accused of a crime that "they have the DNA fit"—whether or not they do! This is legally permitted.

Second, more and more cases will be brought before prosecutors using "cold hits" (that match "known offenders"—which will increasingly include those merely arrested). We know that those "merely arrested" will be heavily distorted by race. From the Arizona database noted above, there were 120 matches, not one in a billion, at nine loci.

Which brings us to a crucial distinction between science and forensic science. One of the most essential elements of science is replication of findings by an independent investigator. If a researcher claims to have discovered some empirically derived finding (think of cold fusion), s/he must make available the method of investigation, and open up for scrutiny the procedures so that other scientists can determine whether the finding was spurious, unique, doctored, a fluke, etc. Not so with empirical evidence on DNA matches in a court of law. The crime labs are routinely held proprietarily, where the government agency *refuses* to permit independent laboratory work by "outsiders" who could use the same "scientific methods" to either corroborate or refute a finding of a DNA match (Murphy 2007). This barrier to comparative laboratory analysis is not science—but it is the current state of forensic science. The stakes are not just scientific reputation of some principal investigator: the stakes can involve the death sentence to an innocent person, the life imprisonment of a citizen falsely accused of rape and homicide.

The Strong Case for Strong Claims of (Even Linked) DNA Evidence[9]

In 2003, after serving eighteen years in prison, Darryl Hunt was exonerated and released from prison in North Carolina. Hunt was serving time for a rape and murder that had occurred in 1984. New analysis showed that his DNA did not match that left at the crime scene. Investigators hoped they could find a match for that DNA sample ("cold hit") from the North Carolina convicted offender databank—which includes DNA from 40,000 individuals. Comparing the data from the 1984 crime scene against the 40,000 available DNA profiles, no perfect matches were found. However, the closest single match was to Anthony Dennard Brown, who matched on sixteen of the possible twenty-six alleles. Alleles associated with Short Tandem Repeats (STR) in DNA sequences are inherited in such a way that the most likely explanation for a near perfect match is that the (DNA evidence) sample belongs to a close relative of the individual whose DNA profile is available. Because Anthony Dennard Brown matched only sixteen of twenty-six alleles, he was not a suspect. But this high proportion of matching alleles immediately cast suspicion on his close relatives—most particularly on his brother, Willard Brown. Police followed Willard Brown and confiscated a discarded cigarette butt for DNA testing. The laboratory found a perfect match at the thirteen-locus Short Tandem Repeats (all twenty-six alleles). Willard Brown was arrested, charged, confessed, pled guilty, and was convicted. He is now serving a life sentence, plus ten years.

While Great Britain's Police Forensic Science departments routinely perform what they call "familial searches" of the variety just described, in the United States there is a wide variety of state policies regarding familial searches. In the U.S., federal law bars the FBI from using DNA information from all but perfect matches. However, New York and Massachusetts encourage familial searches, authorized by specific state statutes. Dan Krane, one of the leading experts in DNA forensic technology,[10] notes that when they are permitted,

> the thresholds of similarity that must be cleared before relatives are investigated tend to be ambiguously defined and described in terms such as matches needing to "be very, very close" (Virginia), "appear useful" (California) or be at 21 or more out of 26 alleles (Florida).

The next case involves DNA as the sole piece of evidence that resulted in a conviction, thirty-five years after the crime was committed. Moreover, the way in which the case unfolded suggested that the laboratory that conducted the DNA analysis most probably made a mistake. On March 20, 1969, Jane Mixer, a University of Michigan law student, was shot and strangled. There was no evidence of sexual assault, nor was there any semen from the perpetrator left at the scene. Thirty-five years later, in November, 2004, the police arrested Gary Lieterman, a sixty-two-year-old man whose DNA was in the database because of a fluke. Several years earlier, Lieterman had undergone neck surgery. He developed an addiction to painkillers. On one occasion, when he could not obtain a physician's signature in time for the next painful episode, he forged one to get a prescription. In Lieterman's only brush with the law, he was remanded to drug treatment. His record was supposed to be expunged after his treatment was finished. However, his DNA was left in the database. This is not uncommon.[11]Even though his sample should have been destroyed, like thousands of others Lieterman's DNA remained in the database for reasons unknown—but which range from incompetence and ineptitude to under-staffing, or from a deliberate policy by some police departments to retain all samples.

Gary Lieterman would now become the subject of a bizarre turn of events that would generate an accusation that he killed Mixer thirty-four years earlier. In 2003, the DNA of two different men was allegedly found on the victim's pantyhose. One of the samples was Lieterman's; the other sample came from someone who would have been four years old at the time of the murder. It turned out that this four-year-old was in the database because he later murdered his own mother in 2003.

Dan Krane, an expert witness for the defense, pointed out in his testimony what should have been obvious: that this was an instance of lab contamination. The same lab was handling the two murder cases at the same time. Although the prosecutor maintained that the DNA of the four-year-old at the crime scene was not a mistake,[12] after only four hours of deliberation the jury voted to convict Lieterman, who is now serving a life sentence.

Police Departments' Organizational Imperative

There are powerful organizational motives for police departments to demonstrate effectiveness in solving crimes. It is a considerable embarrassment for a police department to have a long list of unsolved crimes on its books. No police chief wishes to face a city council with this problem. Thus, there are organizational imperatives for police departments to clean up their books by a procedure known as "cleared by arrest." Few matters count as much as this when it comes to reporting to the public what police are doing. To understand how arrest rates are influenced by "clearing," it is vital to empirically ground this procedure by close observation.

Consider "P," who is arrested and charged with burglary. There have been a number of other burglaries in this police precinct. The arresting officers see a pattern to these burglaries, and decide that the suspect is likely to have committed a number of those on their unsolved burglary list. Thus, it sometimes happens that when "P" is arrested for just one of those burglaries, the police can "clear by arrest" fifteen to twenty crimes with that single arrest. "P" will be considered a "repeat offender," even though there may never be any follow-up empirical research to verify or corroborate that "P's" rap sheet accurately represents his crimes.

But only if one is "riding around in police cars," or doing equivalent close-up observation of police work can crimes be proven to have a pattern. And yet, if social theorists take the FBI Uniform Crime Reports as a reflection of the crime rate, with no observations as to how those rates were calculated, they will make the predictable error of assuming that there are only a very small number of persons who commit a large number of crimes. This kind of bureaucratic decision-making generates a theory of "a few bad apples"—where both the criminological theory and the policy decision lead one to look for the "kind of person" who repeatedly engages in this behavior. In fact, the long rap sheet is frequently generated by the imperative to "clear by arrest."

The U.S. prison population has undergone a dramatic shift in its racial composition in the last thirty years. The convergence of this social trend, to redefine race in terms of DNA, will be a challenge at many levels—from the attempted re-inscription of race as a biological or genetic category, to attempted explanation of a host of complex social behaviors. That challenge can only be met by doing what the social researchers of a previous generation did with police work, namely, going to the very site at which those data are generated.

Unreasonable Search and "Abandoned DNA"

To understand the historical and political context of the right of citizens outlined in the Fourth Amendment "to be secure in the persons, houses, papers, and effects, against unreasonable searches and seizures," we must go back to the period when the British crown ruled the colonies. In this period, according to Chapin (2005), an officer of the crown, armed with only the most general warrant for collecting taxes, could break down the door of a person's home, enter, search for taxable goods, and seize whatever items appeared not to have been taxed, or what were called "uncustomed goods."

Today, the Fourth Amendment does not specify what constitutes "a reasonable search," but most courts have interpreted this to hinge on the government's requirement to obtain a search that is "warranted." However, even without a warrant, a search is sometimes permissible. In issuing a warrant, the state must balance the "government's special needs" against the individual's right to personal privacy. "Special needs," for example, might encompass the safety of airline passengers, so the courts have ruled that it is permissible to test pilots for alcohol and other drugs, as well as bus drivers, train and subway operators, and so forth. Police also need to have other grounds for a warrant, such as the "suspicious behavior" of a suspect.

But a search cannot include a general dragnet of those who exhibit *no* suspicious behavior—unless, of course, *that suspicious behavior is being in a population group that is thought to be containing the likely suspect.* In such a circumstance, there is the "limited privacy expectation," where the courts have ruled that ex-convicts have fewer protections of the expectation of privacy. In *Griffin v. Wisconsin*, the Court upheld a warrantless search. The DNA Act of 2000 provided funds for states to expedite the admission of DNA evidence of crimes without suspects. The lower courts have been challenged on this, but have so far withstood the challenge, and the Supreme Court has yet to rule on it. In late December 2005, the President of the United States acknowledged that he had authorized warrantless electronic eavesdropping on U.S. citizens in the wake of the September 11, 2001, terrorist attacks. It requires little speculation of which socially designated groups would be singled out for such invasions of their privacy. That is, just being in a group becomes "suspicious behavior." Eavesdropping is aimed at those groups thought to be most likely to "harbor terrorists" or to be in contact with terrorists. The parallel, or perhaps analogy, in the criminal justice system is the emerging practice of DNA dragnets. This is a recently developed police tactic, where all "likely suspects" in a wide geographical area around a crime scene are asked to provide a DNA sample in order to exclude them as suspects.

DNA Dragnets

DNA dragnets originated in England, and are most advanced in Europe and the United Kingdom. The first DNA dragnet was conducted in Leicester, England, in 1987. Two teenage girls were raped and murdered in the same area, and police requested voluntary blood samples from more than 4,500 males within a certain radius of the crime scene. When a man asked a friend to submit a DNA sample in his place, he immediately became a prime suspect and turned out to be the killer (Wambaugh 1989). Germany is the site of the largest DNA dragnet ever conducted. In 1998, the police collected samples from more than 16,000 people, and finally matched the DNA of a local mechanic to the sample collected at the crime scene of the rape–murder of an eleven year old (Hansen 2004).

While the United States has only conducted about a dozen DNA dragnets, most notable about them is their focus on specific racial groups. San Diego was among the first jurisdictions to conduct the practice when, in the early 1990s, a serial killer stabbed six persons to death in their homes. The suspect was African American, and more than 750 African Americans were tested. In 1994, Ann Arbor, Michigan, police obtained nearly 200 samples from African Americans in the hunt for yet another serial rapist and murderer. In both the San Diego and Ann Arbor cases, the suspect was apprehended and convicted for committing another crime, not as a result of the success of the dragnet. Then in 2004, Charlottesville, Virginia, had a racially driven dragnet that generated a controversial response from civil liberties groups that ultimately convinced the police to temporarily abandon the dragnet strategy (Glod 2004).

A serial rapist had been active in the Charlottesville area for six years, from 1997 through 2003, frustrating police investigations at every turn. The DNA evidence linked the rapist to at least six assaults. From a number of leads, the police believed the rapist to be African American, and so in the winter of 2003 the chief of police initiated a project to obtain saliva samples from 187 men—185 of whom were black (the two others were Latinos).

However, when two men, both students at the University of Virginia, refused, they raised the whole issue of what constitutes voluntary submission of a DNA sample. In so doing, they brought pressure on both the university and the local black community to take a position. The Dean of the University of Virginia's Office of African American Affairs organized a forum to discuss the situation—drawing national media attention. At one point, the Dean said: "Because the suspect is black, every black man is suspect. What are we going to do about this in the community?" In mid-April of 2004, the police chief suspended the dragnet and restricted its use to a much narrower use of police discretion based more on whether a suspect resembled a composite profile than on race (Glod 2004).

Racial Taxonomies and DNA Databanks

If the United Kingdom was first off the block with DNA dragnets and also led the world's nations in the largest DNA databank and the highest proportion of its citizens who are enrolled in its national DNA database, it also enjoys another distinction. An extraordinary four in ten of the black male population have their DNA in the police database. This is in sharp contrast to the fewer than one in ten whites in the database (Randerson 2006). Of course, one of the responses to these kinds of figures is the speculation that they merely reflect who is committing the crimes. Perhaps blacks are committing about 40 percent of all the crimes in the UK. The dramatic findings of Levine and Small (2008), noted earlier, suggest an answer to this kind of speculation as relates to data collection on race and crime in the United States. However, it is instructive to report the evolving and shifting response of the president of the National Black

Police Association in the UK, Keith Jarrett, to the data about racial disparities in arrest rates and DNA collection. This shift occurred over a very short time period of two years:

> Since April [2005], police have had the power to take DNA from anyone arrested on suspicion of a recordable offence—one that would involve a custodial sentence—meaning the database is not simply a reflection of those convicted of crimes. (Randerson 2006)

At the time, in 2005, Jarrett said that this development was "very worrying" and recommended "an investigation into how the database is compiled." However, in October of 2007, Jarrett delivered a speech in which he urged increased stop-and-search police work when dealing with racial and ethnic minorities:

> Speaking at the group's annual conference, Keith Jarrett [asked] Police Minister Tony McNulty and Sir Ian Blair, Commissioner of the Metropolitan Police, to consider escalating stop-and-searches among black people to reduce the number of shootings that have claimed the lives of another two teenagers in the past week. (Townsend 2007)

But Jarrett went even further, claiming that in the new climate of fear about rampant violence, the black community would welcome random stop-and-search practices by the police:

> Jarrett said he would not oppose a random use of stop-and-search when officers had "reasonable suspicion" an offence had been committed. He argued that as long as police officers used the powers courteously and responsibly, many within the Black community would accept it as a necessary evil. (Townsend 2007)

This remarkable turn-around in the short space of two years reflects the shifting mood in weighing the trade-offs made in the balancing act between security and freedom. And while the British have been in the lead of collecting DNA from their population, whether or not there has been a felony conviction, several states in the U.S. have embarked upon data collection of arrestees as well. The most aggressive programs are in Louisiana and California, but the trendline is clear, so some states are debating whether to include *all* arrestees:

> Lawmakers in South Carolina are considering a bill that would create the nation's most aggressive DNA collection program, instructing police to take genetic samples from people arrested in any crime—including misdemeanors such as shoplifting—and enter them into state and national DNA databases. (Fausset 2007)

There are dramatic implications of this prospective development for how such a database would be heavily racialized. First, consider that incarceration rates for blacks and Latinos are now more than six times higher than for whites; 60 percent of America's prison population is either African American or Latino. Just over 20 percent of black males between the ages of 25 and 44 have served a sentence at some point in their lives, and 8 percent of black men of working age are now behind bars (Austin *et al.* 2007). At current rates, a third of all black males, and one-sixth of Latino males will go to prison at some point during their lives, while the figure for whites is one in 17. These are national figures, but depending upon the urban area, things can look even more heavily racialized. For example, in Baltimore, one in five of black men between the ages of 20 and 30 is incarcerated, and 52 percent are under some form of correctional supervision (Ziedenberg and Lotke 2005). In this kind of setting, familial searching and DNA dragnets take on a particularly ominous racial character: "Six of those 44 states, including California, have approved taking samples from people arrested on suspicion of certain crimes. States maintain their own DNA databases, which are linked to form the national network" (Faussett 2007). Thus we can begin to get a glimpse into the future to see how these various forces (racialized dragnets, expanding offender databases to include arrestees, and the *CSI* effect) can and will further distort the racial bias in the criminal justice system.

A Vital Role for Social Science Research Regarding Human Molecular Genetics

One of the appealing seductions of contemporary work regarding human molecular genetics is for social scientists to partner with their colleagues "across the aisle" in work that tries to integrate genes and environment, illuminating the relationship between nature and nurture. Who could possibly have any concerns, reservations, or *objections* to cross-disciplinary undertakings? In this framing of the research situation, the geneticists are dealing with the "hard science" categories of DNA markers, and the social scientists are consigned to sorting out the myriad environmental forces—*nurture*—that interact with *nature*. Yet if we take a closer look at how molecular geneticists are sorting out those DNA markers, we come to find out that they typically deploy lay categories *as given*. As I shall demonstrate, the far more vital role for social scientists is to investigate, empirically, the way molecular geneticists deploy the categories, not simply take-as-given outcome data that "reveal differences in human populations." Given the findings now being generated by this field, we could easily envision a far more important role for social scientists than "*partnering.*"

Hinterberger on "Population Purity in Genomic Research"

In a recent paper that is a model of how social scientists can contribute to research in human molecular genetics, Hinterberger (2010) has looked at how Canadian scientists have been trying to better understand the sources of complex diseases by using Genome Wide Association Studies (GWAS). The assumption is that about 8,500 French settlers arrived in Canada between 1608 and 1759. They intermarried among themselves, and thus produced what is called a "founder effect":

> the Quebec "founder effect" has provided a large volume of genomic research aimed at understanding the root of common and complex disease. In 2007, a genome-wide association study . . . identified multiple genes underlying Crohn's disease in the Quebec founder populations. (Raelson *et al.* 2007)

GWAS are seen to offer a powerful method for identifying disease susceptibility for common diseases such as cancer and diabetes and are at the cutting edge of genomics-based biomedicine (Hinterberger 2010: 15).

But now there is an explicit lament among these scientists who express concerns that intermarriage rates are threatening the "genetic uniqueness of these groups" and thus the opportunity for this kind of research "may be lost in the next few generations" (Secko 2008). Here is where Hinterberger steps in as the social analyst to point out the deeply flawed empiric and consequently the flawed logic. What genetic researchers regard as a bounded French founder population is actually, upon closer inspection, not so French after all. Specifically, in the strong pressure to convert indigenous people to Christianity, the colonizing French eagerly gave these converts French surnames (Kohli-Laven 2007–2008). An examination of parish records provides documentation of this, and yet it is the French name that demographers and historians have used to set up the assumption that those with French names constituted the *bounded* "French founder" population. This clearly up-ends the otherwise taken-for-granted assumptions about the homogeneity of this population.

One of the most important tools now being deployed to examine human genetic variation is a computer-based program called *Structure*. This program permits the researcher to find patterns and/or clusters of DNA markers, and when an alignment of these clusters overlaps existing categories of race and ethnicity, there is the siren's seductive call to reinscribe these categories as biologically meaningful (Bolnick 2008). As I have suggested elsewhere, any computer program so instructed *could find SNP pattern differences* between randomly selected residents of Chicago and residents of Los Angeles (or between any two cities in the world). To put it in ways that are incontrovertible, no one could expect that SNP patterns would be identical in choosing subjects randomly from two cities. As for Chicago vs Los Angeles, such a proposed research project would be deemed ludicrous, because the theoretical warrant for it would be hard to establish (unless there was some legitimate grounding for hypotheses about smog effects vs sub-zero winter effects). But if all the Chicago residents selected were African American, and all the Los Angeles residents were Asian Americans, and those SNP patterns showed up, some social scientists might begin to accept these findings as having some validity affirming biological or genetic racial differences.

If this seems conjectural, consider a recent publication from the Pan Asian consortium (HUGO Pan-Asian SNP Consortium 2009), in which the authors report that they have found patterned differences between Southeast Asians and those from other parts of Asia. Moreover, in reporting these results, the authors strongly suggest that pharmaceutical products be developed that correspond to the genetic patterns associated with particular ethnic groups. In sharp contrast, another research group (Heyer *et al.* in press) claims that in this very same region, "genetically, there is no such thing as an ethnic group." In this kind of situation, where we have contested terrain, rather than the social scientists accepting the categories used by human geneticists as *given* and pursuing a research agenda as if race and ethnicity are bounded categories, the far more scientifically illuminating strategy would be to empirically pursue how and why these researchers are deploying the categories of race ethnicity. There are two models for this work. The first is the research of Duana Fullwiley (2007), an anthropologist of science who spent many months in the laboratories of researchers doing "admixture" analysis of asthma patients, evaluating how the researchers were using the very categories of "pure" and "admixed." The second is a project of Fujimura and Rajagopalan (2011), in which they examine how researchers are deploying the Eigenstrat SNP variation scores to "determine" differences between populations that have been sorted by ethnicity and race, all the while asserting that they are not using either race or ethnicity in the initial framing of the research. In both instances, the research of the geneticists can be better understood as "co-constructionists" of the categories. The report of the National Academy of Sciences (National Research Council 2009) strongly suggests that a similar or parallel kind of social science investigation needs to be pursued in the forensic laboratories. It is only then, when more sunlight is arrayed along this whole field of inquiry, that we will be able to decipher, defuse, de-construct, and hopefully intercept the forces currently converging to produce the highly combustible intersection of genomics, race and forensics.

Notes

1 And others, including those merely arrested now in several states, but more on that at a later point.

2 Segments of the next few pages are based upon my previously published article, "The Molecular Reinscription of Race," in *Patterns of Prejudice* 40.4/5 (November 2006).

3 Segments of this next section are excerpted from my previously published article, "DNA Dragnets and Race: Larger Social Context, History and Future," in *GeneWatch*, Council for Responsible Genetics, Cambridge, MA, 21.3–4 (November–December 2008).

4 However, recent research indicates that the actual physical fingerprint was never as definitive as forensic scientists claimed (Cole 2002).

5 Coding regions are only 10 percent of the DNA, and it is in these regions that the nucleotides code for proteins that might relate to a full range of matters of concern to researchers, from cancer or heart disease to neuro-transmission and thus, for some, to *possible "coding" for "impulsivity" or biochemical outcomes that might relate to violence.*

6 www.fbi.gov/hq/lab/codis/clickmap.htm (accessed August 25, 2010).

7   There are 3 billion base pairs in the human genome, and even though we are 99.9 per cent alike, that still leaves *several million* points of difference between any two people.
8   Available free to the public from the National Academy Press website, www.nap.edu/catalog/12589.html (accessed September 1, 2009).
9   Segments of the next section are excerpted from my previously published article, "Explaining Differential Trust of DNA Forensic Technology: Grounded Assessment or Inexplicable Paranoia?" *Journal of Law, Medicine and Ethics* 34.2 (Summer, 2006): 293–300.
10 Private communication with Dan Krane, September 11, 2005.
11 The federal DNA Act and most state DNA collection statutes require that the state expunge (from the DNA databank) the profiles of convicted persons whose convictions are reversed. However, in a glaring gap in logic, these statutes do not address what to do with profiles from persons who are not even suspects. The police often retain these DNA profiles in their own, private "suspect databases." For example, Chicago, Miami, and London, Ohio, all keep private police suspect databases (Chapin 2005).
12 This case was the subject of a full hour documentary by the television news program, *48 Hours*, which aired November 26, 2005.

References

Altschuler, Albert W. 1979. "Plea Bargaining and its History," *Columbia Law Review*, 79.1.
Austin, J., T. Clear, T. Duster, D.F. Greenberg, J. Irwin, C. McCoy, A. Mobley, B. Owen, and J. Page. 2007. *Unlocking America: Where and How to Reduce America's Prison Population.* Washington, DC: The JFA Institute.
Bolnick, D.A. 2008. "Individual Ancestry Inference and the Reification of Race as a Biological Phenomenon," in B. Koenig, S. Lee, and S. Richardson, eds, *Revisiting Race in a Genomic Age.* New Brunswick, NJ: Rutgers University Press, 70–88.
Chapin, A.B. 2005. "Arresting DNA: Privacy Expectations of Free Citizens versus Post-Convicted Persons and the Unconstitutionality of DNA Dragnets." *Minnesota Law Review* 89.6 (June): 1842–1874.
Cole, Simon. 2002. *Suspect Identities: A History of Fingerprinting and Criminal Identification.* Cambridge, MA: Harvard University Press.
Fausset, Richard. 2007. *Los Angeles Times*, January 4: Section A.
Fujimura, Joan H. and Ramya Rajagopalan. 2011. "Different Differences: The Use of 'Genetic Ancestry' versus Race in Biomedical Human Genetic Research." *Social Studies of Science* 41.1:5–30.
Fullwiley, Duana. 2007. "The Molecularization of Race: Institutionalizing Human Difference in Pharmacogenetics Practice." *Science as Culture* 16.1 (March): 1–30.
Gavel, Doug. 2000. "Fight Crime Through Science." *Harvard Gazette*, November 30.
Glod, Maria. 2004. "Police in Charlottesville Suspend 'DNA Dragnet.'" *Washington Post*, April 15: B01.
Hansen, Mark. 2004. "DNA Dragnet." *American Bar Association Journal* (May): 38–43.
Heumann, Milton. 1978. *Plea Bargaining: The Experiences of Judges, Jurors, and Defense Attorneys.* Chicago: University of Chicago Press.
Heyer, Evelyne, Patricia Balaresque, Mark A. Jobling, Lluis Quintana-Murci, Raphaelle Chaix, Laure Segurel, Almaz Aldashev, and Tanya Hegay. In press. "Genetic Diversity and the Emergence of Ethnic Groups in Central Asia." *BioMed Central Genetics.*
Hinterberger, Amy. 2010. "Genomic Cartographies: Molecules and the Material of Nation," in K. Wailoo, A. Nelson, C. Lee, and M. Bay, eds, *Genetics and the Unsettled Past: The Collision between DNA, Race, and History.* New Brunswick, NJ: Rutgers University Press.
HUGO Pan-Asian SNP Consortium. 2009. "Mapping Human Genetic Diversity in Asia." *Science* 326: 1541–1545. Available at www.sciencedaily.com/releases/2009/12/091210153546.htm.
Humes, Edward. 2009. "Guilt by the Numbers: How Fuzzy is the Math that makes DNA Evidence Look Compelling to Jurors?" *The Daily Journal.* Available at: http://callawyer.com/common/print.cfm?eid=900572&evid=1 (accessed September 2, 2009).
Jefferson, Jon. 2008. "Cold Hits Meet Cold Facts: Are DNA Matches Infallible?" *Transcript*, University of California, Berkeley—School of Law, 40.1 (Spring): 29–33.
Kahn, Jonathan. 2009. "Race, Genes and Justice: A Call to Reform the Presentation of Forensic DNA Evidence in Criminal Trials." *Brooklyn Law Review* 74.2 (Winter): 325–375.
Kimmelman, Jonathan. 2000. "Risking Ethical Insolvency: A Survey of Trends in Criminal DNA Databanking." *Journal of Law, Medicine and Ethics* 28: 209–221.

Kohli-Laven, N. 2007–2008. "Hidden History: Race and Ethics at the Peripheries of Medical Genetic Research." *Genewatch* 20(6): 5–7.

Kühl, Stefan. 1994. *The Nazi Connection: Eugenics, American Racism, and German National Socialism.* New York: Oxford University Press.

Levine, Harry G. and D.P. Small. 2008. "Marijuana Arrest Crusade: Racial Bias and Police Policy in New York City—1997–2007," New York Civil Liberties Union. Available at: www. NYCLU.org/April 2008.

Lynch, Michael, Simon A. Cole, Ruth McNally and Kathleen Jordan. 2008. *Truth Machine: The Contentious History of DNA Fingerprinting.* Chicago: University of Chicago Press.

Moore, Solomon. 2009. "Damaged DNA Evidence Shrinks Serial Killer Case." *New York Times* A14 (May 22).

Murphy, Erin. 2007. "The New Forensics: Criminal Justice, False Certainty, and the Second Generation of Scientific Evidence." *California Law Review* 95 (June): 1–81.

——. 2008. "The Art in the Science of DNA: A Layperson's Guide to the Subjectivity Inherent in Forensic DNA Typing." *Emory Law Journal* 58.2: 489–512.

National Research Council. 2009. *Strengthening Forensic Science in the United States: A Path Forward.* Washington, DC: Committee on Identifying the Needs of the Forensic Sciences Community.

Nelkin, Dorothy and M. Susan Lindee. 2004. *The DNA Mystique: The Gene as a Cultural Icon.* Ann Arbor: University of Michigan Press.

Prainsack, Barbara and Martin Kitzberger. 2008. "DNA behind Bars—'Other' Ways of Knowing Forensic DNA Technologies," *Social Studies of Science,* 39: 51–79.

Proctor, Robert. 1999. *The Nazi War on Cancer.* Princeton, NJ: Princeton University Press.

Raelson, J.V., R.D. Little, and A. Ruether. 2007. "Genome-wide Association Study for Crohn's Disease in the Quebec Founder Population Identifies Multiple Validated Disease Loci." *Proceedings of the National Academy of Sciences* 104.37: 1474–14752.

Randerson, James. 2006. "DNA of 37% of Black Men Held by Police." *Guardian* January 5. Available at: www.guardian.co.uk/world/2006/jan/05/race.ukcrime (accessed March 11, 2008).

Reilly, Philip R. 1991. *The Surgical Solution: A History of Involuntary Sterilization in the United States.* Baltimore: Johns Hopkins University Press.

Secko, David. 2008. "Rare History, Common Disease," *The Scientist* 22.7 (July): 38–45.

Townsend, Mark. 2007. "Police: Stop More Black Suspects." *Guardian* October 21. Available at: www.guardian.co.uk/uk/2007/oct/21/ukcrime.race (accessed March 11, 2008).

Wambaugh, Joseph. 1989. *The Blooding.* New York: Bantam.

Willig, Richard. 2004. "'CSI Effect' Has Juries Wanting More Evidence." *USA Today,* August 5: 1A.

Ziedenberg, John and Eric Lotke. 2005. *Tipping Point: Maryland's Overuse of Incarceration and the Impact on Public Safety.* Washington, DC: Justice Policy Institute.

Contributors

danah boyd is a senior researcher at Microsoft Research, a research associate at Harvard University's Berkman Center for Internet and Society, and an associate fellow at Tilburg Institute for Law, Technology and Society. She received her doctorate in 2008 from the School of Information at the University of California, Berkeley. In her research, Dr boyd examines everyday practices involving social media, with specific attention to youth engagement. Lately, she has been focused on issues related to privacy, publicity, and visibility. She recently co-authored *Hanging Out, Messing Around, and Geeking Out: Kids Living and Learning with New Media* (MIT Press, forthcoming) and is currently working on a new book. She is co-directing the Youth and Media Policy Working Group, funded by the MacArthur Foundation to examine effective policy interventions in areas related to privacy, safety, and credibility. This builds on her work as a co-director of the Internet Safety Technical Task Force. Dr boyd is on the board of the New Media Consortium, an organization focused on helping educators incorporate new media into their practice. She was a Commissioner on the Knight Commission on Information Needs of Communities in a Democracy, helping examine how technology can be used to help information flow in local communities. Prior to joining Microsoft Research, she has worked for Yahoo! and Google as a researcher. She also created and managed a large online community for V-Day, a non-profit organization working to end violence against women and girls worldwide. Dr boyd has been recognized broadly for her work. In 2010, Dr boyd won the CITASA Award for Public Sociology. The *Financial Times* dubbed Dr boyd "the High Priestess of Internet Friendship" while *Fortune* magazine identified her as the smartest academic in tech. *Technology Review* honored her as one of the top innovators under 35 in 2010. Dr boyd has published dozens of articles in a wide range of scholarly venues, blogs at www.zephoria.org/thoughts/ and tweets at @zephoria.

Peter A. Chow-White is Assistant Professor in the School of Communication at Simon Fraser University in Vancouver, Canada. He has published on race, gender, technology, and genomics in *Communication Theory, Media, Culture & Society*, the *International Journal of Communication*, and *Science, Technology & Human Values*. He is currently writing a scholarly monograph from his research on the social impacts of new forms of knowledge production at the intersection of culture, networks, digital code, information, and data mining.

Wendy Hui Kyong Chun is Professor of Modern Culture and Media at Brown University. She has studied both Systems Design Engineering and English Literature, which she combines and mutates in her current work on digital media. She is author of *Control and Freedom: Power and Paranoia in the Age of Fiber Optics* (MIT Press, 2006) and *Programmed Visions: Software, DNA, Race* (MIT Press, forthcoming 2012). She is also co-editor (with Thomas Keenan) of *New Media, Old Media: A History and Theory Reader* (Routledge, 2006). She has received fellowships from the Radcliffe Institute for Advanced Study at Harvard and from Brown University. She has also been a visiting scholar and visiting associate professor in the History of Science Department at Harvard. She is currently working on a monograph entitled "Imagined Networks."

Sasha Costanza-Chock is a scholar and media maker who works on digital inclusion, the political economy of communication, and the transnational movement for media justice and communication rights. He holds a doctorate in Communications from the Annenberg School for Communication & Journalism at the University of Southern California. Sasha is a community board member of VozMob (Mobile Voices/Voces Móviles): http://vozmob.net. He is a Knight Media Policy Fellow at the New America Foundation, a Postdoctoral Research Associate at USC's Annenberg School, and a Fellow at the Berkman Center for Internet & Society at Harvard University. More info: http://schock.cc

Troy Duster is Silver Professor of Sociology at NYU and he also holds an appointment as Chancellor's Professor at the University of California, Berkeley. He is the past-president of the American Sociological Association (2004–2005), and in 2003–2004 served as chair of the Board of Directors of the Association of American Colleges and Universities. From 1996 to 1998, he served as member and then chair of the joint NIH/DOE advisory committee on Ethical, Legal and Social Issues in the Human Genome Project. He is a member of the Research Advisory Committee of the Innocence Project. Research interests include the social and political implications of developments in human molecular genetics. His relevant books and monographs include *Cultural Perspectives on Biological Knowledge* (co-edited with Karen Garrett; Ablex Publishing, 1984) and *Backdoor to Eugenics* (Routledge, second edition 2003). Recent publications include, "Comparative Perspectives and Competing Explanations: Taking on the Newly Configured Reductionist Challenge to Sociology" in *American Sociological Review* and "Behavioral Genetics and Explanations of the Link between Crime, Violence, and Race," in E. Parens, A.R. Chapman and N. Press, eds, *Wrestling with Behavioral Genetics: Science, Ethics, and Public Conversation* (Johns Hopkins University Press, 2006).

Anna Everett is Professor of Film, Television and New Media Studies in the Department of Film and Media Studies at the University of California, Santa Barbara (UCSB). She has published numerous books and articles, including *Returning the Gaze: A Genealogy of Black Film Criticism, 1909–1949* (Duke University Press, 2001); *The Revolution will be Digitized: Afrocentricity and the*

Digital Public Sphere (Duke University Press, 2002), and *New Media: Theories and Practices of Digitextuality* (with John T. Caldwell; Routledge, 2003), *AfroGEEKS: Beyond the Digital Divide* (with Amber T. Wallace; UCSB Center for Black Studies, 2006), *Learning Race and Ethnicity: Youth and Digital Media*, for the MacArthur Foundation's new series on Digital Media and Learning (MIT Press, 2007), and most recently her newly published monograph *Digital Diaspora: A Race for Cyberspace* (SUNY Press, 2009). Among her articles are "The Other Pleasures: The Narrative Function of Race in the Cinema," "The Black Press in the Age of Digital Reproduction: Two Exemplars," "P.C. Youth Violence: 'What's the Internet or Video Gaming Got to Do With It?'" "Trading Private and Public Spaces @ HGTV and TLS: On New Genre Formations in Transformation TV," and "Serious Play: Playing with Race in Computer Games." She was the lead organizer of the 2004 AfroGEEKS: From Technophobia to Technophilia and the 2005 AfroGEEKS: Global Blackness and the Digital Public Sphere Conferences. She is founding editor of the journal *Screening Noir: A Journal of Film, Video and New Media Culture.*

Rayvon Fouché's work explores the multiple intersections and relationships between cultural representation, racial identification, and technological use. His first book, *Black Inventors in the Age of Segregation* (Johns Hopkins University Press, 2003) created a broader textured understanding of black inventive experiences. He has co-edited *Appropriating Technology: Vernacular Science and Social Power* (University of Minnesota Press, 2004) and edited the four-volume *Technology Studies* (Sage Publications, 2008). He is currently working on two projects. The first examines what happens to communities when the technologies that define their existences change from analog to digital. The second is a study of the ways sport governing bodies construct thresholds of authenticity by legislating technological use.

Alexander R. Galloway is an author and programmer. He is a founding member of the software collective RSG and creator of the Carnivore and Kriegspiel projects. *The New York Times* has described his practice as "conceptually sharp, visually compelling and completely attuned to the political moment." Galloway is the author of *Protocol: How Control Exists After Decentralization* (MIT, 2004), *Gaming: Essays on Algorithmic Culture* (University of Minnesota Press, 2006), and most recently *The Exploit: A Theory of Networks* (University of Minnesota Press, 2007), co-written with Eugene Thacker. He teaches at New York University.

Oscar H. Gandy, Jr is Professor Emeritus of Communication at the University of Pennsylvania. He formerly held the Herbert I. Schiller chair at the Annenberg School for Communication. He is the author of more than seventy articles and chapters and several books in the area of race, communication, and privacy and surveillance, including *Beyond Agenda Setting* (Ablex, 1982), *Communication and Race* (Oxford University Press, 1998), *The Panoptic Sort* (Westview Press, 1993), and a recent book, *Coming to Terms with Chance* (Ashgate, 2009).

Eszter Hargittai is Associate Professor of Communication Studies and Faculty Associate of the Institute for Policy Research at Northwestern University where she heads the Web Use Project. She received her PhD in Sociology from Princeton University where she was a Wilson Scholar. In 2006/2007 she was a Fellow at the Center for Advanced Study in the Behavioral Sciences at Stanford. In 2008/2009 she was a Fellow in residence at Harvard's Berkman Center for Internet & Society where she continues her Fellow affiliation from a distance. Hargittai's research focuses on the social and policy implications of information and communication technologies with a particular interest in how these may contribute to or alleviate social inequalities. She is especially interested in the differences between people's Web-use skills. Her work is regularly featured in the media. Hargittai is editor of *Research Confidential: Solutions to Problems Most Social Scientists Pretend They Never Have* (University of Michigan Press, 2009), which presents a rare behind-the-scenes look at the realities of doing empirical social science research. She writes an academic career advice column at *Inside Higher Ed* called Ph.Do.

Jeong Won Hwang is a recent graduate of Cornell University, where she received a BA in sociology. Originally from South Korea, Jeong Won has lived there and in various parts of the U.S.; exposure to these many different social experiences sparked her interest in the study of inequality, the sociology of culture and socio-cultural studies of science and technology.

Tara McPherson is Associate Professor of Gender and Critical Studies at the University of Southern California's School of Cinematic Arts. Her *Reconstructing Dixie: Race, Gender and Nostalgia in the Imagined South* (Duke University Press, 2003) received the 2004 John G. Cawelti Award for the outstanding book published on American Culture, among other awards. She is co-editor of *Hop on Pop: The Politics and Pleasures of Popular Culture* (Duke University Press, 2003) and editor of *Digital Youth, Innovation and the Unexpected*, part of the MacArthur Foundation series on Digital Media and Learning (MIT Press, 2008). Her writing has appeared in numerous journals and edited anthologies. Her new media research focuses on issues of convergence, gender, and race, as well as upon the development of new tools and paradigms for digital publishing, learning, and authorship. She is the Founding Editor of *Vectors*, www.vectorsjournal.org, a multimedia peer-reviewed journal, and one of three editors for the new MacArthur-supported *International Journal of Learning and Media*. Tara was among the founding organizers of "Race in Digital Space," a multi-year project supported by the Annenberg Center for Communication and the Ford and Rockefeller Foundations. She is a member of the Academic Advisory Board of The Academy of Television Arts and Sciences Archives, has frequently served as an AFI juror, is a core board member of HASTAC, and is on the boards of several journals. With support from the Mellon Foundation, she is currently working with colleagues from Brown, NYU, Rochester, and UC San Diego to explore new modes of scholarship for visual culture research.

Curtis Marez is an Associate Professor in the Ethnic Studies Department at the University of California, San Diego. He is the author of *Drug Wars: The Political Economy of Narcotics* (University of Minnesota Press, 2004), and his essays have appeared in *Cultural Critique*, the *Journal of Visual Culture*, *American Literary History*, *Social Text*, and *Aztlan*. He is former editor of *American Quarterly*, and is working on a book about Mexican farm workers and media technologies.

Lisa Nakamura is the Director of the Asian American Studies Program, Professor in the Institute of Communication Research and Media Studies and Cinema Studies Department and Professor of Asian American Studies at the University of Illinois, Urbana-Champaign. She is the author of *Digitizing Race: Visual Cultures of the Internet* (University of Minnesota Press, 2008), *Cybertypes: Race, Ethnicity and Identity on the Internet* (Routledge, 2002) and co-editor of *Race in Cyberspace* (Routledge, 2000).

Alondra Nelson is Associate Professor of Sociology at Columbia University, where she also holds an appointment in the Institute for Research on Women and Gender. Nelson is author of *Body and Soul: The Black Panther Party and the Fight Against Medical Discrimination* (University of Minnesota Press, 2011) and co-editor of *Genetics and the Unsettled Past: The Collision Between DNA, Race and History* (Rutgers University Press, 2011) and *Technicolor: Race, Technology and Everyday Life* (New York University Press, 2001). She is currently completing a book about genetic ancestry testing and African diasporic culture.

Christian Sandvig is Associate Professor in Communication, Media & Cinema Studies at the Coordinated Science Laboratory at the University of Illinois at Urbana-Champaign. He is also a faculty associate of the Berkman Center for Internet & Society at Harvard University. His research investigates the social science and public policy of new communication infrastructure. He received a PhD in Communication from Stanford University and was previously Markle Foundation Information Policy Fellow at Oxford University. He is a past recipient of the National Science Foundation Faculty Early Career Development Award (the NSF CAREER) in Human-Centered Computing and was named a "next-generation leader" in science and technology policy by the American Association for the Advancement of Science.

Ernest James Wilson III holds the Walter Annenberg Chair in Communication and is Dean of the USC Annenberg School. He has previously served on the faculties of the University of Maryland, University of Michigan and the University of Pennsylvania. His research concentrates on China–Africa relations, global sustainable innovation in high-technology industries, and the role of politics in the diffusion of information and communication technologies. Wilson is chairman of the board of directors of the Corporation for Public Broadcasting. He previously held positions with the National Security Council, the U.S. Information Agency and the Global Information Infrastructure Commission. He served as a policy advisor to candidate and President-Elect Barack Obama in areas of information technology and public diplomacy. Originally from Washington, DC, Wilson earned a PhD and an MA in political science from the University of California, Berkeley, and a BA from Harvard College. He is married to the labor and intellectual historian Francille Rusan Wilson, PhD, and they have two sons.

Index

Page numbers in *italics* denotes an illustration/table